Mass Media 11/12

Seventeenth Edition

EDITOR

Joan Gorham
West Virginia University

Joan Gorham completed her undergraduate work at the University of Wisconsin and received master's and doctoral degrees from Northern Illinois University. She is currently associate dean for academic affairs in the Eberly College of Arts and Sciences and a professor of communication studies at West Virginia University. Dr. Gorham is the author of *Commercial Media and Classroom Teaching* and has published numerous articles on communication in instruction. She has taught classes dealing with mass media and media literacy at the high school and college levels, as well as for teachers throughout the state of West Virginia.

ANNUAL EDITIONS: MASS MEDIA, SEVENTEENTH EDITION

1 2 3 4 5 6 7 8 9 0 QDB/QDB 1 0 9 8 7 6 5 4 3 2 1

ISBN 978-0-07-805090-9
MHID 0-07-805090-1
ISSN 1092-0439 (print)
ISSN 2159-1083 (online)

Managing Editor: *Larry Loeppke*
Developmental Editor: *Dave Welsh*
Senior Permissions Coordinator: *Shirley Lanners*
Senior Marketing Communications Specialist: *Mary Klein*
Marketing Specialist: *Alice Link*
Senior Project Manager: *Joyce Watters*
Design Coordinator: *Margarite Reynolds*
Buyer: *Susan K. Culbertson*
Media Project Manager: *Sridevi Palani*

Compositor: Laserwords Private Limited
Cover Images: The McGraw-Hill Companies, Inc./Mark Dierker, photographer (inset); Ingram
Publishing/SuperStock (background)

Editors/Academic Advisory Board

Members of the Academic Advisory Board are instrumental in the final selection of articles for each edition of ANNUAL EDITIONS. Their review of articles for content, level, and appropriateness provides critical direction to the editors and staff. We think that you will find their careful consideration well reflected in this volume.

ANNUAL EDITIONS: Mass Media 11/12
17th Edition

EDITOR

Joan Gorham
West Virginia University

ACADEMIC ADVISORY BOARD MEMBERS

Editors/Academic Advisory Board continued

Preface

The mass media are a part of the fabric of American society. Learning how to evaluate media messages critically—asking, Who created this message? What is its intent? How objective is it? How does what I am seeing or hearing reflect and/or shape real-world realities?—is a part of being literate in today's world. The organization of articles in this collection reflects this media literacy perspective. Unit 1 offers commentary on mass media use and content and its impact on individuals and society. Unit 2 explores media as sources of news and information. Unit 3 introduces perspectives on media access, ownership, regulation, and ethics. Unit 4 addresses relationships between the content and financial sides of media enterprises.

The articles selected for inclusion in this seventeenth edition of *Annual Editions: Mass Media* reflect the firm entrenchment of "new media" into the traditional media landscape. Issues of access, liberal versus conservative bias, changing interest in and definition of "news," and media effects on kids continue. However, where the "mass" in mass media was traditionally about selected messages reaching large audiences through few channels—narrow on the head end, wide on the receiving end—it is increasingly about mass channels and messages. Articles reviewed over the past year for inclusion in this edition focused overwhelmingly on business models, on changing organizational and financial structures within which media messages are produced, as opposed to message effects.

The eminent media theorist Marshall McLuhan proposed four questions that help predict how new media invariably affect the form and content of old media: (1) What does a new medium enhance or amplify in the culture? (2) What does it make obsolete or push out of a position of prominence? (3) What does it retrieve from the past? and (4) What does a medium "reverse into" or "flip into" when it reaches the limits of its potential? Early adopters of new media tend to use them like old media. Network television, for example, started out with actors reading scripts. It took a while for producers to fully understand how television could tell stories differently from radio, but once they did, folks who had been listening to serial dramas, comedies, and soap operas on radio came to prefer watching them on TV. Radio, in turn, flipped into talk and music programming. DVD players have flipped the way movies are made and marketed. Outtakes and special features such as alternative endings and camera angles became part of the filmmaking craft, saved for the DVD release where "active viewers" can fiddle with them. In return, movie theatres added stadium seating and enhanced sound systems, a return to the grand cinema experience of earlier years, with hopes of making moviegoing a bigger and more sensual, if more passive, experience than watching DVDs at home.

Technology is the conduit through which mass media messages move between senders and receivers. Its development is a scientific experiment, but its use is a social endeavor. Mass media shape the form and content of what is communicated, of who communicates with whom, with what intent and to what effect.

Most of the articles in this collection, even those that are primarily descriptive, include an editorial viewpoint and draw conclusions or make recommendations with which you may disagree. These editorial viewpoints are more frequently critical than they are complimentary. They are not necessarily my opinions and should not necessarily become yours. I encourage you to debate these issues, drawing from the information and insights provided in the readings as well as from your own experiences as a media consumer. If you are an "average" American, you have spent a great deal of time with mass media. Your own observations have as much value as those of the writers whose work is included in these pages.

As always, those involved in producing this anthology are sincerely committed to including articles that are timely, informative, and interesting. We value your feedback and encourage you to complete and return the postage-paid *article rating form* on the last page of the book, to share your suggestions and let us know your opinions.

Joan Gorham
Editor

Contents

UNIT 1
Living with Media

The concepts in bold italics are developed in the article. For further expansion, please refer to the Topic Guide.

UNIT 2
Telling Stories

The concepts in bold italics are developed in the article. For further expansion, please refer to the Topic Guide.

UNIT 3
Players and Guides

The concepts in bold italics are developed in the article. For further expansion, please refer to the Topic Guide.

UNIT 4
A Word from Our Sponsor

The concepts in bold italics are developed in the article. For further expansion, please refer to the Topic Guide.

The concepts in bold italics are developed in the article. For further expansion, please refer to the Topic Guide.

Correlation Guide

The *Annual Editions* series provides students with convenient, inexpensive access to current, carefully selected articles from the public press. **Annual Editions: Mass Media 11/12** is an easy-to-use reader that presents articles on important topics such as *the coverage of war, catastrophes, advertising, the Internet,* and many more. For more information on *Annual Editions* and other *McGraw-Hill Contemporary Learning Series* titles visit www.mhhe.com/cls.

This convenient guide matches the units in **Annual Editions: Mass Media 11/12** with the corresponding chapters in three of our best-selling McGraw-Hill Mass Communication textbooks by Dominick, Rodman, and Baran.

Annual Editions: Mass Media 11/12	Dynamics of Mass Communication: Media in Transition, 11/e by Dominick	Mass Media in a Changing World, 4/e by Rodman	Introduction to Mass Communication: Media Literacy and Culture, 6/e Updated Edition by Baran
Unit 1: Living with Media	**Chapter 1:** Communication: Mass and Other Forms **Chapter 2:** Perspectives on Mass Communication **Chapter 3:** Historical and Cultural Context **Chapter 4:** Newspapers **Chapter 6:** Books **Chapter 9:** Motion Pictures **Chapter 10:** Broadcast Television **Chapter 19:** Social Effects of Mass Communication	**Chapter 1:** Introduction: Media in a Changing World **Chapter 2:** Media Impact: Mass Communication Research and Effects **Chapter 3:** Books: The Durable Medium **Chapter 4:** Newspapers: Where Journalism Begins **Chapter 6:** Movies: Magic from the Dream Factory	**Chapter 1:** Mass Communication, Culture, and Media Literacy **Chapter 3:** Books **Chapter 4:** Newspapers **Chapter 5:** Magazines **Chapter 6:** Film **Chapter 7:** Radio, Recording, and Popular Music **Chapter 8:** Television, Cable, and Mobile Video **Chapter 13:** Theories and Effects of Mass Communication
Unit 2: Telling Stories	**Chapter 4:** Newspapers **Chapter 10:** Broadcast Television **Chapter 13:** News Gathering and Reporting **Chapter 19:** Social Effects of Mass Communication	**Chapter 10:** The Internet: Convergence in a Networked World **Chapter 11:** Electronic Journalism: News in the Age of Entertainment	**Chapter 4:** Newspapers **Chapter 8:** Television, Cable, and Mobile Video **Chapter 15:** Global Media
Unit 3: Players and Guides	**Chapter 16:** Formal Controls: Laws, Rules, Regulations **Chapter 17:** Ethics and Other Informal Controls **Chapter 19:** Social Effects of Mass Communication	**Chapter 7:** Recordings and the Music Industry: Copyright Battles, Format Wars **Chapter 14:** Media Law: Understanding Freedom of Expression **Chapter 15:** Media Ethics: Understanding Media Morality	**Chapter 7:** Radio, Recording, and Popular Music **Chapter 14:** Media Freedom, Regulation, and Ethics
Unit 4: A Word from Our Sponsor	**Chapter 15:** Advertising	**Chapter 4:** Newspapers: Where Journalism Begins **Chapter 10:** The Internet: Convergence in a Networked World **Chapter 13:** Advertising: The Media Support Industry	**Chapter 4:** Newspapers **Chapter 5:** Magazines **Chapter 7:** Radio, Recording, and Popular Music **Chapter 8:** Television, Cable, and Mobile Video **Chapter 12:** Advertising

Topic Guide

This topic guide suggests how the selections in this book relate to the subjects covered in your course. You may want to use the topics listed on these pages to search the Web more easily.

On the following pages a number of websites have been gathered specifically for this book. They are arranged to reflect the units of this Annual Editions reader. You can link to these sites by going to www.mhhe.com/cls

All the articles that relate to each topic are listed below the bold-faced term.

Advertising
9. Peytonplace.com
12. Don't Blame the Journalism
24. A Porous Wall
25. How Can YouTube Survive?
26. But Who's Counting?
27. Brain Candy
28. Multitasking Youth
32. Arianna's Answer

Agenda setting
2. Revolution in a Box
6. Journalist Bites Reality!
7. Girls Gone Anti-Feminist
10. Capital Flight
13. What the Mainstream Media Can Learn from Jon Stewart
14. Whatever Happened to Iraq?: How the Media Lost Interest in a Long-Running War with No End in Sight

Attention economy
1. In the Beginning Was the Word
11. Overload!
28. Multitasking Youth

Blogs
8. The Reconstruction of American Journalism
9. Peytonplace.com
10. Capital Flight

Books
1. In the Beginning Was the Word

Business models
8. The Reconstruction of American Journalism
10. Capital Flight
12. Don't Blame the Journalism
15. What's a Fair Share in the Age of Google?
16. Economic and Business Dimensions: Is the Internet a Maturing Market?
25. How Can YouTube Survive?
29. Tossed by a Gale
30. Open for Business

Children and media
3. Tele[re]vision
28. Multitasking Youth

Copyright
15. What's a Fair Share in the Age of Google?

Craigslist
12. Don't Blame the Journalism

Credibility
5. Wikipedia in the Newsroom
13. What the Mainstream Media Can Learn from Jon Stewart
20. Distorted Picture
21. The Quality-Control Quandary

Cultivation
7. Girls Gone Anti-Feminist

Ethics
18. Too Graphic?
19. Carnage.com
20. Distorted Picture
22. What Would You Do?
23. The Lives of Others
31. Nonprofit News

Fact-checking
5. Wikipedia in the Newsroom
13. What the Mainstream Media Can Learn from Jon Stewart
21. The Quality-Control Quandary

Feedforward
2. Revolution in a Box
7. Girls Gone Anti-Feminist
18. Too Graphic?
22. What Would You Do?

Gatekeeping
14. Whatever Happened to Iraq?: How the Media Lost Interest in a Long-Running War with No End in Sight

Google
15. What's a Fair Share in the Age of Google?
26. But Who's Counting?

Hurricane Katrina
13. What the Mainstream Media Can Learn from Jon Stewart
23. The Lives of Others

Internet
11. Overload!
12. Don't Blame the Journalism
16. Economic and Business Dimensions: Is the Internet a Maturing Market?
26. But Who's Counting?
30. Open for Business

Magazines
23. The Lives of Others

Media effects research
1. In the Beginning Was the Word
3. Tele[re]vision
4. Research on the Effects of Media Violence
28. Multitasking Youth

Media history
1. In the Beginning Was the Word
3. Tele[re]vision
8. *The* Reconstruction *of* American Journalism
15. What's a Fair Share in the Age of Google?
17. Ideastream: *The New* "Public Media"

Internet References

The following Internet sites have been selected to support the articles found in this reader. These sites were available at the time of publication. However, because websites often change their structure and content, the information listed may no longer be available. We invite you to visit www.mhhe.com/cls for easy access to these sites.

Annual Editions: Mass Media 11/12

General Sources

Associated Press Managing Editors
www.apme.com/

Allows you to view all the front pages of newspapers across the nation.

The Center for Communication
www.cencom.org

The Center for Communication is an independent nonpartisan media forum that introduces issues, ethics, people and media business. The site provides archived seminars like the panel discussion on Marshall McLuhan entitled "Oracle of the Electronic Age." Students can tap into these seminars via video-streaming. This site also provides links to numerous other sites.

Current.org
www.current.org/

This is a newspaper about public broadcasting in the U.S. It is editorially independent and is an affiliate of the Educational Broadcasting Corporation.

Digital Forensics and Tampering
www.cs.dartmouth.edu/farid/research/tampering.html

Dartmouth scientist Hany Farid posts examples of photo editing, and illustrations of his work developing mathematical and computational algorithms to detect tampering in digital media. Links to articles including *www.cs.dartmouth .edu/farid/publications/deception07.html* "Digital Doctoring: can we trust photographs?" and *www.cs.dartmouth.edu/farid/ publications/significance06.pdf* "Digital Doctoring: How to tell the real from the fake" (pdf files), well-illustrated with examples, historical and current.

Iowa Scholar's Desktop Resources
www.uiowa.edu/~commstud/resources/scholarsdesktop/

An encyclopedic resource related to a host of mass communication issues, this site is maintained by the University of Iowa's Department of Communication Studies. It provides excellent links covering advertising, cultural studies, digital media, film, gender issues, and media studies.

Media Awareness Network
www.media-awareness.ca/

Media Awareness Network provides resources and support for parents and teachers interested in media and information literacy for kids. Concise, vest-pocket summaries of issues including media stereotyping, media violence, online hate, information privacy. Includes educational games (e.g. *Jo Cool or Jo Fool:* Interactive Module and Quiz on Critical Thinking for the Internet). From Canada.

Netcomtalk/Boston University
http://web.bu.edu/COM/communication.html

The College of Communication at Boston University presents this multimedia publication site for daily perusal of a wide variety of news items and topics in media and communications. Click on "COMNews Today" for the latest happenings in mass media.

NewsPlace
www.niu.edu/newsplace/

This site of Professor Avi Bass from Northern Illinois University will lead you to a wealth of resources of interest in the study of mass media, such as international perspectives on censorship. Links to government, corporate, and other organizations are provided.

The Web Journal of Mass Communication
www.scripps.ohiou.edu/wjmcr/

This site can also be easily accessed from *http://wjmcr.org.* The Web Journal of Mass Communication out of Ohio University focuses on articles that relate to how the web shapes mass communication.

Writers Guild of America
www.wga.org

The Writer's Guild of America is the union for media entertainment writers. The nonmember areas of this site offer useful information for aspiring writers. There is also an excellent links section.

UNIT 1: Living with Media

American Center for Children and Media
www.centerforchildrenandmedia.org

Continually amasses up-to-date research, news and writings about children and media, from which it digests, analyzes and disseminates information on trends and themes.

Children Now
www.childrennow.org

Children Now's site provides access to a variety of views on the impact of media on children. Public opinion surveys of young people, independent research on television and print media, industry conference proceedings, and more are available. An Internet resource list is included.

The Free Child Project: Youth Media Organizations
www.freechild.org/YouthMediaOrgs.htm

Good site covering youth media and current trends.

Freedom Forum
www.freedomforum.org

The Freedom Forum is a nonpartisan, international foundation dedicated to free press, free speech, and free spirit for all people. Its mission is to help the public and the news media understand one another better. The press watch area of this site is intriguing.

UNIT 2: Telling Stories

Cable News Network
www.cnn.com

CNN's interactive site is considered to be an excellent online news site.

Internet References

Fairness and Accuracy in Reporting

www.fair.org

FAIR, a U.S. media watch group, offers well-documented criticism of media bias and censorship. It advocates structural reform to break up the dominant media conglomerates.

Fox News

www.foxnews.com

The Fox News site touts itself as being "fair and balanced."

Organization of News Ombudsmen (ONO)

www.newsombudsmen.org

This ONO page provides links to journalism websites. ONO works to aid in the wider establishment of the position of news ombudsmen on newspapers and elsewhere in the media and to provide a forum for the interchange of experiences, information, and ideas among news ombudsmen.

Television News Archive

http://tvnews.vanderbilt.edu

By browsing through this Vanderbilt University site, you can review national U.S. television news broadcasts from 1968 onward. It will give you insight into how the broadcast news industry has changed over the years and what trends define the industry today.

UNIT 3: Players and Guides

The Electronic Journalist

http://spj.org

This site for The Electronic Journalist, an online service of the Society of Professional Journalists (SPJ), will lead you to a number of articles having to do with journalistic ethics, accuracy, and other topics.

Ethics Matters

A monthly column in *News Photographer* magazine commfaculty. fullerton.edu/lester/writings/nppa.html

Federal Communications Commission (FCC)

www.fcc.gov

The FCC is an independent U.S. government agency whose mission "is to encourage competition in all communications markets and to protect the public interest." Access to information about such topics as laws regulating the media is possible.

Media Ethics Case Studies

www.highered.mcgraw-hill.com/sites/007288259x/student_view0/ case_studies.html

Photo Ethics

www.sree.net/teaching/photoethics.html

Poynter Online: Research Center

www.poynter.org

The Poynter Institute for Media Studies provides extensive links to information and resources on media ethics, media writing and editing, visual journalism, and much more. Many bibliographies and websites are included.

World Intellectual Property Organization (WIPO)

www.wipo.org

Click on the links at WIPO's home page to find general information on WIPO and intellectual property, publications and documents, international classifications, and more.

UNIT 4: A Word from Our Sponsor

Advertising Age

http://adage.com

Gain access to articles and features about media advertising, such as a history of television advertising, at this site.

Citizens Internet Empowerment Coalition (CIEC)

www.ciec.org

CIEC is a broad group of Internet users, library groups, publishers, online service providers, and civil liberties groups working to preserve the First Amendment and ensure the future of free expression. Find discussions of the Communications Decency Act and Internet-related topics here.

Educause

www.educause.edu

Open this site for an e-mailed summary of info-tech news from various major publications and for many other resources meant to facilitate the introduction, use, access to, and management of information resources in teaching, learning, scholarship, and research.

Media Literacy Clearing House

www.frankwbaker.com/default1.htm

Frank Baker's Media Literacy Clearing House provides access to a wealth of resources designed for teaching media literacy and of interest to anyone seeking to improve their own media literacy. Click "Math in the Media" for links to data on 30 second ad costs, calculating ratings and shares, and Nielsen markets.

Young MediaAustralia

www.youngmedia.org.au/mediachildren/03_advertising.htm

This organization's "members share a strong commitment to the promotion of the healthy development of Australian children. Their particular interest and expertise is in the role that media experiences play in that development."

UNIT 1

Living with Media

Unit Selections

Learning Outcomes

The articles in this section will contribute to your being able to

- Critically evaluate the effects of new media on how consumers attend to and process information.

- Assess the potential of feedforward effects in terms of desirable and undesirable outcomes.

- Describe the challenges of researchers' coming to absolute agreement on how media messages affect children and others who consume those messages.

- Summarize criticisms of Wikipedia and other news and information media as sources of accurate and unbiased information.

- Describe the Facebook business model.

Student Website
www.mhhe.com/cls

Internet References

American Center for Children and Media
www.centerforchildrenandmedia.org/
Children Now
www.childrennow.org
Freedom Forum
www.freedomforum.org
The Free Child Project: Youth Media Organizations
www.freechild.org/YouthMediaOrgs.htm

The media have been blamed for just about everything, from a decrease in attention span to an increase in street crime, to undoing our capacity to think. In *Amusing Ourselves to Death* (Penguin, 1986), social critic Neil Postman suggested that the cocktail party, the quiz show, and popular trivia games are reflections of society's trying to find a use for the abundance of superficial information given to us by the media. Peggy Noonan, a former network writer and White House speechwriter, has observed that experiences are not "real" unless they are ratified by media (which is why, she says, half the people in a stadium watch the game on monitors rather than the field). Marie Winn's memorable description of a child transfixed by television—slack-jawed, tongue resting on the front teeth, eyes glazed and vacant (*The Plug-In Drug,* Penguin, 1985, 2002)—has become an oft-quoted symbol of the passivity encouraged by television viewing. In the year 2000 there were four "reality TV" shows, in 2010 there were 320. Americans sent 12 billion emails a day in 2000; in 2010 the number was 247 billion. Time spent online increased from 2.7 hours per week in 2000 to 18 hours per week in 2010. We, as a nation, have a distinct love-hate relationship with mass media.

Questions of whether, and to what extent, media influence our behaviors, values, expectations, and ways of thinking are difficult to answer. While one bibliographer has compiled a list of some 4,000 citations of English-language articles focusing just on children and television, the conclusions drawn in these articles vary. Isolating media as a causal agent in examining human behavior is a difficult task.

Media messages serve a variety of purposes: They inform, they influence public opinion, they sell, and they entertain—sometimes below the level of consumers' conscious awareness. Children watch *Sesame Street* to be entertained, but they also learn to count, to share, to accept physical differences among individuals, and (perhaps) to desire a Sesame Street lunchbox. Adults watch crime dramas to be entertained, but they also learn that they have the right to remain silent when arrested, how (accurately or inaccurately) the criminal justice system works, and that the world is an unsafe place.

Nicholas Johnson, a former chairman of the Federal Communications Commission, has noted, "Every moment of television programming—commercials, entertainment, news—teaches us something." How such incidental learning occurs is most often explained by two theories. Social learning (or modeling) theory suggests that the behavior of media consumers, particularly children, is affected by their imitating role models presented via media. The degree to which modeling occurs depends upon the presence of *inhibitors,* lessons learned in real life that discourage imitation, and *disinhibitors,* experiences in real life that reinforce imitation.

Cultivation theory holds that media shape behavior by influencing attitudes. Media provide a "window to the world," exposing consumers to images of reality that may or may not jibe with personal experience. *Mainstreaming* effects occur when media introduce images of things with which the consumer has no personal experience. *Resonance* effects occur when media images echo personal experience. For example, recent research has found that knowing someone who is openly gay or lesbian is

© Blend Images/Getty Images

the single best predictor of tolerance of same-sex marriage, but seeing likable gay characters on television shows such as *Will & Grace* also has significant effects on attitude. In one study, anti-gay perceptions in students with little personal experience of interacting with gay men decreased by 12% after viewing ten episodes of HBO's *Six Feet Under.* This is a mainstreaming effect. Heavy media consumers are more likely to be affected than light consumers, since they spend more time absorbing information from media. People who have had real-world experiences similar to those in the media they consume may find that the media reinforce their beliefs (resonance). However, consumers who have had personal experiences that differ from the images portrayed in media are not as likely to believe "media reality" over what they have observed in real life.

The readings in this unit examine media use, media content, and media effects. All of them acknowledge the increasingly complex interactions among media producers, technology, forms, formats, and consumers. They share concerns over media influence on daily living and on society. Some take a *feedforward* perspective, holding media accountable for shaping changes in public attitude and behavior. Others argue a *feedback* viewpoint, in which media simply reflect what consumers choose to make popular.

"In the Beginning Was the Word" is about the role of the book in the contemporary media landscape. While the experience of reading (traditional book? Kindle?) and competition for time to read are changing, "our need for stories to translate our experience hasn't changed." The number of books published in 2000 was 282,242; in 2010, 1,052,803. "Revolution in a Box" and "Tele[re]vision" focus on prosocial feedforward effects of television. "Research on the Effects of Media Violence" summarizes some of the key questions that have grounded research on media effects, with findings explained using both social learning and cultivation theories.

"Wikipedia in the Newsroom" provides a different take on Internet information, focusing on creation and ownership of information posted to the website that pops to the first page of most web searches—for better or for worse. "I like much of the new technology," states a Pulitzer Prize-winning reporter. "But to me rules, borders, guidelines, and transparency matter a lot." The argument presented in "Journalist Bites Reality!" is captured in the article's subtitle: "How broadcast journalism is flawed in such a fundamental way that its utility for informing viewers is almost nil."

"Girls Gone Anti-Feminist" takes a feedforward stance: "This is the mass media—exaggerating certain kinds of stories, certain kinds of people, certain kinds of values and attitudes, while minimizing others or rendering them invisible." Finally, "The Great Wall of Facebook" lends insight into the interface of consumer and business perspectives in shaping Google and Facebook.

In the Beginning Was the Word

The book, that fusty old technology, seems rigid and passé as we daily consume a diet of information bytes and digital images. The fault, dear reader, lies not in our books but in ourselves.

CHRISTINE ROSEN

In August, the company that owns *Reader's Digest* filed for bankruptcy protection. The magazine, first cobbled together with scissors and paste in a Greenwich Village basement in 1922 by De Witt Wallace and his wife, Lila, was a novel experiment in abridgement—in 62 pages, it offered Americans condensed versions of current articles from other periodicals. The formula proved wildly successful, and by midcentury *Reader's Digest* was a publishing empire, with millions of subscribers and ventures including Reader's Digest Condensed Books, which sold abridged versions of best-selling works by authors such as Pearl Buck and James Michener. *Reader's Digest* both identified and shaped a peculiarly American approach to reading, one that emphasized convenience, entertainment, and the appearance of breadth. An early issue noted that it was "not a magazine in the usual sense, but rather a co-operative means of rendering a time-saving device."

The fate of *Reader's Digest* would have been of interest to the late historian and Librarian of Congress Daniel Boorstin. In his renowned 1962 book *The Image: A Guide to Pseudo-Events in America,* Boorstin used *Reader's Digest* as an example of what was wrong with a culture that had learned to prefer image to reality, the copy to the original, the part to the whole. Publications such as the *Digest,* produced on the principle that any essay can be boiled down to its essence, encourage readers to see articles as little more than "a whiff of literary ectoplasm exuding from print," he argued, and an author's style as littered with unnecessary "literary embellishments" that waste a reader's time.

Today, of course, abridgement and abbreviation are the norm, and our impatience for information has trained even those of us who never cracked an issue of *Reader's Digest* to prefer 60-second news cycles to 62 condensed pages per month. Free "aggregator" Web sites such as The Huffington Post link to hundreds of articles from other publications every day, and services such as DailyLit deliver snippets of novels directly to our e-mail in-boxes every morning.

Our willingness to follow a writer on a sustained journey that may at times be challenging and frustrating is less compelling than our expectation of being conveniently entertained. Over time, this attitude undermines our commitment to the kind of "deep reading" that researcher Maryanne Wolf, in *Proust and the Squid: The Story and Science of the Reading Brain* (2007), argues is important from an early age, when readers learn to identify with characters and to "expand the boundaries of their lives."

As Boorstin surveyed the terrain nearly half a century ago, his overarching concern was that an image-saturated culture would so distort people's sense of judgment that they would cease to distinguish between the real and the unreal. He criticized the creation of what he called "pseudo-events" such as politicians' staged photo-ops, and he traced the ways in which our pursuit of illusion transforms our experience of travel, clouds our ability to discern the motivations of advertisers, and encourages us to elevate celebrities to the status of heroes. "This is the appealing contradiction at the heart of our passion for pseudo-events: for made news, synthetic heroes, prefabricated tourist attractions, homogenized interchangeable forms of art and literature (where there are no 'originals,' but only the shadows we make of other shadows)," Boorstin wrote. "We believe we can fill our experience with new-fangled content."

Boorstin wrote *The Image* before the digital age, but his book still has a great deal to teach us about the likely future of the printed word. Some of the effects of the Internet appear to undermine Boorstin's occasionally gloomy predictions. For example, an increasing number of us, instead of being passive viewers of images, are active participants in a new culture of online writing and opinion mongering. We comment on newspaper and magazine articles, post our reviews of books and other products online, write about our feelings on personal blogs, and bombard our friends and acquaintances with status updates on Facebook. As the word migrates from printed page to pixilated screen, so too do more of our daily activities. Online we find news, work, love, social interaction, and an array of entertainment. We have embraced new modes of storytelling, such as the interactive, synthetic world of video games, and found new ways to share our quotidian personal experiences, in hyperkinetic bursts, through microblogging services such as Twitter.

Many observers have loudly and frequently praised the new technologies as transformative and democratic, which they undoubtedly are. But their widespread use has sparked broader questions about the relevance and value of the printed word and the traditional book. The book, like the wheel, is merely a technology, these enthusiasts argue, and thus we should welcome improvements to it, even if those improvements eventually lead to the book's obsolescence. After all, the deeply felt human need for storytelling won't fade; it will merely take on new forms, forms we should welcome as signs of progress, not decay. As Boorstin observed in the foreword to the 25th-anniversary edition of *The Image,* "We Americans are sensitive to any suggestion that progress may have its price."

Our screen-intensive culture poses three challenges to traditional reading: distraction, consumerism, and attention-seeking behavior. Screen technologies such as the cell phone and laptop computer that are supposedly revolutionizing reading also potentially offer us greater control over our time. In practice, however, they have increased our anxiety about having too little of it by making us available anytime and anywhere. These technologies have also dramatically increased our opportunities for distraction. It is a rare Web site that presents its material without the clutter of advertisement, and a rare screen reader who isn't lured by the siren song of an incoming e-mail's "ping!" to set aside her work to see who has written. We live in a world of continuous partial attention, one that prizes speed and brandishes the false promise of multitasking as a solution to our time management challenges. The image-driven world of the screen dominates our attention at the same time that it contributes to a kind of experience pollution that is challenging our ability to engage with the printed word.

The digital revolution has also transformed the experience of reading by making it more consumer oriented. With the advent of electronic readers (and cell phones that can double as e-readers), the book is no longer merely a thing you purchase, but a service to which you subscribe. With the purchase of a traditional book, your consumer relationship ends when you walk out of the bookstore. With a wirelessly connected Kindle or iPhone, or your Wi-Fi-enabled computer, you exist in a perpetual state of potential consumerism. To be sure, for most people reading has never been a pure, quasi-monastic activity; everyday life has always presented distractions to the person keen on losing herself in a book. But for the first time, thanks to new technologies, we are making those distractions an integral part of the experience of reading. Embedded in these new versions of the book are the means for constant and elaborate demands on our attention. And as our experience with other screen media, from television to video games to the Internet, suggests, such distractions are difficult to resist.

Finally, the transition from print reading to screen reading has increased our reliance on images and led to a form of "social narcissism" that Boorstin first identified in his book. "We have fallen in love with our own image, with images of our making, which turn out to be images of ourselves," he wrote. We become viewers rather than readers, observers rather than participants. The "common reader" Virginia Woolf prized, who is neither scholar nor critic but "reads for his own pleasure, rather than to impart knowledge or correct the opinions of others," is a vanishing species. Instead, an increasing number of us engage with the written word not to submit ourselves to another's vision or for mere edification, but to have an excuse to share our own opinions.

In August, Stanford University released preliminary results from its Stanford Study of Writing, which examined in-class and out-of-class writing samples from thousands of students over five years. One of the study's lead researchers, Andrea Lunsford, concluded, "We're in the midst of a literacy revolution the likes of which we haven't seen since Greek civilization." The source of this revolution, Lunsford proposed, is the "life writing" students do every day online: The study found that 38 percent of their writing occurred outside the classroom.

But as Emory University English professor Mark Bauerlein pointed out in a blog post on *The Chronicle of Higher Education*'s Web site, this so-called revolution has not translated into concrete improvements in writing skills as measured by standardized tests such as the ACT; nor has it led to a reduction in the number of remedial writing courses necessary to prepare students for the workplace. Of greater concern was the attitude students expressed about the usefulness of writing: Most of them judged the quality of writing by the size of the audience that read it rather than its ability to convey ideas. One of the most prolific contributors to the study, a Stanford undergraduate who submitted more than 700 writing samples ranging from Facebook messages to short stories, told the *Chronicle* that for him a class writing assignment was a "soulless exercise" because it had an audience of one, the professor. He and other students in the study, raised on the Internet, consistently expressed a preference for writing that garnered the most attention from as many people as possible.

Our need for stories to translate our experience hasn't changed. Our ability to be deeply engaged readers of those stories is changing. For at least half a century, the image culture has trained us to expect the easily digestible, the quickly paced, and the uncomplicated. As our tolerance for the inconvenient or complex fades, images achieve even more prominence, displacing the word by appealing powerfully to a different kind of emotional sensibility, one whose vividness and urgency are undeniable but whose ability to explore nuance are not the same as that of the printed word.

What Boorstin feared—that a society beholden to the image would cease to distinguish the real from the unreal—has not come to pass. On the contrary, we acknowledge the unique characteristics of the virtual world and have eagerly embraced them, albeit uncritically. But Boorstin's other concern—that a culture that craves the image will eventually find itself mired in solipsism and satisfied by secondhand experiences—has been borne out. We follow the Twitter feeds of protesting Iranians and watch video of Michael Jackson's funeral and feel connected to the rest of the world, even though we lack context for that feeling and don't make much effort to achieve it beyond logging on. The screen offers us the illusion of participation, and this illusion is becoming our preference. As Boorstin observed, "Every day seeing there and hearing there takes the place of being there."

This secondhand experience is qualitatively different from the empathy we develop as readers. "We read to know we are not alone," C. S. Lewis once observed, and by this he meant that books are a gateway to a better understanding of what it means to be human. Because the pace is slower and the rewards delayed, the exercise of reading on the printed page requires a commitment unlike that demanded by the screen, as anyone who has embarked on the journey of an ambitiously long novel can attest. What the screen gives us is pleasurable, but it is not the same kind of experience as deeply engaged reading; the "screen literacy" praised by techno-enthusiasts should be seen as a complement to, not a replacement of, traditional literacy.

Since the migration of the word from page to screen is still in its early stages, predictions about the future of print are hazardous at best. When *Time* magazine named "YOU!" its person of the year in 2006, the choice was meant as a celebratory recognition of our new digital world and its many opportunities for self-expression. We are all writers now, crafters of our own images and creators of our own online worlds. But so far this power has made us less, not more, willing to submit ourselves to the singular visions of writers and artists and to learn from them difficult truths about the human condition. It has encouraged us to substitute images and simplistic snippets

This Is Your Brain on the Web

As scientists begin to bear down on the cognitive differences between reading online and off, they are discovering that the two activities are not the same at all.

Numerous studies have shown that we don't so much *read* online as *scan*. In a series of studies from the early 1990s until 2006, Jakob Nielsen, a former Sun Microsystems engineer, and Don Norman, a cognitive scientist, tracked the eye movements of Web surfers as they skipped from one page to the next. They found that only 16 percent of subjects read the text on a page in the order in which it appeared. The rest jumped around, picking out individual words and processing them out of sequence. "That's how users read your precious content," Nielsen cautions Web designers in his online column. "In a few seconds, their eyes move at amazing speeds across your Web site's words in a pattern that's very different from what you learned in school."

Nielsen recommends that designers create Web sites that are easy to comprehend by scanning: one idea per paragraph, highlighted keywords, and objective-sounding language so readers don't need to perform the mental heavy-lifting of determining what's fact and what's bias or distortion.

It is particularly hard to hold readers' attention online because of all the temptations dangled before them. Psychologists argue that our brains are naturally inclined to constantly seek new stimuli. Clicking on link after link, always looking for a new bit of information, we are actually revving up our brains with dopamine, the overlord of what psychologist Jaak Panksepp has called the "seeking system."

This system is what drives you to get out of bed each day, and what causes you to check your e-mail every few minutes; it's what keys you up in anticipation of a reward. Most of your e-mail may be junk, but the prospect of receiving a meaningful message—or following a link to a stimulating site—is enough to keep your brain constantly a bit distracted from what you're reading online.

What are the effects on the brain of all this distraction? Scientists are only beginning to answer this question. A recent study by three Stanford researchers found that consummate multitaskers are, in fact, terrible at multitasking. In three experiments, they were worse at paying attention, controlling their memories, and switching between tasks than those who prefer to complete one task at a time. Clifford Nass, one of the researchers, says, "They're suckers for irrelevancy. Everything distracts them." Unable to discriminate between relevant material and junk, multitaskers can get lost in a sea of information.

The things we read on the Web aren't likely to demand intense focus anyway. A survey of 1,300 students at the University of Illinois, Chicago, found that only five percent regularly read a blog or forum on politics, economics, law, or policy. Nearly 80 percent checked Facebook, the social networking site.

Maryanne Wolf, director of the Center for Reading and Language Research at Tufts University, says it's not just what we read that shapes us, but the fact that we read at all. She writes, "With [the invention of reading], we rearranged the very organization of our brain, which in turn expanded the ways we were able to think, which altered the intellectual evolution of our species." When children are just learning to read, their brains show activation in both hemispheres. As word recognition becomes more automatic, this activity is concentrated in the left hemisphere, allowing more of the brain to work on the task of distilling the meaning of the text and less on decoding it. This efficiency is what allows our brains the time to think creatively and analytically. According to Wolf, the question is, "What would be lost to us if we replaced the skills honed by the reading brain with those now being formed in our new generation of 'digital natives'?"

In the end, the most salient difference isn't between a screen and a page but between focused reading and disjointed scanning. Of course, the former doesn't necessarily follow from opening a book and the latter is not inherent to opening a Web browser, but that is the pattern. However, that pattern may not always hold true. Google, for example, recently unveiled Fast Flip, a feature designed to recreate the experience of reading newspapers and magazines offline. Other programs, such as *The New Yorker*'s digital edition or *The New York Times*' Times Reader 2.0, have a similar purpose, allowing readers to see on the screen something much like what they would normally hold between their two hands. And with the Kindle and other e-readers quickly catching on, we may soon find that reading in the future is quite like reading in the past.

Until such innovations move into wider use, the surest bet for undistracted reading continues to be an old-fashioned book. As historian Marshall Poe observes, "A book is a machine for focusing attention; the Internet is [a] machine for diffusing it."

of text for the range, precision, and peculiar beauty of written language, with its unique power to express complex and abstract ideas. Recent surveys by the National Endowment for the Arts reveal that fewer Americans read literature for pleasure than in the past; writers of serious fiction face a daunting publishing market and a reading public that has come to prefer the celebrity memoir to the new literary novel.

There is a reason that the metaphor so often invoked to describe the experience of reading is one of escape: An avid reader can recall the book that first unlocked the door of his imagination or provided a sense of escape from the everyday world. The critic Harold Bloom has written that he was forever changed by his early encounters with books: "My older sisters, when I was very young, took me to the library, and thus transformed my life." As Maryanne Wolf notes, "Biologically and intellectually, reading allows the species to go 'beyond the information given' to create endless thoughts most beautiful and wonderful."

An Avid Reader can recall the book that first unlocked his imagination or provided a sense of escape from the everyday world.

The proliferation of image and text on the Internet has exacerbated the solipsism Boorstin feared, because it allows us to read in a broad but shallow manner. It endorses rather than challenges our sensibilities, and substitutes synthetic images for our own peculiar form of imagination. Over time, the ephemeral, immediate quality of this constant stream of images undermines the self-control required to engage with the written word. And so we find ourselves in the position of living in a highly literate society that chooses not to exercise the privilege of literacy—indeed, it no longer views literacy as a privilege at all.

In *Essays on His Own Times* (1850), Samuel Taylor Coleridge observed, "The great majority of men live like bats, but in twilight, and know and feel the philosophy of their age only by its reflections and refractions." Today we know our age by its tweets and text messages, its never-ending litany of online posts and ripostes. Judging by the evidence so far, the content we find the most compelling is what we produce about ourselves: our tastes, opinions, and habits. This has made us better interpreters of our own experience, but it has not made us better readers or more empathetic human beings.

Critical Thinking

1. Christine Rosen writes, "We live in a world of continuous partial attention, one that prizes speed and brandishes the false promise of multitasking as a solution to our time management challenges." If this is accurate, to what degree is it because of mass media?

2. Summarize Rosen's key differences between the experience of reading words on paper vs. words on screen.

CHRISTINE ROSEN is a senior editor of *The New Atlantis: A Journal of Technology and Society.*

Revolution in a Box

It's not Twitter or Facebook that's reinventing the planet. Eighty years after the first commercial broadcast crackled to life, television still rules our world. And let's hear it for the growing legions of couch potatoes: All those soap operas might be the ticket to a better future after all.

CHARLES KENNY

"The television," science-fiction writer Ray Bradbury lamented in 1953, is "that insidious beast, that Medusa which freezes a billion people to stone every night, staring fixedly, that Siren which called and sang and promised so much and gave, after all, so little." Bradbury wasn't alone in his angst: Television has been as reviled as it has been welcomed since the first broadcasts began in 1928. Critics of television, from disgusted defenders of the politically correct to outraged conservative culture warriors, blame it for poor health, ignorance, and moral decline, among other assorted ills. Some go further: According to a recent *fatwa* in India, television is "nearly impossible to use . . . without a sin." Last year, a top Saudi cleric declared it permissible to kill the executives of television stations for spreading sedition and immorality.

So will the rapid, planetwide proliferation of television sets and digital and satellite channels, to corners of the world where the Internet is yet unheard of, be the cause of global decay such critics fear? Hardly. A world of couch potatoes in front of digital sets will have its downsides—fewer bowling clubs, more Wii bowling. It may or may not be a world of greater obesity, depending on whom you ask. But it could also be a world more equal for women, healthier, better governed, more united in response to global tragedy, and more likely to vote for local versions of *American Idol* than shoot at people.

Indeed, television, that 1920s technology so many of us take for granted, is still coming to tens of millions with a transformative power—for the good—that the world is only now coming to understand. The potential scope of this transformation is enormous: By 2007, there was more than one television set for every four people on the planet, and 1.1 billion households had one. Another 150 million-plus households will be tuned in by 2013.

In our collective enthusiasm for whiz-bang new social-networking tools like Twitter and Facebook, the implications of this next television age—from lower birthrates among poor women to decreased corruption to higher school enrollment rates—have largely gone overlooked despite their much more sweeping impact. And it's not earnest educational programming that's reshaping the world on all those TV sets. The programs that so many dismiss as junk—from song-and-dance shows to *Desperate Housewives*—are being eagerly consumed by poor people everywhere who are just now getting access to television for the first time. That's a powerful force for spreading glitz and drama—but also social change.

Television, it turns out, is the kudzu of consumer durables. It spreads across communities with incredible speed. Just look at the story of expanding TV access in the rural areas of one poor country, Indonesia: Within two years of village electrification, average television ownership rates reached 30 percent. Within seven years, 60 percent of households had TVs—this in areas where average surveyed incomes were about $2 a day. Fewer than 5 percent of these same households owned refrigerators. Television is so beloved that in the vast swaths of the world where there is still no electricity network, people hook up their TVs to batteries—indeed, in a number of poor countries, such as Peru, more homes have televisions than electricity.

As a result, the television is fast approaching global ubiquity. About half of Indian households have a television, up from less than a third in 2001; the figure for Brazil is more than four-fifths. (In comparison, just 7 percent of Indians use the Internet, and about one-third of Brazilians do.) In places like Europe and North America, 90-plus percent of households have a TV. Even in countries as poor as Vietnam and Algeria, rates are above 80 percent. But the potential for real growth in access (and impact) is in the least/developed countries, like Nigeria and Bangladesh, where penetration rates are still well below 30 percent.

If an explosion of access is the first global television revolution, then an explosion of choice will be the second. By 2013, half of the world's televisions will be receiving digital signals, which means access to many more channels. Digital broadcast builds on considerably expanded viewing options delivered through cable or satellite. Indeed, nearly two-thirds of households in India with a TV already have a cable or satellite connection. And in the United States, a bellwether for global television trends, the spread of cable since 1970 has meant an increasing number of broadcast channels are sharing a declining proportion of the audience-down from 80 percent to 40 percent over the last 35 years. The average American

What they're Watching

Soaps, soaps, and more soaps. But not all of the dramas are created equal. In Colombia, viewers enjoy a hard-bitten saga of gang violence; in Iran, they're tuning into tales of Jewish rescue during World War II.

Noor
Turkey

An Arabic-dubbed version of this popular Turkish soap opera became a bona fide pop-culture phenomenon throughout the Middle East during its 2005-2007 run, attracting millions of fans from Egypt to the Persian Gulf to Gaza and the West Bank. It is also "replete with evil, wickedness, moral collapse, and a war on the virtues," said one Saudi cleric. What's so dangerous about the show? It depicts a young couple as an equal partnership in which the husband supports his wife's career aspirations, and their friends are young cosmopolitan Muslims drinking and flirting on screen. Plenty of Muslim women apparently liked what they saw.

The Cartel of the Snitches
Colombia

Drugs, sex, street fights, and money. No, it's not the latest edition of *Grand TheftAuto;* it's Colombia's most popular soap opera, *El Cartel.* The multiseason series traces the lives of characters who are enthralled by the drug trade's prospect of easy wealth, but who learn that their star-studded hopes will not be met in reality; the cartel life is bloody and thankless. The show, based on the book by Andres Lopez Lopez, who was himself once in the drug business, was Colombia's highest rated last year, attracting more than 1 million viewers ages 18 to 49.

Zero Degree Turn
Iran

While Iranian President Mahmoud Ahmadinejad was busy making international headlines by denying the Holocaust, his fellow Iranians were riveted by a drama depicting the terror faced by Jews in Nazi-occupied France. *Zero Degree Turn* tells the true story of an Oskar Schindler-like Iranian diplomat who helped Jews escape Europe by providing them with false Iranian passports. The show was popular with Iranians, but the show's writer and director says he also meant it to show the world that Iran was not the anti-Semitic caricature often depicted in the international media.

Jewel in the Palace
South Korea

This historical soap opera, following the lives and loves of the Korean royal family during the 15th century, is the flagship product of the so-called Korean wave, the onslaught of South Korean pop culture that has swept through East Asia in recent years. Concerned about the shows' "nonsocialist ideas," North Korean authorities have created a special squad of police to crack down on smugglers. Many apparently still try to watch illicit soaps, however, including *Jewel in the Palace* fanboy Kim Jong II, whom then-South Korean President Roh Moo-hyun presented with a DVD boxed set of the show during negotiations in 2007.

Kwanda
South Africa

It's not every day that a prime-time drama written by a nonprofit organization makes it to the top of national ratings. But the Soul City Institute for Health and Development Communication program *Soul City*—with plotlines like a wife presenting her cheating husband with condoms, or a husband's remorse over spousal abuse—has done just that. *Soul City* has been so popular that the NGO is starting a new "community makeover show" this fall. Like *Soul City, Kwanda* won't steer clear of controversy. Episode 7, for example, looks at "sugar daddies that are endangering young girls' lives," according to the NGO's promotional materials.

household now has access to 119 channels, and a similar phenomenon is spreading rapidly around the globe.

The explosion of choice is loosening the grip of bureaucrats the world over, who in many countries have either run or controlled programming directly, or heavily regulated the few stations available. A 97-country survey carried out a few years ago found that an average of 60 percent of the top five television stations in each country were owned by the state, with 32 percent in the hands of small family groupings. Programming in developing countries in particular has often been slanted toward decidedly practical topics—rural TV in China, for example, frequently covers the latest advances in pig breeding. And coverage of politics has often strayed from the balanced. Think Hugo Chavez, who refused to renew the license of RCTV, Venezuela's most popular TV network, after it broadcast commentary critical of his government. He regularly appears on the state channel in his own TV show *Aló Presidente*—episodes of which last anywhere from six to a record 96 hours.

But increasingly, the days when presidential speechmaking and pig breeding were must-see TV are behind us. As choices in what to watch expand, people will have access both to a wider range of voices and to a growing number of channels keen to give the audience what it really wants. And what it wants seems to be pretty much the same everywhere—sports, reality shows, and, yes, soap operas. Some 715 million people worldwide watched the finals of the 2006 soccer World Cup, for example. More than a third of Afghanistan's population tunes into that country's version of *American Idol—Afghan Star.* The biggest television series ever worldwide is *Baywatch*, an everyday tale of lifesaving folk based on and around the beaches of Santa Monica, Calif. The show has been broadcast in 142 countries, and at its peak it had an audience estimated north of 1 billion. (Today, the world's most popular TV show is the medical drama *House*, which according to media consulting firm Eurodata TV Worldwide was watched by 82 million people last year in 66 countries, edging out *CSI* and *Desperate Housewives.*)

Ghulam Nabi Azad, India's health and family welfare minister, has even taken to promoting TV as a form of birth control. "In olden days people had no other entertainment but sex, which is why they produced so many children," he mused publicly in July. "Today, TV is the biggest source of entertainment. Hence, it is important that there is electricity in every village so that people watch TV till late in the night. By the time the serials are over, they'll be too tired to have sex and will fall asleep." Azad is certainly right that television helps slow birthrates, though experience from his own country and elsewhere suggests that it is by example, not exhaustion, that TV programs manage such a dramatic effect.

Since the 1970s, Brazil's Rede Globo network has been providing a steady diet of locally produced soaps, some of which are watched by as many as 80 million people. The programs are no more tales of everyday life in Brazil than *Desperate Housewives* is an accurate representation of a typical U.S. suburb. In a country where divorce was only legalized in 1977, nearly a fifth of the main female characters were divorced (and about a quarter were unfaithful). What's more, 72 percent of the main female characters on the Globo soaps had no kids, and only 7 percent had more than one. In 1970, the average Brazilian woman, in contrast, had given birth nearly six times.

But the soaps clearly resonated with viewers. As the Globo network expanded to new areas in the 1970s and 1980s, according to researchers at the Inter-American Development Bank, parents began naming their kids after soap-opera characters. And women in those parts of the country—especially poor women—started having fewer babies. Being in an area covered by the Globo network had the same effect on a woman's fertility as two additional years of education. This wasn't the result

of what was shown during commercial breaks—for most of the time, contraceptive advertising was banned, and there was no government population-control policy at all. The portrayal of plausible female characters with few children, apparently, was an important social cue.

Cable and satellite television may be having an even bigger impact on fertility in rural India. As in Brazil, popular programming there includes soaps that focus on urban life. Many women on these serials work outside the home, run businesses, and control money. In addition, soap characters are typically well-educated and have few children. And they prove to be extraordinarily powerful role models: Simply giving a village access to cable TV, research by scholars Robert Jensen and Emily Oster has found, has the same effect on fertility rates as increasing by five years the length of time girls stay in school.

The soaps in Brazil and India provided images of women who were empowered to make decisions affecting not only childbirth, but a range of household activities. The introduction of cable or satellite services in a village, Jensen and Oster found, goes along with higher girls' school enrollment rates and increased female autonomy. Within two years of getting cable or satellite, between 45 and 70 percent of the difference between urban and rural areas on these measures disappears. In Brazil, it wasn't just birthrates that changed as Globo's signal spread—divorce rates went up, too. There may be something to the boast of one of the directors of the company that owns *Afghan Star.* When a woman reached the final five this year, the director suggested it would "do more for women's rights than all the millions of dollars we have spent on public service announcements for women's rights on TV."

TV's salutary effects extend far beyond reproduction and gender equality. Kids who watch TV out of school, according to a World Bank survey of young people in the shantytowns of Fortaleza in Brazil, are considerably less likely to consume drugs (or, for that matter, get pregnant). TV's power to reduce youth drug use was two times larger than having a comparatively well-educated mother. And though they might not be as subtly persuasive as *telenovelas* or reality shows, well-designed broadcast campaigns can also make a difference. In Ghana, where as few as 4 percent of mothers were found to wash their hands with soap after defecating and less than 1 percent before feeding their children, reported hand-washing rates shot up in response to a broadcast campaign emphasizing that people eat "more than just rice" if preparers don't wash their hands properly before dinner.

Indeed, TV is its own kind of education—and rather than clash with schooling, as years of parental nagging would suggest, it can even enhance it. U.S. kids with access to a TV signal in the 1950s, for instance—think toddlers watching quality educational programming like *I Love Lucy*—tended to have higher test scores in 1964, according to research by Matthew Gentzkow and Jesse Shapiro of the University of Chicago. Today, more than 700,000 secondary-school students in remote Mexican villages watch the *Telesecundaria* program of televised classes. Although students enter the program with below-average test scores in mathematics and language, by graduation they have caught up in math and halved the language-score deficit.

The World's Most Popular TV Shows

After surveying 66 countries with 1.6 billion viewers between them—from Australia to Japan, Latvia to Venezuela—Eurodata TV Worldwide named the winners for the world's most-watched shows of 2008. What does the world love to watch?

- **Winner:** *House*
- **Category:** Drama
- **Viewers:** 81.8 million worldwide
- **Runners-up:** *CSI: Miami* and *CSI: Las Vegas*

- **Winner:** *Desperate Housewives*
- **Category:** Comedy
- **Viewers:** 56.3 million
- **Runners-up:** *Monk* and *Ugly Betty*

- **Winner:** *The Bold and the Beautiful*
- **Category:** Soap Opera
- **Viewers:** 24.5 million
- **Runners-up:** *Marina* and *The Young and the Restless*

Similarly, evidence that television is responsible for the grim state of civic discourse is mixed, at best. Better television reception in Javanese villages in Indonesia, according to research by Ben Olken, comes with substantially lower levels of participation in social activities and with lower measures of trust in others. Villages with access to an extra TV channel see a decline of about 7 percent in the number of social groups. Similar outcomes have been found in the United States. But improved television reception did not appear to affect the level of discussion in village meetings or levels of corruption in a village road project undertaken during Olken's study. And an examination of the early history of television in the United States by Markus Prior suggests that regions that saw access to more channels in the 1950s and 1960s witnessed increases in political knowledge, interest, and turnout, especially among less-educated TV viewers.

What about television's broader impact on governance? Here, it's the level of competition that seems to matter—a hopeful sign given that the future of global TV is likely to be considerably more competitive. If the only channel that viewers watch is biased in its coverage, then, unsurprisingly, they are likely to be swayed toward that viewpoint. Brazil's Globo channel, for all its positive impact on fertility rates, has played a less positive role in terms of bias-free reporting. It has long had a close relationship with government, as well as a dominant market share. In Brazil's 1989 election—a race in which Globo was squarely behind right-leaning presidential candidate Fernando Collor de Mello—the difference between people who never watched television and those who watched it frequently was a 13 percentage-point increase in the likelihood of voting for Collor, scholar Taylor Boas found. But with channels proliferating nearly everywhere, television controllers may have much less power to sway elections today. In the choice-rich United States, for example, there is no simple relation between hours watched and voting patterns, even if those who watch particular channels are more likely to vote Republican or Democrat.

Then there's corruption. Consider the bribes that Peruvian secret-police chief Vladimiro Montesinos had to pay to subvert competitive newsmaking during the 1990s. It cost only $300,000 per month for Montesinos to bribe most of the congressmen in Peru's government, and about $250,000 a month to bribe the judges—a real bargain. But Montesinos had to spend about $3 million a month to subvert six of the seven available television channels to ensure friendly coverage for the government. The good news here is that competition in the electronic Fourth Estate can apparently make it more expensive to run a country corruptly.

Corruption is one thing, but could television help solve a problem we've had since before Sumer and Elam battled it out around Basra in 2700 B.C.—keeping countries from fighting each other? Maybe.

U.S. researchers who study violence on TV battle viciously themselves over whether it translates into more aggressive behavior in real life. But at least from a broader perspective, television might play a role in stemming the global threat of war. It isn't that TV reporting of death and destruction necessarily reduces support for wars already begun—that's an argument that has raged over conflicts from Vietnam to the Iraq war. It is more that, by fostering a growing global cosmopolitanism, television might make war less attractive to begin with. Indeed, the idea that communications are central to building cross-cultural goodwill is an old one. Karl Marx and Friedrich Engels suggested in the 19th century that railways were vital in rapidly cementing the union of the working class: "that union, to attain which the burghers of the Middle Ages, with their miserable highways, required centuries, the modern proletarians, thanks to railways, achieve in a few years," they wrote in the *Communist Manifesto*. If the Amtraks of the world can have such an impact, surely the Hallmark Channel can do even better.

The fact that Kobe Bryant (born in Philadelphia, plays for the Los Angeles Lakers) sees his basketball shirt considerably outsell those of Yao Ming (born in Shanghai, plays for the Houston Rockets) in China suggests something of that growing global cosmopolitanism at work. The considerable response of

Want to Know More?

- Charles Kenny has written extensively on technology and poverty, beginning with "Development's False Divide" (FOREIGN POLICY, January/February 2003), in which he questions whether the Internet will really be a boon to the world's poor. He elaborates on this idea in his book, *Overselling the Web?: Development and the Internet* (Boulder: Lynne Rienner Publishers, 2006). Kenny looks more broadly at development on his blog, www.charleskenny.blogs.com.

- Matthew Gentzkow and Jesse Shapiro's "Preschool Television Viewing and Adolescent Test Scores: Historical Evidence from the Coleman Study" (*The Quarterly Journal of Economics*, February 2008) finds that childhood TV-viewing improves test scores down the road. In "The Power of TV: Cable Television and Women's Status in India" (*The Quarterly Journal of Economics*, forthcoming), Robert Jensen and Emily Oster find striking correlations between adult TV-watching and lowered fertility rates, among other positive outcomes.

- Steven Johnson agrees that television—even the trashy stuff—can have big social benefits, a theory he details in *Everything Bad Is Good for You: How Today's Popular Culture Is Actually Making Us Smarter* (New York: Riverhead Books, 2005).

- Some skeptics of development include William Easterly, who condemns the whole concept as Western ideology in "The Ideology of Development" (FOREIGN POLICY, July/August 2007). Meanwhile, researchers Dimitri A. Christakis et al. find that television might have its downsides—attentional disorders among children ("Early Television Exposure and Subsequent Attentional Problems in Children," *Pediatrics*, April 2004).

global television viewers to images of famine in Ethiopia, or the tsunami in Asia, also shows how TV is a powerful force for shrinking the emotional distance between peoples within and between countries. In the United States, an additional minute of nightly news coverage of the Asian tsunami increased online donation levels to charities involved in relief efforts by 13 percent, according to research from the William Davidson Institute. And analysis of U.S. public opinion indicates that more coverage of a country on evening news shows is related to increased sympathy and support for that country.

Of course, the extent to which television helps foster cosmopolitanism depends on what people are watching. People in the Middle East who only watched Arab news channels were considerably less likely to agree that the September 11 attacks were carried out by Arab terrorists than those exposed to Western media coverage, researchers Gentzkow and Shapiro found, even after taking into account other characteristics likely to shape their views such as education, language, and age. Similarly, the tone and content of coverage of the ground invasion of Iraq was notably different on Al Jazeera than it was on U.S. and British network broadcasts in the spring of 2003—and surely this helped sustain notably different attitudes toward the war. But with the growing reach of BBC World News and CNN in the Middle East, and the growing reach of Al Jazeera in the West, there is at least a greater potential to understand how the other side thinks.

Just because soap operas and reality shows can help solve real-world problems doesn't mean the world's politicians should now embrace TV as the ultimate policy prescription. There are of course a few things governments could do to harness television's power for good, such as supporting well-designed public service announcements. But for the most part, politicians ought to be paying less attention to TV, not more. They shouldn't be limiting the number of channels or interfering in the news. A vibrant, competitive television market playing *Days of Our Lives or Dias de Nuestras Vidas* on loop might have a bigger impact even than well-meaning educational programs. And competition is critical to ensuring that television helps inform voters, not just indoctrinate them.

In the future, the world will be watching 24 billion hours of TV a day.

In the not-too-distant future, it is quite possible that the world will be watching 24 billion hours of TV a day—an average of close to four hours for each person in the world. Some of those hours could surely be better spent—planting trees, helping old ladies cross the road, or playing cricket, perhaps. But watching TV exposes people to new ideas and different people. With that will come greater opportunity, growing equality, a better understanding of the world, and a new appreciation of the complexities of life for a wannabe Afghan woman pop star. Not bad for a siren Medusa supposedly giving so little.

Critical Thinking

1. Define *feedforward* using examples from this article.
2. Are ethical issues associated with television's feedforward effects different for programs produced in the United States for distribution within the United States than for programs produced for or exported to less developed countries?

CHARLES KENNY, a development economist, is author of the forthcoming book *The Success of Development: Innovation, Ideas and the Global Standard of Living.*

Reprinted in entirety by McGraw-Hill with permission from *Foreign Policy,* November 2009, pp. 70–74. www.foreignpolicy.com. © 2009 Washingtonpost.Newsweek Interactive, LLC.

Tele[re]vision

Researchers are taking a new look at TV. Instead of just filling time or acting as a passive babysitter, can the medium be a good teacher?

JENNY PRICE

Society gives parents plenty of reasons to feel guilty about the time their children spend in front of the television. Nicknames for the medium—boob tube or idiot box, for example—do little to help alleviate their worries.

For years, researchers have shown the negative effects of TV violence and, more recently, they have found links between childhood obesity and too much viewing. President Obama implored parents to "turn off the TV" during a campaign ad pitching his education policy. Still, the average child in the United States spends nearly four hours watching television each day, even though pediatricians recommend no more than two hours of educational programming for kids two years and older.

TV viewing is a given in the average household, but in many cases, parents have no idea what programs their children are watching or whether they understand them at all.

"What we seldom get—and need—is solid, research-based advice about when to turn the TV on," noted Lisa Guernsey, an author and journalist who covers media effects on children, in a column she wrote for the *Washington Post*.

Researchers, including UW-Madison faculty and an alumnus who is behind some groundbreaking work in the field, are working to fill that void, showing that some TV can actually be good for kids.

Their efforts have improved educational programming for children, pinpointing what engages their developing brains and how they learn as they watch. Now the researchers are exploring whether children are really getting the lessons from programs that adults think they are, and how exposure to television might affect children as young as babies and toddlers.

Spoonful of Sugar

Well-crafted shows for children can teach them the alphabet, math, and basic science concepts, as well as manners and social skills. But what really makes for good television when it comes to younger viewers? That's a key question Marie-Louise Mares MA '90, PhD '94, a UW-Madison associate professor of communication arts, is trying to answer.

Much of the educational programming aimed at children falls into the category of "prosocial"—meaning that it's intended to teach lessons, such as healthy eating habits, self-esteem, or how to treat others. The classic example of a prosocial program is *Mister Rogers' Neighborhood.* Mares has shown that a prosocial program's positive influence can be just as strong as a violent program's negative influence.

But good messages can get lost.

"Children's interpretations of what a show is about are very different from what an adult thinks," Mares says. "Some kids take away the completely wrong message."

Mares began studying children's comprehension of prosocial messages after watching the movie *Mary Poppins* with a four-year-old fan. Although the child predicted each scene before it appeared on screen, she had difficulty doing what Mares calls "making sense of the story." The girl did not know why the character Bert, played by Dick Van Dyke, was on the roof dancing or that the "spoonful of sugar" Julie Andrews sings about was a metaphor. As they continued to watch the movie together, Mares learned that what is obvious to an adult doesn't necessarily sink in with children.

She demonstrated that confusion in a study involving a TV episode of *Clifford the Big Red Dog,* in which the cartoon character and friends meet a three-legged dog named K.C. The intent of the program was to teach children to be accepting of those with disabilities. But throughout much of the episode, Clifford and his friends behave badly toward the dog. At one point, one of the dogs expresses fear of catching three-legged dog disease. Sure enough, in follow-up interviews, one-third of the children thought the dogs could catch the disease, and many of them interpreted the lesson of the episode along the lines of this child's comment: "You should be careful . . . not to get sick, not to get germs."

"Showing the fear can actually be more conflicting and more frightening to kids," Mares says.

Her findings are important because much of kids' programming attempts to teach lessons by showing characters behaving badly in some way and then having them learn better behavior. That's confusing for children, Mares says, and could even lead them to focus on the bad behavior.

Her findings are important because much of kids' programming attempts to teach lessons by showing characters behaving badly in some way and then having them learn better behavior. That's confusing for children and could even lead them to focus on the bad behavior.

In the end, 80 percent of the kids in the study said the lesson of the *Clifford* episode was to be nice to dogs with three legs. Although that's a nice sentiment, Mares says, "You don't encounter many [three-legged dogs]."

The producers of prosocial programs also should consider the methods they use to portray the behaviors they're trying to teach kids, Mares says, as well as ensure that the content is relevant and realistic to young viewers. That might be one of the reasons why stories involving dogs or other animal characters don't seem to get the message across to children. One group of youngsters in Mares' study watched a *Clifford* episode that had been edited to remove the dogs showing fear of K.C.—yet the children still interpreted the story as being about dogs, not about inclusiveness and tolerance.

Mares is in new territory; virtually no research has been conducted to identify programming that would effectively foster inclusiveness in children. She has experimented, with mixed results, by embedding some kind of prompt within children's programs that could help young viewers comprehend the intended message, especially since most parents aren't watching along with their kids. Attempts include having the main character start off the show or interrupt mid-lesson to say, "Hey kids, in this story we're going to learn that we shouldn't be afraid of people who are different."

She's still looking for answers on how that practice—which she calls scaffolding—could work effectively. But balance is essential, Mares says, noting that she could create the "ideal" show, but then kids wouldn't want to watch.

Making over *Sesame Street*

The end of the 1960s saw the debut of two landmark educational programs for young people: *Sesame Street* and *Mister Rogers' Neighborhood*. Not long after, Daniel Anderson '66 began trying to discover what exactly was going on with children while they watched TV.

Anderson, a professor at the University of Massachusetts-Amherst who has advised the producers of children's shows including *Sesame Street* and *Captain Kangaroo*, dispelled one of the central myths on the subject—that when the TV is turned on, children's brains turn off. In fact, parents are more likely than their children to become couch potatoes while watching television, says Anderson, who holds a UW bachelor's degree in psychology.

He observed children watching television and witnessed them turning away from the screen several times during a broadcast to play with toys, fight with siblings, or talk to their parents. After they were done watching, he tested their understanding of what they had just seen. Anderson's findings were the exact opposite of what most people thought.

"It was very clear that children were mentally active, that they were constantly posing questions for themselves, [asking], 'What's going to happen next, why are they doing that . . . is this real?' " he says. "And it was also clear that when television invited participation, that kids would become very active—pointing at the screen or talking to the characters on the TV."

This finding ushered in a new era of children's programming, with the cable channel Nickelodeon enlisting Anderson's help to develop a new generation of shows in the late 1990s, most notably *Blue's Clues* and *Dora the Explorer,* that were centered on the concept that children would dance, sing, and follow along with programs they enjoyed rather than sit and stare vacantly at the screen.

Blue's Clues features a mix of animated characters—including a cute blue puppy—and backgrounds, with a live host who invites children who are watching to look for and decipher clues to solve a puzzle, such as, "What does Blue want for her birthday?" Along the way, the show focuses on information such as colors or shapes or numbers.

Anderson pushed producers to make the show visually simple, with very little editing or transitions that require viewers to process jumps in time or location—something young children have a hard time doing, his research showed.

While most researchers "focus on the negative contributions of media," experts such as Anderson and Mares have been "at the forefront of recognizing that television that is designed to be educational really can be beneficial for children," says Amy Jordan, who oversees research on children's media policy for The Annenberg Public Policy Center.

In his best-selling book *The Tipping Point,* which examines how ideas and trends spread, author Malcolm Gladwell labeled *Blue's Clues* as one of the "stickiest"—meaning the most irresistible and involving—television shows ever aired, and noted that its creators "borrowed those parts of *Sesame Street* that did work."

In turn, the success of *Blue's Clues* prompted the producers of *Sesame Street* to seek Anderson's help in giving the long-running staple a makeover. With the new millennium approaching, the show needed to catch up with the way kids watch TV. Rather than the repetitive narrative format children delighted in following as they watched *Blue's Clues, Sesame Street* featured a series of about forty short segments, ranging in length from ten seconds to four minutes.

Even venerable *Sesame Street,* airing since the late 1960s, has evolved, thanks to research about children's TV. The show's original concept assumed short attention spans, cramming as many as forty short segments into each hour.

What Is Educational Television?

POP QUIZ

**Is the TV show *Hannah Montana* educational?
If your answer is no, guess again.**

The ubiquitous Disney Channel sitcom featuring pop star Miley Cyrus airs during ABC's Saturday morning block of shows aimed at children. And, believe it or not, it helps the network's affiliates fulfill their obligation under federal law to air educational and informational (E/I) programming for kids.

Congress first passed legislation in 1990—the Children's Television Act—requiring broadcast stations to increase E/I programming, but what followed were some laughable claims of compliance. For example, *The Jetsons* was labeled educational because it taught children about the future, and stations were sometimes airing educational shows at times when children weren't likely to be awake and watching. So in 1997, lawmakers revisited the act, putting in place what's known as the "three-hour rule," stipulating that the networks air at least three hours of E/I programming for kids per week. Although the rule isn't enforced unless viewers complain, it is used as a guideline when the Federal Communications Commission reviews a station's license for renewal.

So have things gotten better? The FCC has acted on complaints, such as when it fined Univision affiliates $24 million for claiming that serial melodramas known as telenovelas were educational. But even under the three-hour rule, broadcasters maintain shows featuring professional athletes, such as *NBA Inside Stuff* or *NFL Under the Helmet,* count toward the requirement.

Amy Jordan, who oversees research on children's media policy for The Annenberg Public Policy Center and has studied implementation of the three-hour rule, says most commercial network programs are prosocial in nature, aimed at teaching children lessons. *Hannah Montana* falls into that category.

"We actually don't know the take-away value of those kinds of programming," Jordan acknowledges. "And that's an important question, because it speaks to whether or not the broadcasters are living up to the spirit of the Children's Television Act."

A study released last fall by advocacy organization Children Now found that only one in eight shows labeled E/I meets the standard of "highly educational." The majority of the programs studied—a little more than 60 percent—were deemed "moderately educational." The picture looked better at PBS, where the programming for kids was rated significantly higher than E/I shows on commercial stations.

Another issue is that the E/I label is confusing for many parents, with some mistaking programs such as *The Oprah Winfrey Show* and *Who Wants to Be a Millionaire?* as educational.

"In theory, I think parents believe they have a sense of what their kids are exposed to, but in fact, their knowledge is pretty limited," Jordan says. "So to get parents to direct their children to positive programming . . . it's an uphill battle for broadcasters."

Part of the misunderstanding, she says, results from broadcasters doing little to promote which shows carry the E/I label, thereby keeping parents and their children in the dark about which shows are intended to be educational.

"They have this concern about the spinach syndrome—if children think [a program is] good for them, they won't watch it," she says.

—J.P.

"The original conception was that you needed a lot of novelty and change to hold a preschooler's attention. And so they quite explicitly would put things together in unpredictable orders," Anderson says. "A story that was happening on the street with Big Bird and the human characters might be followed by a film about buffalos, which in turn might be followed by a Muppet piece about the letter *H*."

Sesame Street offered children no connection or context among the concepts and segments, and, not surprisingly, it lost viewers when shows like *Blue's Clues* began airing. At Anderson's suggestion, producers made the show more storylike and predictable, reducing the number of characters and sets, and connecting more concepts. Now the typical episode features around ten segments per hour.

"You're dealing with children who don't need complexity," Anderson says. "In a sense, a lot of what they were doing was almost for the adults and not so much for their audience."

Research Gap

The notion of children and television as a research prospect first confronted Anderson when he was a young assistant professor. He had just given an undergraduate lecture on child development, in which he said younger children tend to have more trouble sustaining attention than older children, when one of his students asked, "Well, if those things are true, how come my four-year-old brother can just sit and stare [at *Sesame Street*]?"

"I kind of glibly answered him," Anderson recalls, "that 'Oh, it's because television is just being a distractor. It just looks like your brother's sustaining attention, but the picture is constantly changing and so on.' I just made that up—I had no idea."

Feeling guilty, Anderson sent a graduate student to the library with orders to find out everything he could about children's attention to television.

"He kept coming back and saying he couldn't find anything, and that's what got me started," Anderson says.

> **"Television that has a clear curriculum in mind—that studiously avoids problematic content like violence—has been shown in dozens of studies to really enhance the way children think, the kinds of things that they know, and even how they get along with one another."**
>
> —Amy Jordan

Beginning in the 1980s, Anderson and his colleagues followed 570 children from preschool until high school graduation to see what effect watching *Sesame Street* had on their school performance, behavior, and attitudes. They found that children who had watched when they were young earned better grades in high school, read more books, placed more value on achievement, and showed less aggression. Anderson's study included controls for many other factors, including family size, exposure to media in adolescence, and parents' socioeconomic status.

"We think that the effects are really traceable and cumulative all the way, at least, through high school. So television, I think, can be a powerful educator," Anderson says.

Jordan says those findings hold up in other research. "Television that has a clear curriculum in mind—that studiously avoids problematic content like violence—has been shown in dozens of studies to really enhance the way children think, the kinds of things that they know, and even how they get along with one another," she says.

An Uncontrolled Experiment

So where does that leave guilt-ridden parents looking for answers about television? It seems it comes down to what and how much kids are watching, and at what age.

Anderson, who has been working in the field for decades, thinks that despite educational programming, children are growing up within a vast, uncontrolled experiment. And he draws a sharp distinction about TV's potential value for children over age two.

His recent research focuses on how very young children are affected by simply playing or spending time in a room where adult programming, such as news programs or talk shows, is on the television. Anderson's latest study observed what happened when fifty children ages one to three played in a room for an hour. Half of the time, there was no TV in the room; for the last thirty minutes, the game show *Jeopardy!*—not exactly a toddler favorite—was showing.

The conventional wisdom, based on previous research, was that very young children don't pay attention to programs that they can't understand. But Anderson's study found clear signs that when the television was on, children had trouble concentrating, shortened and decreased the intensity of their play, and cut in half the time they focused on a particular toy.

When the TV was on, the children played about ninety seconds less overall. The concern is whether those effects could add up and harm children's playtime in the long term, impairing their ability to develop sustained attention and other key cognitive skills.

The Annenberg center's Jordan says more studies looking at the effects of TV on younger children are essential, in part because surveys have found that as many as two-thirds of children six years and under live in homes where the TV is on at least half the time, regardless of whether anyone is watching.

"Babies today are spending hours in front of screens . . . and we don't really understand how it's affecting their development," she says. "We can no longer assume children are first exposed to TV when they're two years old because it's happening at a much younger age."

Critical Thinking

1. Define *prosocial programming,* adding your own examples to those in this article.

2. Are *prosocial programming* and *educational programming* synonymous? Why or why not?

JENNY PRICE '96 is a writer for *On Wisconsin.*

Research on the Effects of Media Violence

MEDIA AWARENESS

Whether or not exposure to media violence causes increased levels of aggression and violence in young people is the perennial question of media effects research. Some experts, like University of Michigan professor L. Rowell Huesmann, argue that fifty years of evidence show "that exposure to media violence causes children to behave more aggressively and affects them as adults years later." Others, like Jonathan Freedman of the University of Toronto, maintain that "the scientific evidence simply does not show that watching violence either produces violence in people, or desensitizes them to it."

Many Studies, Many Conclusions

Andrea Martinez at the University of Ottawa conducted a comprehensive review of the scientific literature for the Canadian Radio-television and Telecommunications Commission (CRTC) in 1994. She concluded that the lack of consensus about media effects reflects three "grey areas" or constraints contained in the research itself.

First, media violence is notoriously hard to define and measure. Some experts who track violence in television programming, such as George Gerbner of Temple University, define violence as the act (or threat) of injuring or killing someone, independent of the method used or the surrounding context. Accordingly, Gerber includes cartoon violence in his data-set. But others, such as University of Laval professors Guy Paquette and Jacques de Guise, specifically exclude cartoon violence from their research because of its comical and unrealistic presentation.

Second, researchers disagree over the type of relationship the data supports. Some argue that exposure to media violence causes aggression. Others say that the two are associated, but that there is no causal connection. (That both, for instance, may be caused by some third factor.) And others say the data supports the conclusion that there is no relationship between the two at all.

Third, even those who agree that there is a connection between media violence and aggression disagree about how the one effects the other. Some say that the mechanism is a psychological one, rooted in the ways we learn. For example, Huesmann argues that children develop "cognitive scripts" that guide their own behaviour by imitating the actions of media heroes. As they watch violent shows, children learn to internalize scripts that use violence as an appropriate method of problem-solving.

Other researchers argue that it is the physiological effects of media violence that cause aggressive behaviour. Exposure to violent imagery is linked to increased heart rate, faster respiration and higher blood pressure. Some think that this simulated "fight-or-flight" response predisposes people to act aggressively in the real world. Still others focus on the ways in which media violence primes or cues pre-existing aggressive thoughts and feelings. They argue that an individual's desire to strike out is justified by media images in which both the hero and the villain use violence to seek revenge, often without consequences.

In her final report to the CRTC, Martinez concluded that most studies support "a positive, though weak, relation between exposure to television violence and aggressive behaviour." Although that relationship cannot be "confirmed systematically," she agrees with Dutch researcher Tom Van der Voot who argues that it would be illogical to conclude that "a phenomenon does not exist simply because it is found at times not to occur, or only to occur under certain circumstances."

What the Researchers Are Saying

The lack of consensus about the relationship between media violence and real-world aggression has not impeded ongoing research. Here's a sampling of conclusions drawn to date, from the various research strands:

> Research strand: Children who consume high levels of media violence are more likely to be aggressive in the real world.

In 1956, researchers took to the laboratory to compare the behaviour of 24 children watching TV. Half watched a violent episode of the cartoon *Woody Woodpecker,* and the other 12 watched the non-violent cartoon *The Little Red Hen.* During play afterwards, the researchers observed that the children who watched the violent cartoon were much more likely to hit other children and break toys.

Six years later, in 1963, professors A. Badura, D. Ross and S.A. Ross studied the effect of exposure to real-world violence, television violence, and cartoon violence. They divided 100 pre-school children into four groups. The first group watched a real person shout insults at an inflatable doll while hitting it with a mallet. The second group watched the incident on television. The third watched a cartoon version of the same scene, and the fourth watched nothing.

When all the children were later exposed to a frustrating situation, the first three groups responded with more aggression than the control group. The children who watched the incident on television were just as aggressive as those who had watched the real person use the mallet; and both were more aggressive than those who had only watched the cartoon.

Over the years, laboratory experiments such as these have consistently shown that exposure to violence is associated with increased heartbeat, blood pressure and respiration rate, and a greater willingness to administer electric shocks to inflict pain or punishment on others. However, this line of enquiry has been criticized because of its focus on short term results and the artificial nature of the viewing environment.

Other scientists have sought to establish a connection between media violence and aggression outside the laboratory. For example, a number of surveys indicate that children and young people who report a preference for violent entertainment also score higher on aggression indexes than those who watch less violent shows. L. Rowell Huesmann reviewed studies conducted in Australia, Finland, Poland, Israel, Netherlands and the United States. He reports, "the child most likely to be aggressive would be the one who (a) watches violent television programs most of the time, (b) believes that these shows portray life just as it is, [and] (c) identifies strongly with the aggressive characters in the shows."

A study conducted by the Kaiser Family Foundation in 2003 found that nearly half (47 percent) of parents with children between the ages of 4 and 6 report that their children have imitated aggressive behaviours from TV. However, it is interesting to note that children are more likely to mimic positive behaviours—87 percent of kids do so.

Recent research is exploring the effect of new media on children's behaviour. Craig Anderson and Brad Bushman of Iowa State University reviewed dozens of studies of video gamers. In 2001, they reported that children and young people who play violent video games, even for short periods, are more likely to behave aggressively in the real world; and that both aggressive and non-aggressive children are negatively affected by playing.

In 2003, Craig Anderson and Iowa State University colleague Nicholas Carnagey and Janie Eubanks of the Texas Department of Human Services reported that violent music lyrics increased aggressive thoughts and hostile feelings among 500 college students. They concluded, "There are now good theoretical and empirical reasons to expect effects of music lyrics on aggressive behavior to be similar to the well-studied effects of exposure to TV and movie violence and the more recent research efforts on violent video games."

Research Strand: Children who watch high levels of media violence are at increased risk of aggressive behaviour as adults.

In 1960, University of Michigan Professor Leonard Eron studied 856 grade three students living in a semi-rural community in Columbia County, New York, and found that the children who watched violent television at home behaved more aggressively in school. Eron wanted to track the effect of this exposure over the years, so he revisited Columbia County in 1971, when the children who participated in the 1960 study were 19 years of age. He found that boys who watched violent TV when they were eight were more likely to get in trouble with the law as teenagers.

When Eron and Huesmann returned to Columbia County in 1982, the subjects were 30 years old. They reported that those participants who had watched more violent TV as eight-year-olds were more likely, as adults, to be convicted of serious crimes, to use violence to discipline their children, and to treat their spouses aggressively.

Professor Monroe Lefkowitz published similar findings in 1971. Lefkowitz interviewed a group of eight-year-olds and found that the boys who watched more violent TV were more likely to act aggressively in the real world. When he interviewed the same boys ten years later, he found that the more violence a boy watched at eight, the more aggressively he would act at age eighteen.

Columbia University professor Jeffrey Johnson has found that the effect is not limited to violent shows. Johnson tracked 707 families in upstate New York for 17 years, starting in 1975. In 2002, Johnson reported that children who watched one to three hours of television each day when they were 14 to 16 years old were 60 percent more likely to be involved in assaults and fights as adults than those who watched less TV.

Kansas State University professor John Murray concludes, "The most plausible interpretation of this pattern of correlations is that early preference for violent television programming and other media is one factor in the production of aggressive and antisocial behavior when the young boy becomes a young man."

However, this line of research has attracted a great deal of controversy. Pullitzer Prize-winning author Richard Rhodes has attacked Eron's work, arguing that his conclusions are based on an insignificant amount of data. Rhodes claims that Eron had information about the amount of TV viewed in 1960 for only 3 of the 24 men who committed violent crimes as adults years later. Rhodes concludes that Eron's work is "poorly conceived, scientifically inadequate, biased and sloppy if not actually fraudulent research."

Guy Cumberbatch, head of the Communications Research Group, a U.K. social policy think tank, has equally harsh words for Johnson's study. Cumberbatch claims Johnson's group of 88 under-one-hour TV watchers is "so small, it's aberrant." And, as journalist Ben Shouse points out, other critics say that Johnson's study "can't rule out the possibility that television is just a marker for some unmeasured environmental or psychological influence on both aggression and TV habits."

Research Strand: The introduction of television into a community leads to an increase in violent behaviour.

Researchers have also pursued the link between media violence and real life aggression by examining communities before and after the introduction of television. In the mid 1970s, University of British Columbia professor Tannis McBeth Williams studied a remote village in British Columbia both before and after television was introduced. She found that two years after TV arrived, violent incidents had increased by 160 percent.

Researchers Gary Granzberg and Jack Steinbring studied three Cree communities in northern Manitoba during the 1970s and early 1980s. They found that four years after television was introduced into one of the communities, the incidence of fist fights and black eyes among the children had increased significantly. Interestingly, several days after an episode of *Happy Days* aired, in which one character joined a gang called the Red Demons, children in the community created rival gangs, called the Red Demons and the Green Demons, and the conflict between the two seriously disrupted the local school.

University of Washington Professor Brandon Centerwall noted that the sharp increase in the murder rate in North America in 1955 occurred eight years after television sets began to enter North American homes. To test his hypothesis that the two were related, he examined the murder rate in South Africa where, prior to 1975, television was banned by the government. He found that twelve years after the ban was lifted, murder rates skyrocketed.

University of Toronto Professor Jonathan Freedman has criticized this line of research. He points out that Japanese television has some of the most violent imagery in the world, and yet Japan has a much lower murder rate than other countries, including Canada and the United States, which have comparatively less violence on TV.

Research Strand: Media violence stimulates fear in some children.

A number of studies have reported that watching media violence frightens young children, and that the effects of this may be long lasting.

In 1998, Professors Singer, Slovak, Frierson and York surveyed 2,000 Ohio students in grades three through eight. They report that the incidences of psychological trauma (including anxiety, depression and post-traumatic stress) increased in proportion to the number of hours of television watched each day.

A 1999 survey of 500 Rhode Island parents led by Brown University professor Judith Owens revealed that the presence of a television in a child's bedroom makes it more likely that the child will suffer from sleep disturbances. Nine percent of all the parents surveyed reported that their children have nightmares because of a television show at least once a week.

Tom Van der Voort studied 314 children aged nine through twelve in 1986. He found that although children can easily distinguish cartoons, westerns and spy thrillers from reality, they often confuse realistic programmes with the real world. When they are unable to integrate the violence in these shows

because they can't follow the plot, they are much more likely to become anxious. This is particularly problematic because the children reported that they prefer realistic programmes, which they equate with fun and excitement. And, as Jacques de Guise reported in 2002, the younger the child, the less likely he or she will be able to identify violent content as violence.

In 1999, Professors Joanne Cantor and K. Harrison studied 138 university students, and found that memories of frightening media images continued to disturb a significant number of participants years later. Over 90 percent reported they continued to experience fright effects from images they viewed as children, ranging from sleep disturbances to steadfast avoidance of certain situations.

Research Strand: Media violence desensitizes people to real violence.

A number of studies in the 1970's showed that people who are repeatedly exposed to media violence tend to be less disturbed when they witness real world violence, and have less sympathy for its victims. For example, Professors V.B. Cline, R.G. Croft, and S. Courrier studied young boys over a two-year period. In 1973, they reported that boys who watch more than 25 hours of television per week are significantly less likely to be aroused by real world violence than those boys who watch 4 hours or less per week.

When researchers Fred Molitor and Ken Hirsch revisited this line of investigation in 1994, their work confirmed that children are more likely to tolerate aggressive behaviour in the real world if they first watch TV shows or films that contain violent content.

Research Strand: People who watch a lot of media violence tend to believe that the world is more dangerous than it is in reality.

George Gerbner has conducted the longest running study of television violence. His seminal research suggests that heavy TV viewers tend to perceive the world in ways that are consistent with the images on TV. As viewers' perceptions of the world come to conform with the depictions they see on TV, they become more passive, more anxious, and more fearful. Gerbner calls this the "Mean World Syndrome."

Gerbner's research found that those who watch greater amounts of television are more likely to:

- overestimate their risk of being victimized by crime
- believe their neighbourhoods are unsafe
- believe "fear of crime is a very serious personal problem"
- assume the crime rate is increasing, even when it is not

André Gosselin, Jacques de Guise and Guy Paquette decided to test Gerbner's theory in the Canadian context in 1997. They surveyed 360 university students, and found that heavy television viewers are more likely to believe the world is a more dangerous place. However, they also found heavy viewers are not more likely to actually feel more fearful.

Research Strand: Family attitudes to violent content are more important than the images themselves.

A number of studies suggest that media is only one of a number of variables that put children at risk of aggressive behaviour.

For example, a Norwegian study that included 20 at-risk teen-aged boys found that the lack of parental rules regulating what the boys watched was a more significant predictor of aggressive behaviour than the amount of media violence they watched. It also indicated that exposure to real world violence, together with exposure to media violence, created an "overload" of violent events. Boys who experienced this overload were more likely to use violent media images to create and consolidate their identities as members of an anti-social and marginalized group.

On the other hand, researchers report that parental attitudes towards media violence can mitigate the impact it has on children. Huesmann and Bacharach conclude, "Family attitudes and social class are stronger determinants of attitudes toward aggression than is the amount of exposure to TV, which is nevertheless a significant but weaker predictor."

Critical Thinking

1. Why is it so difficult for researchers to come to definitive conclusions regarding the effects of media violence on media consumers?

2. This article summarizes seven research strands that have investigated cause-effect relationships between media violence and consumer attitudes and/or behaviors. How would you design a study to add to one of these strands?

Wikipedia in the Newsroom

While the line "according to Wikipedia" pops up occasionally in news stories, it's relatively rare to see the user-created online encyclopedia cited as a source. But some journalists find it very valuable as a road map to troves of valuable information.

DONNA SHAW

When the Las Vegas Review-Journal published a story in September about construction cranes, it noted that they were invented by ancient Greeks and powered by men and donkeys.

Michigan's Flint Journal recently traced the origins of fantasy football to 1962, and to three people connected to the Oakland Raiders.

And when the Arizona Republic profiled a controversial local congressman in August, it concluded that his background was "unclear."

What all three had in common was one of the sources they cited: Wikipedia, the popular, reader-written and -edited online encyclopedia. Dismissed by traditional journalism as a gimmicky source of faux information almost since it debuted in 2001, Wikipedia may be gaining some cautious converts as it works its way into the mainstream, albeit more as a road map to information than as a source to cite. While "according to Wikipedia" attributions do crop up, they are relatively rare.

To be sure, many Wikipedia citations probably sneak into print simply because editors don't catch them. Other times, the reference is tongue-in-cheek: The Wall Street Journal, for example, cited Wikipedia as a source for an item on "turducken" (a bizarre concoction in which a chicken is stuffed into a duck that is stuffed into a turkey) in a subscriber e-mail update just before Thanksgiving. In the e-mail, the Journal reporter wrote that some of his information was "courtesy of Wikipedia's highly informative turducken entry. As my hero Dave Barry says, "I'm not making this up. Although, I'll admit that somebody on Wikipedia might have."

And when Time Inc. Editor-in-Chief John Huey was asked how his staffers made sure their stories were correct, he jokingly responded, "Wikipedia."

It's unclear if many newsrooms have formal policies banning Wikipedia attribution in their stories, but many have informal ones. At the Philadelphia Inquirer, which cited Wikipedia in an article about the death of television personality Tom Snyder last July, Managing Editor Mike Leary recently sent an e-mail to staff members reminding them they are never to use Wikipedia "to verify facts or to augment information in a story." A news database search indicates that "according to Wikipedia" mentions are few and far between in U.S. papers, and are found most frequently in opinion columns, letters to the editor and feature stories. They also turn up occasionally in graphics and information boxes.

Such caution is understandable, as for all its enticements, Wikipedia is maddeningly uneven. It can be impressive in one entry (the one on the Naval Battle of Guadalcanal includes 138 endnotes, 18 references and seven external links) and sloppy in another (it misspells the name of AJR's editor). Its topics range from the weighty (the Darfur conflict) to the inconsequential (a list of all episodes of the TV series "Canada's Worst Handyman"). Its talk pages can include sophisticated discussions of whether fluorescent light bulbs will cause significant mercury pollution or silly minutiae like the real birth date of Paris Hilton's Chihuahua. Some of its commentary is remarkable but some contributors are comically dense, like the person who demanded proof that 18th-century satirist Jonathan Swift wasn't serious when he wrote that landlords should eat the children of their impoverished Irish tenants.

Hubble Smith, the Review-Journal business reporter who wrote the crane story, says he was simply looking for background on construction cranes for a feature on the Las Vegas building boom when the Wikipedia entry popped up during a search. It was among the most interesting information he found, so he used it. But after his story went to the desk, a copy editor flagged it.

"He said, 'Do you realize that Wikipedia is just made up of people who contribute all of this?' " Smith recalls. "I had never used it before." The reference was checked and allowed to remain in the story.

Indeed, the primary knock against Wikipedia is that its authors and editors are also its users—an unpaid, partially anonymous army, some of whom insert jokes, exaggeration and even outright lies in their material. About one-fifth of the editing is done by anonymous users, but a tight-knit community of 600 to 1,000 volunteers does the bulk of the work, according to Wikipedia cofounder Jimmy Wales. Members of this group can delete material or, in extreme cases, even lock particularly outrageous entries while they are massaged.

The extent of the potential for misinformation became clearer in August, when a new tool called WikiScanner (wikiscanner .virgil.gr/) began providing an ingenious database to identify propagandists and hoaxers. It gave Wikipedia critics plenty of new ammunition, as it revealed that among those surreptitiously rewriting entries were employees of major corporations, politicians and the CIA trying to make their bosses look better. And then there was the John Seigenthaler Sr. episode, in which someone edited the prominent retired journalist's Wikipedia biography to insinuate that he briefly had been a suspect in the assassinations of John and Robert F. Kennedy. In an op-ed piece for USA Today in 2005, Seigenthaler, who once worked for Bobby Kennedy and was one of his pallbearers, railed against Wikipedia, calling it "a flawed and irresponsible research tool." (A Nashville man later admitted inserting the material as a joke aimed at a coworker, and apologized.)

No one is more aware of such pitfalls than the leadership of Wikipedia, whose online disclaimer reminds users that "anyone with an Internet connection" can alter the content and cautions, "please be advised that nothing found here has necessarily been reviewed by people with the expertise required to provide you with complete, accurate or reliable information." An even more blunt assessment appears in the encyclopedia's "Ten things you may not know about Wikipedia" posting: "We do not expect you to trust us. It is in the nature of an ever-changing work like Wikipedia that, while some articles are of the highest quality of scholarship, others are admittedly complete rubbish." It also reminds users not to use Wikipedia as a primary source or for making "critical decisions."

Wales says it doesn't surprise him to hear that some journalists are cautiously trying it out. "I think that people are sort of slowly learning how to use Wikipedia, and learning its strengths and its weaknesses," he says. "Of course, any reasonable person has to be up front that there are weaknesses. . . . On the other hand, there are lots of sources that have weaknesses." Wales thinks the encyclopedia's best journalistic use is for background research rather than as a source to be quoted.

Wales, a board member and chairman emeritus of the nonprofit Wikimedia Foundation Inc., which owns Wikipedia, says the company constantly strives to improve its product. "Right now we're tightly focused on making sure that, for example, the biographies are well sourced," he says. The foundation is also developing new tools "to block people who are misbehaving," including one for new German-language Wikipedia users that will vet their contributions. If it works, Wales says, it can be rolled out for Wikipedia encyclopedias in other languages.

He also defends the right of Wikipedia—and perhaps even reporters—to have a little fun. "I subscribe to Google alerts and I saw that turducken [item in the Wall Street Journal e-mail] and I thought, well, what other source would you use? Britannica doesn't cover this nonsense," he says.

There are still plenty of journalists who aren't convinced of Wikipedia's worth, among them the denizens of testycopyeditors.org, where contributors to the online conversation have names like "crabby editor" and "wordnerdy." Asked his opinion of Wikipedia, Phillip Blanchard, the Washington Post copy editor who started testycopyeditors, responds, "I'm not sure what I could add, beyond 'don't use it' and 'it's junk.'"

While the Post has no written policy against it, "I can't imagine a circumstance under which a fact would be attributed to Wikipedia," says Blanchard, who works on the financial desk. "'According to Wikipedia' has appeared only a couple of times in the Washington Post, once in a humor column and once in a movie review."

Gilbert Gaul, a Pulitzer Prize-winning reporter at the Post, describes himself as a "dinosaur in the changing world" when it comes to rules about sourcing stories. Wikipedia, he says, doesn't meet his personal test—for one thing, "there is no way for me to verify the information without fact-checking, in which case it isn't really saving me any time." He prefers to do his own research, so he can "see and touch everything," rather than rely on the mostly anonymous content of Wikipedia.

"I like much of the new technology. . . . But to me rules, borders, guidelines and transparency matter a lot," Gaul said in an e-mail

interview. "I need and want to be able to trust the people I am reading or chatting with. If I can't, what is the point?"

Other journalists, though, are at least somewhat won over by what can be an impressive feature: those sometimes lengthy Wikipedia citations that lead to other, more authoritative sources. David Cay Johnston, a Pulitzer-winning reporter for the New York Times, says he recently looked up "thermodynamics" to see where it led him, and found that Wikipedia's entry listed numerous references from reliable sources.

"I have a solid understanding of the concept, but once we get into fine points, I have nothing beyond my skepticism as a reporter to judge the accuracy, validity and reliability of what is there," he says. "However, this entry appears to be useful as a source guide. It has names of researchers whose books were published by eminent organizations, and you can take that as a quick way to find sources. So as a tip sheet, as a road map to reliable sources, Wikipedia seems valuable."

Jim Thomsen, a copy editor at the Kitsap Sun in Bremerton, Washington, has no problem with attributing information to the online encyclopedia in certain cases. "If I see something in Wikipedia I might want to cite for background and context for a story, I trace back the cites to their original sources," Thomsen said in an e-mail interview. "If I feel the origins are solid, I'll use the info."

For a student who just uses a search engine and they use the first thing that pops up . . . this undermines the kind of thing we're trying to teach them.

"I know there's been a lot of hullabaloo about people with agendas seeding Wikipedia with slanted or even false information, but as I see it, that sort of stuff can be easily sniffed out—by looking at the cites, and tracking them back. No cites? Fuhgeddaboudit. The bottom line is that Wikipedia can be a great tool as a central Clearinghouse for contextual information. But not a single syllable there should be taken at face value."

The Los Angeles Times is one of many newspapers that have allowed an occasional "according to Wikipedia" in their pages in the last several months. One was in a commentary piece about Barack Obama; another appeared in a staff-written story about a professional "man in the street" who managed to be interviewed repeatedly. The reference in the latter story drew rapid fire on testycopyeditors.org, with comments including "Shame on the Los Angeles Times" and "No, no, a thousand times no."

Melissa McCoy, the Times' deputy managing editor in charge of copy desks, says the paper occasionally allows Wikipedia attribution. "We're certainly not going to use Wikipedia as a standalone news source, but we're not going to exclude it if it takes us somewhere," she says. "If a reporter spots something in there and it makes them do an extra phone call, it's silly" not to use it.

There's no unanimity about Wikipedia among academic experts, who have engaged in vigorous debates about the online encyclopedia. While many professors refuse to allow students to cite it, it has attracted some prominent defenders, including historians and scientists who have analyzed its content.

"If a journalist were to find something surprising on Wikipedia and the journalistic instincts suggested it was correct, the journalist might add that as an unsubstantiated Wiki-fact and invite Comment," says Cathy Davidson, a professor at Duke University and cofounder of HASTAC (Humanities, Arts, Science, and Technology Advanced Collaboratory, www.hastac.org), a network of researchers developing new ways to collect and share information via technology. "Perhaps an online version of the printed piece, for example, might include a blog inviting people to comment on the Wiki-fact. It may be that there would be Wikifacts online that were not in the printed piece. In other words, why not use the new technologies available to expand knowledge in all kinds of ways?"

Journalists also should consider, Davidson says, whether some of the sources they deem reliable have their own inadequacies. For example, when she recently researched the origins of calculus, she found that standard Western histories generally credited England's Isaac Newton and Germany's Gottfried Wilhelm Leibniz. But Wikipedia went much further, tracing the discovery of basic calculus functions back to the Egyptians in 1800 BC, and then to China, India and Mesopotamia—all hundreds of years before the Europeans.

So while journalists should be cautious no matter what resources they use, "What Wikipedia does reveal to those in the Euro-American world is knowledge which most of our sources, even the most scholarly, have, in the past, neglected because it did not fit in our intellectual genealogies, in our history of ideas," Davidson says.

In December 2005, the science journal Nature published a survey of several experts about the content of comparable Wikipedia and online Encyclopedia Britannica entries. In a conclusion hotly disputed by Britannica, Nature said that Wikipedia "comes close to Britannica in terms of the accuracy of its science entries," in that the average Wikipedia article contained four errors to Britannica's three. Britannica's 20-page response said that "almost everything about the journal's investigation . . . was wrong and misleading . . . the study was so poorly carried out and its findings so error-laden that it was completely without merit." The company further asserted that Nature had misrepresented its own data—its numbers, after all, showed that Wikipedia had a third more inaccuracies than Britannica—and asked for "a full and public retraction of the article." Nature stood by its story.

"The Nature piece profoundly undermined the authority upon which Britannica depends," says Gregory Crane, editor in chief of the Perseus Digital Library at Tufts University. He is a recent convert to the pro-Wikipedia camp, calling it "the most important intellectual phenomenon of the early 21st century."

He recognizes its faults, especially when Wikipedians write about controversial topics. So "people have to do some critical thinking," Crane says, by evaluating their sources, "whether it's Wikipedia or the New York Times."

In an article he wrote in 2005, Crane acknowledged that Wikipedia "is an extreme case whose success so far has shocked skeptical scholars." But he noted as well that other, more mainstream reference works had similar foundations—for example, the Oxford English Dictionary was written over a period of 70 years by thousands of people, including "an inmate at an asylum for the criminally insane."

A 2006 analysis by another scholar and Wikipedia fan, George Mason University historian Roy Rosenzweig, found some inaccuracies, omissions, uneven writing and even plagiarism in selected entries. But his comparison of several Wikipedia biographies against comparable entries in two other encyclopedias found that Wikipedia "roughly matches" Microsoft's Encarta in accuracy while still falling short of the Oxford University Press' American National Biography Online. "This general conclusion is supported by studies comparing Wikipedia to other major encyclopedias," wrote Rosenzweig, who was director of the university's Center for History and New Media until his death last year.

Still, many if not most in the academic community think that Wikipedia, if used at all, should be no more than a secondary source, and they frequently tell their students as much. For Cornell University professor Ross Brann, that position was reinforced in early 2007, after the outing of a salaried Wikipedia employee and editor who called himself "Essjay" and claimed to be a tenured professor with doctorates in theology and canon law. Turns out he had seriously padded his résumé: The New Yorker discovered after interviewing Essjay that he was actually a 24-year-old community college dropout. To Brann, a professor of Judeo-Islamic Studies and director of graduate studies for the Department of Near Eastern Studies, the incident confirmed that Wikipedia could not be trusted as a primary source.

"I just tell students, 'Do not use Wikipedia, do not cite it, do not go there for my classes.' We're trying to teach them how to use sources, how to evaluate different sources, and I think that in general, although obviously a wonderful resource, for a student who just uses a search engine and they use the first thing that pops up . . . this undermines the kind of thing we're trying to teach them," Brann says.

Brann notes that Wikipedia's popularity probably has a lot to do with the fact that its entries so frequently pop up first, because that's the nature of search engines. "Many of them just work by the multiplicity of uses, others by virtue of ad arrangements—somebody is deciding for you what you're going to look at," he says.

And what about college journalists, a group that has never known life without computers? A news database search suggests that they are just as reluctant to cite Wikipedia as their professional colleagues. In August, for example, the University of Iowa newspaper, the Daily Iowan, used the WikiScanner database to determine that thousands of Wikipedia entries had been made or modified by people using the campus computer network. Some involved obvious but harmless enough vandalism: "Hawkeyes Rule" was inserted into text about the college's football stadium; less generously, a former university president was called an "eater of monkey brains," according to the paper's story.

Jason Brummond, editor in chief of the Daily Iowan, says he considers Wikipedia a good initial source, "but you go from there to find what most people would consider a more reputable source." Reporters in his newsroom generally understand that, he adds.

Brummond thinks the age of the journalist doesn't necessarily have that much to do with accepting Wikipedia. "It's more a personal awareness of how Wikipedia works."

In September, the University of Kansas student newspaper ran an editorial calling upon Wikipedia to do a better job of restoring "adulterated pages," noting that "despite a thousand recitations by our professors that Wikipedia is not a genuine source, students trust the site to give them accurate information." Nevertheless, Erick Schmidt, editor of the University Daily Kansan, says he doesn't rely much on Wikipedia, in part because his reporters write mostly about college and community issues. Plus, "we're taught to be cautious of things and skeptical," he says.

Schmidt rejects the notion that college students uncritically accept Wikipedia because they are infatuated with all things Internet. "We don't want to move things to technology because we think it's cool or paper is lame," he says. "But honestly, we are pressed for time, and if technology speeds things up . . . that's why we're being drawn to it."

For his part, Wales maintains that the more people use Wikipedia, the more they'll come to understand and accept it. His conclusion, he says, "comes from people who have used the site for a long time and know, 'I have to be careful'. . . which is what good reporting is supposed to be about anyway."

But whatever the verdict on Wikipedia, one thing should not change, says the New York Times' Johnston: "No matter who your sources are, when you sign your name, you are responsible for every word, every thought, every concept."

Critical Thinking

1. Summarize concerns with Wikipedia's use as a research resource.

2. If Wikipedia information is suspect, why is Wikipedia so popular? Do you think it will be a long-term phenomenon? Why or why not?

Contributing writer **DONNA SHAW** (shaw@tcnj.edu) has written about front-page ads, hyperlocal websites and Pulitzer Prizes for *AJR*.

Journalist Bites Reality!

How broadcast journalism is flawed in such a fundamental way that its utility as a tool for informing viewers is almost nil.

STEVE SALERNO

It is the measure of the media's obsession with its "pedophiles run amok!" story line that so many of us are on a first-name basis with the victims: Polly, Amber, JonBenet, Danielle, Elizabeth, Samantha. And now there is Madeleine. Clearly these crimes were and are horrific, and nothing here is intended to diminish the parents' loss. But something else has been lost in the bargain as journalists tirelessly stoke fear of strangers, segueing from nightly-news segments about cyberstalkers and "the rapist in your neighborhood" to prime-time reality series like *Dateline*'s "To Catch a Predator." That "something else" is reality.

According to the U.S. Department of Justice, in a given year there are about 88,000 documented cases of sexual abuse against juveniles. In the roughly 17,500 cases involving children between ages 6 and 11, strangers are the perpetrators just 5% of the time—and just *3%* of the time when the victim is under age 6. (Further, more than a third of such molesters are themselves juveniles, who may not be true "predators" so much as confused or unruly teens.) Overall, the odds that one of America's 48 million children under age 12 will encounter an adult pedophile at the local park are startlingly remote. The Child Molestation Research & Prevention Institute: "Right now, 90 percent of our efforts go toward protecting our children from strangers, when what we need to do is to focus 90% of our efforts toward protecting children from the abusers who are not strangers." That's a diplomatic way of phrasing the uncomfortable but factually supported truth: that if your child is not molested in your own home—by you, your significant other, or someone else you invited in—chances are your child will never be molested anywhere. Media coverage has precisely inverted both the reality and the risk of child sexual assault. Along the way, it has also inverted the gender of the most tragic victims: Despite the unending parade of young female faces on TV, boys are more likely than girls to be killed in the course of such abuse.

We think we know Big Journalism's faults by its much-ballyhooed lapses—its scandals, gaffes, and breakdowns—as well as by a recent spate of insider tell-alls. When Dan Rather goes public with a sensational exposé based on bogus documents; when the *Atlanta Journal-Constitution* wrongly labels

Richard Jewell the Olympic Park bomber; when *Dateline* resorts to rigging explosive charges to the gas tanks of "unsafe" trucks that, in *Dateline*'s prior tests, stubbornly refused to explode on their own; when the *New York Times*' Jayson Blair scoops other reporters working the same story by quoting sources who don't exist. . . . We see these incidents as atypical, the exceptions that prove the rule.

Sadly, we're mistaken. To argue that a decided sloppiness has crept into journalism or that the media have been "hijacked by [insert least favorite political agenda]" badly misses the real point; it suggests that all we need to do to fix things is filter out the gratuitous political spin or rig the ship to run a bit tighter. In truth, today's system of news delivery is an enterprise whose procedures, protocols, and underlying assumptions all but guarantee that it cannot succeed at its self-described mission. Broadcast journalism in particular is flawed in such a fundamental way that its utility as a tool for illuminating life, let alone interpreting it, is almost nil.

"You Give Us 22 Minutes, and We'll Give You . . . What, Exactly?"

We watch the news to "see what's going on in the world." But there's a hitch right off the bat. In its classic conception, newsworthiness is built on a foundation of anomaly: *man-bites-dog,* to use the hackneyed journalism school example. The significance of this cannot be overstated. It means that, by definition, journalism in its most basic form deals with what life *is not.*

Today's star journalist, however, goes to great lengths to distance himself from his trade's man-bites-dog heritage. To admit that what he's presenting is largely marginalia (or at best "background music") deflates the journalist's relevance in an environment where members of Major Media have come to regard themselves as latter day shamans and oracles. In a memorable 2002 piece, "The Weight of the Anchor," columnist Frank Rich put it this way, regarding the then-Big 3 of Brokaw, Jennings, and Rather: "Not quite movie stars, not quite officialdom, they are more famous than most movie stars and more powerful than most politicians."

Thus, journalism as currently practiced delivers two contradictory messages: that what it puts before you (a) is newsworthy (under the old man-bites-dog standard), but also (b) captures the *zeitgeist.* ("You give us 22 minutes, we'll give you the world," gloat all news radio stations across the country.) The news media cannot simultaneously deliver both. In practice, they fail at both. By painting life in terms of its oddities, journalism yields not a snapshot of your world, but something closer to a photographic negative.

Even when journalism isn't plainly capsizing reality, it's furnishing information that varies between immaterial and misleading. For all its *cinema-verité* panache, embedded reporting, as exemplified in Iraq and in *Nightline*'s recent series on "the forgotten war" in Afghanistan, shows only what's going on in the immediate vicinity of the embedded journalist. It's not all that useful for yielding an overarching sense of the progress of a war, and might easily be counterproductive: To interpret such field reporting as a valid microcosm is the equivalent of standing in a spot where it's raining and assuming it's raining everywhere.

Journalism's paradoxes and problems come to a head in the concept of *newsmagazination,* pioneered on *60 Minutes* and later the staple tactic of such popular clones as *Dateline, 48 Hours,* and *20/20.* One of the more intellectually dishonest phenomena of recent vintage, newsmagazination presents the viewer with a circumstantial stew whipped up from:

- a handful of compelling sound-bites culled from anecdotal sources,
- public-opinion polls (which tell us nothing except what people *think* is true),
- statistics that have no real evidentiary weight and/or scant relevance to the point they're being used to "prove,"
- logical flaws such as *post hoc ergo propter hoc* (after the fact) reasoning,
- faulty or, at best, unproven "expert" assumptions, or "conventional wisdom" that is never seriously examined,
- a proprietary knowledge of people's inner thoughts or motives (as when a White House correspondent discounts a president's actual statements in order to reveal to us that president's "true agenda"), etc.

Case in point: On Nov. 5, 2004, NBC's *Dateline* built a show around the dangers of gastric bypass surgery. The topic was a natural for *Dateline,* inasmuch as *The Today Show*'s own Al Roker, who did much of the reporting, had undergone the surgery and achieved a stunning weight loss. In setting the scene, anchor Stone Phillips noted that the expected mortality rate for gastric bypass is 1 in 200. (Translation: The *survival* rate is 199 in 200, or 99.5%.) Phillips then handed off to Roker; the affable weatherman spent a few cheery moments on his own success, then found his somber face in segueing to the tragic saga of Mike Butler, who died following surgery. The Butler story consumed the next 30 minutes of the hour long broadcast, punctuated by the obligatory wistful soliloquy from Butler's young widow. So, in covering a procedure that helps (or at least doesn't kill) roughly 99.5% of patients, *Dateline* elects to tell the story in terms of the 0.5% *with tragic outcomes.* Had NBC sought to equitably represent the upside and downside of gastric bypass, it would've devoted 1/200th of the show—a mere 18 seconds—to Butler. Further, wouldn't it have been journalistically responsible for *Dateline* to devote a good portion of the broadcast to the risks of morbid obesity itself, which far outweigh the risks of surgical bypass?

Do the Math . . . *Please*

One underlying factor here is that journalists either don't understand the difference between random data and genuine statistical proof, or they find that distinction inconvenient for their larger purpose: to make news dramatic and accessible. The media need a story line—a coherent narrative, ideally with an identifiable hero and villain. As Tom Brokaw once put it, perhaps revealing more than he intended, "It's all storytelling, you know. That's what journalism is about." The mainstream news business is so unaccustomed to dealing with issues at any level of complexity and nuance that they're wont to oversimplify their story to the point of caricature.

The best contemporary example is the Red State/Blue State dichotomy, invoked as an easy metaphor to express the philosophical schism that supposedly divides "the two Americas." Watching CNN's Bill Schneider hover over his maps on Election Night 2004, drawing stark lines between colors, one would've thought there were no Republicans in California, or that a Democrat arriving at the Texas border would be turned back at gunpoint. Well, guess what: The dichotomy doesn't exist—certainly not in the way journalists use the term. It's just a handy, sexy media fiction. Although California did wind up in the Kerry column in 2004, some 5.5 million Californians voted for George W. Bush. They represented about 45% of the state's total electorate and a much larger constituency in raw numbers than Bush enjoyed *in any state he won,* including Texas. Speaking of Texas: That unreconstituted Yankee, John Kerry, collected 2.8 million votes there. *Two point eight million.* Yet to hear the media tell it, California is deep, cool Blue, while Texas is a glaring, monolithic Red. Such fabrications aren't just silly. They become institutionalized in the culture, and they color—in this case literally—the way Americans view the nation in which they live.

The mythical Red State/Blue State paradigm is just one of the more telling indications of a general disability the media exhibit in working with data. A cluster of random events does not a "disturbing new trend!" make—but that doesn't stop journalists from finding patterns in happenstance. Take lightning. It kills with an eerie predictability: about 66 Americans every year. Now, lightning could kill those 66 people more or less evenly all spring and summer, or it could, in theory, kill the lot of them on one *really* scary Sunday in May. But the scary Sunday in May wouldn't necessarily mean we're going to have a year in which lightning kills 79,000 people. (No more than if it killed a half-dozen people named Johanssen on that Sunday would it mean that lightning is suddenly targeting Swedes.) Yet you can bet that if *any* half-dozen people are killed by lightning one Sunday, you'll soon see a special report along the lines of, *LIGHTNING: IS IT OUT TO GET US?* We've seen this propensity on display with shark attacks, meningitis, last year's rash of amusement-park fatalities, and any number of other "random event clusters" that occur for no reason anyone can explain.

Journalists overreact to events that fall well within the laws of probability. They treat the fact that something happened as if we never before had any reason to think it *could* happen—as if it were a brand-new risk with previously unforeseen causation. Did America become more vulnerable on 9/11? Or had it been vulnerable all along? Indeed, it could be argued that America today is far *less* vulnerable, precisely because of the added vigilance inspired by 9/11. Is that how the media play it? Similarly, a bridge collapse is no reason for journalists to assume in knee-jerk fashion that bridges overall are any less safe than they've been for decades. Certainly it's no reason to jump to the conclusion that the nation's infrastructure is crumbling, which is how several major news outlets framed the collapse of the Interstate 35W Bridge this past summer. As Freud might put it, sometimes a bridge collapse is just a bridge collapse. Alas, journalism needs its story line.

For a textbook example of the intellectual barrenness of so much of what's presented even as "headline" news, consider the Consumer Confidence Index and media coverage of same. For decades, such indices have been telling America how it feels about its economic prospects. The best known index has been compiled each month since 1967 by the Conference Board, a nonprofit organization dating to 1916. The Board's index is an arbitrary composite of indicators rooted in five equally arbitrary questions mailed to 5000 households. ("Do you see jobs as being easier or harder to get next year?") On Tuesday, October 30, 2007, the Board reported that its latest CCI had dipped to a two-year low. The media jumped on the story, as is ever the case when the CCI dips. (CCI upticks are seldom reported with the same fervor.) Like many of its counterparts nationally, no doubt, a Philadelphia network affiliate sent its consumer-affairs reporter trudging out to find consumers who lacked confidence. She succeeded.

Few reporters bother to mention that, customarily, there has been only a tenuous connection between CCI numbers and actual consumer spending or the overall health of the economy as objectively measured. In fact, just days after the release of the downbeat CCI, the Labor Department reported that the economy had generated 166,000 new jobs in October—twice the forecast. That statistic, which measures reality, got nowhere near the same play as the CCI, which measures perception.

Let's recap. We have a fanciful metric that's just a compilation of opinion, which is layered with further opinion from passersby, and then subjected to in-studio analysis (still more opinion). All of which is presented to viewers as . . . news.

The problem for society is that giving headline prominence to meaningless or marginal events exalts those events to the status of conventional wisdom. "Reporting confers legitimacy and relevance," writes Russell Frank, Professor of Journalism

Ethics at Penn State University. "When a newspaper puts a certain story on page one or a newscast puts it at or near the top of a 22-minute program, it is saying to its audience, in no uncertain terms, that 'this story is important.'" The self-fulfilling nature of all this should be clear: News organizations decide what's important, spin it to their liking, cover it *ad nauseam,* then describe it—without irony—as "the 800-pound gorilla" or "the issue that just won't go away." This is not unlike network commercials promoting sit-coms and dramas that "everyone is talking about" in the hopes of getting people to watch shows that apparently no one is talking about.

Tonight at 11 . . . the Apocalypse!

Far worse than hyping a story that represents just 0.5% reality, is covering "news" that's *zero* percent reality: There literally is no story. Even so, if the non-story satisfies other requirements, it will be reported anyway. This truism was not lost on the late David Brinkley, who, towards the end of his life, observed, "The one function that TV news performs very well is that when there is no news, we give it to you with the same emphasis as if there were."

On June 9, 2005, as part of its ongoing series of "Security Updates," CNN airs a special report titled "Keeping Milk Safe." Over shots of adorable first-graders sipping from their pint cartons, CNN tells viewers that the farm-to-shelf supply chain is vulnerable at every point, beginning with the cow; with great drama, the report emphasizes the terrifying consequences such tampering could have. Nowhere does the network, mention that in the history of the milk industry, *no incident of supply-chain tampering has ever been confirmed,* due to terrorism or anything else.

Similarly, after the Asian tsunamis struck over Christmas 2004, *Dateline* wasted no time casting about for an alarmist who could bring the tragedy closer to home: the familiar *Could It Happen Here?* motif. The show's producers found Stephen Ward, PhD, of the University of California at Santa Cruz. In January, *Dateline*'s East Coast viewers heard Ward foretell a geological anomaly in their very own ocean that could generate the equivalent of "all the bombs on earth" detonating at once. The event Ward prophesied would unleash on New York City a wave containing "15 or 20 times the energy" of the Asian tsunamis. As a helpful backdrop, *Dateline* treated its viewers to spectacular visuals from *The Day After Tomorrow,* showing Manhattan's heralded landmarks disappearing beneath an onrushing, foamy sea.

But for sheer overwrought absurdity, it's hard to beat what took place in mid-September 1999. For six full days, journalists behaved as if there was one story and one story only: Hurricane Floyd. The TV tempest commenced as the actual tempest still lolled hundreds of miles offshore, with no one certain how much of a threat Floyd posed, or whether it might fizzle before it hit land (as so often happens—Katrina has changed the way we think about hurricanes, but Katrina was a once-in-a-generation event). This was Saturday. By Tuesday the hurricane-in-absentia had engulfed the nightly news. While residents of areas in Floyd's projected path evacuated, the other side of the highway was clotted with news crews on their way *in*. By Wednesday all of the networks had their parka-clad correspondents standing on some coastal beach, each correspondent bent on looking wetter and more windblown than the next. Sprinkled among all this were the requisite interviews with men (and women) on the street—as well as in insurance companies, emergency-services offices, local restaurants, and the like. Bereft of an actual hurricane to show during this feverish build-up, *The Today Show* aired old footage of Hurricane Hugo's plunder of Charleston, in sledgehammer foreshadowing of the disaster to come.

Floyd caused a fair amount of damage when it finally hit on Thursday: 57 deaths and an estimated $6 billion in property loss. But here's where things get curious. By the time Floyd blew in, media interest clearly had ebbed. On television at least, coverage of the aftermath was dispatched in a day or so, with occasional backward glances occupying a few moments of air time in subsequent newscasts. Bottom line, the coverage of Floyd *before* it was a real story dwarfed the coverage given the storm once it *became* a story. Evidently the conjured image of tidal waves crashing on shore was more titillating to news producers than film of real life homeowners swabbing brownish muck out of their basements.

Today's newspeople have substantially improved on one of the timeless axioms of their craft: "If it bleeds, it leads." They prefer the mere prospect of bad news to most other kinds of news that did occur. The result is journalism as Stephen King might do it: the dogged selling of the cataclysm 'round the corner, complete with stage lighting and scenes fictionalized for dramatic purposes. Sure, the camera loves suspense. But . . . is suspense news? Is it really news that someone *thinks* a hurricane *might* kill thousands? It might kill no one, either, which is historically closer to the truth. Honest journalism would wait to see what the storm does, then report it.

Granted, Floyd blew in during a slow week. Following, though, is a sampling of the events that were largely ignored while the assembled media were waiting for Floyd:

- The House of Representatives took a hard stand on soft money, approving limits on campaign spending.
- The Equal Employment Opportunity Commission launched an investigation of corporate America's fondness for cash balance pension plans, an issue that affected millions of workers, and stood to affect millions more.
- The 17-member Joint Security Commission released a chilling report on America's handling of security-clearance applications. This, let us remember, was two years before the terror attacks of 9/11.
- The terrorist bombings in Russia and the gruesome, continuing holocaust in East Timor.

The advance billing given to Floyd bespeaks a gloomy trend in broadcast news' continuing slide toward theater. We witnessed this same phenomenon during the run-up to Desert Storm, Y2K, and the Clinton impeachment, among others.

The Crusades— Postmodern Style

Nowhere are these foibles more noticeable—or more of a threat to journalistic integrity—than when they coalesce into a cause: so-called "advocacy" or "social" journalism. To begin with, there are legitimate questions about whether journalism should even have causes. Does the journalist alone know what's objectively, abstractly good or evil? What deserves supporting or reforming? The moment journalists claim license to cover events sympathetically or cynically, we confront the problem of what to cover sympathetically or cynically, where to draw such lines and—above all—who gets to draw them. There are very few issues that unite the whole of mankind. Regardless, as Tom Rosenstiel of the Project for Excellence in Journalism told *USA Today,* "News outlets have found they can create more . . . identity by creating franchise brands around issues or around a point of view."

Even worse, the data on which journalists premise their crusades are drawn from the same marginalia discussed above. When Francisco Serrano was discovered to be living in the Minnesota high school he once attended, the media covered the 2005 story as if every American high school had a half-dozen homeless people living in it. The actual episode, though exceedingly rare if not one-of-a-kind, became a window to the nation's social failings.

In his thinking and methodology, today's journalist resembles the homicide cop who, having settled on a suspect, begins collecting evidence specifically against that suspect, dismissing information that counters his newfound theory of the crime. Too many journalists think in terms of buttressing a preconceived argument or fleshing out a sense of narrative gained very early in their research. This mindset is formalized in journalism's highest award: the Pulitzer Prize. Traditionally, stories deemed worthy of Pulitzer consideration have revealed the dark (and, often as not, statistically insignificant) underbelly of American life. In 2007 the Pulitzer for "public-service journalism" went to *The Wall Street Journal,* for its "creative and comprehensive probe into backdated stock options for business executives. . . ." The *Journal* reported on "possible" violations then under investigation at 120 companies. There are 2764 listed companies on the New York Stock Exchange; NASDAQ adds another 3200. Not to dismiss the sincerity and diligence of the *Journal's* work, but what's the final takeaway here? That 120 companies (0.02) "possibly" cheated? Or that—so far as anyone knows—at least 5844 others didn't?

Food for thought: Every time I fly, I'm amazed that these huge, winged machines get off the ground, stay off the ground, and don't return to ground until they're supposed to. Think about the failure rate of commonplace products: Light bulbs burn out. Fan belts snap. Refrigerators stop refrigerating. But planes don't crash. Actuarially speaking, they simply don't. The entire process of commercial flight and the systems that support it is remarkable. Do you fully understand it? I don't. I'm sure lots of people don't. Still, you won't win a Pulitzer for a piece that sheds light on the myriad "little miracles" that conspire to produce aviation's normalcy, stability and success. You'd be laughed out of today's newsrooms for even proposing such a piece (unless you were doing it as the kind of feel-good feature that editors like to give audiences as gifts for the holidays). Have a flight go down, however—*one* flight, *one* time—and have a reporter find some overworked ATC operator or other aberration that may have caused the disaster, and *voila!* You're in Pulitzer territory for writing about something that—statistically—never happens.

Just as journalists who run out of news may create it, journalists who run out of real causes may invent them. It's not hard to do. All you need is a fact or two, which you then "contextualize" with more so-called expert opinion. December 10, 2004 was a banner night for exposing those well-known dens of iniquity that masquerade as Amish settlements. Stories about rape and incest among the Amish appeared on both *Dateline* and *20/20*. The *Dateline* story even made reference to the principal character in the story that aired an hour later on *20/20*—which gives you some idea how common the abuse may be, if seasoned journalists must choreograph their exposés around the same incident. That brings us to Elizabeth Vargas and her question for *20/20*'s expert on Amish affairs: Just how widespread *is* this abuse? Amid stock footage of adorable children strolling down a dusky road in suspenders and bonnets, the expert tells America that it's "not a gross exception."

What kind of reporting is that? Does it indicate that 1% of Amish children are abused? Ten percent? Forty percent? Who knows?

This is what passes for investigative journalism nowadays.

Their World . . . and They're Welcome to It

The world we're "given" has an indisputable impact on how Americans see and live their lives. (How many other events are set in motion by the "truths" people infer from the news?) Here we enter the realm of iatrogenic reporting: provable harms that didn't exist until journalism itself got involved.

In science journalism in particular, the use of anecdotal information can create impressions that would be comical, were it not for the amount of public alarm they generate.

Pop quiz: How many Americans have died of Mad Cow Disease? Before you answer, let's look to Britain, where the scare began in earnest around 1995 after a few herd of cattle were found to be infected. First of all, in the cows themselves, what we call "Mad Cow" is technically *bovine spongiform encephalopathy,* or BSE. When BSE species-jumps to humans, it manifests itself as something called *variant Creutzfeldt Jacob Disease,* or *v*CJD. ("Non-variant" CJD occurs independently of cows and can even be inherited.) A link between BSE and *v*CJD was established in 1996. British reporters went scurrying to find epidemiologists who were alarmed by the discovery, some of whom obligingly put the death toll in the coming years above 500,000.

By late 2006, the end of Mad Cow's first documented decade, the U.K. had confirmed a total of 162 human deaths—nothing to be glib about. But that's a long way from 500,000. And here in the U.S.? The CDC describes two confirmed deaths, both involving people born and raised abroad. A third case involves a man from Saudi Arabia who remains alive at this writing.

Not what you might've expected, eh?

Nevertheless, when a New Jersey woman, Janet Skarbek, became convinced that an outbreak had killed off her neighbors, she found a warm welcome in newsrooms. Her dire pronouncements touched off a mini-hysteria. Even after the CDC eliminated *v*CJD as a factor, the media kept fanning the fires of public concern, typically by quoting Dr. Michael Greger, a part-time chef and full-time alarmist who labels Mad Cow "the plague of the 21st Century." When journalists want a fatalistic sound bite on the disease, they dial Greger's number.

However history may remember Mad Cow as an actual pathology, this much is sure: The media-inflamed scare has been fatal to jobs—most directly in the meat-packing industry, but in related enterprises as well. It has soured consumers on beef. It has caused volatile swings in livestock prices. It has mandated new protocols that add hundreds of thousands of dollars to the average cattle rancher's cost of doing business. It has caused us to cut ourselves off from key beef suppliers, fomenting minor crises in diplomacy and commerce. A 2005 survey reckoned the total cost of Mad Cow to U.S. agricultural interests at between $3.2 billion and $4.7 billion. This, for something that has killed far fewer Americans in 10 years than the 200 who die each month from *choking* on food or food substances.

To hear the media tell it, we're under perpetual siege from some Terrifying New Disease That Threatens to End Life as We Know It. It's too soon to render verdicts on the ultimate impact of avian flu, but that pathogen would have to wipe out many millions in order to justify the hype. Lyme Disease? The Cleveland Clinic has this to say: "Although rarely fatal and seldom a serious illness, Lyme Disease has been widely publicized, frequently overdramatized, and sometimes linked to unproven conditions." Is it coincidence that visits to national parks began tracking downward in 1999, amid media coverage that made it sound as if deer ticks and the rest of Mother Nature's foot-soldiers had declared war on humankind? Maybe. Maybe not.

In science reporting and everywhere else, there's no minimizing the psychic effects of regularly consuming a world-view rooted in peculiarity, much of which is pessimistic. In a 2003 Gallup poll, just 11% of respondents rated crime in their own neighborhoods as "very serious" or "extremely serious," yet 54% of those same respondents deemed crime in America as a whole "very serious" or "extremely serious." The catch-22 should be apparent: If crime were that pervasive, it would have to be occurring in a lot more than 11% of the respondents' "own neighborhoods." Such an enigmatic skew can only be explained in terms of the difference between what people personally experience—what they know firsthand—and the wider impressions they get from the news.

Figuratively speaking, we end up drowning in the tides of a hurricane that never makes shore.

I give you, herewith, a capsule summary of your world, and in far less than 22 minutes:

- The current *employment* rate is 95%.
- Out of 300 million Americans, roughly 299.999954 million were not murdered today.
- Day after day, some 35,000 commercial flights traverse our skies without incident.
- The vast majority of college students who got drunk last weekend did not rape anyone, or kill themselves or anyone else in a DUI or hazing incident. On Monday, they got up and went to class, bleary-eyed but otherwise okay.

It is not being a Pollyanna to state such facts, because they *are* facts. Next time you watch the news, keep in mind that what you're most often seeing is trivia framed as Truth. Or as British humorist/philosopher G.K. Chesteron whimsically put it some decades ago, "Journalism consists in saying 'Lord Jones is dead' to people who never knew Lord Jones was alive."

Critical Thinking

1. If ratings and sales figures indicate that the public is attracted to "intellectually bare" content, should media owners give media consumers what they want? Why or why not?

2. Should feedforward standards and rules differ for news vs entertainment media? Why or why not?

From *Skeptic* by Steve Salerno, volume 14, Number 1, 2008, pp. 52–59. Copyright © 2008 by Skeptic Magazine. Reprinted by permission of Millenium Press.

Girls Gone Anti-Feminist

Is '70s feminism an impediment to female happiness and fulfillment?

SUSAN J. DOUGLAS

This was the Spice Girls moment, and debate: Were these frosted cupcakes really a vehicle for feminism? And how much reversion back to the glory days of prefeminism should girls and women accept—even celebrate—given that we now allegedly had it all? Despite their Wonderbras and bare thighs, the Spice Girls advocated "girl power." They demanded, in their colossal, intercontinental hit "Wannabe," that boys treat them with respect or take a hike. Their boldfaced liner notes claimed that "The Future Is Female" and suggested that they and their fans were "Freedom Fighters." They made Margaret Thatcher an honorary Spice Girl. "We're freshening up feminism for the nineties," they told the *Guardian.* "Feminism has become a dirty word. Girl Power is just a '90s way of saying it."

Fast-forward to 2008. Talk about girl power! One woman ran for president and another for vice president. Millions of women and men voted for each of them. The one who ran for vice president had five children, one of them an infant, yet it was verboten to even ask whether she could handle the job while tending to a baby. At the same time we had a female secretary of state, and the woman who had run for president became her high-profile successor. And we have Lady Gaga, power girl of the new millennium. Feminism? Who needs feminism anymore? Aren't we, like, so done here? Okay, so some women moaned about the sexist coverage of Hillary Clinton, but picky, picky, picky.

Indeed, eight years earlier, career antifeminist Christina Hoff Sommers huffed in her book, *The War Against Boys: How Misguided Feminism Is Harming Our Young Men,* that girls were getting way too much attention and, as a result, were going to college in greater numbers and much more likely to succeed while boys were getting sent to detention, dropping out of high school, destined for careers behind fast-food counters, and so beaten down they were about to become the nation's new "second sex." Other books like *The Myth of Male Power and The Decline of Males* followed suit, with annual panics about the new "crisis" for boys. Girl power? Gone way too far.

Fantasies of Power

In 1999, one year before Sommers' book came out, the top five jobs for women did not include attorney, surgeon or CEO. They were, in order, secretaries, retail and personal sales workers (including cashiers), managers and administrators, elementary school teachers and registered nurses. Farther down among the top 20 were bookkeepers, receptionists, cooks and waitresses. In 2007, when presumably some of the privileged, pampered girls whose advantages over boys Sommers had kvetched about had entered the workforce, the top five jobs for women were, still, secretaries in first place, followed by registered nurses, elementary and middle school teachers, cashiers and retail salespersons.

Farther down the line? Maids, child care workers, office clerks and hairdressers. Not a CEO or hedge fund manager in sight. And, in the end, no president or vice president in 2008. But what about all those career-driven girls going to college and leaving the guys in the dust? A year out of college, they earn 80 percent of what men make. And 10 years out? A staggering 69 percent.

Since the early 1990s, much of the media have come to overrepresent women as having made it—completely—in the professions, as having gained sexual equality with men, and having achieved a level of financial success and comfort enjoyed primarily by the Tiffany's-encrusted doyennes of Laguna Beach. At the same time, there has been a resurgence of dreck clogging our cultural arteries—*The Man Show, Maxim, Girls Gone Wild.* But even this fare was presented as empowering, because while the scantily clad or bare-breasted women may have *seemed* to be objectified, they were really on top, because now they had chosen to be sex objects and men were supposedly nothing more than their helpless, ogling, crotch-driven slaves.

What the media have been giving us, then, are little more than fantasies of power. They assure girls and women, repeatedly, that women's liberation is a *fait accompli* and that we are stronger, more successful, more sexually in control, more fearless and more held in awe than we actually are. We can believe that any woman can become a CEO (or president), that women have achieved economic, professional and political parity with men, and we can expunge any suggestion that there might be anyone living on the national median income, which for women in 2008 was $36,000 a year, 23 percent less than their male counterparts.

Yet the images we see on television, in the movies, and in advertising also insist that purchasing power and sexual power are much more gratifying than political or economic power. Buying stuff—the right stuff, a lot of stuff—emerged as the dominant way to empower ourselves. Women in fictional settings can be in the highest positions of authority, but in real life maybe not such a good idea. Instead, the wheedling, seductive message to young women is that being decorative is the highest form of power—when, of course, if it were, Dick Cheney would have gone to work every day in a sequined tutu.

Enter Enlightened Sexism

Not that some of these fantasies haven't been delectable. I mean, Xena single-handedly trashing, on a regular basis, battalions of stubblefaced, leather-clad, murdering-and-raping barbarian hordes? Or *Buffy the Vampire Slayer* letting us pretend, if just for an hour, that only a teenage girl can save the world from fang-toothed evil? What about an underdog law student, dismissed by her fellow classmates as an airheaded bimbo, winning a high-profile murder case because she understood how permanents work, as Elle did in *Legally Blonde?* Or let's say you've had an especially stupid day at work and as you collapse on the sofa desperately clutching a martini (hold the vermouth), you see a man on TV tell his female boss that the way she does things is "just not the way we play ball," and she responds drolly, "Well, if you don't like the way I'm doing things, you're free to take your balls and go straight home"? (Yes, *The Closer.*) Oooo-weeee.

So what's the matter with fantasies of female power? Haven't the media always provided escapist fantasies; isn't that, like, their job? And aren't many in the media, belatedly, simply addressing women's demands for more representations of female achievement and control? Well, yes. But here's the odd, somewhat unintended consequence: These demanded-and-delivered, delicious media-created fantasies have been driven by marketing, and they use that heady mix of flattery and denigration to sell us everything from skin cream to glutestoning shoes.

So it's time to take these fantasies to the interrogation room and shine a little light on them.

One force at work is embedded feminism: the way in which women's achievements, or their desire for achievement, are simply part of today's cultural landscape.

But the media's fantasies of power are also the product of another force that has gained considerable momentum since the early and mid-1990s: enlightened sexism. Enlightened sexism is a response, deliberate or not, to the perceived threat of a new gender regime. It insists that women have made plenty of progress because of feminism—indeed, full equality, has allegedly been achieved. So now it's okay, even amusing, to resurrect sexist stereotypes of girls and women. Enlightened sexism sells the line that it is precisely through women's calculated deployment of their faces, bodies, attire, and sexuality that they gain and enjoy true power—power that is fun, that men will not resent, and indeed will embrace. True power here has nothing to do with economic independence or professional achievement: it has to do with getting men to lust after you and other women to envy you. Enlightened sexism is especially targeted to girls and young women and emphasizes that now that they "have it all," they should focus the bulk of their time and energy on being hot, pleasing men, competing with other women, and shopping.

Enlightened sexism is a manufacturing process that is constantly produced by the media. Its components—anxiety about female achievement; renewed and amplified objectification of young women's bodies and faces; dual exploitation and punishment of female sexuality; dividing of women against each other by age, race and class; and rampant branding and consumerism—began to swirl around in the early 1990s, consolidating as the dark star it has become in the early 21st century.

The Seed of Feminism's Demise

Some, myself included, have referred to this state of affairs and this kind of media mix as "postfeminist." But I am rejecting this term. It has gotten gummed up by many conflicting definitions. And besides, this term suggests that somehow feminism is at the root of this when it isn't— it's good, old-fashioned, grade-A sexism that reinforces good, old-fashioned, grade-A patriarchy. It's just much better disguised, in seductive Manolo Blahniks and a million-dollar bra.

Enlightened sexism is feminist in its outward appearance (of course you can be or do anything you want) but sexist in its intent (hold on, girls, only up to a certain point, and not in any way that discomfits men). While enlightened sexism seems to support women's equality, it is dedicated to the undoing of feminism. In fact, because this equality might lead to "sameness"—way too scary—girls and women need to be reminded that they are still fundamentally female, and so must be emphatically feminine.

Thus, enlightened sexism takes the gains of the women's movement as a given, and then uses them as permission to resurrect retrograde images of girls and women as sex objects, still defined by their appearance and their biological destiny.

Consequently, in the age of enlightened sexism there has been an explosion in makeover, matchmaking and modeling shows, a renewed emphasis on breasts (and a massive surge in the promotion of breast augmentation), an obsession with babies and motherhood in celebrity journalism (the rise of the creepy "bump patrol"), and a celebration of "opting out" of the workforce.

Feminism thus must remain a dirty word, with feminists (particularly older ones) stereotyped as man-hating, child-loathing, hairy, shrill, humorless and deliberately unattractive lesbians. More to the point, feminism must be emphatically rejected because it supposedly prohibits women from having any fun, listening to Lil' Wayne or Muse, or dancing to Lady Gaga, or wearing leggings. As this logic goes, feminism is so 1970s—grim, dowdy, aggrieved and passé—that it is now an impediment to female happiness and fulfillment. Thus, an amnesia about the women's movement, and the rampant, now illegal, discrimination that produced it, is essential, so we'll forget that politics matters.

Because women are now "equal" and the battle is over and won, we are now free to embrace things we used to see as sexist, including hypergirliness. In fact, this is supposed to be a relief.

Thank God girls and women can turn their backs on stick-in-the-mud, curdled feminism and now we can jiggle our way into that awesome party. Now that women allegedly have the same sexual freedom as men, they actually prefer to be sex objects because it's liberating. According to enlightened sexism, women today have a choice between feminism and antifeminism, and they just naturally and happily choose the latter because, well, antifeminism has become cool, even hip.

The Irony of It All

Enlightened sexism has cranked out media fare geared to girls and young women in which they compete over men, many of them knuckleheads (*The Bachelor, Flavor of Love*); compete with each other (*America's Next Top Model*); obsess about relationships and status (*The Hills*) or about pleasing men sexually (most music videos); and are fixated by conspicuous consumption (*Rich Girls, My Super Sweet 16, Laguna Beach,* and that wonderful little serpent of a show *Gossip Girl*). Yet I can assure you that my female students at the University of Michigan—academically accomplished, smart and ambitious—have flocked to these shows. Why?

This is the final key component to enlightened sexism: irony, the cultivation of the ironic, knowing viewer and the deployment of ironic sexism. Irony offers the following fantasy of power: the people on the screen may be rich, spoiled, or beautiful, but you, oh superior viewer, get to judge and mock them, and thus are above them. With a show like MTV's *My Super Sweet 16,* in which a spoiled brat has her parents buy her everything from a new Mercedes to a Vegas-style show to make sure her Sweet 16 party is, like, the most totally awesome ever, viewers are not merely (or primarily) meant to envy the girl. Animated stars superimposed on the scenes accompanied by a tinkling sound effect signal that we are also meant to see the whole exercise as over-the-top, ridiculous, exaggerated, the girl way too shallow and narcissistic. The show—indeed many 'reality' shows—elbow the viewer in the ribs, saying, "We know that you know that we know that you know that you're too smart to read this straight and not laugh at it."

For media-savvy youth, bombarded their entire lives by almost every marketing ploy in the book, irony means that you can look as if you are absolutely not seduced by the mass media, while then being seduced by the media, wearing a knowing smirk. Viewers are flattered that they are sophisticated, can see through the craven self-absorption, wouldn't be so vacuous and featherbrained as to get so completely caught up in something so trivial. The media offers this irony as a shield.

What so much of this media emphasizes is that women are defined by our bodies. This is nothing new, of course, but it was something millions of women hoped to deep-six back in the 1970s. Indeed, it is precisely because women no longer have to exhibit traditionally "feminine" *personality* traits—like being passive, helpless, docile, overly emotional, dumb and deferential to men—that they must exhibit hyperfeminine *physical* traits—cleavage, short skirts, pouty lips—and the proper logos linking this femininity to social acceptance. The war between embedded feminism and enlightened sexism gives with one hand and takes away with the other. It's a powerful choke leash, letting women venture out, offering us fantasies of power, control and love and then pulling us back in.

This, then, is the mission at hand: to pull back the curtain and to note how these fantasies distract us from our ongoing status—still, despite everything—as second-class citizens.

Trapped in the Media's Funhouse

Many producers insist that mass media are simply mirrors, reflecting reality, whatever that is, back to the public. Whenever you hear this mirror metaphor, I urge you to smash it. Because if the media are mirrors, they are funhouse mirrors. You know, the wavy kind, where your body becomes completely distorted and certain parts—typically your butt and thighs—become huge while other parts, like your knees, nearly disappear. This is the mass media—exaggerating certain kinds of stories, certain kinds of people, certain kinds of values and attitudes, while minimizing others or rendering them invisible.

This is even more true today than it was thirty years ago because specific media outlets targeted to specific audiences traffic in an ever-narrower range of representations. These media also set the agenda for what we are to think about, what kinds of people deserve our admiration, respect and envy, and what kinds don't.

Thus, despite my own love of escaping into worlds in which women solve crimes, can buy whatever they want, perform life-saving surgeries and find love, I am here to argue, forcefully, for the importance of wariness, with a capital W. The media have played an important role in enabling us to have female cabinet members, in raising awareness about and condemning domestic violence, in helping Americans accept very different family formations than the one on *Leave It to Beaver,* and even in imagining a woman president. But let's not forget that in the United States, we have the flimsiest support network for mothers and children of any industrialized country, nearly 2 million women are assaulted each year by a husband or boyfriend, and 18 percent of women have reported being the victim of a completed or attempted rape. White women still make 75 cents to a man's dollar, and it's 62 cents for Black women and only 53 cents for Latinas. The majority of families with children in poverty are headed by single women.

It is only through tracing the origins of these images of female power that we can begin to untangle how they have offered empowerment at the cost of eroding our self-esteem, and keeping millions in their place. Because still, despite everything, what courses through our culture is the belief—and fear—that once women have power, they turn into Miranda Priestly in *The Devil Wears Prada*—evil, tyrannical, hated. And the great irony is that if some media fare is actually ahead of where most women are in society, it may be thwarting the very advances for women that it seeks to achieve.

This essay was adapted from Susan J. Douglas' new book, Enlightened Sexism: The Seductive Message that Feminism's Work is Done *(Times Books, March).*

Critical Thinking

1. What factors, in what proportion, would you estimate are salient in forming a preteen girl's self perception? Where do media fit on your list?

2. How does the article *enlightened sexism?* In your experience, do media consumers get the irony?

SUSAN J. DOUGLAS is a professor of communications at the University of Michigan and an *In These Times* columnist. Her latest book is *Enlightened Sexism: The Seductive Message That Feminism's Work is Done* (2010).

UNIT 2
Telling Stories

Unit Selections

Learning Outcomes

The articles in this section will contribute to your being able to

• Summarize factors that have contributed to newspapers' decline.

• Assess the potential of proposals to reinvent and reinvigorate news media.

• Describe changes in media coverage of politics in terms of feedforward and feedback agendas of reporting.

• Analyze the implications of the American public's changing relationship with news media.

• Describe the media implications of the attention economy.

Student Website

www.mhhe.com/cls

Internet References

Cable News Network
www.cnn.com
Fox News
www.foxnews.com
Fairness and Accuracy in Reporting
www.fair.org
Organization of News Ombudsmen (ONO)
www.newsombudsmen.org
Television News Archive
www.tvnews.vanderbilt.edu

The reporting of news and information was not, in the beginning, considered an important function within broadcast media organizations. Television news was originally limited to 15-minute commercial-free broadcasts, presented as a public service. Over the years, however, the news business became big business. News operations grew intensely competitive, locked in head-to-head popularity races in which the loss of one ratings point translated into a loss of millions of dollars in advertising revenue. The government spent time debating how many newspapers and television stations a single company could own. There were articles written speculating on how online news and information would change business-as-usual, and traditional news media took steps to become online players. In the past several years, however, layoffs and buyouts have rocked the most noble of news organizations.

News, by definition, is timely: It is "news," not "olds." Decisions regarding what stories to play and how to play them are made under tight deadlines. Media expert Wilbur Schramm has noted that "hardly anything about communication is so impressive as the enormous number of choices and discards and interpretations that have to be made between [an] actual news event and the symbols that later appear in the mind of a reporter, an editor, a reader, a listener, or a viewer. Therefore, even if everyone does his job perfectly, it is hard enough to get the report of an event straight and clear and true." Schramm's comments point to the tremendous impact of selectivity in crafting news messages. The process is called *gatekeeping.*

Gatekeeping is necessary. News operations cannot logistically cover or report every event that happens in the world from one edition or broadcast or posting to the next. The concerns associated with the reality of gatekeeping relate to whether the gatekeepers abuse the privilege of deciding what information or viewpoints mass audiences receive. Simply being selected for media coverage lends an issue, an event, or an individual a certain degree of celebrity—the "masser" the medium, the greater the effect.

Traditional news media are under enormous pressure to remain competitive in a changing media environment. Daily U.S. newspaper circulation peaked at 62.3 million in 1990. Since then, market share in large markets has dropped as much as ten% per year. In 2000 there were 1,480 daily newspapers in the United States; in 2010 the number dropped to 1,302. A 2010 survey of 1,040 adults ages 18 and over indicated 20% of respondents ages 18–49 read a newspaper daily, compared with 42% of respondents age 50 and older. Television remained the most preferred source of news (52% ages 18–49; 69% age 50 +), followed by print newspapers (19% ages 18–49; 35% age 50 +) and online sites (34% ages 18-49; 16% age 50 +). Among online news sites, CNN has the most monthly unique visitors (65,657,000 in mid-2010 data), followed by Yahoo! News (56,038,000), MSNBC (47,950,000), the *New York Times* (32,360,000), AOL News (29,858,000), and the Huffington Post (24,393,000). The average time spent per person on a *New York Times* site visit in 2009 was 12 minutes and 36 seconds, a drop of 24 minutes from 2008. Time spent at the *Wall*

© Jeffrey Coolidge/Photodisc/Getty Images

Street Journal site was on average 7 minutes, at USATODAY.com 12 minutes, at Washingtonpost.com 11 minutes.

In his novel *The Evening News,* Arthur Hailey observed: "People watch the news to find out the answers to three questions, Is the world safe? Are my home and family safe? and, Did anything happen today that was interesting?" Given cursory answers to those questions, viewers are satisfied that they are "keeping up," although the total amount of news delivered in a half-hour newscast would, if set in type, hardly fill the front page of a daily newspaper. Many adults report that they are too busy to follow the news, or are suspicious of the media, or find the news too depressing. In one recent study, 27% of television viewers described themselves as "stressed" while watching the evening news (51% reported feeling "stressed" watching Martha Stewart). Availability and consumption of *information,* however, is on the rise. Knowledge of sports and celebrities has increased, while knowledge of local and national politics has decreased.

The articles in this section explore the changing landscape of contemporary news and information coverage and consumption, significant changes in the news business that both reflect and shape messages in the media pipeline. "The Reconstruction of American Journalism" and "Don't Blame the Journalism" review turning points in the collapse of newspapers, which depend on diminishing advertising revenue to run their businesses. "Capital Flight" analyzes the implications of reduction in the Washington, DC–based press corps. "Peytonplace.com" discusses how blog sites compete for advertising revenue. "Overload!" offers an intriguing application of insights from cognitive psychology to analyzing media consumers' response to information overload. "What the Mainstream Media Can Learn from Jon Stewart" proposes "lessons for newspapers and networks struggling to hold on to fleeting readers, viewers, and advertisers in a tumultuous era of transition for old media." Jon Stewart aficionados fare well.

Communicating news and information is a critical function of mass media, and the degree to which media perform and are perceived to perform their gatekeeping and watchdog functions are of critical importance. In his book *Tuned Out: Why Americans Under 40 Don't Follow the News,* David T.Z. Mindich writes,

Robert Putnam's 2000 book, *Bowling Alone,* charted the decay of what the author called "social capital," the important resource of public and quasi-public dialogue. For example, Putnam discovered that more people bowl than ever before, but fewer bowl in leagues; hence, the title of his book. But bowling is just the start. The last half century has seen a decline in membership in unions, Elks clubs, and PTAs; fewer people give dinner parties, speak in public, go to church, and attend the theater. . . . Putnam convincingly demonstrated a correlation between the lack of social capital and news consumption. The same people who join groups and write their representatives also read newspapers. The same people who have trust in the system, and their ability to change it, use the news for ammunition. The same people who distrust each other, drop out of society, and become isolated, find news irrelevant to their lives.

It is arguable that a decline in careful and credible coverage of important events and issues among media has contributed to decline in social capital. However, in a market-driven media climate, it is difficult for news media to sustain an economically viable hard news orientation when a declining number of consumers express interest in that product.

The Reconstruction *of* American Journalism

Many recent articles have addressed the perilous future of journalism. What is different about this one, aside from the breadth of the authors' research, is that it focuses resolutely on a particular function of the press, what it calls "accountability journalism," and that it lays out a series of usable—though ambitious—ideas that, taken together, would build an ecosystem beneficial to the health of accountability journalism in the commercial, nonprofit, and public news sectors. We hope you see the report as framing the discussion, and that you will join in a conversation about it on our website at cjr.org/reconstruction. —The Editors

LEONARD DOWNIE JR. AND MICHAEL SCHUDSON

American journalism is at a transformational moment, in which the era of dominant newspapers and influential network news divisions is rapidly giving way to one in which the gathering and distribution of news is more widely dispersed. As almost everyone knows, the economic foundation of the nation's newspapers, long supported by advertising, is collapsing, and newspapers themselves, which have been the country's chief source of independent reporting, are shrinking—literally. Fewer journalists are reporting less news in fewer pages, and the hegemony that near-monopoly metropolitan newspapers enjoyed during the last third of the twentieth century, even as their primary audience eroded, is ending. Commercial television news, which was long the chief rival of printed newspapers, has also been losing its audience, its advertising revenue, and its reporting resources.

Newspapers and television news are not going to vanish in the foreseeable future, despite frequent predictions of their imminent extinction. But they will play diminished roles in an emerging and still rapidly changing world of digital journalism, in which the means of news reporting are being re-invented, the character of news is being reconstructed, and reporting is being distributed across a greater number and variety of news organizations, new and old.

The questions that this transformation raises are simple enough: What is going to take the place of what is being lost, and can the new array of news media report on our nation and our communities as well as—or better than—journalism has until now? More importantly—and the issue central to this report—what should be done to shape this new landscape, to help assure that the essential elements of independent, original, and credible news reporting are preserved? We believe that choices made now and in the near future will not only have far-reaching effects but, if the choices are sound, significantly beneficial ones.

Some answers are already emerging. The Internet and those seizing its potential have made it possible—and often quite easy—to gather and distribute news more widely in new ways. This is being done not only by surviving newspapers and commercial television, but by startup online news organizations, nonprofit investigative reporting projects, public broadcasting stations, university-run news services, community news sites with citizen participation, and bloggers. Even government agencies and activist groups are playing a role. Together, they are creating not only a greater variety of independent reporting missions but different definitions of news.

Reporting is becoming more participatory and collaborative. The ranks of news gatherers now include not only newsroom staffers, but freelancers, university faculty members, students, and citizens. Financial support for reporting now comes not only from advertisers and subscribers, but also from foundations, individual philanthropists, academic and government budgets, special interests, and voluntary contributions from readers and viewers. There is increased competition among the different kinds of news gatherers, but there also is more cooperation, a willingness to share resources and reporting with former competitors. That increases the value and impact of the news they produce, and creates new identities for reporting while keeping old, familiar ones alive. "I have seen the future, and it is mutual," says Alan Rusbridger, editor of Britain's widely read *Guardian* newspaper. He sees a collaborative journalism emerging, what he calls a "mutualized newspaper."

The Internet has made all this possible, but it also has undermined the traditional marketplace support for American journalism. The Internet's easily accessible free information and low-cost advertising have loosened the hold of large, near-monopoly news organizations on audiences and advertisers. As this report will explain, credible independent news reporting cannot flourish without news organizations of various kinds, including the print and digital reporting operations of surviving newspapers. But it is unlikely that any but the smallest of these news organizations can be supported primarily by existing online revenue. That is why—at the end of this report—we will explore a variety and mixture of ways to support news reporting, which must include non-market sources like philanthropy and government.

The way news is reported today did not spring from an unbroken tradition. Rather, journalism changed, sometimes dramatically, as the nation changed—its economics (because of the growth of large retailers in major cities), demographics (because of the shifts of population from farms to cities and then to suburbs), and politics (because early on political parties controlled newspapers and later lost power over them). In the early days of the republic, newspapers did little or no local reporting—in fact, those early newspapers were almost all four-page weeklies, each produced by a single proprietor-printer-editor. They published much more foreign than local news, reprinting stories they happened to see in London papers they received in the mail, much as Web news aggregators do today. What local news they did provide consisted mostly of short items or bits of intelligence brought in by their readers, without verification.

Most of what American newspapers did from the time that the First Amendment was ratified, in 1791, until well into the nineteenth century was to provide an outlet for opinion, often stridently partisan. Newspaper printers owed their livelihoods and loyalties to political parties. Not until the 1820s and 1830s did they begin to hire reporters to gather news actively rather than wait for it to come to them. By the late nineteenth century, urban newspapers grew more prosperous, ambitious and powerful, and some began to proclaim their political independence.

In the first half of the twentieth century, even though earnings at newspapers were able to support a more professional culture of reporters and editors, reporting was often limited by deference to authority. By the 1960s, though, more journalists at a number of prosperous metropolitan newspapers were showing increasing skepticism about pronouncements from government and other centers of power. More newspapers began to encourage "accountability reporting" that often comes out of beat coverage and targets those who have power and influence in our lives—not only governmental bodies, but businesses and educational and cultural institutions. Federal regulatory pressure on broadcasters to take the public service requirements of their licenses seriously also encouraged greater investment in news.

A serious commitment to accountability journalism did not spread universally throughout newspapers or broadcast media, but abundant advertising revenue during the profitable last decades of the century gave the historically large staffs of many urban newspapers an opportunity to significantly increase the quantity and quality of their reporting. An extensive *American Journalism Review* study of the content of ten metropolitan newspapers across the country, for the years 1964–65 and 1998–99, found that overall the amount of news these papers published doubled.

The concept of news also was changing. The percentage of news categorized in the study as local, national, and international declined from 35 to 24 percent, while business news doubled from 7 to 15 percent, sports increased from 16 to 21 percent, and features from 23 to 26 percent. Newspapers moved from a preoccupation with government, usually in response to specific events, to a much broader understanding of public life that included not just events, but also patterns and trends, and not just in politics, but also in science, medicine, business, sports, education, religion, culture, and entertainment.

These developments were driven in part by the market. Editors sought to slow the loss of readers turning to broadcast or cable television, or to magazines that appealed to niche audiences. The changes also were driven by the social movements of the 1960s and 1970s. The civil rights movement taught journalists in what had been overwhelmingly white and male newsrooms about minority communities that they hadn't covered well or at all. The women's movement successfully asserted that "the personal is political" and ushered in such topics as sexuality, gender equity, birth control, abortion, childhood, and parenthood. Environmentalists helped to make scientific and medical questions part of everyday news reporting.

Is that kind of journalism imperiled by the transformation of the American news media? To put it another way, is independent news reporting a significant public good whose diminution requires urgent attention? Is it an essential component of public information that, as the Knight Commission on the Information Needs of Communities in a Democracy recently put it, "is as vital to the healthy functioning of communities as clean air, safe streets, good schools, and public health?"

Those questions are asked most often in connection with independent reporting's role in helping to create an informed citizenry in a representative democracy. This is an essential purpose for reporting, along with interpretation, analysis and informed opinion, and advocacy. And news reporting also provides vital information for participation in society and in daily life.

Much of newspaper journalism in other democracies is still partisan, subsidized by or closely allied with political parties. That kind of journalism can also serve democracy. But in the plurality of the American media universe, advocacy journalism is not endangered—it is growing. The expression of publicly disseminated opinion is perhaps Americans' most exercised First Amendment right, as anyone can see and hear every day on the Internet, cable television, or talk radio.

What is under threat is independent *reporting* that provides information, investigation, analysis, and community knowledge, particularly in the coverage of local affairs. Reporting the news means telling citizens what they would not otherwise know. "It's so simple it sounds stupid at first, but when you think about it, it is our fundamental advantage," says Tim McGuire, a former editor of the Minneapolis *Star Tribune*. "We've got to tell people stuff they don't know."

Reporting is not something to be taken for granted. Even late in the nineteenth century, when American news reporting was well established, European journalists looked askance, particularly at the suspicious practice of interviewing. One French critic lamented disdainfully that the "spirit of inquiry and espionage" in America might be seeping into French journalism.

Independent reporting not only reveals what government or private interests appear to be doing but also what lies behind their actions. This is the watchdog function of the press— reporting that holds government officials accountable to the legal and moral standards of public service and keeps business and professional leaders accountable to society's expectations of integrity and fairness.

Reporting the news also undergirds democracy by explaining complicated events, issues, and processes in clear language. Since 1985, explanatory reporting has had its own Pulitzer Prize category, and explanation and analysis is now part of much news and investigative reporting. It requires the ability to explain a complex situation to a broad public. News reporting also draws audiences into their communities. In America, sympathetic exposes of "how the other half lives" go back to the late nineteenth century, but what we may call "community knowledge reporting" or "social empathy reporting" has proliferated in recent decades. Everyone remembers how the emotionally engaging coverage by newspapers and television of the victims of Hurricane Katrina made more vivid and accessible issues of race, social and economic conditions, and the role of government in people's lives. At its best, this kind of reporting shocks readers, as well as enhances curiosity, empathy, and understanding about life in our communities.

In the age of the Internet, everyone from individual citizens to political operatives can gather information, investigate the powerful, and provide analysis. Even if news organizations were to vanish en masse, information, investigation, analysis, and community knowledge would not disappear. But something else would be lost, and we would be reminded that there is a need not just for information, but for news judgment oriented to a public agenda and a general audience. We would be reminded that there is a need not just for news but for newsrooms. Something is gained when reporting, analysis, and investigation are pursued collaboratively by stable organizations that can facilitate regular reporting by experienced journalists, support them with money, logistics, and legal services, and present their work to a large public. Institutional authority or weight often guarantees that the work of newsrooms won't easily be ignored.

Something is gained when reporting, analysis, and investigation are pursued collaboratively by stable organizations.

The challenge is to turn the current moment of transformation into a reconstruction of American journalism, enabling independent reporting to emerge enlivened and enlarged from the decline of long-dominant news media. It may not be essential to save any particular news medium, including printed newspapers. What is paramount is preserving independent, original, credible reporting, whether or not it is popular or profitable, and regardless of the medium in which it appears.

Accountability journalism, particularly local accountability journalism, is especially threatened by the economic troubles that have diminished so many newspapers. So much of the news that people find, whether on television or radio or the Internet, still originates with newspaper reporting. And newspapers are the source of most local news reporting, which is why it is even more endangered than national, international or investigative reporting that might be provided by other sources.

At the same time, digital technology—joined by innovation and entrepreneurial energy—is opening new possibilities for reporting. Journalists can research much more widely, update their work repeatedly, follow it up more thoroughly, verify it more easily, compare it with that of competitors, and have it enriched and fact-checked by readers. "Shoe leather" reporting is often still essential, but there are extraordinary opportunities for reporting today because journalists can find so much information on the Internet. *Los Angeles Times* reporters Bettina Boxall and Julie Cart won the 2009 Pulitzer Prize for explanatory reporting by using both the Internet and in-person reporting to analyze why the number and intensity of wildfires has increased in California. They found good sources among U. S. Forest Service retirees by typing "Forest Service" and "retired" into a Google search and then interviewing the people whose names came up. "The Internet," Boxall said, "has made basic research faster, easier, and richer. But it can't displace interviews, being there, or narrative." At the same time, consumers of news have more fresh reporting at their fingertips and the ability to participate in reportorial journalism more readily than ever before. They and reporters can share information, expertise, and perspectives, in direct contacts and through digital communities. Taking advantage of these opportunities requires finding ways to help new kinds of reporting grow and prosper while existing media adapt to new roles.

These are the issues that this report—based on dozens of interviews, visits to news organizations across the country, and numerous recent studies and conferences on the future of news—will explore, and that will lead to its recommendations.

What is happening to independent news reporting by newspapers? Metropolitan newspaper readership began its long decline during the television era and the movement of urban populations to the suburbs. As significant amounts of national and retail advertising shifted to television, newspapers became more dependent on classified advertising. Then, with the advent of multichannel cable television and the largest wave of non-English-speaking immigration in nearly a century, audiences for news became fragmented. Ownership of newspapers and television stations became increasingly concentrated in publicly traded corporations that were determined to maintain large profit margins and correspondingly high stock prices.

Quarterly earnings increasingly became the preoccupation of some large newspaper chain owners and managers who were far removed from their companies' newsrooms and the communities they covered. To maintain earnings whenever advertising revenues fell, some owners started to reverse some of their previous increases in reporting staffs and the space devoted to news. Afternoon newspapers in remaining multipaper cities were in most cases merged with morning papers or shut down. In many cities, by the turn of the century—even before websites noticeably competed for readers or Craigslist attracted large amounts of classified advertising—newspapers already were doing less news reporting.

The Internet revolution helped to accelerate the decline in print readership, and newspapers responded by offering their content for free on their new websites. In hindsight, this may have been a business mistake, but the motivation at the time was to attract new audiences and advertising for content on the Internet, where most other information was already free. Although the readership of newspaper websites grew rapidly, much of the growth turned out to be illusory—just momentary and occasional visits from people drawn to the sites through links from the rapidly growing number of Web aggregators, search engines, and blogs. The initial surge in traffic helped to create a tantalizing but brief boomlet in advertising on newspaper websites. But the newfound revenue leveled off, and fell far short of making up for the rapid declines in revenue from print advertising that accelerated with the recession.

The economics of newspapers deteriorated rapidly. Profits fell precipitously, despite repeated rounds of deep cost-cutting. Some newspapers began losing money, and the depressed earnings of many others were not enough to service the debt that their owners had run up while continuing to buy new properties. The Tribune chain of newspapers, which stretched from the *Los Angeles Times* and the *Chicago Tribune* to *Newsday, The Baltimore Sun,* and the *Orlando Sentinel,* went into bankruptcy. So did several smaller chains and individually owned newspapers in large cities such as Minneapolis and Philadelphia. In Denver, Seattle, and Tucson—still two-newspaper towns in 2008—longstanding metropolitan dailies stopped printing newspapers. More than one hundred daily papers eliminated print publication on Saturdays or other days each week.

In just a few years' time, many newspapers cut their reporting staffs by half and significantly reduced their news coverage. *The Baltimore Sun*'s newsroom shrank to about 150 journalists from more than 400; the *Los Angeles Times*'s to fewer than 600 journalists from more than 1,100. Overall, according to various studies, the number of newspaper editorial employees, which had grown from about 40,000 in 1971 to more than 60,000 in 1992, had fallen back to around 40,000 in 2009.

In most cities, fewer newspaper journalists were reporting on city halls, schools, social welfare, life in the suburbs, local business, culture, the arts, science, or the environment, and fewer were assigned to investigative reporting. Most large newspapers eliminated foreign correspondents and many of their correspondents in Washington. The number of newspaper reporters covering state capitals full-time fell from 524 in 2003 to 355 at the beginning of 2009. A large share of newspaper reporting of government, economic activity, and quality of life simply disappeared.

A large share of newspaper reporting of government, economic activity, and quality of life simply disappeared.

Will this contraction continue until newspapers and their news reporting no longer exist? Not all newspapers are at risk. Many of those less battered by the economic downturn are situated in smaller cities and towns where there is no newspaper competition, no locally based television station, and no Craigslist. Those papers' reporting staffs, which never grew very large, remain about the same size they have been for years, and they still concentrate on local news. A number of them have sought to limit the loss of paid circulation and advertising in their print papers by charging non-subscribers for access to most of their Web content. They are scattered across the country from Albuquerque, New Mexico, to Lawrence, Kansas, to Newport, Rhode Island. Although they have not attracted many paid Web-only subscribers, their publishers say they have so far protected much of their print circulation and advertising.

Larger newspapers are seriously looking into ways to seek payment for at least some of the news they put online. Their publishers have been discussing various proposals from Internet entrepreneurs, including improved technologies for digital subscriptions, micropayments (on the model of iTunes) to read individual news stories, single-click mechanisms for readers to make voluntary payments, and business-to-business arrangements enabling newspapers to share in the ad revenue from other sites that republish their content. Whether "information wants to be free" on the Internet has become a highly charged, contentious issue, somewhat out of proportion to how much money may be at stake or its potential impact on news reporting.

Only a few large newspapers are already charging for digital news of special interest. Both *The Wall Street Journal* and the *Financial Times* sell subscriptions for access to their websites, and the *Journal* also has decided to charge for its content on mobile devices like BlackBerrys and iPhones. The *Milwaukee Journal Sentinel* sells subscriptions to avid Green Bay Packers football fans for its Packer Insider site, and the *Pittsburgh Post-Gazette* offers paid membership to a niche website of exclusive staff blogs, videos, chats, and social networking.

One entrepreneurial venture, Journalism Online, claims that publishers of hundreds of daily and weekly newspapers have signed letters of intent to explore its strategy for enabling online readers to buy digital news from many publications through a single password-protected website. A Silicon Valley startup named Attributor has developed technology to "fingerprint" each news organization's digital content to determine where it shows up on other websites and what advertising is being sold with it. Attributor offers to negotiate with Internet advertising networks to share that revenue with publishers who join its Fair Syndication Consortium. The Associated Press recently announced a strategy for tracking news produced by AP and its member newspapers through the Internet, and then seeking payment for it.

Entrepreneurs have also proposed ways in which news consumers could allow their reading habits on the Internet to be monitored so that news organizations could sell highly targeted groups of readers to advertisers at high prices. Google offers publishers some ways to use its search engine to seek payment for their digital news. But given the Internet's culture of relatively free access to an infinite amount of information, no one knows whether any of these approaches would lead to new economic models for journalism.

There have been suggestions that philanthropists or foundations could buy and run newspapers as endowed institutions, as though they were museums. But it would take an endowment of billions of dollars to produce enough investment income to run a single sizeable newspaper, much less large numbers of papers in communities across the country.

U. S. Senator Ben Cardin of Maryland has introduced legislation to allow newspapers to become nonprofits for educational purposes under section 501(c)(3) of the tax code, similar to charities and educational and cultural nonprofits. Philanthropic contributions to them would be tax-deductible. But the bill, which has not moved anywhere in Congress, does not address how a newspaper that is losing money, especially one saddled with significant debt or other liabilities, could be converted into a viable nonprofit.

For all this, many newspapers are still profitable, not counting some of their owners' overhanging debt, which may be resolved through ongoing bankruptcy reorganizations and ownership changes. And many newspapers are extensively restructuring themselves to integrate their print and digital operations, creating truly multimedia news organizations in ways that should produce both more cost savings—and more engaging journalism.

A growing number of newspapers also are supplementing their reduced resources for news reporting by collaborating with other newspapers, new kinds of news organizations, and their own readers. In the most extensive collaboration, Ohio's eight largest newspapers—*The Plain Dealer* in Cleveland, *The Akron Beacon Journal, The* (Canton) *Repository, The Columbus Dispatch, The* (Cincinnati) *Enquirer,* the *Dayton Daily News, The* (Toledo) *Blade*, and *The* (Youngstown) *Vindicator*—have formed the Ohio News Organization. They share state, business, sports, arts, and entertainment news reporting, various kinds of features, editorials, photographs, and graphics. The newspapers work independently and competitively on enterprise and investigative reporting, to which their editors say they can each now devote more of their smaller number of reporters.

A growing number of newspapers are collaborating on stories with other newspapers, new kinds of news organizations, and their own readers.

The Star-Ledger in Newark has created a separate community news service that hired three-dozen younger, lower-paid journalists to report from surrounding New Jersey towns. *The Seattle Times* has agreed to share news website links and some reporting with what editor David Boardman calls Seattle's "most respected neighborhood blogs," to which residents contribute news to be edited by professional journalists.

As newspapers sharply reduce their staffs and news reporting to cut costs and survive, they also reduce their value to their readers and communities. At the same time, they are disgorging thousands of trained journalists who are now available to start and staff new kinds of local news organizations, primarily online. This sets the stage for a future for local news reporting in which the remaining economically viable newspapers—with much smaller staffs, revenues, and profits—will try to do many things at once: publish in print and digitally, seek new ways to attract audience and advertisers, invent new products and revenue streams, and find partners to help them produce high-quality news at lower cost. They will do all of this in competition—and in collaboration—with the new, primarily online, news organizations that are able to thrive.

Why can't television and radio make up for the loss of reporting by newspapers? Some local television stations sometimes produce exemplary local and regional reporting, as demonstrated by the winners of the 2009 DuPont Award. A two-year investigation by WTVT, a Fox affiliate in Tampa, of criminal justice in nearby Hardee County led to the release of a truck driver wrongfully imprisoned for vehicular manslaughter. WFAA in Dallas, an ABC affiliate that has won more than a dozen national awards, received a special citation for three notable investigative reports in a single year.

Still, even in their best years, most commercial television stations had far fewer news reporters than local newspapers, and a 1999 study of fifty-nine local news stations in nineteen cities found that 90 percent of all their stories reported on accidents, crimes, and scheduled or staged events. In recent years, with their ratings and ad revenues in rapid decline and their once extravagant profit margins imperiled, many local television stations have made further cuts in already small news staffs. The number of television stations producing local news of their own is steadily shrinking. Some stations, such as KDNL, the ABC affiliate in St. Louis, and WYOU, serving Scranton and Wilkes-Barre in Pennsylvania, have dropped local news altogether. At 205 stations around the country, newscasts are now produced by other stations in the same cities.

In the past, the Federal Communications Commission required station owners to show they were serving the public interest before their broadcasting licenses could be renewed. But the FCC no longer effectively enforces the public-service requirement. Some cable television systems offer all-news local channels produced by the cable company itself or by broadcast station owners. The cable news channels, which recycle a relatively few news programs throughout the day, are usually lower cost, smaller-audience versions of host or collaborating broadcast stations.

On radio, with the exception of all-news stations in some large cities, most commercial stations do little or no local news reporting. A growing number of listeners have turned to public radio stations for national and international news provided by National Public Radio. But only a relatively small number of those public radio stations also offer their listeners a significant amount of local news reporting. And even fewer public television stations provide local news coverage.

Congress created the current system of public radio and television in 1967. Through the quasi-independent Corporation for Public Broadcasting, the federal government funnels about $400 million a year to program producers and to hundreds of independent public radio and television stations that reach every corner of the country. The stations, which are owned by colleges and universities, nonprofit community groups, and state and local governments, supplement relatively small CPB grants with fundraising from individual donors, philanthropic foundations, and corporate contributors. Most of the money is used for each station's overhead costs and fundraising, rather than news reporting.

Three-fourths of the CPB's money goes to public television, which has never done much original news reporting. The Public Broadcasting Service, collectively owned by local public television stations and primarily funded by the CPB, is a conduit for public affairs programs produced by some larger stations and independent producers that consist mostly of documentaries, talk shows, and a single national news discussion program, *The NewsHour with Jim Lehrer,* on weeknights.

Because PBS has no production capacity of its own, it does not do any news reporting. But as a distributor of programming, it is exploring how to improve public television news in what a Pew Foundation-funded PBS consultant described as an often dysfunctional, entrenched culture with "too many silos"— meaning the many individual stations, production organizations, and programming groups—that have not worked well together on news reporting. An internal PBS study reportedly recommends the creation of a destination public news website, with content from throughout public television and radio. David Fanning, the longtime executive producer of *Frontline,* has proposed going further. Fanning wants to create a full-fledged national reporting organization for public television with its own staff and funding. Realizing either his proposal or the vision of the PBS study would require a major realignment of public media relationships and funding. Neither would increase independent local news reporting by public television stations.

While the audience for public radio of about 28 million listeners each week is just over one-third of the 75 million weekly viewers of public television, it has been growing substantially for several decades, driven largely by its national news programs. NPR's *Morning Edition* and *All Things Considered* are the most popular programs on public radio or television. And *Morning Edition*'s audience of nearly 12 million listeners alone has been about a third larger than that for NBC's *Today.* Although NPR also has lost revenue during the recession and laid off staff for the first time in a quarter century, it recently launched an ambitious website with national news updates and stories. It also hired its first editor for investigative reporting, Brian Duffy, who is working on accountability journalism projects with reporters at NPR and local public radio stations. NPR has seventeen foreign bureaus, more than all but a few American newspapers, and six U.S. regional bureaus.

But only a small fraction of the public radio stations that broadcast NPR's national and international news accompany it with a significant amount of local news reporting. Those that do tend to be large city, regional, or state flagship stations. Some of these operations are impressive. Northern California Public Broadcasting, for instance, with stations in San Francisco, San Jose, and Monterey, has a thirty-person news staff reporting on the state's government and economy, education, environment, and health. Its KQED public radio and television stations in San Francisco have announced a collaboration with the Graduate School of Journalism at the University of California, Berkeley to launch in 2010 an independent nonprofit Bay area news organization with $5 million seed money from local businessman Warren Hellman. The new entity's reporters, working with KQED journalists and Berkeley students, will cover local government, education, culture, the environment and neighborhoods for its own website, other digital media, and public radio and television.

Some public radio stations have sought advice from CPB, asking how they could expand and finance local news coverage, using journalists who had worked at local newspapers. A just-completed CPB Public Radio Task Force Report put "supporting significant growth in the scale, quality, and impact of local reporting" near the top of its recommendations for further increasing the audience for public radio.

Under Vivian Schiller, National Public Radio's new CEO, NPR has taken steps to help member stations with local news coverage. NPR is a nonprofit that supplies national and international news and cultural programming—but not local news—to about 800 public radio stations. These stations are owned and managed by 280 local and state nonprofits, colleges, and universities that support NPR with their dues. Schiller says her goal, approved by the board of member station representatives that governs NPR, is "to step in where local newspapers are leaving." In its most ambitious project, NPR has created a digital distribution platform on which it and member stations can share radio and website reporting on subjects of local interest in various parts of the country, such as education or the environment.

Overall, however, local news coverage remains underfunded, understaffed, and a low priority at most public radio and television stations, whose leaders have been unable to make—or uninterested in making—the case for investment in local news to donors and Congress.

What are the new sources of independent news reporting? Different kinds of news organizations are being started by journalists who have left print and broadcast, and also by universities and their students, Internet entrepreneurs, bloggers, and so-called "citizen journalists." Many of these new organizations report on their communities. Others concentrate on investigative reporting. Some specialize in subjects like national politics, state government, or health care. Many are tax-exempt nonprofits, while others are trying to become profitable. Most publish only online, avoiding printing and delivery costs. However, some also collaborate with other news media to reach larger audiences through newspapers, radio, and television, as well as their own websites. Many of the startups are still quite small and financially fragile, but they are multiplying steadily.

The startups are financially fragile. Their staffs and audiences are small, and they are scattered unevenly around the country.

Several new local news organizations, each different from the others, can be found in San Diego. The reporting staff of the daily newspaper there, *The San Diego Union-Tribune,* has been halved by a series of cuts both before and after its sale by the Copley family in May 2009 to a Los Angeles investment firm, Platinum Equity, which had no previous experience in journalism.

Five years ago, frustration with the *Union-Tribune*'s coverage of the city prompted a local businessman, Buzz Woolley, to fund the launch of an online-only local news organization, Voice of San Diego. The dozen reporters who work out of its light-filled newsroom in a new Spanish mission-style building near San Diego Bay focus on local accountability journalism. The site has no recipes or movie reviews or sports. The young journalists, most of whom came from newspapers, do enterprise and investigative reporting about San Diego government, business, housing, education, health, environment, and other "key quality of life issues facing the region," said executive editor Andrew Donohue. "We want to be best at covering a small number of things. We're very disciplined about not trying to do everything."

Voice of San Diego's impact has been disproportionate to its steadily growing but still relatively modest audience of fewer than 100,000 unique visitors a month. Its investigations of fraud in local economic development corporations, police misrepresentation of crime statistics, and the city's troubled pension fund, among other subjects, have led to prosecutions, reforms, and the kind of national journalism awards—from Sigma Delta Chi and Investigative Reporters and Editors—typically given to newspapers. To increase their reach, Voice journalists appear regularly on the local NBC television station, the all-news commercial radio station, and the public radio station, giving those outlets reporting they otherwise would not have.

Voice of San Diego's investigations have led to prosecutions, reforms, and national journalism awards.

The current $1 million annual budget of the Voice of San Diego, which is a nonprofit, comes from donors like Woolley, from foundations, advertising, corporate sponsorships, and contributions from citizen "members," like those who support local public radio and television and cultural institutions. "We don't count on mass traffic, but rather a level of loyalty," said publisher Scott Lewis. "We're seeking loyal people like those who give to the opera, museums or the orchestra because they believe they should be sustained."

They rent newsroom space from one of their supporters, the San Diego Foundation, which, like hundreds of other community foundations around the country, is a collection of local family funds with a professional staff to offer advice to the donors of these funds. Lewis said the foundation recommends contributions to the Voice. At the same time, the national Knight Foundation has been encouraging such foundations to support news and information needs in their communities through a program of matching grants. Knight and the San Diego Foundation recently gave Voice of San Diego matching grants of $100,000 each to increase its coverage of local neighborhoods and communities "underserved" by other news media.

Across town, the San Diego News Network has launched a quite different, for-profit local news website that resembles the *Union-Tribune* newspaper's website much more than it does Voice of San Diego. SDNN aggregates news and information from its own small reporting staff, freelancers, San Diego-area weekly community newspapers, radio, and television stations, and bloggers. It covers most of the subjects the newspaper does, from local events, business, and sports to entertainment, food, and travel, but with less independent reporting. Local entrepreneurs Barbara Bry and her husband Neil Senturia, and former *Union-Tribune* website editor Chris Jennewein, have raised $2 million from local investors and want to create a network of similar sites in as many as forty cities; they hope to attract more advertisers and become profitable. Jennewein said that he expects cities like San Diego, which long had a single dominant newspaper, to spawn many kinds of news entities. "There's going to be fragmentation," he said. "It may be a good thing. We have to think of there being a new news ecosystem."

The most unusual San Diego startup is The Watchdog Institute, an independent nonprofit local investigative reporting project based on the campus of San Diego State University. Lorie Hearn, who was a senior editor at the *Union-Tribune,* persuaded her former newspaper's new owner, Platinum Equity, to contribute money to the startup so that Hearn could hire investigative reporters who had worked for her at the *Union-Tribune.* In return, Hearn will provide the newspaper with investigative stories at a cost lower than if Hearn and the other Watchdog Institute journalists were still on its payroll. She intends to seek more local media partners, along with philanthropic donations, while training San Diego State journalism students to help with the reporting.

There are other examples of local news startups around the country. The nonprofit website St. Louis Beacon, launched by Margaret Freivogel and a dozen of her colleagues who were bought out or laid off by the venerable *St. Louis Post-Dispatch,* does in-depth reporting and analysis in targeted "areas of concentration," including the local economy, politics, race relations, education, health, and the arts. Freivogel's budget of just under $1 million comes primarily from foundations and local donors, advertisers, and corporate sponsors. In Minneapolis, the nonprofit MinnPost website relies on a mix of full-time, part-time, contract, and freelance journalists for the site's news reporting, commentary, and blogs. Editor Joel Kramer's budget of more than $1 million a year includes foundation grants and a significant amount of advertising.

Some of the startups are experimenting with what is being called "pro-am" journalism—professionals and amateurs working together over the Internet. This includes, for example, ProPublica, the nation's largest startup nonprofit news organization with three-dozen investigative reporters and editors. Amanda Michel, its director of distributed reporting, recruited a network of volunteer citizen reporters to monitor progress on a sample of 510 of the six thousand projects approved for federal stimulus money around the country. "We recruited people who know about contracts," Michel said. "We need a definable culture" of people with expertise on targeted subjects, "not just everybody."

Much smaller local and regional websites founded by professional journalists—ranging from the for-profit New West network of websites in Montana and neighboring states to the nonprofit New Haven Independent in Connecticut—regularly supplement reporting by their relatively tiny staffs with contributions from freelancers, bloggers, and readers. The fast-increasing number of blog-like hyperlocal neighborhood news sites across the country depend even more heavily for their news reporting on freelancers and citizen contributors that is edited by professional journalists. In Seattle, among the most Internet-oriented metropolitan areas in the country, pro-am neighborhood news sites are proliferating. "We believe this could become the next-generation news source" in American cities, said Cory Bergman, who started Next Door Media, a group of sites in five connecting Seattle neighborhoods. "The challenge is to create a viable economic model." Bergman and his wife Kate devised a franchise model, in which the editor of each site, a professional journalist, reports news of the neighborhood and curates text, photo, and video contributions from residents. Editors earn a percentage of their site's advertising revenue.

Several affluent suburban New Jersey towns outside New York City also have become test tubes for these kinds of hyperlocal news websites, some of which have been launched by big news organizations experimenting with low-cost local newsgathering. At the state level, other new, nonprofit news organizations are trying to help fill the gap left when cost-cutting newspapers pulled reporters out of state capitals. The Center for Investigative Reporting, a three-decade-old Berkeley-based nonprofit that had long produced award-winning national stories for newspapers and television, has started California Watch with foundation funding to scrutinize that state's government, publishing its reporting in dozens of news media throughout California and on its own website.

The Center for Independent Media, with funding from a variety of donors and foundations, operates a network of nonprofit, liberal-leaning political news websites in the capitals of Colorado, Iowa, Michigan, Minnesota, and New Mexico, all battleground states during the 2008 presidential election. David Bennahum, a journalist and business consultant, launched the sites in 2006 with the stated mission of producing "actionable impact journalism" about "key issues." Meanwhile, Texas venture capitalist John Thornton and former *Texas Monthly* editor Evan Smith have raised $3.5 million from Thornton and his wife, other Texas donors, including entrepreneur T. Boone Pickens, and foundations to start the nonprofit Texas Tribune in Austin, where they are hiring fifteen journalists to do independent, multimedia reporting about state government, politics, and policy for its website and other Texas news media.

Not surprisingly, most of these startups are financially fragile. In Chicago, a former *Tribune* reporter, Geoff Dougherty, trained scores of volunteers to help a handful of paid reporters find news in the city's neighborhoods for his nonprofit website, the Chi-Town Daily News. But, in the summer of 2009, after four years of operation with a variety of foundation grants, Dougherty announced he could not raise enough money to keep going as a nonprofit. He said he would instead seek investors for some of kind of commercial local news site.

There are notable startups on the national and international front as well. The for-profit GlobalPost, for example, with money from investors, Web advertising, and fee-paying clients, produces independent foreign reporting with a string of sixty-five professional stringers. On the home front, Politico has a news staff of seventy, and delivers scoops, gossip, and commentary on national politics and government. Revenue comes mostly from advertising online and via its weekly print version, and by corporations and groups seeking to influence legislation and policy.

Meanwhile, as it separates from Time Warner and transitions from an Internet portal to a generator of Web content, AOL also is betting on special-interest, advertising-supported, professionally produced news websites like Politico's. AOL has launched or purchased such Web startups as Politics Daily for politics and government, Fanhouse for sports, Bloging Stocks for business, and TMZ for celebrities and entertainment. It also is experimenting with small local new sites like Patch.com in suburban Connecticut and New Jersey. And like Politico, AOL has been hiring experienced journalists from struggling news media.

The quality of news reporting by most of the national, regional, and local startups is generally comparable to, and sometimes better than, that of newspapers, as can be seen by their collaboration with traditional newspapers on some stories. Small neighborhood news startups generally report on their communities in more detail than newspapers can, even though the quality of reporting and writing may not be comparable.

Collectively, the newcomers are filling some of the gaps left by the downsizing of newspapers' reporting staffs, especially in local accountability and neighborhood reporting. However, the staffs of most of the startups are still small, as are their audiences and budgets, and they are scattered unevenly across the country. Their growth, role, and impact in news reporting are still to be determined by a variety of factors explored later in this report.

What kind of news reporting has been spawned by the blogosphere? The boon and bane of the digital world is its seemingly infinite variety. It offers news, information and, especially, opinion—on countless thousands of websites, blogs, and social networks. Most are vehicles for sharing personal observations, activities, and views in words, photographs, and videos—sometimes more than anyone would want to know. A large number also pass along, link to, or comment on news and other content originally produced by established news organizations. And many of the participants—bloggers, political and special interest activists and groups, governments and private companies, and Internet entrepreneurs—generate various kinds of news reporting themselves.

Lumped together as the "blogosphere," these sites are sometimes seen as either the replacement for—or the enemy of—established news media. In fact, the blogosphere and older media have become increasingly symbiotic. They feed off each other's information and commentary, and they fact-check each other. They share audiences, and they mimic each other through evolving digital journalistic innovation.

A few blogs have grown into influential, for-profit digital news organizations. Upstairs in a loft newsroom in New York's Chelsea neighborhood, Josh Marshall's Talking Points Memo staff is combining traditional news reporting with an openly ideological agenda to create an influential and profitable national news website. TPM has grown from former print reporter Marshall's one-man opinion blog into a full-fledged, advertising-supported digital news institution with a small group of paid reporters and editors in New York and Washington. In 2008, TPM won a George Polk Award for its investigation of the political firings of U.S. attorneys during the Bush administration.

Marshall described TPM as "narrating with reporting and aggregation"—including the involvement of "an audience with high interest and expertise. We have a consistent, iterative relationship with our audience—people telling us where to look," Marshall said. "But all the information, stories, and sources are checked professionally by our journalists."

Marshall also believes in "the discipline of the marketplace," and has not taken foundation money or philanthropic donations. Only advertising and small contributions from readers support TPM's still relatively small $600,000 annual budget. Its first outside investment is coming from a group led by Netscape founder Marc Andreesen to help Marshall expand his reporting staff and advertising sales.

TPM's combination of news reporting, analysis, commentary, and reader participation is the model in varying forms for many blogs on the Internet. Some of the more widely read and trusted independent bloggers specialize in subjects they know and have informed opinions about, such as politics, the economy and business, legal affairs, the news media, education, health care, and family issues. Freelance financial journalist Michelle Leder, for example, turned her interest in the fine print of SEC filings into the closely watched Footnoted blog, which is supported by both her freelance income and expensive subscriptions for investors to an insider version of her blog.

They also are creating new ways to report news. In 2008, Kelly Golnoush Niknejad, a Columbia University journalism school graduate, launched a blog called Tehran Bureau, to which Iranian and other journalists contribute reporting from inside Iran and from the diaspora of Iranian exiles. In 2009, Tehran Bureau joined in a partnership with the public television program *Frontline,* which provides the blog with editorial and financial support and hosts its website. *Frontline* and Tehran Bureau also are collaborating on a documentary.

For most of the millions of its practitioners, blogging is still a hobby for which there is little or no remuneration, even if the blog is picked up or mentioned by news media or aggregation sites. Residents of Baltimore, for example, can currently choose among a variety of blogs about life there. Baltimore Crime posts contributions from readers about what they see happening in the streets. Investigative Voice, started by two journalists from the defunct *Baltimore Examiner* newspaper, and Bmore News, owned by a public relations firm, focus on the city's African-American community. Inside Charm City posts press releases from local businesses and government agencies. Blog Baltimore aggregates reader contributions with stories from local news media. The anonymous Baltimore Slumlord Watch blogger posts photos of abandoned and derelict buildings, identifies the property owners, names the city council members in whose districts the buildings are located, provides links to city and state agencies.

The most ambitious local blog there is Baltimore Brew, launched in 2009 by Fern Shen, a former reporter for *The Baltimore Sun* and *The Washington Post,* who has recruited freelancers, including other former *Sun* journalists, to contribute reporting about the city and its neighborhoods, mostly without pay for the moment. Shen, who runs the blog from her kitchen table with money from an initial angel investor, acknowledged taking advantage of buyouts and layoffs that took about 120 journalists out of the *Sun*'s newsroom in less than a year. "The folks that used to do things for a paycheck are now doing them for cheap or for free," she said. "Somebody has to get these reporters back to work again." She is hoping to take advantage of being named "best local blog" by the *Baltimore City Paper* to raise revenue from prospective advertisers and eventually create a paying business for herself and her contributors.

National online news aggregators have created business models for mass audiences and advertising they hope will make them profitable. They aggregate blogs and some reporting of their own with links to and summaries of news reported by other media, along with plentiful photographs and videos. The small staff at Newser, for example, rewrites stories taken from news media websites. The Drudge Report's Matt Drudge, who has been at it much longer, simply links to other sites' content, along with bits of occasionally reliable media and political gossip. Founders Ariana Huffington of Huffington Post and Tina Brown of The Daily Beast, who are media celebrities themselves, have attracted numerous freelance contributors and volunteer bloggers, including big-name writers, to supplement their relatively small writing and editing staffs. Huffington Post on the left and Drudge on the right also display clear ideological leanings in their selection of stories, links and blogs.

Newspapers complain that some aggregators violate copyrights by using their work without payment or a share of the aggregators' advertising revenue, although the aggregators also link to the original stories on the papers' websites. At issue, besides the trade between paying the papers on the one hand and driving some readers to their sites on the other, is the current state of copyright law, which has not kept up with issues raised by digital publication. It has not been decided, for example, how much of a story can be republished, or in what form, before the prevailing principle of "fair use" is violated.

In a departure from other for-profit aggregators, The Huffington Post has joined with the American News Project, a non-profit print and video investigative reporting entity, to invest in a The Huffington Post Investigative Fund, a legally separate nonprofit based in Washington with about a dozen investigative journalists and initial funding of $1.75 million, including $500,000 from Huffington Post. The fund's editor, former *Washington Post* investigative editor Larry Roberts, said it will provide reporting on national subjects for use by The Huffington Post and other news media, much the way that ProPublica does. He said that he has a commitment from Huffington that the project would be editorially independent and nonpartisan.

The fast-growing number of digital startups, ambitious blogs, experiments in pro-am journalism, and other hybrid news organizations are not replacing newspapers or broadcast news. But they increasingly depend on each other—the old media for news and investigative reporting they can no longer do themselves and the newcomers for the larger audiences they can reach through newspapers, radio, and television—and for the authority that these legacy media outlets still convey. The many new sources of news reporting have become, in the span of a relatively few years, significant factors in the reconstruction of American journalism.

How are colleges and universities contributing to independent news reporting? A number of universities are publishing the reporting of their student journalists on the states, cities, and neighborhoods where the schools are located. The students work in journalism classes and news services under the supervision of professional journalists now on their faculties. The students' reporting appears on local news websites operated by the universities and in other local news media, some of which pay for the reporting to supplement their own. In southern Florida, for example, *The Miami Herald, The Palm Beach Post,* and *Sun Sentinel* have agreed to use reporting from journalism students at Florida International University.

The University of Missouri is unique in having run its own local daily newspaper, the *Columbia Missourian,* since 1908, when its journalism school opened. This valuable journalism laboratory has professional editors and a reporting staff of journalism students. Other universities, meanwhile, publish local news websites. In New York, Columbia's journalism school operates several sites with reporting by its students in city neighborhoods, and investigative reporting by students in the school's Stabile Center for Investigative Journalism has appeared in several major news outlets.

Students at the Graduate School of Journalism at the University of California at Berkeley also do reporting in several San Francisco area communities for the school's neighborhood news websites, and the graduate school has plans for its 120 students to work with professional journalists, beginning next year, at the local news website it is starting with San Francisco's KQED public radio and television. The Walter Cronkite School of Journalism at Arizona State University in Phoenix operates the Cronkite News Service, which provides student reporting to about thirty client newspapers and television stations around the state. And the Capital News Service of the University of Maryland's Philip Merrill College of Journalism operates news bureaus in Washington and Maryland's capital in Annapolis. Northwestern University students staff a similar Medill School of Journalism news service in Washington.

Universities also are becoming homes for independent nonprofit investigative reporting projects started by former newspaper and television journalists. Some are run by journalists on their faculties, while others, such as The Watchdog Institute at San Diego State University, are independent nonprofits that use university facilities and work with faculty and students. For example, Andy Hall, a former *Wisconsin State Journal* investigative reporter, started the Wisconsin Center for Investigative Journalism as an independent, foundation-supported nonprofit on the campus of the University of Wisconsin in Madison. Its reporting by professional journalists, interns, and students appears in Wisconsin newspapers, public radio and television stations, and their websites.

In Boston, Walter Robinson, a former Pulitzer Prize-winning *Globe* investigative reporter, and students in his investigative reporting seminars at Northeastern have produced eleven front-page pieces for the *Globe* since 2007. And a group of former local television and newspaper journalists on the faculty at Boston University recently launched the New England Center for Investigative Journalism in its College of Communications, staffed by the journalist faculty members and their students, in collaboration with the *Globe,* New England Cable News, and public radio station WBUR.

How can fledgling news reporting organizations keep going? Money is obviously a major challenge for nonprofit news organizations, many of which are struggling to stay afloat. Raising money from foundations and other donors and sponsors consumes a disproportionate amount of their time and energy. Advertising and payments from media partners for some stories account for only a fraction of the support needed by most news reporting nonprofits.

Nearly twenty nonprofit news organizations—ranging from the relatively large and well-established Center for Investigative Reporting and Center for Public Integrity to relatively small startups like Voice of San Diego and MinnPost—met last summer to form an Investigative News Network to collaborate on fundraising, legal matters, back-office functions, website development, and reporting projects. Joe Bergantino, a former Boston television investigative reporter who is director of the New England Center for Investigative Reporting at Boston University, said such collaboration is vital "if we're all going to be back next year."

A number of national foundations—led by Knight and including Carnegie, Ford, Hewlett, MacArthur, Open Society Institute, Pew, and Rockefeller, among others—have made grants to a variety of nonprofit reporting ventures in recent years. A study by the Knight-funded J-Lab at American University in Washington estimated that, altogether, national and local foundations provided $128 million to news nonprofits from 2005 into 2009.

Nearly half of that money, however, has been given by major donors to a handful of relatively large national investigative reporting nonprofits, including ProPublica, the Center for Investigative Reporting at Berkeley, and the Center for Public Integrity in Washington. Some foundations fund only national reporting on subjects of particular interest to their donors or managers—such as health, religion, or government accountability. Grants for local news reporting are much smaller and usually not high priorities for foundations, many of which do not make any grants for journalism.

But the future of news reporting is a priority for the Knight Foundation, whose money comes from a family that once owned twenty-six newspapers. Knight has given tens of millions of dollars to nonprofit reporting projects and university journalism instruction, and is encouraging the hundreds of community foundations around the country to join with it in supporting local journalism, as the San Diego Foundation has done with the Voice of San Diego and the Greater St. Louis Community Foundation with the St. Louis Beacon. Knight conducts an annual seminar with leaders of community foundations to encourage grants to local news nonprofits and has started its matching grants initiative to donate with them. "The bottom line," said Eric Newton, Knight's vice president, "is that local news needs local support." Knight foundation president Alberto Ibarguen has also been talking with national foundations for the past two years to encourage more of them to provide more support for local news reporting.

Some foundations have recognized the importance of news reporting to the advancement of their other objectives, while trying to protect the independence of the reporting. The Kaiser Family Foundation, which has long supported health care policy research, started its own nonprofit news organization in 2009. The California Healthcare Foundation, which also funds research, has given $3.2 million to the Annenberg School of Communication and Journalism at the University of Southern California to support a team of six California newspaper journalists for three years to expand health care reporting in the state. Michael Parks, an Annenberg faculty member and a former *Los Angeles Times* executive editor, directs the team, which has helped newspapers in half a dozen California cities report on local hospitals, the pattern of Medicare reimbursements to doctors, and causes of mortality in the state's central valley. "We went to newspapers and asked what stories they have wanted to do, but were unable to do—no resources, no expertise, whatever," Parks said. "We can help."

What other new sources are there for public information?
The Internet has greatly increased access to large quantities of "public information" and news produced by government and a growing number of data-gathering, data-analyzing, research, academic, and special interest activist organizations. Altogether, these sources of public information appear to be a realization of what Walter Lippmann envisioned nearly ninety years ago when he argued that, in an increasingly complex world, journalism could serve democracy only by relying on agencies beyond journalism for dependable data. He urged journalists to make greater use of what he termed "political observatories"—organizations both in and out of government that used scientific methods and instruments to examine human affairs.

Digital databases, for example, enable journalists and citizens to find information in a fraction of the time it would have taken years ago—if it could have been found at all. Routine documents a reporter once had to obtain in a reading room of a government agency or by filing a Freedom of Information Act request can now be found online and are easy to download.

Access to much of the information is dependent on new online intermediaries. Neither house of Congress, for instance, nor any city council of the twenty-five largest American cities nor most state legislative houses make an individual legislator's roll-call votes available in easily usable form, for example. However, that information is now available online for a fee from three different Congress-watching organizations and for free on the websites OpenCongress.org, GovTrack.us, and Washingtonpost.com. Princeton's Center for Information Technology Policy has created a keyword-searchable online database of federal court records that is much less cumbersome to use than the database maintained by the courts themselves.

Some of this public information comes from government agencies that have been around for a long time, like the Government Accountability Office or the Security and Exchange Commission. Others, like the Federal Election Commission (1975) or the Environmental Protection Agency, which produces the Toxic Release Inventory (1986), or the individual departments' and agencies' inspectors general (most of them established through the Inspectors General Act of 1978) are products of the past several decades. All produce abundant information and analysis about government and what it regulates, information that both resembles and assists news reporting.

Outside government, advocacy groups and nongovernmental organizations have sometimes created what resemble news staffs to report on the subjects of their special interest. It is then up to journalists to separate the groups' activist agendas from their information gathering, which, in many cases, the journalists have grown to trust. Taxpayers for Common Sense, founded in 1995, for example, has painstakingly gathered data on congressional "earmarking" that is the starting point for journalists who report on how members of Congress add money to appropriation bills for projects sought by special interests, constituents, and campaign contributors.

Besides their own version of reporting, governments and interest groups also are opening up increasing numbers of digital databases to journalists and citizens. For instance, ProPublica and the Washington-based Sunlight Foundation have created a downloadable database of two years of federal filings from 300 foreign agents on their lobbying of Congress.

A database is not journalism, but, increasingly, sophisticated journalism depends on reliable, downloadable, and searchable databases. The federal government alone has fourteen statistical agencies and about sixty offices within other agencies that produce statistical data. Such data, said Columbia professor of public affairs Kenneth Prewitt, a former director of the U.S. Census Bureau, "has an assumed precision that the journalistic world is trained to question." It needs to be evaluated carefully and skeptically.

The accessibility of so much more public information changes the work of journalists and the nature of news reporting. It provides reporters new shortcuts to usable, usually reliable information, saving them and their news organizations time and money. It runs the risk of drowning reporters in deep seas of data, but it makes possible richer and more comprehensive and accurate reporting.

What needs to be done to support independent news reporting? We are not recommending a government bailout of newspapers, nor any of the various direct subsidies that governments give newspapers in many European countries, although those subsidies have not had a noticeably chilling effect on newspapers' willingness to print criticism of those governments. Nor are we recommending direct government financing or control of television networks or stations.

Most Americans have a deep distrust of direct government involvement or political influence in independent news reporting, a sentiment we share. But this should not preclude government support for news reporting any more than it has for the arts, the humanities, and sciences, all of which receive some government support.

There has been a minimum of government pressure in those fields, with a few notable exceptions. The National Endowment for the Arts came under fire in the 1990s, for example, for the controversial nature of some of the art it helped sponsor with federal funds. So any use of government money to help support news reporting would require mechanisms, besides the protections of the First Amendment, to insulate the resulting journalism as much as possible from pressure, interference, or censorship.

From its beginning, the U.S. government has enacted laws providing support for the news media, with varying consequences. In the year following enactment of the First Amendment, Congress passed the Post Office Act of 1792 that put the postal system on a permanent foundation and authorized a subsidy for newspapers sent through the mail, as many were at the time. Those early newspapers also could mail copies to one another free of charge, creating the first collaborative news reporting. This subsidy assisted the distribution of news across the growing country for many years. While the First Amendment forbade the federal government from abridging freedom of the press, the founders' commitment to broad circulation of public information produced policies that made a free press possible.

Nearly two centuries later, the Newspaper Preservation Act of 1970, in a specific exception to antitrust laws, allowed newspapers in the same city to form joint operating agreements to share revenue and costs in what proved to be a futile attempt to prevent single-newspaper monopolies in most cities. This intervention did not work as intended, and most joint operating agreements ended with just one of the newspapers surviving.

An antitrust exemption that would allow newspapers to act together to seek payment for the digital distribution of their news would not be any wiser or do much more to support independent reporting. Antitrust laws forbid industries from setting prices in concert, which we do not think is desirable or necessary for newspapers. Individually, newspapers are already contemplating various ways to charge for digital content, and they do not need an antitrust exemption to continue.

We are not advocating or discouraging specific ways for news organizations to seek payment for digital content. We believe the marketplace will determine whether any of the many experiments will ultimately be successful. And we believe that managers of news organizations are best positioned to shape and test responses to them. For example, newspapers should develop detailed information about their digital audience to sell more targeted, and higher-priced, advertising to accompany specific digital content, while protecting individual readers' privacy. They also should experiment with digital commerce that does not conflict with their news reporting, such as facilitating the purchase of books they review. To borrow a phrase from another digital news context, we see a long tail of possible revenue sources—payment for some kinds of unique digital content, online commerce, higher print subscription prices, even new print products—being added to diminished but still significant advertising revenues.

There is unlikely to be any single new economic model for supporting news reporting. Many newspapers can and will find ways to survive in print and online, with new combinations of reduced resources. But they will no longer produce the kinds of revenues or profits that had subsidized large reporting staffs, regardless of what new business models they evolve. The days of a kind of news media paternalism or patronage that produced journalism in the public interest, whether or not it contributed to the bottom line, are largely gone. American society must take some collective responsibility for supporting independent news reporting in this new environment—as society has, at much greater expense, for public needs like education, health care, scientific advancement, and cultural preservation—through varying combinations of philanthropy, subsidy, and government policy.

American society must take some collective responsibility for supporting independent news reporting in this new environment.

Our recommendations are intended to support independent, original, and credible news reporting, especially local and accountability reporting, across all media in communities throughout the United States. Rather than depending primarily on newspapers and their waning reporting resources, each sizeable American community should have a range of diverse sources of news reporting. They should include a variety and mix of commercial and nonprofit news organizations that can both compete and collaborate with one another. They should be adapting traditional journalistic forms to the multimedia, interactive, real-time capabilities of digital communication, sharing the reporting and distribution of news with citizens, bloggers, and aggregators.

To support diverse sources of independent news reporting, we specifically recommend:

1. The Internal Revenue Service or Congress should explicitly authorize any independent news organization substantially devoted to reporting on public affairs to be created as or converted into a nonprofit entity

or a low-profit Limited Liability Corporation serving the public interest, regardless of its mix of financial support, including commercial sponsorship and advertising. The IRS or Congress also should explicitly authorize program-related investments by philanthropic foundations in these hybrid news organizations—and in designated public service news reporting by for-profit news organizations.

Any of the startup news reporting entities are already tax-exempt nonprofits recognized by the IRS under section 501(c)(3) of the tax code. Some magazines with news content, including *Harper's* and *Mother Jones,* as well as public radio and television stations, also have been nonprofits for years. All are able to receive tax-deductible donations, along with foundation grants, advertising revenue, and other income, including revenue from for-profit subsidiaries. Their nonprofit status helps assure contributors and advertisers that they are primarily supporting news reporting rather than the maximization of profits. Tax deductibility is an added incentive for donors, and the nonprofit's tax exemption allows any excess income to be re-invested in resources for reporting.

However, neither the IRS nor Congress has made clear what kinds of news organizations qualify as nonprofits under section 501(c)(3), which specifies such charitable activities as the advancement of education, religion, science, civil rights, and amateur sports. News reporting is not one of the "exempt purposes" listed by the IRS, which has granted 501(c)(3) nonprofit recognition to startup news organizations individually by letter rather than categorically. News organizations cannot be certain whether they would qualify—or whether they would be able to keep their 501(c)(3) status, depending, for example, on how much advertising or other commercial income they earn or the extent to which they express political opinions.

The IRS has not made clear whether a certain amount of a nonprofit news organization's advertising revenue might be considered "unrelated business income" subject to tax or even might be regarded as an impediment to continued nonprofit status. And, while its regulations stipulate that a 501(c)(3) nonprofit "may not attempt to influence legislation as a substantial part of its activities and it may not participate in any campaign activity for or against political candidates," it is not clear whether that restricts political editorial opinion apart from the endorsement of candidates.

Congress should add news organizations substantially devoted to public affairs reporting to the list of specifically eligible nonprofits under section 501(c)(3), regardless of the amount of their advertising income. Or the IRS itself should rule that such news organizations are categorically eligible under the criteria already established by Congress. The IRS also should explicitly allow news nonprofits to express editorial opinions about legislation and politics without endorsing candidates or lobbying. The Obama administration, in which the president and some officials have expressed their openness to ways to help preserve public interest news reporting, should weigh in on these policy decisions.

A possible alternative for news organizations is a Low-profit Limited Liability Corporation, known as an L3C, a hybrid legal entity with both for-profit and nonprofit investments to carry out socially useful purposes. Both private investors and foundations could invest in an L3C, with private investors able to realize a limited profit. A small but growing number of states, beginning with Vermont in 2008, have passed laws enabling the creation of L3Cs to make it more economically feasible to set up businesses for charitable or education purposes that might have difficulty attracting sufficient capital as either commercial firms or nonprofits. Illinois, Michigan, Wyoming, and North Dakota also have recently enacted L3C laws.

Each of the state laws was written to enable foundations to make "program-related investments" in the new hybrid organizations. The IRS created the concept of program-related investments in the 1960s to enable foundations to make socially useful grants to for-profit ventures. But foundations have been hesitant to make such grants because they are not certain which ones the IRS would allow. Congress or the IRS should provide a process by which a qualifying journalistic organization seeking a program-related investment from a foundation could be assured that it would qualify.

Nonprofit news organizations should, as some already have, individually and collectively through collaboration, develop professional fundraising capabilities like those of advertising departments for commercial news organizations. They also should develop other sources of revenue, including advertising, partnerships, and innovative marketing of their reporting to other news media and news consumers.

2. Philanthropists, and national foundations, and community foundations should substantially increase their support for news organizations that have demonstrated a substantial commitment to public affairs and accountability reporting.

Philanthropically supported institutions are central to American society. Philanthropy has been essential for educational, research, cultural, and religious institutions, health and social services, parks and the preservation of nature, and much more. With the exception of public radio and television, philanthropy has played a very small role in supporting news reporting, because most of it had been subsidized by advertising.

Led by the Knight Foundation and individual donors like Buzz Woolley and Herbert and Marion Sandler, foundations and philanthropists have begun to respond to the breakdown of that economic model by funding the launch of nonprofit news startups and individual reporting projects, as discussed earlier. But foundations are not yet providing much money to sustain those startups or to underwrite all of their journalism rather than only their reporting on subjects of special interest to each foundation or donor.

Foundations should consider news reporting of public affairs to be a continuous public good rather than a series of specific projects under their control or a way of generating interest and action around causes and issues of special interest to them. They should ensure that there is an impermeable wall between each foundation's interests and the news reporting it supports, and they should make their support of accountability journalism a much higher priority than it has been for all but a few like the Knight Foundation.

These steps would represent major shifts in the missions of most national foundations. Their model of grant-making has relied on documenting specific "outcomes," explained Eric Newton of the Knight Foundation, and it is not easy to measure the impact of news reporting. "News is not like electricity," Newton said. "When there's a news blackout, you don't know what you're not getting." But what communities are now missing in news reporting is becoming increasingly apparent as newspaper and television station newsrooms empty out.

It is time for other national foundations to join with Knight in a concerted effort to preserve public affairs news reporting, and because of the importance of local news, the nation's more than 700 community foundations should take the lead in supporting news reporting in their own cities and towns. Community foundations, which manage collections of donor-advised local philanthropic funds, have large assets and make large gifts. Donations from the twenty-five largest community foundations alone in 2007 totaled $2.4 billion. If community foundations were to allocate just 1 percent of their giving to local news reporting, it would roughly equal all the money that all foundations have spent annually to support news reporting in recent years.

Some community foundations have taken the first steps in this direction. Several donor-advised funds of the Greater St. Louis Community Foundation are among donors to the St. Louis Beacon. The San Diego Foundation has been a key supporter of the Voice of San Diego. The Minneapolis Foundation received a Knight grant to encourage its donors to help MinnPost pay for reporting on local subjects like education and poverty, in which the foundation has a longstanding interest and record of grant-giving.

Community foundations also should consider funding public affairs and accountability reporting not only by nonprofits but also by local commercial newspapers that no longer have the resources to fund all of it themselves. For example, James Hamilton, director of Duke University's DeWitt Wallace Center for Media and Democracy has proposed that local foundations finance specific accountability reporting projects, individual reporters, or the coverage of some subjects at the Raleigh *News & Observer*. That would not be such a big step beyond the journalism produced by nonprofits like ProPublica or the Center for Investigative Reporting that many commercial news media are already publishing and broadcasting.

3. Public radio and television should be substantially reoriented to provide significant local news reporting in every community served by public stations and their websites. This requires urgent action by and reform of the Corporation for Public Broadcasting, increased congressional funding and support for public media news reporting, and changes in mission and leadership for many public stations across the country.

The failure of much of the public broadcasting system to provide significant local news reporting reflects longstanding neglect of this responsibility by the majority of public radio and televisions stations, the Corporation for Public Broadcasting, and Congress. The approximately $400 million that Congress currently appropriates for the CPB each year is far less per capita than public broadcasting support in countries with comparable economies—roughly $1.35 per capita for the United States, compared to about $25 in Canada, Australia, and Germany, nearly $60 in Japan, $80 in Britain, and more than $100 in Denmark and Finland. The lion's share of the financial support for public radio and television in the United States comes from listener and viewer donations, corporate sponsorships, foundation grants, and philanthropic gifts.

It is not just a question of money, but how it is spent. Most of the money that the CPB and private donors and sponsors provide public broadcasting is spent on broadcast facilities, independent television production companies, and programming to attract audiences during fund-raising drives. In many metropolitan areas, the money supports more stations and signals than are necessary to reach everyone in the community.

At the same time, outside of a relatively few regional public radio station groups, very little money is spent on local news coverage by individual public radio and television stations. The CPB itself, in its new Public Radio Audience Task Force Report, acknowledged that "claiming a significantly larger role in American journalism requires a much more robust news-gathering capacity—more 'feet on the street' with notebooks, recorders, cameras, and more editors and producers to shape their work" for broadcast and digital distribution by public radio stations. "The distance between current reality and the role we imagine—and that others urge upon public radio—is large," the report concluded. And that distance is immense for the vast majority of public television stations that do no local news reporting at all.

The CPB should declare that local news reporting is a top priority for public broadcasting and change its allocation of resources accordingly. Local news reporting is an essential part of the public education function that American public radio and television have been charged with fulfilling since their inception.

The CPB should require a minimum amount of local news reporting by every public radio and television station receiving CPB money, and require stations to report publicly to the CPB on their progress in reaching specified goals. The CPB should increase and speed up its direct funding for experiments in more robust and creative local news coverage by public stations both on the air and on their websites. The CPB should also aggressively encourage and reward collaborations by public stations with other local nonprofit and university news organizations.

National leaders of public radio and television who have been meeting privately to discuss news reporting should bring their deliberations into the open, reduce wasteful rivalries among local public stations, regional and national public media, and production entities, and launch concerted initiatives to increase local news coverage. The CPB should encourage changes in the leadership of public stations that are not capable of reorienting their missions.

Congress should back these reforms. In its next reauthorization of the CPB and appropriation of its budget, Congress should change its name to the Corporation for Public Media, support its efforts to move public radio and television into the digital age, specify public media's local news reporting mission, and significantly increase its appropriation. Congress should also reform the governance of the reformed corporation by broadening the membership of its board with appointments by such nonpolitical sources as the Librarian of Congress or national media organizations. Ideological issues that have surfaced over publicly supported arts, cultural activities, or national news coverage should not affect decisions about significantly improving local news reporting by public media.

4. Universities, both public and private, should become ongoing sources of local, state, specialized subject, and accountability news reporting as part of their educational missions. They should operate their own news organizations, host platforms for other nonprofit news and investigative reporting organizations, provide faculty positions for active individual journalists, and be laboratories for digital innovation in the gathering and sharing of news and information.

In addition to educating and training journalists, colleges and universities should be centers of professional news reporting, as they are for the practice and advancement of medicine and law, scientific and social research, business development, engineering, education, and agriculture. As discussed earlier, a number of campuses have already started or become partners in local news services, websites and investigative reporting projects, in which professional journalists, faculty members and students collaborate on news reporting. It is time for those and other colleges and universities to take the next step and create full-fledged news organizations.

Journalists on their faculties should engage in news reporting and editing, as well as teach these skills and perform research, just as members of other professional school faculties do. The most proficient student journalists should advance after graduation to paid residencies and internships, joining fully experienced journalists on year-round staffs of university-based, independently edited local news services, websites, and investigative reporting projects.

As in many professional fields, integrating such practical work into an academic setting can be challenging. Although much basic news reporting is routine, enterprise and accountability journalism, which by definition bring new information to light, can grow into society-changing work not so dissimilar from academic research that makes original contributions to knowledge in history and the social sciences. The capacity of the best journalists to combine original investigation with writing and other communications skills can enhance the teaching and research missions of universities.

Funding for university news organizations should come from earmarked donations and endowments, collaborations with other local news organizations, advertising, and other sources. Facilities, overhead, and fund-raising assistance should be provided by the colleges and universities, as is the case for other university-based models of professional practice. Reporting on specialized subjects in which university researchers can offer

relevant expertise in such fields as the arts, business, politics, science, and health could be assisted by faculty and students in those disciplines, funded in part by research grants, so long as independent news judgment is not compromised.

University news organizations should increase their collaboration with other local news nonprofits, including local public radio and television stations, many of which are owned by colleges and universities themselves and housed on their campuses. They also should collaborate with local commercial news media, providing them with news coverage and reporting interns, as some journalism schools and their news services do now. They should provide assistance for hyperlocal community news sites and blogs.

Universities should incubate innovations in news reporting and dissemination for the digital era. They could earn money for this from news media clients, as the Walter Cronkite School at Arizona State University does for research and development work for Gannett. Universities are among the nation's largest nonprofit institutions, and they should play significant roles in the reconstruction of American journalism.

5. A national Fund for Local News should be created with money the Federal Communications Commission now collects from or could impose on telecom users, television and radio broadcast licensees, or Internet service providers and which would be administered in open competition through state Local News Fund Councils.

The federal government already provides assistance to the arts, humanities, and sciences through independent agencies that include the National Endowment for the Arts, the National Endowment for the Humanities, the National Science Foundation, and the National Institutes of Health. The arts and humanities endowments each have budgets under $200 million. The National Science Foundation, with a budget of $6 billion, gives out about 10,000 grants a year. The National Institutes of Health has a budget of $28 billion and gives 50,000 grants. In these and other ways, the federal government gives significant support to individuals and organizations whose work creates new knowledge that contributes to the public good.

The Federal Communications Commission uses money from a surcharge on telephone bills—currently more than $7 billion a year—to underwrite telecom service for rural areas and the multimedia wiring of schools and libraries, among other things. In this way, the FCC supports the public circulation of information in places the market has failed to serve. Local news reporting, whose market model has faltered, is in need of similar support.

The FCC should direct some of the money from the telephone bill surcharge—or from fees paid by radio and television licensees, or proceeds from auctions of telecommunications spectrum, or new fees imposed on Internet service providers—to finance a Fund for Local News that would make grants for advances in local news reporting and innovative ways to support it. Commercial broadcasters who no longer cover local news or do not otherwise satisfy unenforced public-service requirements could also pay into such a fund instead.

In the stimulus bill passed in early 2009, Congress required the FCC to produce by February 17, 2010, a strategic plan for universal broadband access that specifies its national purposes. One of those purposes should be the gathering and dissemination of local news in every community, and the plan should include roles for the FCC and the federal government in achieving it.

The Fund for Local News would make grants through state Local News Fund Councils to news organizations—nonprofit and commercial, new media and old—that propose worthy initiatives in local news reporting. They would fund categories and methods of reporting and ways to support them, rather than individual stories or reporting projects, for durations of several years or more, with periodic progress reviews.

Local News Fund Councils would operate in ways similar to the way state Humanities Councils have since the 1970s, when they emerged as affiliates of the National Endowment for the Humanities. Organized as 501(c)(3) nonprofits, they have volunteer boards of academics, other figures in the humanities, and, in some places, gubernatorial appointees, all serving limited terms. Local News Fund Council boards should be comprised of journalists, educators, and community leaders representing a wide range of viewpoints and backgrounds.

Grants should be awarded in a transparent, public competition. The criteria for grants should be journalistic quality, local relevance, innovation in news reporting, and the capacity of the news organization, small or large, to carry out the reporting. A Fund for Local News national board of review should monitor the state councils and the quality of news their grants produced, all of which should be available on a public Fund for Local News website.

We understand the complexity of establishing a workable grant selection system and the need for strict safeguards to shield news organizations from pressure or coercion from state councils or anyone in government. As stated earlier, we recognize that political pressure has played a role at times in the history of the arts and humanities endowments and in public broadcasting. But these organizations have weathered those storms, and funding for the sciences and social sciences has generally been free of political pressure. With appropriate safeguards, a Fund for Local News would play a significant role in the reconstruction of American journalism.

6. More should be done—by journalists, nonprofit organizations and governments—to increase the accessibility and usefulness of public information collected by federal, state, and local governments, to facilitate the gathering and dissemination of public information by citizens, and to expand public recognition of the many sources of relevant reporting.

With the Internet, the compilation of—and access to—public information, such as government databases, is far easier than ever before. Yet much of this information is not easily available, and the already useable information is not being fully exploited by journalists. Optimal exploitation of these information sources is central to the mission of journalism, as it is to the practice of democratic governance. Governments, nongovernmental organizations, and news organizations should accelerate their efforts to make public information more accessible and to use it for news reporting.

With the Obama administration taking the lead, governments should fulfill "open government" promises by rapidly making more information available without Freedom of Information Act requests. News organizations should work with government agencies to use more of this information in their reporting. The federal government has some 24,000 websites, a massive bounty of information that should be made more accessible by opening closed archives, digitizing what is not yet available online, and improving its organization and display so everyone can use it easily.

News organizations should also move more quickly and creatively to involve their audiences and other citizens in the gathering and analysis of news and information, as Josh Marshall has done with readers of his TPM blogs, Minnesota Public Radio has done with its Public Insight Network of radio listeners, and ProPublica's Amanda Michel is doing with her citizen reporters. Local news organizations should collaborate with community news startups that utilize citizen reporting, as *The Seattle Times* has committed to do with neighborhood blogs. University scholars should archive and analyze these experiments and produce guidelines for "best practices."

Involving thousands of citizens in the collection and distribution of public information began long before computers and the Internet. For over a century, the Audubon Society has relied on thousands of local volunteers for a national bird count that might be termed pro-am scientific research. This is similar to the reporting that volunteers all over the world do for Human Rights Watch, or the information-gathering that health workers do for the Centers for Disease Control and Prevention. The original gathering and reporting of information also includes expert investigations like those of the inspectors general in federal agencies. All of this work amounts to "adjunct journalism"—public information gathering, analysis, and reporting that is adjunct to the news reporting journalists do and available for them to use. It should be fully integrated into what journalists, scholars, and the public recognize as reporting in the public interest.

Where Do We Go from Here?

What is bound to be a chaotic reconstruction of American journalism is full of both perils and opportunities for news reporting, especially in local communities. The perils are obvious. The restructuring of newspapers, which remain central to the future of local news reporting, is an uphill battle. Emerging local news organizations are still small and fragile, requiring considerable assistance—as we have recommended—to survive to compete and collaborate with newspapers. And much of public media must drastically change its culture to become a significant source of local news reporting.

Yet we believe we have seen abundant opportunity in the future of journalism. At many of the news organizations we visited, new and old, we have seen the beginnings of a genuine reconstruction of what journalism can and should be. We have seen struggling newspapers embrace digital change and start to collaborate with other papers, nonprofit news organizations, universities, bloggers, and their own readers. We have seen energetic local reporting startups, where enthusiasm about new forms of journalism is contagious, exemplified by Voice of San Diego's Scott Lewis when he says, "I am living a dream." We have seen pioneering public radio news operations that could be emulated by the rest of public media. We have seen forward-leaning journalism schools where faculty and student journalists report news themselves and invent new ways to do it. We have seen bloggers become influential journalists, and Internet innovators develop ways to harvest public information, such as the linguistics doctoral student who created the GovTrack .us Congressional voting database. We have seen the first foundations and philanthropists step forward to invest in the future of news, and we have seen citizens help to report the news and support new nonprofit news ventures. We have seen into a future of more diverse news organizations and more diverse support for their reporting.

We have seen into a future of more diverse news organizations and more diverse support for their reporting. It is all within reach.

All of this is within reach. Now, we want to see more leaders emerge in journalism, government, philanthropy, higher education, and the rest of society to seize this moment of challenging changes and new beginnings to ensure the future of independent news reporting.

Critical Thinking

1. What is *accountability journalism?* Do you agree that it is "as vital to the functioning of communities as clean air, safe streets, good schools, and public health"?

2. Summarize the writers' six recommendations for supporting diverse sources of independent news reporting. All of them assume sources of non-commercial financial support, most of them governmental. What are pros and cons of each?

Leonard Downie Jr. is vice president at large and former executive editor of *The Washington Post* and Weil Family Professor of Journalism at Arizona State University's Walter Cronkite School of Journalism and Mass Communication. **Michael Schudson** is a professor of communication at Columbia University's Graduate School of Journalism. Additional research was provided by Christopher W. Anderson, an assistant professor of communications at the College of Staten Island.

This version of The Reconstruction of American Journalism is drawn from a longer report commissioned by Columbia's Graduate School of Journalism and its dean, Nicholas Lemann. The full version is available in pdf format at columbiajournalismreport.org. The school thanks the Charles H. Revson Foundation for its support of this project, as well as the Surdna Foundation and Barbara G. Fleishman.

Peytonplace.com

Bloggers across the country are obsessively chronicling small-town life. Is Maplewood, N.J., ready for its own Bob Woodward?

Johnnie L. Roberts

Until recently, a fender bender or a gas leak in Millburn, N.J., was treated like the minor event that it is. Then Jennifer Connic arrived in town. Connic, 32, is the editor of a website called Millburn.Patch.com, part of a chain of local sites called Patch.com, and since February she's been covering mundane events in this suburban town of 20,000 residents with a zeal most journalists re-serve for a big scoop. Connic shows up at so many auto accidents that for a time Millburn Fire Chief Michael Roberts began going too, just so he could deal with Connic's questions while his firefighters worked. At Millburn town hall, town administrator Timothy Gordon often spends part of his week alerting the Millburn Township Committee about what news Connic is likely to break next—so they hear it from him, not from her blog. For decades the locals got their news from a sleepy weekly newspaper, but now, with Connic, rival bloggers, and the "citizen journalists" they recruit walking the Millburn beat 24/7, Gordon sometimes has trouble staying abreast of town controversies. "They can come across problems before [town officials] know about them," Gordon says.

Millburn is ground zero in what is fast becoming America's first post-newspaper media war. Dailies like the nearby Newark *Star Ledger* or *The New York Times* once had local reporters who'd cover places like Millburn, but as newspapers' finances have unraveled, coverage of outlying villages has shrunk: in April the *Times* cut its news sections for New Jersey, Connecticut, Long Island, and Westchester County, N.Y., to one page. In the last year, however, a group of community-focused blogs, run by journalists but relying heavily on citizen-commentators, have risen up to take their place. For them, no event is too local. Millburn.Patch.com recently reported on efforts of town officials to encourage use of parking-meter tokens, while rival The-Local showcased "Rainbow Fish," a colorful drawing by a local 9-year-old.

As humble as it sounds, that coverage is making three New Jersey towns—Maplewood, South Orange, and Millburn (including its hamlet Short Hills)—a hotbed for cutting-edge ventures in hyper-local journalism. At last count, 10 different websites were focusing on the three communities—including

the newly launched blogs Patch.com, funded by AOL; The-Local, a *New York Times*–owned site; and Maplewoodian.com, run part-time by a Maplewood resident. Bloggers and media companies were drawn in part by the areas' affluent demographics and quaint, commercially vibrant downtowns filled with potential advertisers. And New Jersey is merely a launch-pad for the hyperlocal upstarts. The *Times*, for example, has pondered the idea of franchising TheLocal to various communities. Patch.com already is swiftly expanding. At stake is the $100 billion market for local advertising, typically extracted from merchants such as dry cleaners and pizza parlors. Even as the overall ad market has declined during the recession, forecasters at Borrell Associates estimate local online ad spending will rise from about $13 billion in 2008 to $14 billion in 2009. In New Jersey, the invasion of journo-bloggers has amazed local officials. "We've gone from being sleepy little news towns to being boomtowns," says Maplewood Mayor Victor DeLuca.

The hyperlocal concept dates back to the early to mid-1990s. Microsoft, for example, experimented with an urban-focused entertainment-listings site called Sidewalk.com in 1996. But the concept really gained momentum this decade, with high-profile sites, such as Backfence.com, launched by hyperlocal-ism evangelist Mark Potts, and LoudounExtra.com, which The Washington Post Company (NEWSWEEK's owner) launched in 2007 to cover prosperous Loudoun County, Va. Thousands of hyperlocal sites have now sprouted nationwide. But the model has yet to produce a seminal success story—and in fact there have been significant failures, including LoudonExtra, which shuttered last month. Yet the *Times*'s entry into the game is an encouraging sign that big players still see a future in hyperlocal coverage, a model that virtually eliminates the huge printing and delivery costs that burden newspaper publishers. The sites typically employ one or two experienced reporters, supplemented by mostly unpaid amateur commentators and interns.

If you live in one of the towns where hyperlocal sites are taking root, you're sure to notice the phenomenon. I live in South Orange, and first became aware of Patch's outpost there about a month after it went live. At the town's old brick train station, the South Orange editor, Cotton Delo, was handing out fliers to Manhattan-bound commuters. Several weeks later, walking into the Starbucks two doors from the station entrance, I noticed Tina Kelley, hunched over a laptop sporting a logo for TheLocal and a notice reading THE JOURNALIST IS IN. *The New York Times* launched TheLocal in March. Kelley, a veteran *Times* reporter who lives in Maplewood, covers her hometown and the two next door with three unpaid student interns and as many citizen journalists as she can muster for user-generated content. In a "Why We're Here" post that explains the site's philosophy, its editors proclaim that TheLocal will be "what you want it to be."

There's still wariness among locals unaccustomed to being covered so closely by bloggers. One Friday at 3:30 P.M., Millburn.Patch editor Connic is interviewing town administrator Gordon. He dutifully answers questions about the agenda at the next Township Committee meeting. As the interview concludes, Gordon reflects on his new life in the hyperlocal media spotlight. "They drive me crazy," he says. "You have a lot of people blogging who may not know the facts—what is rumor becomes fact, [and] I have to worry about running the town, not rumors." At times Gordon longs for the days when the weekly newspaper, *The Item*, was Millburn's sole watchdog. "It was slower, and [its] reporters mostly stayed in their office," he says. So Gordon is adapting. When the town's phone system went down recently, he relied on Patch to explain why town hall couldn't be contacted.

Patch.com was founded in 2008 by Tim Armstrong, 38, who was Google's top advertising executive until March of this year. That's when AOL named Armstrong its CEO; three months later AOL purchased Patch for an undisclosed sum. Now it has local bloggers like Connic and Delo running sites in 11 towns in New Jersey and Connecticut. That makes Patch, which plans to expand nationwide, one of the fastest-growing of the hyperlocal empires. In August MSNBC.com bought EveryBlock.com, which was founded by Adrian Holovaty, a rising star in Web-journalism circles. The site offers news about social, civic, and commercial life on neighborhood blocks (listed by ZIP code) in 15 U.S. cities, including Chicago and Miami. Three big newspaper chains—Gannett, McClatchy, and Tribune Co.—own Topix.com, which bills itself as a federation of hyperlocal sites. In August ESPN launched a series of city-focused sites. Even nonprofits are getting in on the act: the John S. and James L. Knight Foundation put up seed money for EveryBlock.com and other hyperlocal sites such as PlaceBlogger.com and Rural News Network.

The influx of new sites may be the first real threat to small-time bloggers who helped pioneer the hyperlocal concept. Maplewood native Jamie Ross founded MaplewoodOnline.com in 1997. Back then the site was an old-fashioned digital bulletin board, but lately it has added Web video and what he calls "nog," or newsy blogs. When Patch and TheLocal came to the area, Ross says, they picked off some of his bloggers and online commentators. He admits that it's nerve-racking to suddenly find himself facing the likes of AOL and the *Times*. "They have millions of dollars and I don't," he says. Outside observers say the bigger worry is that too many sites are trying to subsist off the same small base of advertisers.

Still, the sites are attracting readers, and with low expenses, they may prove to be viable businesses. Data from Compete .com, a Web analytics company, suggests that in any given month, no less than one fifth—and often far more—of the average population of the towns covered by the local bloggers is clicking on the sites. Patch cites internal data suggesting it's already reaching more than half the population in areas it's covering. Web-news guru Jeff Jarvis, director of the interactive-journalism program at the City University of New York, has done an extensive study of hyper-local economics, and he's optimistic. "The most startling and hopeful number I have found is this: some hyper-local bloggers, serving markets of about 50,000, are bringing in up to $200,000 a year in advertising," he says. That's small beans to big media companies, but if an operation like AOL's Patch can link together a network of $200,000-a-year sites each run by a single reporter, and then amortize big expenses (like technology and ad sales) across multiple sites, you could start to see decent profits. The low overhead is crucial: not only are startups like Patch using less costly labor, but they also believe readership and revenue will grow as networks of hyperlocal blogs link to each other, and as they become adept at persuading small businesses that never advertised in newspapers to give online advertising a shot—a key to Patch's strategy.

Journalistically, it's easy to dismiss the ambitions of sites manned by citizen journalists and unpaid interns—but lately they've begun to garner legitimate scoops. In September, Alternative—press.com, another hyperlocal site, broke a story of hazing at the highly regarded Millburn High School. Then Millburn.Patch posted an explosive story, including graphic details, of how female members of the senior class had circulated a "slut list" describing the alleged sexual escapades of incoming freshman girls. Other local bloggers jumped in, with TheLocal and MaplewoodOnline both advancing the story. Within days, the "slut list" scandal hit *The New York Times* and NBC's *Today* show. It's not exactly the Pentagon Papers, but as America's newsrooms continue to empty, the hyperlocal blogs are allowing a new generation of watchdogs to walk the beat—when they're not hanging out at Starbucks.

Critical Thinking

1. Research any blogs in your local area. How many are there? What are their themes?

2. Do you see a time where local blogs will be bought out by large websites, just as local newspapers have increasingly been bought out by larger papers/media companies, or does the nature of blogging negate this possibility?

Capital Flight

Watchdog reporting is at an alarming low at many federal agencies and departments whose actions have a huge impact on the lives of American citizens.

JODI ENDA

After an explosion killed 29 coal miners in West Virginia in early April, the Washington Post and the New York Times quickly produced lengthy exposés detailing a plethora of safety breaches that preceded the nation's worst coal mining disaster in a quarter century. The Times reported that mining companies thwarted tough federal regulations enacted after a spate of deaths four years earlier simply by appealing citations. The Post wrote that federal regulators had cited the Upper Big Branch mine for a whopping 1,342 safety violations in the past five years, 50 times in the previous month alone.

These are the kind of powerful stories that can goad public officials to make changes—sometimes life-saving changes—by shedding light on dangerous conditions. They also are the kind of stories that more and more often come too late, or not at all.

Just ask the families of the 29 miners.

As daily newspapers continue to shed Washington bureaus and severely slash their staffs, fewer reporters than ever are serving as watchdogs of the federal government. Rare is the reporter who is assigned to cover one of the many federal departments, agencies or bureaus that are not part of the daily news cycle. Even if they are large, even if they are central to how Americans live their lives, most parts of the federal government—the very offices that write the rules and execute the decisions of Congress and the president—remain uncovered or undercovered by the mainstream media. Consider that not one newspaper has a reporter who works in the newsroom of the Department of Agriculture, which, with a staff of 104,000, is one of the government's largest employers. Trade publications and bloggers pick up a bit of the slack but have neither the audience nor the impact of more traditional media outlets.

Throughout much of this nation's history, it has been newspapers that set the standard for reporting that is hard-hitting, meaningful, thought-provoking, exhaustive, consequential. In the last half century, in particular, newspapers sought to be more impartial and professional, and less partisan, as they disclosed misdeeds involving Democrats and Republicans alike. Think Pentagon Papers, Watergate, Iran-contra, Jack Abramoff, campaign finance.

Networks and cable television news outlets certainly have reporters in Washington, but they concentrate on politics and the story of the day out of the White House, the Capitol and the most visible departments, such as Defense, State, Justice and Homeland Security. National Public Radio has beefed up its Washington coverage the past several years, and its reporters—many of them former newspaper writers—do have time for enterprise. Yet when it comes to departments, it sticks to the same handful as television.

Now that so many newspapers have forsaken the capital, it should not be surprising that the quality of reporting on the federal government has slipped. The watchdogs have abandoned their posts. How that plays out in the long run—for journalism, for democracy—has yet to be determined. Perhaps one day, websites, or a future medium, will pick up where newspapers left off. In the short term, though, the dearth of in-depth government reporting is palpable.

Newspaper reporters who remain in the capital tend to focus on the big issues of the moment (health care, Wall Street), their congressional delegations and politics. Scoops are measured in nanoseconds and posted online the moment they are secured (and sometimes prior to that). Good, old-fashioned shoe-leather reporting? You can find it here and there, kind of like the typewriter.

"Dealing with agencies can be very time-consuming," says Bill Lambrecht, the lone reporter remaining in the once-exalted Washington bureau of the St. Louis Post-Dispatch, a Lee Enterprises-owned newspaper. "The kind of source work that you need to do—calling people at night, filing FOIAs [Freedom of Information Act requests]—to bird-dog the agencies that invariably try to put up obstructions to giving you what you should get takes a lot of time."

Perhaps that's why only one Washington-based newspaper reporter covers the Mine Safety and Health Administration, which oversees mines in every state in the country, on anything close to a regular basis.

"The Courier-Journal [in Louisville] historically has had a great interest and desire to cover the coal mining industry and safety issues related to coal mining. That commitment hasn't diminished at all in recent years," says James Carroll, the Gannett newspaper's Washington reporter. "Being a one-man bureau, however, you have to pick your shots. Disasters obviously get a lot of media that don't normally cover this. And we do that ourselves. If there's an accident, we spend a lot of time on it. But in between, we try to keep an eye on anything significant that MSHA does. We know it will have a great impact on Kentucky."

Carroll, who has won numerous awards for regional reporting from Washington, says he keeps tabs on MSHA "when they're proposing safety initiatives and when they're not putting out safety initiatives. . . . With MSHA, we try to revisit issues that nobody else is covering." For years, he's been tracking government activity on "float dust," coal dust that floats in the air and can lead to black lung disease and cause fires in underground mines. In the 1990s, the Courier-Journal reported that mining companies were falsifying records on coal dust, prompting the federal government to crack down.

"Over the years since then we've tried to revisit this story from time to time, absent any immediate event," Carroll says. "With the changing administrations, now it looks like there is going to be some new energy coming up with regulations on coal dust."

It is those types of stories, the "in-between" ones that track government's progress or lack of it, that so many Washington reporters either choose to or are forced to skip. Many have little interest in what they consider to be "unsexy" process stories that take a lot of time to report, require research and source-building, and don't necessarily pan out or land on the front page. But for reporters like Lambrecht and Carroll, who made their names by patiently following turn-of-the-screw stories, the issue is one of time.

It is those types of stories, the "in-between" ones that track government's progress or lack of it, that so many Washington reporters either choose to or are forced to skip.

"It goes without saying that when bureaus are operating with fewer people and fewer resources, they have to be more selective about what they go after," says Lambrecht, whose own bureau gradually decreased from seven full-time reporters and one part-time reporter in the late 1980s to five, then three and, since the end of 2008, just him. Since then, he has had to scale back on the type of hard-hitting stories he previously wrote about the Environmental Protection Agency, the Agriculture Department and the Food and Drug Administration, to name a few. His plight is shared by countless Washington reporters, survivors of layoffs, buyouts and closures. "Part of the bureau reduction around town also meant focusing much more, and sometimes exclusively, on congressional delegations

and issues that have a direct impact on a region or locality," Carroll says.

Like Lambrecht, Carroll has to sandwich reporting on regulatory agencies—in addition to MSHA, he follows specific issues at the Federal Aviation Administration, the National Transportation Safety Board, the FDA and the Pentagon—in between stories about politics and Kentucky's congressional delegation, which includes Senate Minority Leader Mitch McConnell, the Republican who has led his party's efforts to block President Obama's agenda.

"It's a real challenge because you have day-to-day things that are breaking all the time. And you have additional responsibilities, like blogs," Carroll says. "You have to treat your enterprise stories like daily stories. . . . Otherwise, you'll never get to them."

To be sure, the decline in coverage of federal departments, bureaus and agencies started long before newspapers began shuttering their Washington bureaus.

Nine years ago, AJR documented how newspapers and wire services had shifted from covering government "buildings"— shorthand for a blanket approach to reporting on departments and agencies—to covering issue-oriented beats. Reporters abandoned their desks in what once had been bustling press-rooms in stately federal buildings all across the capital and worked from modern news bureaus in staid rooms that often resembled insurance offices. At the time, bureau chiefs explained in what might be described as lockstep language that the change was a way to bring alive coverage of dry policy issues, to engage readers who had tuned out incremental Washington stories.

"There's been a real castor-oil quality of coverage," Kathleen Carroll, then Knight Ridder's Washington bureau chief and now executive editor of the Associated Press, said in 2001. "If you look back at the way Washington stories were written in the past, you see that it's just boring as hell."

Bureau chiefs trumpeted their move to issue-related coverage, saying that by leaving the daily drudgery to the wires, they had more time and more resources to devote to investigative and enterprise reporting.

But toward what end? Did journalists use their newfound freedom from daily coverage to keep closer tabs on what really was happening behind the imposing façades of federal buildings? Did they do a better job of telling readers what was going on before and after, rather than during, press conferences? Did they forgo the dull, incremental stuff to better serve the American people, to make sure their elected and appointed officials were using taxpayers' money wisely and honestly, using sound judgment, serving the public good? Were they better watchdogs?

The evidence suggests the answer is no. Certainly, there have been some standout stories in the past decade—Knight Ridder stood virtually alone in questioning the Bush administration's march to war in Iraq; Copley News Service sent a corrupt member of Congress to prison. But it is no secret that the story of Washington newspaper bureaus in the 2000s is one of cutbacks and closures, and less coverage.

"When I joined the Dallas Morning News' D.C. bureau in early 2003, we had 11 people. We now have three. Back then, we did indeed have a full-time Pentagon writer, a Supreme Court writer and a writer who covered the Justice Department, homeland security and immigration. All three took buyouts several years ago," says Todd Gillman, Washington bureau chief for the Belo-owned newspaper. "Now, with three reporters, we no longer structure any coverage around agencies. We are more scattershot. Or flexible. However you prefer."

A near-revolutionary shift in the Washington press corps was well documented in a 2009 report by the Pew Research Center's Project for Excellence in Journalism. The report concluded that newspapers with Washington bureaus declined by more than half from the mid-1980s to 2008 (when additional reductions took place). Conversely, there was tremendous growth in special interest or niche media, including newsletters, and nearly a tenfold increase in the number of foreign reporters in the capital.

The widespread constriction of newspaper bureaus, coming as it did after the move toward issue-based reporting, has served to further limit coverage of the "real" Washington, the workaday, off-camera Washington charged with getting things done.

"To me, what's happening—and it goes back over a period of time—is that there are some parts of Washington that I would argue are overcovered, like the White House. There's a tremendous amount of pack journalism going on over there; everybody has to do a stand-up in front," says Clark Hoyt, who is completing a three-year stint as the New York Times' public editor in mid-June and was formerly Washington editor for now-defunct Knight Ridder. (The chain was acquired by McClatchy in 2006.) "The numbers of reporters in Washington have not necessarily gone down. It's just the composition of the press corps and what they cover has changed dramatically."

Parts of the capital are woefully ignored, says Hoyt, who makes clear he does not speak for the Times. A case in point, he says, is the Agriculture Department. In years past, the Des Moines Register "had a powerhouse Washington bureau" whose reporters landed the paper four Pulitzer Prizes for national reporting between 1968 and 1985 and were finalists for two others. "These were stories that grew out of intense coverage of the Agriculture Department," Hoyt says. "I don't know how many people are in the pressroom of the Agriculture Department on a daily basis, but I'll bet you that most of them work for special-interest publications."

"To me, that story has been replicated all over town in different places where newspapers once identified local affinities that were important to the economy, that were important to local readers because they really touched their lives in some ways. I think a lot of that coverage has dried up."

Chris Mather, communications director at the Agriculture Department, concurs. The USDA is covered by smaller local papers in communities that are beneficiaries of its largesse, especially as a result of the federal stimulus, but much less frequently by the Washington press corps, she says. The department's pressroom, or what's left of it, is dominated by wire services—Thomson Reuters, Bloomberg News, the Associated Press and Dow Jones—National Journal and Agri-Pulse, which has a website and weekly e-newsletter on farming and rural issues. The Register's sole remaining Washington reporter was, remarkably, not on her radar. (Philip Brasher, whose blog says he covers agriculture, energy and climate issues for the Gannett-owned Register, did not return repeated phone calls from AJR.)

At a time when critical or salacious stories are in vogue, many communications officials are content to be ignored. Mather, though, is keen for her department to receive attention. "The difficulty we have at USDA is that there are very few people out there who understand the breadth of our portfolio," Mather says. "Reporters think that we are here just to advocate for farmers and ranchers. We definitely do that, but we do a lot more than that."

For instance, she says, the department made 113,000 home loans last year through its Rural Development Agency. It also financed fire stations, schools and infrastructure in rural areas, as well as broadband support for telemedicine. Now, she says, Agriculture Secretary Tom Vilsack is focusing on ways to rebuild and revitalize rural America with greater access to broadband Internet connections, development of biofuels, programs to mitigate climate change and ways for consumers to connect with local food producers. Publicity for the programs is sparse, particularly out of Washington.

"Rural America continues to suffer," Mather says. "The poverty level is higher, the education level lower. It's suffering because people are leaving those communities. They don't have water treatment systems that work; the schools aren't what they used to be."

It could be a great story: Where are these people going? What kind of jobs can they get? Are they putting pressure on the social service system? Who's doing the work they left behind? What's the impact on the cities and suburbs that receive them? What about the schools? Does this migration affect the nation's food supply?

It's a story Mather would love to see. "When we start talking about our new approach," she says, "you see this light bulb go off in reporters' heads after about 20 minutes."

Agriculture—like mining—might be a hard sell to readers of large, urban papers whose closest connection with rural America often is a neighborhood farmers market. But it is up to reporters to connect the dots, to explain the impact of rural poverty on the food that makes its way to grocers in Manhattan or Los Angeles, for example, or of mining issues on electricity and climate change nationwide.

"We're making the largest broadband investment in rural America in history," Mather says. "It will bolster the national economy if these businesses are able to thrive and people stay in these communities. It's unfortunate people are not interested in the story."

The happiest press secretary in Washington might well be Scott Wolfson of the Consumer Product Safety Commission. Having endured a period of bad press in the final years of the Bush administration, the CPSC now is on the offensive, fighting unsafe products and reveling in coverage. Wolfson credits the new chairman, Inez Tenenbaum, whom he characterizes as something of a publicity machine. Tenenbaum has made herself available for countless interviews, and she traveled the country and even the world to demonstrate that the Obama administration takes consumer safety seriously, he says.

"We do not want there to be a downtime in the media's coverage of CPSC. We are trying to be transparent and proactive, to let the media know how we are trying to solve the problems of the past for two key reasons: to give parents greater confidence in the safety of products in the marketplace and to give them confidence that their children or themselves won't be hurt by products in their homes."

The press office also is putting out videos on YouTube, writing blogs and tweeting. And the press is responding, Wolfson says. But that's hardly the case for many other departments, bureaus and agencies. Indeed, a clear majority get little, if any, coverage. Even large departments often go begging for coverage out of Washington.

The Department of Housing and Urban Development has been the subject of more stories than usual in the past year because of the foreclosure crisis, says Jerry Brown, deputy assistant secretary for the Office of Public Affairs. But normally, he says, no newspaper or wire service reporters are assigned to cover HUD full time, and the number of newspaper reporters who check in with the department from time to time has dropped as papers have eliminated real estate sections and housing beats. Still, HUD gets publicity from trade publications and housing magazines as well as blogs, Brown says. And, as with the Agriculture Department, local papers cover it when HUD grants money to community projects.

But is anyone serving as a watchdog? During the Bush administration, National Journal's Edward Pound broke a story that federal prosecutors were investigating whether then-HUD Secretary Alphonso R. Jackson had steered contracts to friends. This May, Jackson's lawyers announced that the Justice Department had decided not to file charges. Even so, Jackson was plagued by so many allegations of misconduct regarding contracts and favoritism that he resigned in 2008.

Pound, a well-known Washington investigative reporter and veteran of U.S. News & World Report, the New York Times, the Wall Street Journal and USA Today, no longer works as a journalist. He left National Journal last year to be director of communications for the federal Recovery Accountability and Transparency Board. He laments the lack of coverage of nuts-and-bolts Washington, saying it never was great, and now it's worse.

"A lot of these agencies never were covered the way they should have been covered because they weren't sexy stories. It's not some sex scandal on the Hill or some intelligence screwup," Pound says. "HUD is a very good example of how reporters aren't really covering these agencies very well. I'm loath to stick it to the reporters. I know what the pressures are on people to just churn it out, churn it out. The economics of the business are so much a factor now."

A lot of these agencies never were covered the way they should have been covered because they weren't sexy stories. It's not some sex scandal on the Hill or some intelligence screwup.

What's more, he says, "So much of what's out here in Washington is glitz reporting."

It's a sure bet that more Americans recognize the names Tareq and Michaele Salahi than could identify Shaun Donovan. The former are the Virginia socialites whose claim to fame is crashing President Obama's first state dinner in November. So notable are they that the president included a quip about them in his address to the White House Correspondents' Association dinner in May. The latter is the secretary of HUD, who oversees 9,000 employees and a $43.5 billion 2010 budget, plus stimulus money.

Likewise, how many Americans can name the chairman of the Federal Trade Commission? It is Jon Leibowitz. According to the commission's website, the FTC "deals with issues that touch the economic life of every American." Certainly, the commission receives attention on big stories about consumer rip-offs and unfair trade practices. But much of the publicity comes from blogs and websites, making it unavailable to those without Internet access. Like so many other places in town, this one has seen a diminution of its traditional corps of newspaper reporters. Consequently, to get the word out, its press office has learned to be "creative," says Cecelia J. Prewett, the public affairs director.

"It definitely makes for an on-your-toes press person," Prewett says. "Evidently, it used to be much simpler. You'd know who your contact was, you'd call and—boom!—they'd be interested. Now there's much targeting to be done." Prewett, who started at the FTC in late November, says she frequently has to help reporters—even those from the largest, most-respected newspapers—sell stories to their editors. "You have to do a lot more embargoing of information so that you can help them convince their editor, because the resources are so tight. You have to help them pitch it to their editor. You're not having to convince one person, you have to convince two."

The FTC has adjusted to the shift away from newspapers with Washington bureaus and toward websites without bureaus by changing tactics, from the way it conducts press conferences to the way it issues press releases, says Claudia Bourne Farrell, a senior press officer who has been with the commission for 16 years.

"Five years ago, if we were having a press conference, we'd send out a release and expect 8 to 10 cameras and a roomful of reporters. That no longer happens. Because we don't fill up the room, we do Webcasts of our news releases and two-way audio conferences so reporters can call up and listen and ask questions," she explains. "Five years ago, material produced by the Division of Consumer and Business Education was largely written—paper publications and/or Web-based publications. They were words. In the last several years, that division has taken to producing videos."

"It underscores what I said about having to work smarter," Farrell continues. Still, there's a downside. "I think our Division of Consumer and Business Education is very creative and gifted at developing consumer education. But about 45 percent of the country is on the other side of the digital divide."

Ralph Nader does not mince words. As far as the consumer advocate and frequent presidential candidate is concerned, the failure of the Washington press corps to cover departments, agencies and bureaus—the guts of the federal government—has cost American lives.

"The danger is *danger*," he says. "Health and safety agencies are letting people die that they can save . . . It's a very, very sad state of affairs."

Example No. 1 in his mind is the National Highway Traffic Safety Administration's treatment of Toyota Motor Corp., maker of the popular Toyota and Lexus vehicles. "NHTSA has had six investigations on Toyota in the last two to three years. They haven't subpoenaed one document yet from Toyota. That's a story," Nader said earlier this spring.

In November, a Los Angeles Times investigation by Ralph Vartabedian and Ken Bensinger reported that, since 2001, more than 1,000 Toyota and Lexus owners had complained that their vehicles accelerated suddenly, against the drivers' wishes. Many instances ended in crashes, and 19 people died. They wrote that those complaints led NHTSA to open eight investigations, and that Toyota responded to two of them by recalling 85,000 vehicles. NHTSA closed the other six investigations because it did not find a defect.

But the Times disclosed that the investigations "systematically excluded or dismissed the majority of complaints by owners that their Toyota and Lexus vehicles had suddenly accelerated, which sharply narrowed the scope of the probes." A second story by the same reporters later in November called Toyota to task for blaming the cases of sudden acceleration solely on floor mats. The L.A. Times' own investigation pointed to electronic throttles, the reporters wrote. Subsequently, the National Academy of Sciences undertook a 15-month investigation to determine whether electronic vehicle controls can cause sudden acceleration.

Similar to the mining stories by the New York Times and the Washington Post, these were strong and damning. Also similar to those stories, they came after disaster struck. In late September, Toyota issued what, at the time, was its largest U.S. recall—of 3.8 million vehicles. The recall was prompted by a fiery crash near San Diego in August, when a California Highway Patrol officer and three members of his family were killed after their Lexus ES 350 suddenly took off, sped out of control, flew off an embankment, rolled several times and burst into flames.

In April, NHTSA slapped Toyota with a $16.4 million fine—the maximum it is allowed to levy—for failing to disclose for months that faulty pedals in 2.3 million vehicles could cause them to accelerate suddenly. NHTSA has been criticized for acting too slowly as thousands of consumers complained—and dozens died—and congressional Democrats began work this spring on legislation to grant NHTSA greater authority.

Vartabedian and Bensinger were Pulitzer Prize finalists, and their reporting shed needed light on a deadly issue, light that likely helped prod the Obama administration and Congress to take another look at NHTSA as well as at Toyota. Not a bad feat from 3,000 miles away—the reporters are based not in Washington, but in California. Some argue that makes no difference, that with access to records on the Internet, reporters can cover Washington from anywhere.

Washington-based reporters from just four news organizations—the AP, the Detroit News, the Detroit Free Press and Automotive News—regularly check in with NHTSA, says a public affairs specialist there, who was one of just a handful of spokespersons who refused to speak for attribution for this article. Reporters from Bloomberg and USA Today call fairly often, as does the Los Angeles Times (from L.A.) and Jalopnik, a car blog, the spokesperson says. Routine NHTSA press conferences (not those about Toyota) attract just two or three print reporters.

One of those reporters is Justin Hyde, a business writer who represents half of the Detroit Free Press' Washington bureau. Hyde's beat is automotive news, a high-profile job for a Motor City daily. And Hyde says he is given a lot of time by the Gannett-owned paper to do his job well. Last year, he co-wrote an eight-part series on the bankruptcies of General Motors and Chrysler.

The Toyota story, he says, was hard to get because the Japanese company withheld much of the pertinent information about sudden acceleration. However, Hyde says that NHTSA officials were "fairly responsive" and that data about complaints are available online.

So why didn't the Washington press corps write about the Toyota investigations earlier? Nader blames the migration away from "building" coverage.

"These agencies are not being covered on a regular basis," he says. "They're being covered thematically. So if EPA puts out something on carbon dioxide regulation, they'll cover that. But if OSHA [the Occupational Safety and Health Administration] doesn't put out anything for four years, they don't cover that. It's the end of the beat reporter. There's nobody I can consistently call on NHTSA or FDA and know that they're there every day."

When reporters aren't on top of an agency or department, they often miss inaction. Advocates argue that was the real story of the first decade of this century. The Bush administration systematically rolled back regulatory enforcement, but little was written about it. As Nader puts it: "You don't want to be investigated or covered? Don't do anything."

The Center for Auto Safety, a consumer organization founded by Nader in 1970, lists an overwhelming amount of information about recalls, defects and complaints on its Website, autosafety.org. Clarence Ditlow, the group's executive director, says that during the second term of George W. Bush's presidency, NHTSA "virtually stopped issuing any fines. And there was no journalistic coverage of that."

It's only now, with the Obama administration confronting record-setting Toyota recalls, that fines are coming back into fashion, he says. But that doesn't mean journalists should be less vigilant.

"You simply need to have journalists who are willing to pull teeth," Ditlow says. "Could Toyota have been discovered earlier? I think so . . . If there'd been coverage of Toyota and NHTSA reaching deals to exclude certain types of complaints, I think that would have precluded what they did." For instance, Ditlow says that NHTSA excluded from its investigations complaints in which Toyota drivers said the brakes failed to stop runaway vehicles or the sudden acceleration lasted a long time. "If you look at the San Diego event where four people were killed, the brakes couldn't stop the vehicle and it was a long-duration event," he says. "The very premise on which they curtailed the investigation was false.

"A death is a death!"

And a death is a story.

In fact, Nader says about the only things he can count on reporters to cover are disasters—plane crashes, mine explosions, auto deaths. He called it a "tombstone mentality." But after the initial flood of coverage, the follow-up is noticeably minuscule.

The words "regulatory agencies" are eye-glazing for many, if not most, Washington journalists. Give 'em a juicy story about politics—the sleaze of a John Edwards, the slide of a Charlie Crist, the slurs and slams that fly between the powers on Pennsylvania Avenue and K Street—over a substantive (read: boring) policy (read: homework) story any day of the week. Without a doubt, many a Washington journalist would rather pore over transcripts of Sunday morning talk shows for a mini-scoop that anyone else on the planet could find online than wade through government records that might yield an exclusive yet hard-to-find exposé of the Pulitzer variety.

Perhaps that's why an article in the New York Times Sunday magazine recently posited that Politico's Mike Allen, author of a popular e-mail tip sheet called "Playbook" that dishes scooplets and news summaries along with birthday wishes for insiders, might be the most powerful journalist in Washington. Some bloggers and columnists have disputed the title, but not the fact that Allen is one of the capital's best known scribes. To be sure, Allen is a hard-working, knowledgeable journalist. He has reported for the Washington Post, the New York Times and Time magazine. He has covered the White House and presidential campaigns. Like many Washington writers of the 21st century, he has enhanced his fame by appearing regularly on TV. But Allen's selling point is his ability to be a human vacuum cleaner. He is on top of everything, but he's not an expert at any one thing. And while Allen is fortunate to work for one of the few news outlets that actually has increased its Washington presence the past few years, he also is symbolic of the direction this town's reporting has taken of late.

Short is in.

Blogs are in.

And.

Tweets.

R.

In.

Coverage of the inner workings of the bureaucracy, the behind-the-scenes actions that affect everyday Americans? Not so much.

"It's changed dramatically, and all for the worse," George Condon, former Washington bureau chief for Copley News Service, says of Washington journalism. Condon was forced to close down the bureau in November 2008, two years after its reporters won a Pulitzer for the chain and Copley's flagship paper, the San Diego Union-Tribune, for revealing that Rep. Randy "Duke" Cunningham, a California Republican, had taken millions in bribes. Condon, who now covers the White House for CongressDaily, ticked off a few of the Washington bureaus that have closed in recent years: Newhouse, Cox, Media General. There are more that have shut down, of course, including numerous one- or two-person bureaus. And many that have merged (most notably Tribune Co. bureaus, including the Los Angeles Times') and shrunk.

Each bureau had expertise based on the industries in the areas where their newspapers were located, Condon notes. For Copley, with its Southern California base, that meant immigration and border policies and the military; for Media General, which has several outlets in Florida, that meant NASA. Reporters assigned to those beats developed deep and reliable sources in agencies and departments, expertise that their newspapers no longer have.

"You're not getting the voice filled by AP," Condon says. "Just calling a press secretary or the person whose name is on a press release is not the same thing as knowing who the decision maker is before the decision is made."

Few reporters who have been laid off or bought out (Condon represents the latter) end up at other newspapers, given that they generally aren't hiring, especially in Washington bureaus. CongressDaily, part of National Journal Group, is published twice a day, on paper and online, when Congress is in session. Condon points out that none of the 11 reporters who worked for Copley's Washington bureau landed at a newspaper.

Where are all these old-fashioned newspaper reporters going? Some have left the field, putting their skills to use at think tanks, nonprofits, research organizations, foundations and public relations firms. Some have gone to brand-name websites, such as Politico, The Daily Beast, AOL News and Politics Daily. For the most part, those reporters cover politics or breaking news and have little opportunity to develop the sources and do the kind of digging required to uncover the stories people don't know about, but should.

After two decades at the Los Angeles Times, one of them in the Washington bureau, Josh Meyer quit early this year to become director of education and outreach for Northwestern University's Medill National Security Journalism Initiative in Washington. Meyer says he took the job for the entrepreneurial opportunities it provides, but he acknowledges that he became frustrated when real estate developer Sam Zell bought Tribune Co. and combined and slashed staff in all of its papers'

Washington bureaus. His national security and terrorism beat was broadened to include the Justice Department, making it difficult to cover any of them as well as he would have liked, Meyer says.

"People don't want specialists anymore," he says. "It takes a long time to understand how things work and to get people to talk to you and crack intelligence agencies and the FBI and even the White House. If you don't have that, you're relegated to writing off the news."

Now, through Northwestern's Washington journalism program, Meyer will be conducting investigative projects on national security issues with groups of 10 graduate students assigned to him for three months at a time.

"We're also trying to figure out," he says, "who's going to pick up the slack from the carnage of the major media outlets."

Mary Jacoby, for one.

A former reporter for the Wall Street Journal and several other publications, Jacoby now is a media entrepreneur. In 2009, she founded Main Justice (mainjustice. com), a website that covers "insider news" about the Justice Department. It is just one of the upstart specialty or niche publications attempting to fill the void left by newspaper bureaus—and providing jobs to the capital's many unemployed or underemployed journalists.

"I saw that no one was really covering Justice," Jacoby explains. "The big papers never covered it in depth," and when cutbacks came, coverage "really fell off a cliff." Jacoby says there's "hardly anyone" in the Justice Department's pressroom and "dust on the desks." Further, she says, "very few people show up for the daily press gaggle."

Jacoby, who used her own money and raised some venture capital to start the site, teamed up with Kenny Day, now her publisher, when Legal Times laid him off and closed its Washington operation. They have hired five reporters and employ others on a contract basis. Jacoby says she wants to "revolutionize" how the department and its employees are covered by delving into certain legal topics, such as white-collar crime, and writing about lawyers "as personalities."

She likens her website to the Politico of the Justice set.

Other specialty sites have popped up to cover topics newspapers have pulled back on, including Scotusblog.com, which focuses on the Supreme Court. That newspapers have reduced their coverage of the High Court—the pinnacle of an entire branch of government—would have been unthinkable in an earlier time. But that withdrawal has left an opening for the site, which boasts that it hired the "dean" of the Supreme Court press corps, Lyle Denniston, a 52-year veteran of the beat (and onetime AJR columnist). Denniston, who previously wrote about the court for the Baltimore Sun and other papers, says he is reveling in his newfound editorial freedom and virtually unlimited space. The downside of the new outlet, he says, is that the audience is relatively small. "Now my audience is in the tens of thousands, not the hundreds of thousands," he says. The upside is that it is sophisticated, composed mainly of professionals and academics, so "we can write at a level of technicality and scope greater than any daily newspaper could use."

Perhaps the best-known of the specialty Websites is Kaiser Health News, which is funded primarily by the Kaiser Family Foundation and launched on June 1, 2009, the same day Congress opened its debate on health care legislation, says Laurie McGinley, executive editor for news.

"We're a niche operation. We're writing for people who are interested in health care," says McGinley, formerly the Wall Street Journal's deputy Washington bureau chief for global economics. "The great thing is, given what happened in Congress, there's a lot more general interest than there was before."

KHN, as it is known, lists 16 reporters and editors and one Web producer on the site. Its stories read much as they would if written for a mainstream newspaper—and other news outlets are encouraged to reproduce them for free. The ultimate goal, McGinley says, is to reach a wider audience, not just Washington insiders.

Although plenty of reporters covered the health care debate during the past year, many wonder to what extent they will follow up as the administration drafts the rules and regulations that will determine exactly how the new law is applied. After all, congressional reporters who covered the politics and the substance of the legislation before it passed now must move on to other hot-button issues facing Congress, such as financial regulation, immigration and the Supreme Court nomination of Elena Kagan, not to mention what could be game-changing midterm elections in November.

"That's where we can make a big contribution," McGinley says. "Now that the traditional media are moving on to other things," KHN can "fill in the blanks."

A number of other newspaper refugees have gone to Environment & Energy Publishing, known as E&E, which hired 45 reporters and editors for four daily online publications on environment and energy policy. "Most of the people we've hired over the last three years have been laid off from regional papers," says Editor in Chief Kevin Braun, who put that number at 18. (See "Endangered Species," December 2008/January 2009.)

But Braun, who co-founded E&E in 1998, is careful to say that his sites are not intended to replace traditional media. His 2,000 subscribers pay in the neighborhood of $5,000 a year, he says, adding that total readership is about 40,000. E&E's target audience is not Mr. and Ms. Public, but insiders: Congress members and staffers, lobbyists and officials at federal agencies, major law firms, multinational corporations, energy companies and utilities, financial institutions, environmental organizations, foreign governments, universities and state governments.

"Our bread-and-butter issues are not of interest to the general public," Braun says. On the occasions that it does have general-interest stories, E&E makes them available through a partnership with the New York Times.

The fact is that niche or specialty publications tend to be geared toward specialty audiences, not the broad readership that newspapers have long targeted. Even if there are more reporters than ever before in the capital, the question arises as to whether they are covering federal departments, agencies and bureaus in a way that is useful to most Americans.

Who has replaced the newspaper reporters who once filled the pressroom desks at places like the departments of Agriculture, Justice, and Housing and Urban Development?

The answer seems to be no one and everyone.

Beyond the professional journalists seeking refuge at Websites are the now-ubiquitous citizen journalists and others, such as bloggers at nonprofits and advocacy groups, who also are working to "fill in the blanks." These are dedicated individuals, some of whom have a point of view, some of whom do not, with varying degrees of training and commitment to the values that journalists hold dear. Many journalists scorn them; others rationalize that, given the demise of traditional outlets, there's no alternative. This can be described as an "if not them, who?" approach to the world of untrained scribes.

To those inside and outside government who want their issues covered accurately and without bias, the "who" makes a big difference.

"The level of expertise has largely disappeared," says Caroline Smith DeWaal, food safety director at the Center for Science in the Public Interest, a consumer advocacy organization. She says most major news outlets, in the past, had reporters who focused primarily on food safety. Now, few do. "One possible effect of this is that when the administration makes a major announcement, you don't have the quality of questions or the quality of analysis that you used to have. The media act strictly as reporters of information. They can't dissect the policy at the level they used to."

Even at places like the Pentagon, which, thanks to two wars, has not shed its corps of print reporters, press secretaries field regular queries from online reporters, bloggers and other "nontraditional media," including advocates, says Marine Col. Dave Lapan, director of press operations there.

"One of the biggest changes I have encountered in my career in public affairs is the exponential increase in newsgathering organizations and individuals and the volume of requests for information," Lapan said in an e-mail interview. "I don't think the effect on defense policy of these changes is yet known."

As a result of the mushrooming number of news outlets, there is a split between experienced beat journalists who understand the practices, policies, and unique culture and language of the Defense Department and the drop-ins, who do not. "One of our challenges," Lapan says, "is in providing information to the myriad sources who don't cover the beat and don't have the depth of knowledge and understanding."

Eliot Brenner, director of public affairs for the Nuclear Regulatory Commission, has watched the transformation of Washington coverage. He outlines a progression in which newspaper reporters have gone from producing in-depth stories to following a wire-service approach of filing and updating and, now, to writing in the fast, nonstop method of the digital world.

"We're seeing a transition where reporters are consumed with feeding the electronic ether," he says.

Every reporter knows what that means: less depth, less triple- or even double-checking, a greater chance for errors. Brenner says he has no problems with newspaper coverage of the NRC—the Washington Post, Wall Street Journal and New York Times still cover it regularly—but that he must stay on top of non-newspaper Websites and quickly correct any mistakes. Further, he says, because these niche sites tend to concentrate on narrow issues, they don't offer the benefits of mainstream outlets—that is, a general readership.

"Now, we're paying more attention to blogs, but you have to take them with a grain of salt," he says. "Their readership tends to be smaller and made up of true believers."

Gary Bass, executive director of OMB Watch, a nonprofit research and advocacy organization that closely monitors the White House Office of Management and Budget, says nonjournalism Websites can be useful if they provide links to the underlying materials they are writing about. Otherwise, he says, it's hard to know which sites are reliable. As an example, he says that last year, there were "thousands upon thousands of citizen inspector generals" who wrote about how federal stimulus money was being used.

"As the news media has cut back, I think we've seen this growth in citizen journalism," Bass says. "The strength is that a lot of these accountability issues are covered. The weakness is that you don't have editors—not only for the writing quality, but also for accuracy."

A common refrain among regulatory agency staffers and advocates alike is that things haven't been the same since Cindy Skrzycki left the Washington Post. In 1993, Skrzycki began writing a weekly column called "The Regulators," and she later wrote a book called *The Regulators: The Anonymous Power Brokers Who Shape Your Life.* The title explains exactly how she views coverage of departments, bureaus and agencies: not as the regurgitation of mind-numbing bureaucratic gobbledygook, but as the discovery, interpretation and exploration of the truly important stuff of Washington, the otherwise hidden decisions that touch real people in beyond-the-Beltway America.

Skrzycki is addicted to regulation in the same way a baseball writer might be addicted to the game. She practically breathes it. "I just thought it was the most fascinating part of government and the most unsupervised part of government. These people are not elected. They really affect our lives," she says. She might have been the only reporter at the Post who regularly covered numerous agencies and bureaus, but she was ever vigilant. When she left the Post in 2005, Skrzycki continued her column at Bloomberg News until last year.

She eagerly rattles off some of the regulatory issues she covered over the years: auto safety, distracted driving among truck drivers, federal preemption of regulatory matters, tires, immigration and employment, liquor regulations, lobbying, food safety (chicken, eggs, meat), ergonomics, the environment, communications, nuclear power, alcohol labeling, import laws regarding socks—socks!—Internet gambling, ozone, mercury, airplane drinking water, lead, Medicare, Medicaid, small and big business, and spyware.

"I don't think there's anyone in Washington now who has a 20-year overview of how these things have played out over the years and how they repeat themselves and how the problems don't get fixed," says Skrzycki, who now teaches nonfiction writing at the University of Pittsburgh and is a business correspondent for GlobalPost, a Website that launched last year to fill another emerging gap—international reporting. "Covering regulation is a long, tedious process. It doesn't happen by press conference. If you don't have people dedicated to doing that, it's likely not to get done. . . . I was spread pretty thin, but I did know all the major legislation that was moving, everything that was going on at the agencies. I had great sources."

It is through the slow, methodical, old-school skill of source development that government reporters often get their best stories. That can take time, and it's harder to do when deadlines are measured in hours or minutes and not days. But it is these sources, people in little-known offices of agencies and bureaus, who are bothered by what they see, who might pick up the phone and tip off a trusted reporter. Skrzycki says she was the beneficiary of many such calls over the years, the kind of call she would have hoped someone in NHTSA would have made concerning Toyota.

"If you have fewer and fewer reporters out there who are recognizable, who people can call, tip, it's likely things are going to go on for longer than they might," Skrzycki says. "It's always good to have reporters watching, checking in."

If you have fewer and fewer reporters out there who are recognizable, who people can call, tip, it's likely things are going to go on for longer than they might.

Some of her sources (who also are her fans) echo that sentiment. "Cindy used to track regulatory issues. Unless there is a silo-based issue [one that fits neatly into a beat], there isn't someone you can go to at the Washington Post, New York Times, Wall Street Journal and say, 'Look what OMB is doing,'" says OMB Watch's Bass.

Apparently, no one called a reporter to say, "Look what the Minerals Management Service is doing." Prior to the explosion of the Deepwater Horizon drilling platform in the Gulf of Mexico in April, little had been written about the MMS in recent years, save for a sex scandal from 2002 to 2006. After the rig exploded, killing 11 workers and dumping millions of gallons of oil into the Gulf of Mexico, journalists and Congress members alike started paying attention to the Interior Department agency, which granted permission to BP and other oil companies to drill in the gulf. Among the revelations that came out in the weeks after the explosion was that the agency, which both promotes and regulates offshore drilling, failed to get permits intended to protect endangered species.

Interior Secretary Ken Salazar announced that he would reduce the conflict of interest within MMS by abolishing the agency and dividing its functions among three new entities. Skrzycki's book addresses the built-in tensions in a number of federal agencies.

"You have agencies that have these dual missions both to promote the industry and to police them," she says. "These things often come into conflict. And the recent blowup with BP and the Minerals Management agency is an example of that."

Even though President Obama announced before the spill that he was going to expand offshore drilling, it appears that no one was looking into the agency that would regulate it. "You have all these inherent conflicts," Skrzycki said. "It means that the enforcement part of the regulatory system is not pure. And, sometimes, you get results like this. This is something that the press certainly never looks into or even probably knows about until you have a big incident like this."

MMS spokesman Nicholas Pardi says there are a number of reporters who contact the agency regularly, though none covers it full time. Most of the reporters cover issues such as energy (especially oil and gas) or the environment, and report on other agencies as well, he says. Still, Pardi insists the agency is frequently in the news because it provides oil and gas production numbers and information about offshore rig safety during hurricanes. He declines to speculate about whether the press should have been writing about the inherent conflict between MMS's dual functions.

"Our movements are pretty closely monitored, because we're responsible for regulating such a large industry," Pardi says. Since the Gulf of Mexico explosion, he adds, "people have been doing a lot of research about the agency. And we welcome that. We want to be transparent."

Skrzycki cut her journalistic teeth covering the steel industry for the American Metal Market, a trade publication that she credits with teaching her the importance of the people who write the regulations. Take the health care law: "There will be hundreds of rules coming out of HHS [the Department of Health and Human Services] and the Centers for Medicare and Medicaid Services. That's a huge story. The implementation of that law will be in regulations. And they're going to be so important, and there's going to be so much lobbying."

It's a valid point. While most reporters cover lobbyists as they work to persuade members of Congress and their staffs, few pay attention to (or even see) the lobbyists who roam the halls of other government buildings, meeting with administrators who write rules and regulations. It's not surprising, since few reporters roam those halls themselves. For sure, it is more difficult to wander around government buildings, poking your head in offices, than it used to be. In the post-9/11 era, it's impossible to walk into many buildings without an appointment. Nevertheless, with some effort, it can be done.

Neil Kerwin, president of American University and, like Skrzycki, a regulatory aficionado, says it must be done. Casting a spotlight on the writing and enforcement of regulations "changes priorities," says Kerwin, who founded AU's Center for the Study of Rulemaking and wrote a book titled *Rulemaking: How Government Agencies Write Law and Make Policy*. Public pressure on agencies, he says, "will cause them to try to fix the faults of the system. That's where I would encourage journalists to spend more time. . . ."

"I believe the most important law in America is being written by administrative agencies," Kerwin says. And, more than ever before, the administrators writing the rules are receiving information from advocacy groups and lobbyists, he says. It's not their fault, Kerwin asserts, because the government doesn't have the money to provide independent research on every issue that needs a rule. But that makes it even more important for journalists to watch over the regulatory process.

"The person who needs to be educated is the average American," Kerwin says. "You sit here and you watch the health care bill going through what it went through. As an afterthought, we won't know the impact until HHS writes the rules. How are they going to write them? Who's going to write them? How much guidance will they get from the Congress?. . . . Does the government have resources? I rarely see that covered. . . .

"Cindy," he says of Skrzycki, "was a lonely voice out there."

The Post did not replace Skrzycki. But it did run her column for a while after she went to Bloomberg. And National Editor Kevin Merida insists that, despite repeated rounds of buyouts that have reduced the Post's editorial staff, the paper's devotion to federal coverage remains strong.

"I think buyouts have an effect on a newsroom. But it hasn't reduced our commitment to covering the federal government, because that's the heart of what we do," Merida says. "That's central for us. That's kind of where we live. Politics and government is the heart of our core franchise coverage."

Like so many of its counterparts, the Post shifted years ago from covering "buildings" to covering issues. That means a number of reporters follow topics that require them to touch base with more than one department or agency. It may or may not mean that they follow the agency closely. "We don't have people attached to buildings per se, for instance, the Agriculture Department or HUD," Merida says. "But through issues, we intersect with the federal government."

Lyndsey Layton writes for the Post about food safety and consumer issues, and Kimberly Kindy writes about government accountability, an assignment that has led to post-disaster investigations of both Toyota and mining. Further, Merida says, the Post is strengthening its coverage of the federal government, regulatory agencies in particular, through blogs. Cecilia Kang is writing about the Federal Communications Commission on her technology blog, and Zach Goldfarb covers the SEC on a new blog called Market Cop.

The blog posts tend to be faster and shorter than newspaper stories, and some compete with niche publications. "There are a lot of specialized audiences that want selected news given to them any time they want it wherever they are," Merida says, adding that blogs provide the Post a way to develop more mobile "apps" for agency coverage. "We'll find ways to serve those specialized audiences."

As Washington bureaus grapple with contracting staffs and increasing pressures to produce for multiple media platforms, there is one that has had the luxury—in terms of staff and money—to set its own course. And the course Bloomberg News has chosen is to beef up coverage of departments and agencies, says Washington Executive Editor Al Hunt. The bureau went so far as to create a regulatory team of 10 reporters and three editors. Some reporters still cover issue-oriented beats, but all in all, Hunt says, "we think it's better to cover buildings."

Hunt says the need to cover agencies has increased because the Obama administration is much more given to regulation than administrations past, both because the financial crisis shone a spotlight on some of government's shortcomings and because the deficit has limited Washington's options to solve problems in more expensive ways.

"We think it's very important in most agencies," he says. "The FTC, the SEC and the FDIC [Federal Deposit Insurance Corporation] particularly now are in a period of tremendous regulatory attention. If you don't focus on those agencies, you're going to miss a lot of that. Fifteen or 20 years ago, the FDIC was a pretty sleepy agency. No one would accuse it of being a sleepy agency today. . . .

"I've been in Washington for 40 years, and I have never seen a time where there is so much attention paid to the regulatory issue" by the federal government.

Bloomberg is able to place one, two and occasionally three reporters on departments and agencies because of its remarkable size. Unlike so many Washington bureaus, this one has grown—substantially—in recent years. The bureau now numbers 140, about double what it was a decade ago and 30 percent larger than it was five years ago, Hunt says. It has a seasoned staff peopled with many illustrious former newspaper reporters, including Hunt, a veteran of the Wall Street Journal and a familiar television commentator. Along with its staff, the bureau's reach has grown significantly. Once a financial media outlet primarily for wealthy CEOs, investors, bankers and the like, Bloomberg now distributes a much broader daily report through its famed (and pricey) terminals, but also on its Website; in Bloomberg Businessweek magazine, which it bought late last year; through its global television operation; and to hundreds of newspapers that subscribe to the Washington Post's newswire.

Hunt is reluctant to criticize bureaus that don't cover agencies. "I think a lot of people don't do it that way because they've cut back," he says. "If instead of 10 reporters, you only have five reporters, it's tough to cover institutions."

The New York Times makes no bones about the manner in which it covers the capital. "We don't cover buildings, which would be a remarkably bureaucratic and reader-unfriendly way of organizing ourselves," Richard Stevenson, deputy Washington bureau chief, said in an e-mail interview. "We cover subject matter, and encourage our reporters to follow the story when it cuts across the boundaries of departments or agencies, or between Washington and the rest of the world."

Perhaps if the Times or another paper had written about the conflicted relationship between MMS and the oil industry it regulates before the latest disaster, no one would have paid attention and nothing would have changed. It likely would have been viewed as a dullish insider story about a flawed government bureaucracy, something to bury inside the A section. After the explosion, it was a front-page story that definitely grabbed attention.

Too late.

Talk to anyone about coverage of the Mine Safety and Health Administration and you'll undoubtedly hear about Ellen Smith. Smith is managing editor of Mine Safety & Health News, a biweekly newsletter published from Pittsford, New York. She has been covering mining since 1987 and has won 29 journalism awards. It's easy to see why. She's a walking encyclopedia of mining information, about flammability and inspection requirements, about underground conveyor belts and rescue chambers. And she has the ability to explain the intricacies to a general, non-mining audience. But she doesn't. Smith's newsletter, which costs $525 to $625 a year, is distributed to insiders.

Smith understands why Washington newspaper reporters don't cover MSHA— "It's not sexy . . ."—so whenever disasters occur, she finds herself translating mining-ese to non-mining reporters. She teaches them how to search MSHA's database and what the information they find there means. She did that in April in West Virginia, just as she did following three mining disasters in five months in 2006.

Eventually, Smith knows, most of the reporters will go back to their newspapers and ignore mining until the next disaster. Except, primarily, for Smith (who has two part-time reporters under contract in Washington), plus James Carroll of Louisville's Courier-Journal and Ken Ward Jr. of the Charleston Gazette in West Virginia. Each of these journalists covers the mining industry differently, and each goes out of his or her way to praise the other two. Carroll, the only one in Washington, asserts that he has the advantage of being able to show his face at MSHA's office and at hearings on Capitol Hill.

"Within the limits of the time you have as a one-person bureau, it does really help when you're at a committee hearing to spend time chatting with the staff," he says. "It's helpful to have that face-to-face contact. They know who you are. It shows your level of interest in the subject matter. It's one of those intangible things that helps you do your job as a reporter.

"Newspapers would say they don't need to have people in Washington," he continues. "By the same token, you could say you don't need to have somebody in City Hall, in the police headquarters, you could just dial it in. They—editors—would argue about that. Well, I'd say the same thing for Washington . . . I think it's a mistake for newspapers not to see Washington as just as vital to local coverage as any other beat."

Ward, who covers not only mining but all things environmental, says his paper hasn't had a reporter in Washington for more than two decades. In the 19 years he has been with the independently owned Gazette, Ward has been to MSHA's national office exactly once, when he came to the capital because he won a journalism fellowship and wanted to attend the luncheon. He doesn't view his location as a disadvantage.

"If I were in Washington, I might have different and higher-level sources in the agency that I went to lunch with or had drinks with or something, but a sense of perspective outside the Beltway is not necessarily a bad thing," he says.

In fact, Ward does something to unearth stories that a lot of Washington reporters *used* to do: He reads the Federal Register.

"The job of these agencies is to implement a law that Congress passed. They do that by writing regulations and by enforcement. You can find out what they're doing without being in Washington. You can read the regulations. You can file FOIA requests. You can do that from afar."

Like Carroll, Ward tries to cover MSHA and other agencies "in between" disasters. "We started doing stories in 2001 about how the Bush administration was tearing down the safety net for miners," he says. "They were halting work on new regulations. They were reversing existing regulations. They were trying to be more friendly to coal.

"We were doing stories about that in 2001–2005. Then in 2006, six miners died in the Sago mine [in West Virginia], and all of a sudden reporters discovered that, oh, the Bush administration was dismantling MSHA."

But the Gazette, with its circulation of less than 50,000, doesn't have the influence that large newspapers have. And the large papers don't provide the kind of sustained day in day out coverage of agencies that might bring change.

Not one large, national paper covers MSHA consistently, according to spokeswoman Amy Louviere. She says that in addition to the three regulars, she occasionally hears from reporters who work for papers in Salt Lake City, Pittsburgh and Lexington, Kentucky. In the 15 years that Louviere has been with MSHA, the press operation has shrunk from four people to just her.

Phil Smith, director of communications for the United Mine Workers, says that since the April mine explosion in West Virginia, he has tried to persuade more reporters to stick with the story. "I think it would make a difference," he says. "When the mine operators know that there's going to be media scrutiny of what they're doing and MSHA knows there's going to be scrutiny in how they are enforcing the law, I think it's obvious they would do things differently.

"I have talked to several hundred reporters from print media, from radio, from television and bloggers. I encouraged all them: 'You guys can't do what you always do when the story's not so sexy and the funerals are over.'

"But something else always comes up."

This year it's the oil spill in the gulf.

Attention spans are short. News bureaus, those that remain, are thin. The federal bureaucracy is massive, and no newspaper could possibly cover all of it. However, when Washington teemed with newspaper bureaus fully stocked with reporters, there was always a chance that one or two would pay attention to this department or that agency. It's still possible.

But it happens less and less.

"I like to think a lot of us got into this profession because we did want to make government accountable and help people understand how government works," Carroll says. "That should be one of our top priorities—to be watchdogs. But in this environment, it's more of a challenge. If you're the only guy answering the phone, doing the blog, doing the Web update and writing for tomorrow's paper? Then you want to go talk to sources? You just do the very best you can."

> **"I like to think a lot of us got into this profession because we did want to make government accountable and help people understand how government works. That should be one of our top priorities—to be watchdogs."**

"Tomorrow's paper" may well prove to be anachronistic. The question for Washington is whether "yesterday's" reporting—the time-consuming, source-building, questioning, triple-checking and following up that hold officials' feet to the fire; the painstaking digging that tells readers or viewers or clickers or scrollers things that no one else is telling them—will become a relic as well.

Critical Thinking

1. Summarize Jodi Enda's concerns is terms of *feedforward* and *feedback* agendas of reporting. Which loss is the greater concern?

2. Why have many of the Washington bureaus shut down? Is diminishing depth of coverage driven more by lack of resources or lack of audience interest? Would greater audience interest lead to increased reporting resources? Would increased reporting resources lead to greater audience interest?

Jodi Enda (jaenda@gmail.com) writes about politics and government from Washington. Previously, she covered the White House, presidential campaigns and Congress for Knight Ridder and was a national correspondent for the Philadelphia Inquirer. AJR Assistant Editor Lori Miller (lammiller@comcast.net) contributed to this story.

Overload!

Journalism's Battle for Relevance in an Age of Too Much Information

BREE NORDENSON

In 2007, as part of the third round of strategic planning for its digital transformation, The Associated Press decided to do something a little different. It hired a research company called Context to conduct an in-depth study of young-adult news consumption around the world. Jim Kennedy, the AP's director of strategic planning, initially agreed to the project because he thought it would make for a "fun and entertaining" presentation at the annual meeting. It turned out to be more than that; the AP believed that the results held fundamental implications for the role of the news media in the digital age. Chief among the findings was that many young consumers craved more in-depth news but were unable or unwilling to get it. "The abundance of news and ubiquity of choice do not necessarily translate into a better news environment for consumers," concluded the researchers in their final report. "Participants in this study showed signs of news fatigue; that is, they appeared debilitated by information overload and unsatisfying news experiences. . . . Ultimately news fatigue brought many of the participants to a learned helplessness response. The more overwhelmed or unsatisfied they were, the less effort they were willing to put in."

The idea that news consumers, even young ones, are overloaded should hardly come as a surprise. The information age is defined by output: we produce far more information than we can possibly manage, let alone absorb. Before the digital era, information was limited by our means to contain it. Publishing was restricted by paper and delivery costs; broadcasting was circumscribed by available frequencies and airtime. The Internet, on the other hand, has unlimited capacity at near-zero cost. There are more than 70 million blogs and 150 million websites today—a number that is expanding at a rate of approximately ten thousand an *hour.* Two hundred and ten billion e-mails are sent each day. Say goodbye to the gigabyte and hello to the exabyte, five of which are worth 37,000 Libraries of Congress. In 2006 alone, the world produced 161 exabytes of digital data, the equivalent of three million times the information contained in all the books ever written. By 2010, it is estimated that this number will increase to 988. Pick your metaphor: we're drowning, buried, snowed under.

The information age's effect on news production and consumption has been profound. For all its benefits—increased transparency, accessibility, and democratization—the Internet has upended the business model of advertising-supported journalism.

This, in turn, has led news outlets to a ferocious focus on profitability. Over the past decade, they have cut staff, closed bureaus, and shrunk the newshole. Yet despite these reductions, the average citizen is unlikely to complain of a lack of news. Anyone with access to the Internet has thousands of free news sources at his fingertips. In a matter of seconds, we can browse *The New York Times* and *The Guardian, Newsweek* and *The Economist,* CNN and the BBC.

News is part of the atmosphere now, as pervasive—and in some ways as invasive—as advertising. It finds us in airport lounges and taxicabs, on our smart phones and PDAS, through e-mail providers and Internet search engines. Much of the time, it arrives unpackaged: headlines, updates, and articles are snatched from their original sources—often as soon as they're published—and excerpted or aggregated on blogs, portals, social-networking sites, RSS readers, and customizable homepages like My MSN, My Yahoo, myAOL, and iGoogle. These days, news comes at us in a flood of unrelated snippets. As Clay Shirky, author of *Here Comes Everybody: The Power of Organizing without Organizations,* explains, "The economic logic of the age is unbundling." But information without context is meaningless. It is incapable of informing and can make consumers feel lost. As the AP noted in its research report, "The irony in news fatigue is that these consumers felt helpless to change their news consumption at a time when they have more control and choice than ever before. When the news wore them down, participants in the study showed a tendency to passively receive versus actively seek news."

There has always been a large swath of the population that is not interested in news, of course, just as there has always been a portion that actively seeks it out. What's interesting about the current environment is that despite an enormous increase in available news and information, the American public is no better informed now than it has been during less information-rich times. "The basic pattern from the forties to today is that the amount of information that people have and their knowledge about politics is no worse or no better than it's been over that sixty-year period," explains Michael X. Delli Carpini, dean of the Annenberg School for Communication at the University of Pennsylvania. For example, a 2007 survey conducted by the Pew Research Center for the People & the Press found that 69 percent of Americans could correctly name the vice president, only a slight decrease from the 74 percent who could in 1989.

This phenomenon can be partially explained by our tendency to become passive in the face of too much information. It can also be attributed to the fact that the sheer number of specialized publications, the preponderance of television channels, the wide array of entertainment options, and the personalization and customization encouraged by digital technologies have made it far easier to avoid public-affairs content. "As choice goes up, people who are motivated to be politically informed take advantage of these choices, but people who are not move away from politics," explains Delli Carpini. "In the 1960s, if you wanted to watch television you were going to watch news. And today you can avoid news. So choice can be a mixed blessing."

Markus Prior writes in his book, *Post-Broadcast Democracy: How Media Choice Increases Inequality in Political Involvement and Polarizes Elections,* "Political information in the current media environment comes mostly to those who want it." In other words, in our supersaturated media environment, serendipitous exposure to political-affairs content is far less common than it used to be. Passive news consumers are less informed and less likely to become informed than ever before.

The tragedy of the news media in the information age is that in their struggle to find a financial foothold, they have neglected to look hard enough at the larger implications of the new information landscape—and more generally, of modern life. How do people process information? How has media saturation affected news consumption? What must the news media do in order to fulfill their critical role of informing the public, as well as survive? If they were to address these questions head on, many news outlets would discover that their actions thus far—to increase the volume and frequency of production, sometimes frantically and mindlessly—have only made things more difficult for the consumer.

To win the war for our attention, news organizations must make themselves indispensable by producing journalism that helps make sense of the flood of information that inundates us all.

While it is naïve to assume that news organizations will reduce their output—advertising dollars are involved, after all—they would be wise to be more mindful of the content they produce. The greatest hope for a healthy news media rests as much on their ability to filter and interpret information as it does on their ability to gather and disseminate it. If they make snippets and sound bites the priority, they will fail. Attention—our most precious resource—is in increasingly short supply. To win the war for our attention, news organizations must make themselves indispensable by producing journalism that helps make sense of the flood of information that inundates us all.

The Limits of Human Attention

Ours is a culture of multitasking, of cramming as many activities as possible into as short a period of time as possible. We drive and talk on our cell phones, check e-mail during meetings and presentations, eat dinner while watching TV. In part, says Maggie Jackson, author of *Distracted: The Erosion of Attention and the Coming Dark Age,* such multitasking "is part of a wider value system that venerates speed, frenetic activity, hyper-mobility, etcetera, as the paths to success. That's why we're willing to drive like drunks or work in frenzied ways, although it literally might kill us."

Many young people multitask to the extreme, particularly when it comes to media consumption. I've witnessed my twenty-two-year-old brother watch television while talking on the phone, IMing with several friends, composing an e-mail, and updating his Facebook page. A widely cited 2006 study by the Henry J. Kaiser Family Foundation found that 81 percent of young people engage in some form of media multitasking during a given week. But as cognitive psychologists have long known, human attention is quite limited. Despite our best efforts, when we try to do more than one thing at once, we are less efficient and more prone to error. This is because multitasking is actually a process of dividing attention, of toggling back and forth between tasks.

Acquiring new information requires particularly focused attention, which includes the ability to ignore distractions. In order to absorb the information contained in a CNN newscast, for example, we must not only direct our attention to the person talking, but also filter out the running headlines, news updates, and financial ticker on the lower part of the screen. Torkel Klingberg, a professor of cognitive neuroscience at Karolinska Institute in Sweden and author of *The Overflowing Brain,* puts it simply: "If we do not focus our attention on something, we will not remember it." In other words, attention is a critical component of learning.

Michael Posner, a researcher who has dedicated his career to studying attention and a professor emeritus of psychology at the University of Oregon, explains attention as a system of three networks—alerting, orienting, and executive. Alerting refers to the state of wakefulness necessary to attend to information, while orienting is the process by which we respond to stimuli, such as movement, sound, or noise. Executive attention is the highest-order network, the one that we have conscious control over. If we are trying to study for a test or read a novel, we use it to direct and maintain our focus, as well as to suppress our reaction to competing stimuli like the din of a nearby conversation or television.

The information-saturated environment that we live in is, unsurprisingly, extremely demanding of our attention. Modern life—both at work and at home—has become so information-rich that Edward Hallowell, a Boston-area psychiatrist, believes many of us suffer from what he calls an attention-deficit trait, a culturally induced form of attention-deficit disorder. As he pointed out in a 2005 interview with CNET News, "We've been able to overload manual labor. But never before have we so routinely been able to overload brain labor." According to Hallowell and other psychiatrists, all these competing inputs prevent us from assimilating information. "What your brain is best equipped to do is to think, to analyze, to dissect, and create," he explains. "And if you're simply responding to bits of stimulation, you won't ever go deep." Journalist John Lorinc noted as much in an elegant article on distraction in the April 2007 issue of *The Walrus:*

> It often seems as though the sheer glut of data itself has supplanted the kind of focused, reflective attention that might make this information useful in the first place. The dysfunction of our information environment is an outgrowth of its extraordinary fecundity. Digital communications technology

has demonstrated a striking capacity to subdivide our attention into smaller and smaller increments; increasingly, it seems as if the day's work has become a matter of interrupting the interruptions.

In a recent report, *Information Overload: We Have Met the Enemy and He Is Us,* the research firm Basex concluded that interruptions take up nearly 30 percent of a knowledge worker's day and end up costing American businesses $650 billion annually. Other studies show that interruptions cause significant impairments in performance on IQ tests.

In many ways, the modern age—and the Internet, in particular—is a veritable minefield of distractions. This poses a central challenge to news organizations whose mandate is to inform the public. Research by Pablo Boczkowski, who teaches communication studies at Northwestern University, has revealed that when we consume news online we do so for significantly less time than in print and that we do it while we're working. Further complicating matters is the disruptive nature of online advertising. Intrusive Web advertisements—washingtonpost.com recently featured one in which a Boeing helicopter flies right across the text of a news story—exploit our orienting network, which evolved to respond quickly to novel stimuli. Could we train ourselves to suppress our tendency to be distracted by such advertising? "You can get somewhat better, but it's hard to resist because it'll produce orienting," Posner explains. "The way you resist it is you bring your attention back as quickly as you can." Yet even if we were somehow able to eliminate ads, the sheer number of articles, headlines, and video and audio feeds on news websites makes focused attention difficult. Having to decide where to direct our attention and then maintain it makes reading and retaining news online a formidable task.

The Attention Economy

One of the most useful frameworks for understanding journalism's challenges and behavior in the information age is the notion of the attention economy. Economics is the study of the allocation of resources and the basic principles of supply and demand, after all, and about a decade ago a handful of economists and scholars came up with the concept of the attention economy as a way of wrestling with the problem of having too much information—an oversupply, if you will—and not enough time or people to absorb it all.

The dynamics of the attention economy have created a complicated and hypercompetitive arena for news production and consumption. News media must not only compete with one another, as well as with an ever-increasing assortment of information and entertainment options, but also with the very thing that supports their endeavors—advertising. In fact, the advertising industry has been struggling with the dynamics of the attention economy for a couple of decades now. As the advertising landscape becomes more saturated, advertisers must work harder to get their messages to the consumer. But as Mark Crispin Miller, professor of media ecology at New York University, notes in the *Frontline* documentary *The Persuaders:*

> Every effort to break through the clutter is just more clutter. Ultimately, if you don't have clean, plain borders and backdrops for your ads, if you don't have that blank space, that commons, that virgin territory, you have a very hard time

making yourself heard. The most obvious metaphor is a room full of people, all screaming to be heard. What this really means, finally, is that advertising is asphyxiating itself.

The news media also run the risk of self-asphyxiation in an information landscape crowded with headlines, updates, and news feeds. In order to garner audience attention and maintain financial viability, media outlets are increasingly concerned with the "stickiness" of their content. According to Douglas Rushkoff, host of *The Persuaders* and author of the forthcoming book *Life Incorporated,* the question for these organizations has become, "How do we stick the eyeballs onto our content and ultimately deliver the eyeballs to our sponsors?" As he dryly points out, "That's a very different mandate than how do we make information—real information—available to people. The information economy, then, is a competitive space. So as more people who are information providers think of themselves as competing for eyeballs rather than competing for a good story, then journalism's backwards." The rise of sound bites, headlines, snippets, infotainment, and celebrity gossip are all outgrowths of this attempt to grab audience attention—and advertising money. Visit a cable-news website most any day for an example along the lines of POLICE: WOMAN IN COW SUIT CHASED KIDS (CNN); or MAN BEATS TEEN GIRL WAITING IN MCDONALD'S LINE (Fox News). As Northwestern's Boczkowski points out, "Unlike when most of the media were organized in monopolistic or oligopolistic markets, now they are far more competitive; the cost of ignoring customer preferences is much higher."

Meanwhile, the massive increase in information production and the negligible cost of distributing and storing information online have caused it to lose value. Eli Noam, director of the Columbia Institute for Tele-Information, explains that this price deflation is only partly offset by an increase in demand in the digital age, since the time we have to consume information is finite. "On the whole—on the per-minute, per-line, per-word basis—information has continuously declined in price," says Noam. "The deflation makes it very difficult for many companies to stay in business for a long time."

Thus, we come to the heart of journalism's challenge in an attention economy: in order to preserve their vital public-service function—not to mention survive—news organizations need to reevaluate their role in the information landscape and reinvent themselves to better serve their consumers. They need to raise the value of the information they present, rather than diminish it. As it stands now, they often do the opposite.

More-Faster-Better

"Living and working in the midst of information resources like the Internet and the World Wide Web can resemble watching a firefighter attempt to extinguish a fire with napalm," write Paul Duguid and John Seely Brown, information scientists, in *The Social Life of Information.* "If your Web page is hard to understand, link to another. If a 'help' system gets overburdened, add a 'help on using help.' If your answer isn't here, then click on through another 1,000 pages. Problems with information? Add more."

Like many businesses in the information age, news outlets have been steadily increasing the volume and speed of their output. As the proliferation of information sources on the Web continues at a breakneck pace, news media compete for attention by adding content and features—blogs, live chat sessions with journalists, video and audio streams, and slideshows. Much of this is of excellent quality. But taken together, these features present a quandary: Do we persevere or retreat in the face of too much information? And as the AP study showed, even young news consumers get fatigued.

In psychology, passivity resulting from a lack of control is referred to as "learned helplessness." Though logic would suggest that an increase in available news would give consumers more control, this is not actually the case. As Barry Schwartz, the Dorwin Cartwright Professor of Social Theory and Social Action at Swarthmore College, argues in his book *The Paradox of Choice: Why More is Less,* too many choices can be burdensome. "Instead of feeling in control, we feel unable to cope," he writes. "Freedom of choice eventually becomes a tyranny of choice."

Too many choices can be burdensome: 'Instead of feeling in control, we feel unable to cope. Freedom of choice becomes a tyranny of choice.'

A recent study by Northwestern University's Media Management Center supports this phenomenon. It found that despite their interest in the 2008 election, young adults avoid political news online "because they feel too much information is coming at them all at once and too many different things are competing for their attention." The study participants said they wanted news organizations to display *less* content in order to highlight the essential information. "Young people want the site design to signal to them what's really important . . . instead of being confronted by a bewildering array of choices," write the researchers in their final report, *From "Too Much" to "Just Right": Engaging Millennials in Election News on the Web.*

The instinct that more is better is deeply ingrained in the modern psyche. David Levy, a professor at The Information School of the University of Washington, uses the phrase "more-better-faster" to describe the acceleration of society that began with the Industrial Revolution. According to Levy, we tend to define productivity in terms of speed and volume rather than quality of thought and ideas. "We are all now expected to complete more tasks in a smaller amount of time," writes Levy in a 2007 journal article. "And while the new technologies do make it remarkably efficient and easy to search for information and to collect masses of potentially relevant sources on a huge variety of topics, they can't, in and of themselves, clear the space and time needed to absorb and to reflect on what has been collected." In the case of news production, Swarthmore's Schwartz agrees. "The rhythm of the news cycle has changed so dramatically that what's really been excluded," he says, "is the time that it takes to think."

Implications for Democracy

Our access to digital information, as well as our ability to instantly publish, share, and improve upon it at negligible cost, hold extraordinary promise for realizing the democratic ideals of journalism. Yet as we've seen, many news consumers are unable or unwilling to navigate what Michael Delli Carpini refers to as the "chaotic and gateless information environment that we live in today."

When people had fewer information and entertainment options, journalistic outlets were able to produce public-affairs content without having to worry excessively about audience share. As the Internet and the 24/7 news cycle splinter readership and attention

spans, this is no longer the case. "Real journalism is a kind of physician-patient relationship where you don't pander to readers," says Bob Garfield, a columnist for *Advertising Age* and co-host of NPR's *On the Media.* "You give them some of what they want and some of what you as the doctor-journalist think they ought to have." Unfortunately, many news outlets feel they can no longer afford to strike the right balance.

As information proliferates, meanwhile, people inevitably become more specialized both in their careers and their interests. This nichification—the basis for *Wired* editor Chris Anderson's breakthrough concept of the Long Tail—means that shared public knowledge is receding, as is the likelihood that we come in contact with beliefs that contradict our own. Personalized home pages, newsfeeds, and e-mail alerts, as well as special-interest publications lead us to create what sociologist Todd Gitlin disparagingly referred to as "my news, my world." Serendipitous news—accidentally encountered information—is far less frequent in a world of TiVo and online customization tools.

Viewed in this light, the role of the journalist is more important than ever. "As society becomes splintered," writes journalist and author David Shenk in *Data Smog,* "it is journalists who provide the vital social glue to keep us at least partly intact as a common unit." Journalists work to deliver the big picture at a time when the overload of information makes it hard to piece it together ourselves. "The journalist's job isn't to pay attention simply to one particular field," explains Paul Duguid. "The job is to say, 'Well, what are all the different fields that bear on this particular story?' They give us the breadth that none of us can have because we're all specialists in our own particular area." In other words, the best journalism does not merely report and deliver information, it places it in its full and proper context.

Journalism's New Role

The primacy placed on speed and volume in the information age has led to an uneven news landscape. "There is an over-allocation of resources on breaking and developing news production and constant updates," observes Boczkowski. "I think many news organizations are overdoing it." While headlines and updates are undoubtedly important, their accumulation is problematic. "Increasingly, as the abundance of information overwhelms us all, we need not simply more information, but people to assimilate, understand, and make sense of it," write Duguid and Seely Brown.

The question, then, is how?

As David Shenk presciently noted more than a decade ago, "In a world with vastly more information than we can process, journalists are the most important processors we have." The researchers who conducted the study for the AP concluded that the news fatigue they observed among young adults resulted from "an overload of basic staples in the news diet—the facts and updates that tend to dominate the digital news environment." In other words, the news they were encountering was underprocessed.

"In a world with vastly more information than we can process, journalists are the most important processors we have."

—David Shenk

In order to address the problem, the AP has made a number of changes in the way it approaches news production. For starters, it instituted a procedure it calls 1-2-3 filing, which attempts to reduce news clutter and repetition (the days of endless write-throughs are over) while also acknowledging the unpackaged and real-time nature of news in the digital world. With 1-2-3 filing, reporters produce news content in three discrete parts, which they file separately: a headline, a short present-tense story, and, when appropriate, a longer in-depth account. By breaking down the news in this way, the AP hopes to eliminate the redundancy and confusion caused by filing a full-length article for every new story development. In 1-2-3 filing, each component replaces the previous component: the headline is replaced by the present-tense story, which is then replaced by the in-depth account.

The AP has also launched a series of initiatives aimed at providing consumers with deeper, more analytical content. It has created a Top Stories Desk at its New York headquarters to identify and "consider the big-picture significance" of the most important stories of the day. It has also begun developing interactive Web graphics to help explain complicated and ongoing stories like Hurricane Katrina and the Minnesota bridge collapse. And for 2008, the AP launched "Measure of a Nation," a multimedia series dedicated to examining the election "through the prism of American culture, rather than simply the candidates and the horse race." "Measure of a Nation" packages take a historical approach to covering such notions as myth, elitism, and celebrity in American presidential politics. In one article published in late August, for example, journalist Ted Anthony explains the powerful political influence of the Kennedy family over the past fifty years, drawing parallels between the campaigns of JFK and RFK and that of Barack Obama. As the AP writes in its report, these changes in approach represent "a concerted effort to think about the news from an end-user's perspective, re-emphasizing a dimension to news gathering and editing that can get lost in the relentless rush of the daily news cycle."

Much like educational institutions, the best news organizations help people convert information into the knowledge they need to understand the world. As Richard Lanham explains in *The Economics of Attention,* "Universities have never been simply data-mining and storage operations. They have always taken as their central activity the conversion of data into useful knowledge and into wisdom. They do this by creating attention structures that we call curricula, courses of study." Institutions of journalism do it by crafting thoughtful and illuminating stories. "Journalists who limit their role to news flashes are absolving themselves of any overarching obligation to the audience," writes Shenk in *The End of Patience.* "Mere telling focuses on the mechanics of transmitting information of the moment, while education assumes a responsibility for making sure that knowledge sticks." The most valuable journalism is the kind that *explains.* "The first and foremost role that a journalist plays is to provide the information in a context that we wouldn't be able to get as amateurs," says Delli Carpini. "And I think that's where journalism should be focusing."

As it turns out, explanatory journalism may have a promising future in the market for news. On May 9, in partnership with NPR News, *This American Life* dedicated its hour-long program to explaining the housing crisis. "The Giant Pool of Money" quickly became the most popular episode in the show's thirteen-year history. *CJR* praised the piece (in "Boiler Room," the essay by Dean Starkman in our September/October issue) as "the most comprehensive and insightful look at the system that produced the credit crisis." And on his blog, *PressThink,* Jay Rosen, a journalism professor at New York University, wrote that the program was "probably the best work of explanatory journalism I have ever heard." Rosen went on to note that by helping people understand an issue, explanatory journalism actually creates a market for news. It gives people a reason to tune in. "There are some stories—and the mortgage crisis is a great example—where until I grasp the *whole,* I am unable to make sense of *any* part," he writes. "Not only am I not a customer for news reports prior to that moment, but the very frequency of the updates alienates me from the providers of those updates because the news stream is adding daily to my feeling of being ill-informed, overwhelmed, out of the loop."

> **"There are some stories—and the mortgage crisis is a great example—where until I grasp the *whole,* I am unable to make sense of *any* part."**
>
> —Jay Rosen

Rather than simply contributing to the noise of the unending torrent of headlines, sound bites, and snippets, NPR and *This American Life* took the time to step back, report the issue in depth, and then explain it in a way that illuminated one of the biggest and most complicated stories of the year. As a result of the program's success, *NPR News* formed a multimedia team in late August to explain the global economy through a blog and podcast, both of which are called "Planet Money." And on October 3, *This American Life* and *NPR* aired a valuable follow-up episode, "Another Frightening Show About the Economy," which examined the deepening credit crisis, including how it might have been prevented and Washington's attempts at a bailout.

Along with supplying depth and context, another function of the modern news organization is to act as an information filter. No news outlet better embodies this aim than *The Week,* a magazine dedicated to determining the top news stories of the week and then synthesizing them. As the traditional newsweeklies are struggling to remain relevant and financially viable, *The Week* has experienced steady circulation growth over the past several years. "The purpose of *The Week* is not to tell people the news but to make sense of the news for people," explains editor William Falk. "Ironically, in this intensive information age, it's in some ways harder than ever to know what's important and what's not. And so I often say to people, 'With *The Week,* you're hiring this group of really smart, well-versed people that read for you fifty hours a week and then sit down and basically give you a report on what they learned that week.' "

Rather than merely excerpting and reprinting content, this slim magazine takes facts, text, and opinions from a variety of sources—approximately a hundred per issue—to create its own articles, columns, reviews, and obituaries. As Falk explains, there's a certain "alchemy" that occurs when you synthesize multiple accounts of a news story. And *The Week*'s success suggests that consumers are willing to pay for this. "We're a service magazine as much as we are a journalism magazine," says Falk. "People work ten, eleven hours a day. They're very busy. There are tremendous demands on their time. There are other things competing for your leisure time—you can go online, you can watch television or a DVD. So what we do is deliver to you, in a one-hour package or less, is a smart distillation of what happened last week that you need to pay attention to."

One ally in journalism's struggle to deal with information overload, meanwhile, may be the digital machinery that brought it about in the first place. While digital archiving and data tagging cannot replace human interpretation and editorial judgment, they have an important role to play in helping us navigate the informational sea. As any news consumer knows, searching for or following a story can be frustrating on the Internet, where information is both pervasive and transient. In its study, the AP observed that young consumers struggled to find relevant in-depth news. So the wire service stepped up an effort begun in 2005 to tag all its articles, images, and videos according to a classification system of major news topics and important people, places, and things. These tags allow consumers, as well as news organizations and aggregators, to more effectively find and link to AP content. A number of other organizations, including *The New York Times* (check out the Times Topics tab on nytimes.com), *The Washington Post,* and CNN have similar projects under way, promising an opportunity to rapidly—and often automatically—provide consumers with a high level of detail, context, and graphical means of explanation.

The website for BBC News may be the best example of how journalistic organizations can deliver context in the digital environment. A news story about the Russia-Georgia crisis, for example, is displayed alongside a list of links to a map of the region, a country profile, an explanation of the crisis, a summary of Russian foreign policy, and related news articles and video footage. All online BBC News stories are presented in this manner, giving consumers multiple ways to learn about and understand an issue. While no American site is this comprehensive, a handful of major news outlets, from CNN to NPR to the *National Journal,* have used this approach in creating special election 2008 Web pages. By linking stories to one another and to background information and analysis, news organizations help news consumers find their way through a flood of information that without such mediation could be overwhelming and nearly meaningless.

Why Journalism Won't Disappear

While it's true that the Web allows the average individual to create and disseminate information without the help of a publishing house or a news organization, this does not mean journalism institutions are no longer relevant. "Oddly enough, information is one of the things that in the end needs brands almost more than anything else," explains Paul Duguid. "It needs a recommendation, a seal of approval, something that says this is reliable or true or whatever. And so journalists, but also the institutions of journalism as one aspect of this, become very important."

Moreover, the flood of news created by the production bias of the Internet could, in the end, point to a new role for journalistic institutions. "We're expecting people who are not librarians, who are not knowledge engineers to do the work of knowledge engineers and librarians," says Jonathan Spira, CEO and chief analyst for the business research firm Basex and an expert in information overload.

In other words, most of us lack the skills—not to mention the time, attention, and motivation—to make sense of an unrelenting torrent of information. This is where journalists and news organizations come in. The fact that there is more information than there are people or time to consume it—the classic economy-of-attention problem—represents a financial opportunity for news organizations. "I think that the consumers, being subjects to this flood, need help, and they know it," says Eli Noam. "And so therefore they want to have publications that will be selecting along the lines of quality and credibility in order to make their lives easier. For that, people will be willing to pay." A challenge could become an opportunity.

In fact, journalism that makes sense of the news may even increase news consumption. As Jay Rosen points out on his blog, explanatory journalism creates a "scaffold of understanding in the users that future reports can attach to, thus driving demand for the updates that today are more easily delivered." In a similar fashion—by providing links to background information and analysis alongside every news story—the BBC gives consumers frameworks for understanding that generate an appetite for more information.

The future of news depends on the willingness of journalistic organizations to adjust to the new ecology and new economy of information in the digital age. "I think in some ways, we need a better metaphor," says Delli Carpini. "The gatekeeping metaphor worked pretty well in the twentieth century, but maybe what news organizations should be now is not gatekeepers so much as guides. You don't want gatekeepers that can say you can get this and you can't get that. You want people who can guide you through all this stuff."

> **"Maybe what news organizations should be now is not gatekeepers so much as guides. You want people who can guide you through all this stuff."**
>
> —Delli Carpini

Ironically, if out of desperation for advertising dollars, news organizations continue to chase eyeballs with snippets and sound bites, they will ultimately lose the war for consumer attention. Readers and viewers will go elsewhere, and so will advertisers. But if news organizations decide to rethink their role and give consumers the context and coherence they want and need in an age of overload, they may just achieve the financial stability they've been scrambling for, even as they recapture their public-service mission before it slips away.

Critical Thinking

1. To what degree do you want news media to filter and interpret information you receive?
2. Describe the media implications of *the attention economy*.

BREE NORDENSON is a freelance writer.

Don't Blame the Journalism

The Economic and Technological Forces behind the Collapse of Newspapers

Paul Farhi

When the obituaries are written for America's newspapers, count on journalists to indict themselves in their own demise. You've heard it before, from a thousand bloggers and roundtable know-it-alls: We were too slow to adapt, too complacent, too yoked to our tried-and-true editorial traditions and formulas. We could have saved ourselves, goes the refrain, if only we had been more creative and aggressive and less risk averse.

To which I can only reply: Oh, please.

As newspapers shuffle toward the twilight, I'm increasingly convinced that the news has been the least of the newspaper industry's problems. Newspapers are in trouble for reasons that have almost nothing to do with newspaper journalism, and everything to do with the newspaper business. Even a paper stocked with the world's finest editorial minds wouldn't have a fighting chance against the economic and technological forces arrayed against the business. The critics have it exactly backward: Journalists and journalism are the victims, not the cause, of the industry's shaken state.

We've lost readers, to be sure. But that's been happening for decades, and not necessarily because of editorial quality. Disagree? Then try answering this: Did editorial quality kill afternoon newspapers?

Contemporary newspapers have their own problems, but the usual analysis about what ails us misses the point. Let's take a quick tour:

Fact No. 1

Despite everything you've heard, newspapers, even these days, remain remarkably popular. Some readers have left us (and many, it should be said, were dropped by cost-conscious publishers who no longer wanted to deliver papers to far-flung subscribers). But what's largely overlooked in the gloom is how many people newspapers reach each day. Almost 50 million buy one daily, and nearly 117 million read one, according to the Newspaper Association of America's research. Throw in 66 million unique visitors to newspaper websites each month, and the conclusion is inescapable: Lots of people want what newspaper journalists produce.

Fact No. 2

Newspaper readers—so often derided as old and unattractive to advertisers—are actually better educated and more affluent than TV news viewers. The average newspaper, for example, reaches about seven in 10 households with incomes of more than $60,000 annually, compared with about four in 10 for CNN and Fox News, according to Mediamark Research.

Fact No. 3

Every traditional news medium has lost market share, and some have lost more than newspapers. According to the Project for Excellence in Journalism, ratings for late local newscasts on network-affiliated stations across the country were 6.7 percent lower during the November 2007 sweeps than the previous year—a faster decline than newspaper circulation (down 2.6 percent daily, 3.5 percent on Sunday) during roughly the same period. This isn't a one-time aberration, either. Local TV stations in Washington, D.C., for example, have seen the ratings for their 6 P.M. newscasts plunge 37 percent from 1997 to 2007. Over the same period, the *Washington Post's* Sunday circulation has dropped 16 percent. Yet the local TV news business remains relatively strong, with far fewer layoffs and cutbacks and less end-of-an-era weariness than in most print newsrooms.

So if the problem with newspapers really isn't too few customers, or too many undesirable ones, why are they so threatened these days?

The problem has little to do with the reporting, packaging and selling of information. It's much bigger than that. The gravest threats include the flight of classified advertisers, the deterioration of retail advertising and the indebtedness of newspaper owners. Wrap all these factors together and you've set in motion the kind of slash-and-burn tactics that will hasten, not forestall, the end.

For decades, newspapers enjoyed what economists call a "scarcity" advantage. In most cities, there was only one outfit that could profitably collect, print and distribute the day's news, and it could raise prices even as it delivered fewer readers each year. Indeed, monopoly daily newspapers enjoyed enormous profit margins—sometimes as much as 25 percent or more—until very recently. But the scarcity advantage has faded; the Internet has essentially handed a free printing press and a distribution network to anyone with a computer.

The real revelation of the Internet is not what it has done to newspaper readership—it has in fact expanded it—but how it has sapped newspapers' economic lifeblood.

The real revelation of the Internet is not what it has done to newspaper readership—it has in fact expanded it—but how it has sapped newspapers' economic lifeblood. The most serious erosion has occurred in classified advertising, which once made up more than 40 percent of a newspaper's revenues and more than half its profits. Classified advertisers didn't desert newspapers because they disliked our political coverage or our sports sections, but because they had alternatives. Craigslist and eBay and dozens of other low-cost and no-cost classified sites began gobbling newspapers' market share a few years ago. What they didn't wipe out, the tanking economy did. During the first half of 2008, print classified advertising nosedived more than 25 percent, as withering job, real-estate and auto listings erased $1.8 billion in revenue from newspaper companies' books. Newspapers have been uniquely hurt—television never had classifieds to lose.

Similarly, the disappearance of local chain stores over the past two decades has fallen like a series of hammer blows on newspapers. In my city, the names of the dearly departed included such homegrown advertisers as Hechinger hardware stores, Trak Auto Parts, Crown Books, Dart Drug, Peoples Drug, Raleigh's clothing stores and the department stores Woodward & Lothrop, Garfinckel's and Hecht's. TV lost some of these advertisers, too, but has gained the likes of Wal-Mart and other big-box outlets, which tend to buy airtime, not newspaper space.

Newspapers that were hoping to be rescued by their online ad businesses woke up to a sobering reality in mid-2007. By then, it was becoming clear that online advertising wasn't growing fast enough to make up for the rapid disappearance of print ads (see "Online Salvation?" December 2007/January 2008). In fact, at the moment, online ads aren't growing at all. Sales at newspaper websites fell 2.4 percent in the second quarter of 2008. This may be as ominous a development as the meltdown of print. Online newspaper revenues had grown smartly in every quarter since the Newspaper Association of America began tracking them in 2003. No longer.

There's still much that many newspapers can do to improve their websites: adding Twitter feeds, social networking applications, Google map mashups (maps over-laid with data), on-demand mobile information and, of course, more video. All good. But let's not kid ourselves. The online business model is still uncertain, at best. An online visitor isn't as valuable to advertisers as a print customer. Online readers tend to dart in and out, spending far less time on a newspaper site than a subscriber spends with a paper. And a portion of the traffic (how much depends on the paper) comes from outside the paper's circulation area, making these visitors irrelevant to local advertisers. I'm not really surprised that newspapers haven't figured out how to make the Web pay for all the things that print traditionally has. There may not even be a business model for it. But again: Can you really blame the newsroom for that?

Newspapers that were hoping to be rescued by their online ad businesses woke up to a sobering reality in mid-2007.

The last wound is self-inflicted. Newspaper companies and other investors completed highly leveraged takeover deals just as the newspaper business rolled off the table. It's no coincidence that the most troubled newspapers are the ones owned by companies that took on enormous IOUs just as the newspaper apocalypse began. Some of these companies—Tribune, McClatchy, Journal Register, MediaNews Group, Avista Capital Partners, GateHouse Media—are now cutting like mad to stay ahead of the debt boulder bearing down on them. Meanwhile, Copley, Advance, Cox, Landmark and Blethen have all put some of their newspaper holdings up for sale. This all but guarantees more debt for the papers' new owners—assuming, of course, that the sellers can find buyers in the first place.

So add it up. Could smarter reporting, editing and photojournalism have made a difference? Can a spiffy new website or paper redesign win the hearts of readers? Surely, they can't hurt. But if we, and our critics, were realistic, we'd admit that much is beyond our control, and that insisting otherwise is vain. As British media scholar and author Adrian Monck put it in an essay about the industry's troubles earlier this year: "The crops did not fail because we offended the gods."

As is, I fear we're deep into the self-fulfilling prophecy stage now. In many ways, newspapers are dying . . . because they're dying. As their cash flow shrivels, owners aren't willing, or able, to invest in their papers to arrest the rate of decline, if not reverse it. Each cut in editorial staffing and newshole makes the newspaper less useful and attractive, which makes the next round of cuts inevitable, and so on. Some newspapers entered their death spiral months ago.

I suspect someday our former readers will be peering forlornly toward their empty doorsteps and driveways and wondering where the paper they once loved has gone. I will share their sadness, but not their shock. I've got some news for you, dear readers: Our disappearance wasn't your fault. And as a journalist, I can safely say, it wasn't ours, either.

Critical Thinking

1. According to Paul Farhi, what is the biggest threat to newspapers?
2. If it is true that newspapers remain remarkably popular, and that newspaper readers are better educated and more affluent than TV news viewers, what actions might reverse the advertising erosion?

PAUL FARHI (farhip@washpost.com), a *Washington Post* reporter, writes frequently about the media for the *Post* and *AJR*.

From *American Journalism Review,* October/November 2008 , pp. 14–15. Copyright © 2008 by the Philip Merrill College of Journalism at the University of Maryland, College Park, MD 20742–7111. Reprinted with permission.

What the Mainstream Media Can Learn from Jon Stewart

No, not to be funny and snarky, but to be bold and to do a better job of cutting through the fog.

RACHEL SMOLKIN

When Hub Brown's students first told him they loved "The Daily Show with Jon Stewart" and sometimes even relied on it for news, he was, as any responsible journalism professor would be, appalled.

Now he's a "Daily Show" convert.

"There are days when I watch 'The Daily Show,' and I kind of chuckle. There are days when I laugh out loud. There are days when I stand up and point to the TV and say, 'You're damn right!'" says Brown, chair of the communications department at Syracuse University's S.I. Newhouse School of Public Communications and an associate professor of broadcast journalism.

Brown, who had dismissed the faux news show as silly riffing, got hooked during the early days of the war in Iraq, when he felt most of the mainstream media were swallowing the administration's spin rather than challenging it. Not "The Daily Show," which had no qualms about second-guessing the nation's leaders. "The stock-in-trade of 'The Daily Show' is hypocrisy, exposing hypocrisy. And nobody else has the guts to do it," Brown says. "They really know how to crystallize an issue on all sides, see the silliness everywhere."

Whether lampooning President Bush's disastrous Iraq policies or mocking "real" reporters for their credulity, Stewart and his team often seem to steer closer to the truth than traditional journalists. The "Daily Show" satirizes spin, punctures pretense and belittles bombast. When a video clip reveals a politician's backpedaling, verbal contortions or mindless prattle, Stewart can state the obvious—ridiculing such blather as it deserves to be ridiculed—or remain silent but speak volumes merely by arching an eyebrow.

Stewart and his fake correspondents are freed from the media's preoccupation with balance, the fixation with fairness. They have no obligation to deliver the day's most important news, if that news is too depressing, too complicated or too boring. Their sole allegiance is to comedy.

Or, as "The Daily's Show's" website puts it: "One anchor, five correspondents, zero credibility. If you're tired of the stodginess of the evening newscasts, if you can't bear to sit through the spin-meisters and shills on the 24-hour cable news networks, don't miss "The Daily Show" with Jon Stewart, a nightly half-hour series unburdened by objectivity, journalistic integrity or even accuracy."

That's funny. And obvious. But does that simple, facetious statement capture a larger truth—one that may contain some lessons for newspapers and networks struggling to hold on to fleeing readers, viewers and advertisers in a tumultuous era of transition for old media?

Has our slavish devotion to journalism fundamentals—particularly our obsession with "objectivity"—so restricted news organizations that a comedian can tell the public what's going on more effectively than a reporter? Has Stewart, whose mission is to be funny, sliced through the daily obfuscation more effectively than his media counterparts, whose mission is to inform?

This is, perhaps, a strange premise for a journalism review to explore. *AJR's* mission is to encourage rigorous ethical and professional standards, particularly at a time when fake news of the non Jon Stewart variety has become all too prevalent. Stewart's faux news is parody, a sharp, humorous take on the actual events of the day, not to be confused with fake news of the Jayson Blair, Jack Kelley, National Guard memos or even *WMD* variety, based only loosely on actual events yet presented as real news.

As I posed my question about lessons of "The Daily Show" to various journalism ethicists and professionals, some carefully explained why mainstream news organizations should refrain from engaging in such whimsy.

Ed Fouhy, who worked for all three broadcast networks in his 22-year career as a producer and network executive before retiring in 2004, is a regular "Daily Show" watcher. "Sometimes conventional journalism makes it difficult for a journalist to say what he or she really thinks about an incident. Sometimes you can cut closer to the bone with another form, another creative form, like a novel or a satire on television," Fouhy says. "I think what we're seeing is just a daily dose of it. You think back to 'Saturday Night Live,' and they've satirized the news for a long time with their 'Weekend Update.' 'That Was the Week That Was' was an early television satire on the news."

But Fouhy cringes at the idea that real journalists should model themselves after such a show. When readers pick up a newspaper or viewers turn on a news broadcast, they're looking for serious information, and they should be able to find it. "When you begin to blur the line . . . to attract more viewers and younger viewers, I think that's a lousy idea," he says.

Adds Robert Thompson, director of the Bleier Center for Television and Popular Culture at Syracuse University, "Journalists have a really inconvenient thing they've got to go through: a process of trying to get [the story] right. . . . I don't think journalists should try to be more hip. Journalists have to learn the one lesson which is important, which is to try to get it right."

Fouhy and Thompson are correct, of course. But Thompson's colleague Hub Brown and some others interviewed for this piece believe the lesson of "The Daily Show" is not that reporters should try to be funny, but that they should try to be honest.

"Stop being so doggone scared of everything," Brown advises journalists. "I think there is much less courageousness than there needs to be. There are people out there who stick out because of their fearlessness. Somebody like Lara Logan at CBS," the network's chief foreign correspondent who has reported extensively from Iraq and Afghanistan, "is a great example who is fearless about saying the truth."

In the hours and days following Hurricane Katrina, state and federal officials dithered while New Orleanians suffered inside the filth and chaos of the Louisiana Superdome. Many journalists, notably CNN's Anderson Cooper, jettisoned their usual care in handling all sides equally. They were bewildered, appalled and furious, and it showed.

"We saw a lot of that during Hurricane Katrina, but it shouldn't take a Hurricane Katrina to get journalists to say the truth, to call it as they see it," Brown says. "The thing that makes 'The Daily Show' stick out is they sometimes seem to understand that better than the networks do." He adds: "I think it's valuable because when the emperor has no clothes, we get to say the emperor has no clothes. And we have to do that more often here. . . . The truth itself doesn't respect point of view. The truth is never balanced. . . . We have to not give in to an atmosphere that's become so partisan that we're afraid of what we say every single time we say something."

Venise Wagner, associate chair of the journalism department at San Francisco State University, argues with her students over whether "The Daily Show" is real journalism. They think it is; she tells them it isn't, explaining that journalism involves not just conveying information but also following a set of standards that includes verification, accuracy and balance.

But she says "The Daily Show" does manage to make information relevant in a way that traditional news organizations often do not, and freedom from "balance" shapes its success.

" 'The Daily Show' doesn't have to worry about balance. They don't have to worry about accuracy, even. They can just sort of get at the essence of something, so it gives them much more latitude to play around with the information, to make it more engaging," Wagner says. "Straight news sometimes places itself in a box where it doesn't allow itself—it doesn't give itself permission to question as much as it probably should question." Instead, the exercise becomes one of: "I'm just going to take the news down and give it to you straight."

But what exactly is straight news, and what is balance? Is balance a process of giving equal weight to both sides, or of giving more weight to the side with more evidence? Does accuracy mean spelling everybody's name right and quoting them correctly, or does it also mean slicing to the heart of an issue? "Nowhere is the comedy show balanced," says Wagner, "but it allows them more balance in showing what is really going on."

As journalists, by contrast, "We've presented a balanced picture to the public. But is it accurate? Is it authentic?" She cites coverage of the global warming debate, which, until recently, often was presented as an equal argument between scientists who said global warming was occurring and scientists who denied it. "That reality was not authentic. There were very few scientists who refuted the body of evidence" supporting global warming, Wagner says, yet the coverage did not always reflect that.

Martin Kaplan, associate dean of the University of Southern California's Annenberg School for Communication, dislikes journalists' modern perception of balance. "Straight news is not what it used to be," he says. "It has fallen into a bizarre notion that substitutes something called 'balance' for what used to be called 'accuracy' or 'truth' or 'objectivity.' That may be because of a general postmodern malaise in society at large in which the notion of a truth doesn't have the same reputation it used to, but, as a consequence, straight journalists both in print and in broadcast can be played like a piccolo by people who know how to exploit that weakness."

"Every issue can be portrayed as a controversy between two opposite sides, and the journalist is fearful of saying that one side has it right, and the other side does not. It leaves the reader or viewer in the position of having to weigh competing truth claims, often without enough information to decide that one side is manifestly right, and the other side is trying to muddy the water with propaganda."

Kaplan directs USC's Norman Lear Center, which studies how journalism and politics have become branches of entertainment, and he has worked in all three worlds: former editor and columnist for the now-defunct Washington Star; chief speechwriter for Vice President Walter Mondale; deputy presidential campaign manager for Mondale; Disney studio executive and motion picture and television producer.

He borrows Eric Alterman's phrase "working the ref" to illustrate his point about balance. Instead of "reading a story and finding out that black is black, you now read a story and it says, 'Some say black is black, and some say black is white'. . . . So whether it's climate change or evolution or the impact on war policy of various proposals, it's all being framed as 'on the one hand, on the other hand,' as though the two sides had equal claims on accuracy."

Therein lies "The Daily Show's" appeal, he says. "So-called fake news makes fun of that concept of balance. It's not afraid to have a bullshit meter and to call people spinners or liars when they deserve it. I think as a consequence some viewers find that helpful and refreshing and hilarious."

In addition to the user-generated satire on YouTube, Kaplan thinks the Web is bursting with commentators, including Alterman and Salon's Glenn Greenwald, who brilliantly penetrate the fog—sometimes angrily, sometimes amusingly, sometimes a bit of both.

Broadcasters have tackled this least successfully, he says, citing CBS' ill-fated "Free Speech" segment. Launched on and then discarded from "The CBS Evening News with Katie Couric," the segment gave personalities such as Rush Limbaugh uninterrupted airtime to trumpet their views. And "the challenge for the great national papers," Kaplan adds, "is to escape from this straightjacket in which they're unable to say that official A was telling the truth, and official B was not."

Part of "The Daily Show's" charm comes from its dexterity in letting public figures from Bush to House Speaker Nancy Pelosi (D-Calif.) speak for—and contradict—themselves, allowing the truth to emanate from a politician's entanglement over his or her own two feet. It's one way to hold government officials accountable for their words and deeds. Some might even call it fact-checking.

Brooks Jackson directs FactCheck.org, a project of the Annenberg Public Policy Center of the University of Pennsylvania, which monitors the accuracy of prominent politicians' statements in TV ads, debates, speeches, interviews and press releases. Jackson himself is a former reporter for the Associated Press, Wall Street Journal and CNN who pioneered "ad watch" coverage at the cable network during the '92 presidential race.

"I'm totally buying it," he told me after I stumbled through my fake-news-gets-at-the-truth-better premise. "I am in awe of the ability of Stewart and however many people he has working for him to cull through the vast wasteland of cable TV and pick out the political actors at their most absurd. They just have an unerring eye for that moment when people parody themselves. And I guess while the cable news hosts are obliged to take those moments of idiocy seriously, Jon Stewart can give us that Jack Benny stare—Does anybody remember Jack Benny?—give us that Jon Stewart stare and let the hilarity of the moment sink in, often without saying a word."

Does this qualify as fact-checking? Not exactly, Jackson replies, but "one thing he does do that is fact-checking: If somebody says, 'I never said that,' and next thing you know, there's a clip of the same guy three months ago saying exactly that, that's great fact-checking," and a great lesson for journalists. Jackson thinks NBC's Tim Russert is the master of that art in the mainstream media, confronting his subjects as he puts their quotes on-screen and reading them verbatim. "Stewart does it for laughs, and Russert does it for good journalistic reasons, and we all can learn from the two of them."

The form has its limits as a fact-checking technique. Jackson doesn't envision Stewart giving a State of the Union address rigorous ad-watch-type treatment, complete with statistical analysis of the president's proposed budget. Why would he? He'd

put his audience to sleep. "Not every misleading statement can be debunked out of the person's own mouth," notes Jackson. "That's a particular kind of debunking that's very effective as comedy. . . . There's plenty that needs debunking that isn't funny."

Asked about Stewart's influence on mainstream reporters, Jackson says: "Jon's been holding up the mirror to them for quite a while without any particular effect. The forces that are making the news more trivial and less relevant are frankly much more powerful than a show like Jon Stewart's can change."

Much of the allure of Stewart's show lies in its brutal satire of the media. He and his correspondents mimic the stylized performance of network anchors and correspondents. He exposes their gullibility. He derides their contrivances.

On March 28, the broadcast media elite partied with their government sources at the annual Radio and Television Correspondents' Association dinner. The disquieting spectacle of White House adviser Karl Rove rapping in front of a howling audience of journalists quickly appeared on YouTube. Quipped Stewart, only too accurately, the next night: "The media gets a chance to, for one night, put aside its cozy relationship with the government for one that is, instead, nauseatingly sycophantic."

His 2004 textbook satire, "America (The Book): A Citizen's Guide to Democracy Inaction," devotes a section to media in the throes of transformation and punctures this transition far more concisely, and probably more memorably, than the millions of words *AJR* has devoted to the subject:

"Newspapers abound, and though they have endured decades of decline in readership and influence, they can still form impressive piles if no one takes them out to the trash. . . . Television continues to thrive. One fifteen-minute nightly newscast, barely visible through the smoky haze of its cigarette company benefactor, has evolved into a multi-channel, twenty-four hour a day infotastic clusterfuck of factish-like material. The 1990s brought the advent of a dynamic new medium for news, the Internet, a magnificent new technology combining the credibility of anonymous hearsay with the excitement of typing."

Phil Rosenthal, the *Chicago Tribune's* media columnist, thinks part of the reason "The Daily Show" and its spinoff, "The Colbert Report," resonate is that they parody not only news but also how journalists get news. "It's actually kind of a surefire way to appeal to people because if the news itself isn't entertaining, then the way it's covered, the breathless conventions of TV news, are always bankable," Rosenthal says. "You can always find something amusing there."

He adds that "so much of the news these days involves managing the news, so a show like Stewart's that takes the larger view of not just what's going on, but how it's being manipulated, is really effective. I think there's general skepticism about the process that this plays into. . . . The wink isn't so much we know what's really going on. The wink is also we know you know what we're doing here. It's down to the way the correspondents stand [in front of] the green screen, offering commentary and intoning even when their commentary may not be important."

Irony-deficient journalists have rewarded Stewart over the last five years by devoting more than 150 newspaper articles alone to his show and to studies about his show. Most have discussed the program's popularity. ("The Daily Show" attracted an average 1.5 million viewers nightly from January 1 through April 19, according to Nielsen Media Research. Couric's beleaguered CBS newscast, by contrast, netted an average 7.2 million viewers nightly during the same period.)

Many stories have pondered whether "The Daily Show" has substance and credibility; mourned young people's alleged propensity to rely on such lighthearted fare for news; brooded over what this reliance says about the state of the news media; and grieved that the show poisons young people's outlook on government, leaving them cynical and jaded. Stewart, who declined to be interviewed for this article, has patiently explained that his show is supposed to be funny.

That hasn't stopped the onslaught of serious discourse and research about "The Daily Show." A 2004 survey by the Pew Research Center for the People and the Press found that 21 percent of people age 18 to 29 cited comedy shows such as "The Daily Show" and "Saturday Night Live" as places where they regularly learned presidential campaign news, nearly equal to the 23 percent who regularly learned something from the nightly network news or from daily newspapers.

Even if they did learn from his show, a more recent study indicates Stewart's viewers are well-informed. An April 15 Pew survey gauging Americans' knowledge of national and international affairs found that 54 percent of regular viewers of "The Daily Show" and "Colbert Report" scored in the high-knowledge category, tying with regular readers of newspaper websites and edging regular watchers of "The NewsHour with Jim Lehrer." Overall, 35 percent of people surveyed scored in the high-knowledge category.

In October, Julia R. Fox, who teaches telecommunications at Indiana University, and two graduate students announced the results of the first scholarly attempt to compare Stewart's show with traditional TV news as a political information source. Their study, which will be published this summer by the Journal of Broadcasting & Electronic Media, examined substantive political coverage in 2004 of the first presidential debate and political conventions on "The Daily Show" and the broadcast television networks' nightly newscasts. Fox concluded Stewart's show is just as substantive as network news.

Fox says she wasn't surprised by the study results, but she was surprised by the general lack of surprise. "People have e-mailed me and said, 'I think you're absolutely wrong. I think 'The Daily Show' is more substantive.'"

Beyond the debate over whether Stewart's show is a quality source of information or whether wayward young fans have lost their minds, the media have treated him with admiration bordering on reverence. In early 2005, press reports handicapped his chances of landing on the "CBS Evening News," which, like "Comedy Central," was then owned by Viacom. After Dan Rather had announced his abrupt retirement following revelations that alleged memos about President Bush's National Guard

Service had not been authenticated, CBS chief Leslie Moonves said he wanted to reinvent the evening news to make it more relevant, "something that younger people can relate to." Asked at a news conference whether he'd rule out a role for Stewart, Moonves took a pass, fueling more speculation.

In 2004, the Television Critics Association bestowed the outstanding achievement in news and information award not on ABC's "Nightline" or PBS' "Frontline," but on "The Daily Show." Stewart, who had won for outstanding achievement in comedy the previous year, seemed bemused by the honor. Instead of accepting in person, he sent a tape of himself sitting at "The Daily Show" anchor desk. "We're fake," he informed the TV critics. "See this desk? . . . It folds up at the end of the day, and I take it home in my purse."

But Melanie McFarland, the critic who presented Stewart's award, calls him a "truth teller" who speaks plainly about the news and offers a "spoonful of sugar that helps the medicine, the news, go down."

That sugar is not just delightful; it's provocative. "Any comedian can do sort of a 'Saturday Night Live' presentation and just do the punch line," says McFarland, who writes for the Seattle Post-Intelligencer. "He actually gives you some stuff to consider in addition to the punch line. He and his staff show an awareness of the issues and [are] able to take a longer view than a 24-hour news cycle can, which is funny because it's also a daily show." Other news programs and journalists, including "Frontline" and Bill Moyers, do this also, she says, but not as often. "So much of the news is not digestion but regurgitation. He's sort of looking at the raw material and making a commonsense assessment of what it means."

McFarland says Stewart's mockery of the media should galvanize journalists to perform better. "If there's a guy who's making great headway in giving people information by showing people what you're not doing in giving them information, let's try to do our jobs."

For serious news organizations, change is easier advised than enacted. Take Stewart's imitation of the stylized anchor persona, which—with precious little exaggeration—makes TV personalities look silly and stilted. Altering that persona is no easy task, as Katie Couric discovered when she tried to make the nightly news chattier.

"While Jon Stewart is a guy in a suit pretending to be a newscaster, and he acts like a guy in a suit pretending to be a newscaster, there's a certain formality and rigidity we've come to expect from our news, so much so that when Katie Couric opens the news with 'Hi,' or now I think it's 'Hello,' this is thought of as some kind of breakdown in the proper etiquette of newscasting," says the Chicago Tribune's Rosenthal. He thinks perhaps the time has come to abandon the old formality of newscasting but says such a process will be evolutionary.

In other broadcast formats, incorporating a more sardonic tone can work well. Rosenthal cites MSNBC's "Countdown with Keith Olbermann" as one news program that does a pretty good job incorporating the same sorts of elements that make "The Daily Show" successful. "Keith Olbermann gets a lot of attention for his editorializing, but the meat of that show is this hybrid blend of the news you need to know, the news that's entertaining, with a little bit of perspective [in] taking a step back from what the news is and what the newsmakers want it to be," he says. (See "Is Keith Olbermann the Future of Journalism?" February/March.)

Rosenthal thinks ABC's quirky overnight show, "World News Now," also has achieved a more detached, looser tone, and says it's no accident that the program has been "such a fertile breeding ground for unorthodox newspeople," including Anderson Cooper and Aaron Brown.

Public radio, known for its sober (and sometimes stodgy) programming, is experimenting with a more freewheeling search for truth as well. In January, Public Radio International launched "Fair Game from PRI with Faith Salie," a one-hour satirical news and entertainment show that airs on weeknights. The Sacramento Bee's Sam McManis likened the new show to "the quirky love child of 'The Daily Show With Jon Stewart' and 'All Things Considered.' It's smart enough to slake the traditional public-radio fans' thirst for intellectual programming but satiric enough to catch the attention of the prematurely cynical Gen X and Gen Y sets."

Salie is a comedian and a Rhodes Scholar with a bachelor's degree from Harvard and a master of philosophy from Oxford in modern English literature. "I'm not a journalist, and I don't have to pretend to be one," she says, describing herself as her listeners' proxy. When she interviews newsmakers—topics have included the Taliban, Hillary Clinton and the Dixie Chicks—"I don't feel like I have to mask my incredulousness. I can say, 'For real? Are you kidding me?' That leads to spontaneity."

Sometimes humor results from a certain framing of the news. Each Monday, the show revisits metaphors from the Sunday morning news shows. On "Fox News Sunday" on April 8, Juan Williams first compared Republican presidential hopeful John McCain to a "deflated balloon," then declared the Arizona senator was on the "wrong path" with his Iraq policy and concluded that he shouldn't be "tying his tail" to such an albatross. On NBC's "Meet the Press," Judy Woodruff in January described the administration's Iraq policy as akin to "putting a fist in a sink full of water, leaving it there for a few minutes and taking it out."

Salie says "The Daily Show" has demonstrated that young people are savvier than many elders believe, and the mainstream media should learn from that. Young people "are aware of the news and can recognize the preposterousness of some of it." But don't try too hard to be funny, she cautions. "I don't think real news shows should try the scripted, cutesy, pithy banter. It gives me the heebie-jeebies. It makes me feel sad for them, and it feels pathetic."

For an informal, satirical or even humorous take on the news to work in a mainstream newspaper, the format must be exactly right. Gene Weingarten, the Washington Post humor writer, thinks the media would do their jobs better if they had more fun, and he cringes whenever editors insist on labeling his pieces as satire. "Nothing could be worse for satire than labeling it satire," he laments.

But he concedes his editors may have a point. In August, Paul Farhi, a reporter for the Post's Style section (and an AJR contributor), reviewed the debut of colleague Tony Kornheiser on ESPN's "Monday Night Football." The critique was not flattering, and an apoplectic Kornheiser retaliated by publicly trashing Farhi as "a two-bit weasel slug," whom he would "gladly run over with a Mack truck."

The smackdown drew national attention, and Weingarten decided he wanted a piece of the action. So he skewered Kornheiser's second show with an outrageous, over-the-top rant on the front of Style about the "failed Kornheiser stewardship" taking "yet another bumbling misstep toward its inevitable humiliating collapse."

"It was patently unfair," Weingarten says of his tongue-in-cheek diatribe, which was not labeled as satire. "A child would have understood this piece. No one could have misunderstood this."

And yet they did. Weingarten got hundreds, possibly thousands, of complaints from sports lovers pummeling him for attacking Kornheiser unfairly. (Kornheiser himself called Weingarten, unsure how to interpret the piece.) "The mail I got was just absolutely hilarious," Weingarten says. "There is a problem of applying irony, humorous satire, in a newspaper when readers are not accustomed to seeing it there."

Did he learn from the experience? "No," he replies. "Because my reaction was, 'These people are idiots.'"

P erhaps the hardest lesson to take away from "The Daily Show" is the most important one. How can journalists in today's polarized political climate pierce the truth, Edward R. Murrow-style, without a) being ideological, or b) appearing ideological?

Olbermann's show, cited in several interviews as a serious news program that excels in revealing hypocrisy, is unabashedly liberal, and "The Daily Show" itself is frequently tagged with that label. In February, Fox News Channel debuted "The 1/2 Hour News Hour," billed as the conservative riposte to Stewart's liberal bent; after two pilot shows, the network has agreed to pick up 13 additional episodes.

"Unfortunately, people are heading for news that sort of reinforces their own beliefs," says Washington Post reporter Dana Milbank. "That may be Jon Stewart on the left, or that may be Rush Limbaugh on the right. . . . Limbaugh isn't funny, but he's starting with something that has a kernel of truth and distorting it to the point of fakery as well, so I think they are parallel."

Milbank is the author of Washington Sketch, an experiment at slashing through the hazy words and deeds of federal power players. Milbank pitched the idea, based on British newspapers' parliamentary sketches, and argued for a few years before getting the green light in early 2005. "There was a lot of sort of figuring out the place, and first it really floated in the news section," he says. "I think we fixed that problem [by] putting it consistently on page two, and it's labeled more clearly."

Occasionally, Washington Sketch has appeared on page one, as it did March 6 when Milbank tartly contrasted the style of two generals who testified before Congress on the deplorable conditions at Walter Reed Army Medical Center. Then and at other times, Milbank's acerbic take has proved more enlightening than the longer, more traditional accompanying news story.

The column lacks a consistent ideology. Milbank says his goal is a "pox on both their houses sort of thing," and adds, "I'm not trying to be 50-50, particularly. The goal is to pick on all of them. . . . It's observational as opposed to argumentative." Too often, he says, "We seem to make the mistake of thinking that if you're not being ideological, you therefore have to be boring, and all sort of 50-50 down the middle and follow the inverted pyramid."

Jeff Jarvis, the blogger behind BuzzMachine.com, says journalists should engage in more open, honest conversations with readers. "I think what Stewart et al do is remind us of what our mission and voice used to be and should be," says Jarvis, who also is a media consultant and head of the interactive journalism program at the City University of New York Graduate School of Journalism. He notes that Stewart is "very much a part of the conversation. He's joking about things we're talking about. And then the next day, we're talking about him talking about it."

Jarvis wants journalists to unleash their inner Stewart. "After enough drinks, reporters talk like Stewart: 'You won't BELIEVE what the mayor said today!' Why don't we talk to our readers that way?" he asks, and then acknowledges: "OK. There's a lot of arguments: 'The mayor won't talk to us again.' 'It's biased.' 'We don't want to turn everything into blogs'."

Jarvis doesn't mean that every story should become a first-person diatribe, and obviously the mainstream media can't fall back on Stewart's I'm-just-joking excuse after they've infuriated a thin-skinned politician. But there are instances when a little unorthodoxy may be appropriate, and speaking frankly may enhance credibility.

Eric Deggans, the TV and media critic for the St. Petersburg Times, also wants to see a little more pluck. "'The Daily Show' is pushing us to be less traditional about how we deliver people information," Deggans says. "Are we going to turn around and turn into the Onion?" (The cult publication parodies news in print and online; its facetious Onion News Network debuted on March 27.) "Of course not. But if you've got a longtime state capitol bureau chief, and they see something go down in the capitol, and they have a great, acerbic take on it, why not let them go at it in a column?"

Or, he suggests, experiment just a bit with the sacred space on page one. "Sometimes editors have really rigid ideas about what can go on the front page," he says. "If somebody has a really good column on [Don] Imus, why wouldn't you put it on the front page, as long as you label it clearly as opinion? There are some editors who would say your first next-day story about Don Imus has to be traditional. Why? Why does it have to be traditional? As long as the reader isn't fooled, why do you let yourself be handcuffed like that?"

Deggans is quick to add some caveats, including the importance of fairness. "You always have to be careful because there's a good reason why we had those rules," Deggans says. "But we have to challenge ourselves to subvert them more often. You have to be subversive in a way that maintains your credibility. When you have smart, capable people who want to write in a different way, let them try it."

The mainstream media can not, should not and never will be "The Daily Show." The major news of our time is grimly serious, and only real news organizations will provide the time, commitment and professionalism necessary to ferret out stories such as the Washington Post's exposé of neglected veterans at Walter Reed or the New York Times' disclosures of secret, warrantless wiretapping by the federal government.

But in the midst of a transition, our industry is flailing. Our credibility suffers mightily. The public thinks we're biased despite our reluctance to speak plainly. Our daily newspapers often seem stale. Perhaps "The Daily Show" can teach us little, but remind us of a lot: Don't underestimate your audience. Be relevant. And be bold.

Says Deggans: "In a lot of news organizations, it's the fourth quarter. It's fourth down, man. It's time to show a little pizzazz. It's time to reinvent what's going on, so people get engaged."

Critical Thinking

1. What's the appeal of "The Daily Show with Jon Stewart"? (If you haven't watched it, do.)

2. What lessons might straight news take from Jon Stewart, without itself turning into faux news?

RACHEL SMOLKIN (rsmolkin@ajr.umd.edu) is *AJR*'s managing editor. *AJR* editorial assistant Emily Groves contributed research to this report.

Whatever Happened to Iraq?

How the Media Lost Interest in a Long-Running War with No End in Sight

SHERRY RICCHIARDI

A rmando Acuna, public editor of the Sacramento Bee, turned a Sunday column into a public flogging for both his editors and the nation's news media. They had allowed the third-longest war in American history to slip off the radar screen, and he had the numbers to prove it.

The public also got a scolding for its meager interest in a controversial conflict that is costing taxpayers about $12.5 billion a month, or nearly $5,000 a second, according to some calculations. In his March 30 commentary, Acuna noted: "There's enough shame . . . for everyone to share."

He had watched stories about Iraq move from 1A to the inside pages of his newspaper, if they ran at all. He understood the editors' frustration over how to handle the mind-numbing cycles of violence and complex issues surrounding Operation Iraqi Freedom. "People feel powerless about this war," he said in an interview in April.

Acuna knew the Sacramento Bee was not alone.

For long stretches over the past 12 months, Iraq virtually disappeared from the front pages of the nation's newspapers and from the nightly network newscasts. The American press and the American people had lost interest in the war.

T he decline in coverage of Iraq has been staggering. During the first 10 weeks of 2007, Iraq accounted for 23 percent of the newshole for network TV news. In 2008, it plummeted to 3 percent during that period. On cable networks it fell from 24 percent to 1 percent, according to a study by the Project for Excellence in Journalism.

The numbers also were dismal for the country's dailies. By Acuna's count, during the first three months of this year, front-page stories about Iraq in the Bee were down 70 percent from the same time last year. Articles about Iraq once topped the list for reader feedback. By mid-2007, "Their interest just dropped off; it was noticeable to me," says the public editor.

A daily tracking of 65 newspapers by the Associated Press confirms a dip in page-one play throughout the country. In September 2007, the AP found 457 Iraq-related stories (154 by the AP) on front pages, many related to a progress report delivered to Congress by Gen. David Petraeus, the top U.S. commander in Iraq. Over the succeeding months, that number fell to as low as 49. A spike in March 2008 was largely due to a rash of

stories keyed to the conflict's fifth anniversary, according to AP Senior Managing Editor Mike Silverman.

During the early stages of shock and awe, Americans were glued to the news as Saddam Hussein's statue was toppled in Baghdad and sweat-soaked Marines bivouacked in his luxurious palaces. It was a huge story when President Bush landed on the aircraft carrier USS Abraham Lincoln on May 1, 2003, and declared major combat operations were over.

By March 2008, a striking reversal had taken place. Only 28 percent of Americans knew that 4,000 military personnel had been killed in the conflict, according to a survey by the Pew Research Center for the People & the Press. Eight months earlier, 54 percent could cite the correct casualty rate.

TV news was a vivid indicator of the declining interest. The three broadcast networks' nightly newscasts devoted more than 4,100 minutes to Iraq in 2003 and 3,000 in 2004. That leveled off to 2,000 annually. By late 2007, it was half that, according to Andrew Tyndall, who monitors the nightly news (tyndall report.com).

In broadcast, there's a sense that the appetite for Iraq coverage has grown thin.

"In broadcast, there's a sense that the appetite for Iraq coverage has grown thin. The big issue is how many people stick with it. It is not less of a story," said Jeffrey Fager, executive producer of "60 Minutes," during the Reva and David Logan Symposium on Investigative Reporting in late April at the Graduate School of Journalism at the University of California, Berkeley. The number of Iraq-related stories aired on "60 Minutes" has been consistent over the past two years. The total from April 2007 through March 2008 was 15, one fewer than during the same period the year before.

D espite the pile of evidence of waning coverage, news managers interviewed for this story consistently maintained there was no conscious decision to back off. "I wasn't hearing that in our newsroom," says Margaret Sullivan, editor of the Buffalo News. Yet numbers show that attention to the war plummeted at the Buffalo paper as it did at other news outlets.

Why the dramatic drop-off? Gatekeepers offer a variety of reasons, from the enormous danger for journalists on the ground in Iraq (see "Obstructed View," April/May 2007) to plunging newsroom budgets and shrinking news space. Competing megastories on the home front like the presidential primaries and the sagging economy figure into the equation. So does the exorbitant cost of keeping correspondents in Baghdad.

No one questioned the importance of a grueling war gone sour or the looming consequences for the United States and the Middle East. Instead, newsroom managers talked about the realities of life in a rapidly changing media market, including smaller newsholes and, for many, a laser-beam focus on local issues and events.

Los Angeles Times' foreign editor Marjorie Miller attributes the decline to three factors:

The economic downturn and the contentious presidential primaries have sucked oxygen from Iraq. "We have a woman, an African American and a senior running for president," Miller says. "That is a very big story."

With no solutions in sight, with no light at the end of the tunnel, war fatigue has become a factor. Over the years, a bleak sameness has settled into accounts of suicide bombings and brutal sectarian violence. Insurgents fighting counterinsurgents are hard to translate to an American audience.

The sheer cost of keeping correspondents on the ground in Baghdad is trimming the roster of journalists. The expense is "unlike anything we've ever faced. We have shouldered the financial burden so far, but we are really squeezed," Miller says. Earlier, the L.A. Times had as many as five Western correspondents in the field. The bureau is down to two or three plus Iraqi staff.

Other media decision-makers echo Miller's analysis.

When Lara Logan, the high-profile chief senior foreign correspondent for CBS News, is rotated out of Iraq, she might not be replaced, says her boss, Senior Vice President Paul Friedman. The network is sending in fewer Westerners from European and American bureaus and depending more on local staff, a common practice for media outlets with personnel in Iraq. "We won't pull out, but we are making adjustments," Friedman says.

Friedman defends the cutbacks: "One of the definitions of news is change, and there are long periods now in Iraq when very little changes. Therefore, it's difficult for the Iraq story to fight its way on the air against other news where change is involved," such as the political campaign, he says.

John Stack, Fox News Channel's vice president for newsgathering, has no qualms about allotting more airtime to the presidential campaign than to Iraq. "This is a very big story playing out on the screen every night . . . . The time devoted to news is finite," Stack says. "It's a matter of shifting to another story of national interest."

Despite diminished emphasis on the war, Fox has no plans to cut back its Baghdad operation. "We still have a full complement of people there, operating in a very difficult environment. That hasn't gone down at all," he says. Fox has two full reporting teams in Iraq as well as a bureau chief and some local staff, for a total of 25 to 30 people, according to Stack.

In late 2007, the networks—CBS, NBC, ABC, CNN and Fox—entertained the notion of pooling resources in Iraq to cut expenses. After much discussion, the idea was tabled. "It turned out not to be possible," Friedman says. "To some extent, our needs are very different." Cable TV is all about constant repetition; even during lulls it features correspondents standing in front of cameras making reports. "The networks don't do that and don't need the same kind of facilities," Friedman says.

McClatchy Newspapers maintains a presence in Baghdad—a bureau chief, a rotating staffer generally from one of the chain's papers and six local staffers—but the decline in violence since the U.S. troop buildup last year has resulted in fewer daily stories, says Foreign Editor Roy Gutman. "We produce according to the news. During the [Iraqi] government's offensive in Basra [in March], we produced lengthy stories every day." To add another dimension to the coverage, McClatchy tapped into its Iraqi staff for compelling first-person accounts posted on its Washington bureau's website (mcclatchydc.com—see "A Blog of Heartbreak," April/May 2007).

New York Times Foreign Editor Susan Chira says she is content to run fewer stories than in the past. "But we want them to have impact. And, of course, when there are big running stories, we will stay on them every day."

Midsize dailies around the country face a different set of challenges. Many operate under mandates from their bosses to push local stories over national or international news in hope of boosting readership and advertising. In those publications, it often takes a strong community tie to propel Iraq onto page one.

Case in point: During the first week of February, the one story about Iraq that made 1A in the Buffalo News was headlined, "Close to home while far off at war." It told how the latest gadgetry helps local service members stay in touch with loved ones. During the same week a year ago, four Iraq-related stories made 1A. None appeared to have a local angle.

"There is strong local interest because we have a lot of service members over there and we have had quite a few deaths of local soldiers," Editor Sullivan says. "In my mind, there is no bigger nonlocal story. It's the expense, the lives, the policy issues, and what it means to the country's future. There is a general feeling that the media have tired of Iraq, but I have not."

At Alabama's Birmingham News, it takes a significant development to get an Iraq-related story prominent play without a local link, says Executive Editor Hunter George. During the first week in February, the Birmingham paper ran only one story related to the war. The topic: "Brownies send goodies, cards to troops in Iraq."

Editors did not sit in a news budget meeting and make a conscious decision to cut back on Iraq coverage, George says. He believes the repetitiveness of the storyline has something to do with the decline. "I see and hear it all the time. It seems like a bad dream, and the public's not interested in revisiting it unless there is a major development. If I'm outside the newsroom and Iraq comes up, I hear groans. People say, 'More bad news,' Stories about the economy are moving up the news scale."

It was big news for Pennsylvania's Reading Eagle when a wounded soldier came home from Iraq and was met by some 50 bikers at the airport. The "Patriot Guard," as they are called, provided an escort. Townspeople slapped together a carnival to help raise money for a wheelchair ramp. "For us, it comes down to the grassroots level," says Eagle reporter Dan Kelly.

Earlier that day, Kelly's editor had handed him an assignment about a Marine from nearby Exeter Township who rushed home from the war zone to visit his ailing grandfather. By the time he got there, he was facing a funeral instead. "We look for special circumstances like this," Kelly says. "We pick our battles."

The Indianapolis Star ramped up coverage in January when the 76th Infantry Brigade Combat Team from the Indiana National Guard was redeployed to Iraq. The newspaper created a special Web page to help readers stay in touch with the more than 3,000 soldiers from around the state, including graphics showing their hometowns and how the combat gear they wear works in the war zone.

"I don't want to mislead you and say our coverage has been consistent over the past 12 months. It has rolled and dipped. We have had calls from people who believe we underplay events like bombings where several people are killed," says Pam Fine, the Star's managing editor until early April. Front-page coverage of Iraq was the same in the first three months of 2007 and 2008. A total of 23 stories ran in each period. Fine left the paper to become the Knight Chair in News, Leadership and Community at the University of Kansas.

The reader representative for the San Francisco Chronicle doesn't think placement of stories about Iraq makes much difference. He reasons that five years in, most readers have formed clear opinions about the war. They're not likely to change their minds one way or another if a story runs on page one or page three, says Dick Rogers. "The public has become accustomed to the steady drumbeat of violence out of Iraq. A report of 20 or 30 killed doesn't bring fresh insight for a lot of people."

Americans might care if they could witness more of the human toll. That's the approach the Washington Post's Dana Milbank took in an April 24 piece titled, "What the Family Would Let You See, the Pentagon Obstructs."

When Lt. Col. Billy Hall was buried in Arlington National Cemetery in April, his family gave the media permission to cover the ceremony—he is among the highest-ranking officers to be killed in Iraq. But, according to Milbank, the military did everything it could to keep the journalists away, isolating them some 50 yards away behind a yellow rope.

The "de facto ban on media at Arlington funerals fits neatly" with White House efforts "to sanitize the war in Iraq," and that, in turn, has helped keep the bloodshed out of the public's mind, Milbank wrote in his Washington Sketch feature. There have been similar complaints over the years about the administration's policy that bans on-base photography of coffins returning from Iraq and Afghanistan. (See Drop Cap, June/July 2004.)

Despite the litany of reasons, some journalists still take a "shame on you" attitude toward those who have relegated the Iraq war to second-class status.

Sig Christenson, military writer for the San Antonio Express-News, has made five trips to the war zone and says he would go back in a heartbeat. "This is not a story we can afford to ignore," he says. "There are vast implications for every American, right down to how much gasoline costs when we go to the pump."

Christenson, a co-founder of the organization MRE—Military Reporters and Editors—believes the media have an obligation to provide context and nuance and make clear the complexities of

the war so Americans better understand its seriousness. "That's our job," he says.

Along the same lines, Greg Mitchell, editor of Editor & Publisher, faults newsroom leaders for shortchanging "the biggest political and moral issue of our time."

"You can forgive the American public for being shocked at the recent violence in Basra [in March]. From the lack of press coverage that's out there, they probably thought the war was over," says Mitchell, who wrote about media performance in the book "So Wrong for So Long: How the Press, the Pundits—and the President—Failed on Iraq."

Both journalists point to cause and effect: The public tends to take cues from the media about what is important. If Iraq is pushed to a back burner, the signal is clear—the war no longer is a top priority. It follows that news consumers lose interest and turn their attention elsewhere. The Pew study found exactly that: As news coverage of the war diminished, so too did the public interest in Iraq.

Ellen Hume, research director at the MIT Center for Future Civic Media and a former journalist, believes the decline in Iraq news could be linked to a larger issue—profits. "The problem doesn't seem to be valuing coverage of the war; it's more about the business model of journalism today and what that market requires," Hume says.

"There is no sense that [the media] are going to be able to meet the numbers that their corporate owners require by offering news about a downer subject like Iraq. It's a terrible dilemma for news organizations."

Still, there has been some stunningly good reporting on Iraq over the past year.

Two of the Washington Post's six Pulitzer Prizes were war-related. Anne Hull and Dana Priest won the public service award for revealing the neglect of wounded soldiers at Walter Reed Army Medical Center (see Drop Cap, April/May 2007). Steve Fainaru won in the international reporting category for an examination of private security contractors in Iraq.

McClatchy's Baghdad bureau chief, Leila Fadel, collected the George R. Polk Award for outstanding foreign reporting. Judges offered high praise for her vivid depictions of the agonizing plight of families in ethnically torn neighborhoods.

CBS took two Peabody Awards, one for Scott Pelley's report on the killings of civilians in the Iraqi city of Haditha (see "A Matter of Time," August/September 2006) on "60 Minutes," another for Kimberly Dozier's report about two female veterans who lost limbs in Iraq on "CBS News Sunday Morning." Dozier herself was wounded in Iraq in May 2006.

ABC News correspondent Bob Woodruff, who was injured in Iraq in January 2006, received a Peabody Award for "Wounds of War," a series of reports about injured veterans.

There have been a series of groundbreaking investigations over the past year. In one of the most recent, the New York Times' David Barstow documented how the Pentagon cultivated military analysts to generate favorable news for the Bush administration's wartime performance. Many of the talking heads, including former generals, were being coached on what to tell viewers on television.

The Times continues to have a dominant presence on the ground in Iraq, sinking millions into maintaining its Baghdad complex, home and office to six or seven Western correspondents and a large Iraqi staff. Foreign Editor Chira says it has been more challenging to recruit people to go to Baghdad, but "we remain completely committed to maintaining a robust presence in Iraq."

Those are notable exceptions; no doubt there are more. But overall, Iraq remains the biggest nonstory of the day unless major news is breaking.

Mark Jurkowitz, associate director of the Project for Excellence in Journalism, points to May 24, 2007, as a major turning point in the coverage of U.S. policy toward Iraq. That's the day Congress voted to continue to fund the war without troop withdrawal timetables, giving the White House a major victory in a clash with the Democratic leadership over who would control the purse strings and thus the future of the war. Democrats felt they had a mandate from Americans to bring the troops home. President Bush stuck to a hard line and came out the victor. "The political fight was over," Jurkowitz says. "Iraq no longer was a hot story. The media began looking elsewhere."

Statistics from a report by Jurkowitz released in March 2008 support his theory. From January through May 2007, Iraq accounted for 20 percent of all news measured by PEJ's News Coverage Index. That period included the announcement of the troop "surge."

"But from the time of the May funding vote through the war's fifth anniversary on March 19, 2008, coverage plunged by about 50 percent. In that period, the media paid more than twice as much attention to the presidential campaigns than the war," according to PEJ.

"You could see the coverage of the political debate [over Iraq] shrink noticeably. The drop was dramatic," says Jurkowitz, who believes the press has an obligation to cover stories about Iraq even when the political landscape changes. "It is hard to say that the media has spurred any meaningful debate in America on this."

Is there anything to the concept of war fatigue or a psychological numbing that comes with rote reports of violence? Susan Tifft, professor of journalism and public policy at Duke University, believes there is.

She reasons that humans do adapt when the abnormal gradually becomes normal, such as a bloody and seemingly endless conflict far from America's shores. Tifft explains that despite tensions of the Cold War, America's default position for many years had been peace. Now the default position—the environment in which Americans live—is war. "And somehow we have gotten used to it. That's why it seems like wallpaper or Muzak. It's oddly normal and just part of the atmosphere," she says.

Does an acceptance of the status quo indicate helplessness or rational resignation on the part of the public and the press? Is it a survival mechanism?

Harvard University Professor Howard Gardner, a psychologist and social scientist, has explored what it is about the way humans operate that might allow this to happen.

Gardner explains that when a news story becomes repetitive, people "habituate"—the technical term for what happens when they no longer take in information. "You can be sure that if American deaths were going up, or if there was a draft, then there would not be acceptance of the status quo," Gardner wrote in an April 17 e-mail.

"But American deaths are pretty small, and the children of the political, business and chattering classes are not dying, and so the war no longer is on the radar screen most of the time. The bad economy has replaced it, and no one has yet succeeded in tying the trillion-dollar war to the decline in the economy."

New York Times columnist Nicholas D. Kristof is one who has tried. In a March 23 op-ed column, he quoted Nobel Prize-winning economist Joseph Stiglitz as saying the "present economic mess" is very much related to the Iraq war, which also "is partially responsible for soaring oil prices." Stiglitz calculated the eventual total cost to be about $3 trillion.

Kristof tossed out plenty of fodder for stories: "A congressional study by the Joint Economic Committee found that the sums spent on the Iraq war each day could enroll an additional 58,000 children in Head Start or give Pell Grants to 153,000 students to attend college. . . . [A] day's Iraq spending would finance another 11,000 border patrol agents or 9,000 police officers."

In Denver, Jason Salzman has been thinking along the same lines. The media critic for the Rocky Mountain News suggested in a February 16 column that news organizations "treat the economic costs of the war as they've treated U.S. casualties." After the death of the 3,000th American soldier, for instance, his newspaper printed the names of all the dead on the front page. To mark economic milestones, Salzman would like to see page one filled with graphics representing dollars Colorado communities have lost to the war.

"It's hard for me to realize why more reporters don't do these stories about the impact of the cost of the war back home," he said in an interview.

Another aspect of the war that could use more scrutiny is the Iraqi oil industry: Where is the money going? Who is benefiting? Why isn't oil money paying for a fair share of reconstruction costs?

Similarly, much more attention could be paid to the ramifications of stretching America's military to the limit.

And what about the impact of the war on the lives of ordinary Iraqis (see "Out of Reach," April/May 2006)? In April, Los Angeles Times correspondent Alexandra Zavis filed a story about a ballet school in Baghdad that had become an oasis for children of all ethnic and religious backgrounds.

"Now, more than ever," Zavis wrote in an e-mail interview, it "is the responsibility of journalists to put a name and a face on the mind-numbing statistics, to take readers in to the lives of ordinary Iraqis, and to find ways to convey what this unimaginable bloodshed means to the people who live it."

Jurkowitz's March 2008 report cited the "inverse relationship between war coverage and the coverage of the 2008 presidential campaign—an early-starting, wide-open affair that has fascinated the press since it began in earnest in January 2007. As attention to Iraq steadily declined, coverage of the campaign continued to grow in 2007 and 2008, consuming more of the press' attention and resources.

"Moreover, the expectation that Iraq would dominate the campaign conversation proved to be wrong," the report said. It was the economy instead. Jurkowitz cites what he calls an eye-catching statistic: In the first three months of 2008, coverage of the campaign outstripped war coverage by a ratio of nearly 11 to 1, or 43 percent of newshole compared with 4 percent.

But all that soon could change. "The [Iraq] story, we believe, remains as important as ever, and the debate about the future conduct of the war and the level of American troop presence in Iraq during the presidential campaign makes it crucial for the American public to be well informed," says the New York Times' Chira.

Jurkowitz agrees. That's why he's predicting a renaissance in Iraq coverage in the coming months. Battle lines already have been drawn: Sen. John McCain, the presumed Republican candidate, has vowed to stay the course in Iraq until victory is achieved. The Democrats favor withdrawing U.S. forces, perhaps beginning as early as six months after taking the oath of office.

"When we get in the general election mode, Iraq will be a big issue. The candidates will set the agenda for the discussion and the media will pick it up. This could reinvigorate the debate," Jurkowitz says. "The war will be back in the headlines."

Critical Thinking

1. Can you explain why some journalists don't look at the Iraq conflict as a "second-rate war."

2. Do you believe the United States will ever see economic benefits from nation building in Iraq?

Senior contributing writer **SHERRY RICCHIARDI** (sricchia@iupui .edu), who writes frequently about international coverage for AJR, assessed reporting on Iran in the magazine's February/March issue. Editorial assistant Roxana Hadadi (rhadadi@ajr.umd.edu) contributed research to this report.

UNIT 3
Players and Guides

Unit Selections

Learning Outcomes

The articles in this section will contribute to your being able to

- Propose reasonable standards of "fair use" and "fair compensation" for Internet content.

- Contrast the Hulu and PBS business models: Where does the content come from? Who provides financial support? What kinds of partnerships are involved?

- Propose rules of ethical practice for publishing or posting graphic photographs and for altering photographs.

- Propose rules of ethical practice for obtaining and reporting news and "reality" entertainment stories.

- Discuss the case for and against strict separation of information and advertising functions of media.

Student Website

www.mhhe.com/cls

Internet References

The Electronic Journalist
> www.spj.org

Federal Communications Commission (FCC)
> www.fcc.gov

Poynter Online: Research Center
> www.poynter.org

World Intellectual Property Organization (WIPO)
> www.wipo.org

Ethics Matters
> www.commfaculty.fullerton.edu/lester/writings/nppa.html

Photo Ethics
> www.sree.net/teaching/photoethics.html

Media Ethics Case Studies
> www.highered.mcgraw-hill.com/sites/007288259x/student_view0/case_studies.html

The freedom of speech and of the press are regarded as fundamental American rights, protected under the U.S. Constitution. These freedoms, however, are not without restrictions. The media are held accountable to legal and regulatory authorities whose involvement reflects a belief that the public sometimes requires protection.

Regulatory agencies, such as the Federal Communications Commission (FCC), exert influence over media access and content through their power to grant, regulate, and revoke licenses to operate. Ownership regulations have traditionally centered on radio and television because of the historically limited number of broadcast bands available in any community (called spectrum scarcity). The courts exert influence over media practice through hearing cases of alleged violation of legal principles such as the protection from libel and the right to privacy. Antitrust law has been summoned in attempts to break up media monopolies. Copyright laws protect an author's right to control distribution of her or his "intellectual property." Shield laws grant reporters the right to promise informants confidentiality. The courts have heard cases based on product liability law, in which plaintiffs have—sometimes successfully and sometimes not—sued media companies for harmful acts attributed to a perpetrator's exposure to violent media content. The Federal Trade Commission (FTC) and the U.S. Food and Drug Administration (FDA) have regulatory controls that affect advertising.

The first four articles in this section contribute differing perspectives on media business practice and access—the "players" of the unit's title. "What's a Fair Share in the Age of Google?" describes tension regarding application of fair use and copyright law to the Internet, noting "there is a growing sense among the 'legacy' media, at least, that Google facilitates a corrosive move away from paying content providers for their work." "Economic and Business Dimensions: Is the Internet a Maturing Market?" draws on product life cycle theory and dominant design theory to position the Internet in relation to appropriateness of regulation. "Ideastream: *The New* 'Public Media'" lends insight to the Public Broadcast System (PBS), a nonprofit public television service funded largely by the Corporation for Public Broadcasting.

Beyond the reach of legal and regulatory sanction, there is a wide grey zone between an actionable offense and an error in judgment. For example, while legal precedence makes it difficult for public figures to prevail in either libel or invasion-of-privacy cases, it is not necessarily right to print information that might be hurtful to them. Nor is it necessarily wrong to do so. Sometimes a "good business decision" from one player's perspective impedes another's success. Sometimes being "truthful" is insensitive.

U.S. Air Force/Tech. Sgt. James L. Harper Jr.

Sometimes being "interesting" means being exploitive. Some media organizations seem to have a greater concern for ethical policy than do others; however, even with the best intentions, drawing the line is not always simple.

The remaining articles in this unit raise questions of ethical practice. "Too Graphic," "Carnage.com," and "Distorted Picture" address ethical questions regarding photographs. "Too Graphic" is about news photos covering the January 2010 earthquake that devastated the island nation of Haiti. "Carnage.com" is about online posting of graphic images of war. "Distorted Pictures" addresses the ethics of altering photographs. Technology such as Photoshop makes it easy to edit photos, and often photo editing is done for aesthetic reasons rather than with intent to deceive. What are the limits of acceptable practice?

"The Quality-Control Quandary" discusses immediacy versus accuracy as traditional journalists struggle with acceptable expectations for proofreading and fact-checking prior to online posting. "What Would You Do?" ponders the ethics of investigative experimenters, who "step out of their customary role as observers and play with reality to see what will happen." "The Lives of Others" is about gatekeeping in the context of reality shows such as *America's Most Wanted.* "A Porous Wall" addresses the traditional boundary between news and advertising copy in newspapers, and how newspapers come to terms with changing rules as they fight to sustain revenue.

What rules of practice should be applied in balancing the public's right to know against potential effects on individuals and society at large? Which great photograph shouldn't run? Which facts shouldn't be printed? Who owns media channels and makes these decisions? Is it ethical for journalists to cover stories on issues about which they have strong personal views, or does such practice compromise objectivity? Is it fair to become a "friend" to win trust, then write a story that is not flattering or does not support the source's views or actions? Should the paparazzi be held legally responsible for causing harm to those they stalk, or should that responsibility be borne by consumers who buy their products? What about the well-intentioned story that attempts to right a social wrong, but hurts people in the process?

These are not easy questions, and they do not have easy answers. Media in the United States are grounded in a legacy of fiercely protected First Amendment rights and shaped by a code for conducting business with a strong sense of moral obligation to society. But no laws or codes of conduct can prescribe an appropriate behavior for every possible situation. When people tell us something in face-to-face communication, we are often quick to "consider the source" to evaluate the message. Media-literate consumers do the same in evaluating media messages.

What's a Fair Share in the Age of Google?

How to Think about News in the Link Economy

Peter Osnos

The buzz inside Google is overwhelmingly positive about what the company does and how we will all benefit from the results—including the embattled denizens of newspapers and magazines who increasingly see Google as an enabler of their demise. Barely a decade ago, Google received its first $25 million investment, based on search technology developed by Sergey Brin and Larry Page, the company's co-founders. By the time it went public just five years later, "Google" was a verb. Today it is the dominant force in what has turned out to be the central organizing principle of the Internet's impact on our lives: the search function and the accompanying links, keywords, and advertising that make sense and commerce out of the vast universe of information and entertainment on the Web. Google is as important today as were Microsoft, IBM, and the original AT&T, linchpins of our culture and economy, in the development of modern computation and communications.

By contrast, the great twentieth-century print companies, such as Time Inc., Tribune, and The New York Times Company, are in a battle for survival, or at least reinvention, against considerable odds. Google has become a kind of metaphor for the link economy and the Internet's immense power to organize content. Yet as the global leader among Web-based enterprises, it has also become a subject of debate and controversy, even though its sense of itself is still as benign as the playful tenor of its Manhatttan offices, where the fittings include scooters for zipping around the halls and a lavish free cafeteria.

At lunch there, I was surrounded by an animated crowd that included Brin, Google's thirty-six-year-old co-founder, wearing jeans, a sweater, and a demeanor indistinguishable from the rest of his eager young crew. Google maintains that it is actively working to make journalism and literature truly democratic and, functionally, easier to do. Google's "Office of Content Partnerships" sent me a list of "free tools journalists could use today for nearly every aspect of their work," including Blogger, a platform for publishing online; Google Analytics, for measuring Web traffic; Google website Optimizer; and other tools. The publishers of newspapers, magazines, and books, recognize that Google and the link-referral service it represents have become inextricable from their audiences' lives, and indispensable to reaching that audience in large numbers.

And yet there is a growing sense among the "legacy" media, at least, that Google facilitates a corrosive move away from paying content providers for their work. Proceeds go instead to those who sell advertising and other services while aggregating and/or lifting material they did not create. It is true that the content providers have submitted to the link economy of their own accord. Still, in a piece last winter, I wrote that the notion that "information wants to be free" is absurd when the referral mechanism makes a fortune and the creators get scraps. That position was excoriated by some bloggers, including one who, in a quote cited on The New York Times's Opinionator blog, called it "sheer idiocy."

Maybe. But only two months later, the Associated Press (clearly acting on behalf of the news organizations that own it) made a similar point and initiated a process that could end in lawsuits. Addressing the Newspaper Association of America, the chairman of the AP's board of directors, William Dean Singleton, CEO of MediaNews, said: "We can no longer stand by and watch others walk off with our work under misguided legal theories."

The full quote from which "information wants to be free" was lifted, by the way, is more ambiguous and complicated than that widely-quoted excerpt. The line comes from the futurist Stewart Brand, who first said it at a programmer's convention in 1984 and elaborated in his book, *The Media Lab: Inventing the Future at MIT,* in 1987, where he wrote:

Information Wants To Be Free. Information also wants to be expensive. Information wants to be free because it has become so cheap to distribute, copy, and recombine—too cheap to meter. It wants to be expensive because it can be immeasurably valuable to the recipient. That tension will not go away. It leads to endless wrenching debate about price, copyright, 'intellectual property,' the moral rightness of casual distribution, because each round of new devices makes the tension worse, not better.

Brand leaves out another factor—that valuable information is expensive to produce. But two decades later, the battles he foresaw are fully engaged.

An ecosystem in which all stakeholders in the content economy have a fair share. That is one media executive's succinct summary of what is necessary to redress the growing imbalance of power and resources between traditional content creators and those who provide links to or aggregate that material. But the effort to find that formula is complicated because it involves technologies upgrading at warp speed, sweeping changes in popular habits, collapsing and emerging business models, and one of the basic pillars of our democracy—what we have always called a free press.

As this century began, newspapers, especially those in metro areas with dominant positions, were reporting profits of 20, 30, and even 40 percent. *The New York Times* was selling over a billion dollars a year in advertising and *Time* magazine held its seventy-fifth-anniversary gala celebration at Radio City Music Hall, which had been specially redone for the occasion. Fortunes disappeared in the tech bust of 2000–01, which seemed to underscore the fact that Internet-based commerce was in its formative stages. The news products on the Web—CompuServe, Prodigy, and America Online—seemed, on the whole, complementary to newspapers and magazines rather than competitive against them.

Yet the unlimited expanse that the Internet provides and the amazing capacity of Google (and Yahoo and MSN, etc.) to search it, soon began to change everything. Vending services like eBay and Craigslist flourished; sensations like MySpace and YouTube, where users provide the content, were born at the intersection of creativity and engineering; audiences were suddenly huge for essentially brand-new Web news providers online, such as MSNBC and CNN. Sites like The Drudge Report showed the potential of aggregation and, later, The Huffington Post showed the potential for garnering large crowds partly by recycling material created elsewhere.

Significantly, most of the established news organizations reached the same conclusion about how to take advantage of what was happening on the Web. They went for the model that had supported network television for decades—mass audiences attracted by free access that would justify high advertising rates. Virtually overnight, Google et al were delivering hundreds of millions of readers to media companies which, in turn, believed they could monetize those visitors.

This approach contrasted with the one adopted in the 1980s by the emerging cable systems for television. Those companies negotiated subscription fees with the providers of their most popular programming, such as ESPN and dozens of other channels, including some that carried news. (The average cable subscriber, for example, pays 77 cents per month for Fox News, whether they watch it or not.) Most cable networks also have copious advertising, from inexpensive pitches for local establishments to national campaigns. This flow of subscription revenues, combined with advertising, made cable programming a lucrative business—which, ironically, resembles the way newspapers and magazines operated until they unilaterally decided they were better off giving content away. (There are differences, of course, especially since barriers to a cable system are high, while barriers to launching on the Web are low, even though moguls like Barry Diller at The Daily Beast and others have found themselves investing real money there to get started.)

As the scale of the global economic implosion became clear, accelerating negative trends in circulation and advertising already under way, it became increasingly obvious that the free-content model was not working. News audiences were huge. On September 29, 2008, the day the Bush administration's first bailout proposal was voted down by the House of Representatives and the Dow fell almost eight hundred points, nytimes.com had 10 million visitors and 42.7 million page views. But revenues for The New York Times Company were disappearing so fast that this respected gatherer of news had to beg and borrow just to meet its debt obligations and maintain its news operation while also sustaining morale for the myriad innovations necessary to stay extant. This spring it threatened to shut down *The Boston Globe,* another financially sick newspaper with healthy traffic on its website. Unless new ways of attracting and sharing revenue are devised with the same breathtaking speed with which they have disappeared, the gathering of news by reputable, experienced institutions that are cornerstones of their community and the nation will be irreversibly damaged.

Print journalism bought into the free-news online model. Still, it is hardly surprising that the winners in the transformation of news dissemination, the distributors and aggregators, would become the focus of grievances by those they have trounced, willfully or not. So what is to be done to manage the consequences of this inexorable transformation of news delivery? If there is a simple, all-encompassing answer to that question, I did not find it in discussions with practitioners and pundits on all sides of the problem. But in the haze, I did find a tripartite framework for understanding the major aspects of the issue—let's call them the doctrines of Fair Conduct, Fair Use, and Fair Compensation.

Fair Conduct

On Saturday afternoon, February 7, 2009, SI.com, the website of *Sports Illustrated,* broke a huge story: Alex Rodriguez, the mega-rich Yankees star, had taken performance-enhancing drugs while playing for the Texas Rangers. *Sports Illustrated* released the story on its website rather than in the magazine, according to the editors involved, in an effort to enhance SI.com's standing as a destination for fans increasingly conditioned to getting sports news online. Within hours the story was everywhere, but if you went through Google to find it, what you likely got instead were the pickups that appeared elsewhere, summaries or even rewrites, with attribution. Most galling was that The Huffington Post's use of an Associated Press version of *SI*'s report was initially tops on Google, which meant that it, and not SI.com, tended to be the place readers clicking through to get the gist of the breaking scandal would land.

Traffic on SI.com did go up on that Saturday and for days thereafter, but not nearly as much as the editors had projected.

As long as the value of advertising on the Web is measured by the number of visitors a site receives, driving those numbers is critical, and therein lies the dilemma. Why did The Huffington Post come up ahead of SI.com? Because, even Google insiders concede, Huffington is effective at implementing search optimization techniques, which means that its manipulation of keywords, search terms, and the dynamics of Web protocol give it an advantage over others scrambling to be the place readers are sent by search engines. What angered the people at *Sports Illustrated* and Time Inc. is that Google, acting as traffic conductor, seemed unmoved by their grievance over what had happened to their ownership of the story. An *SI* editor quoted to me Time Inc's editor-in-chief, John Huey, noting crisply that, "talking to Google is like trying to talk to a television."

The rules of the road for distributing traffic on the Internet need to include recognition, in simple terms, of who got the story. The algorithm needs human help; otherwise, valuable traffic goes to sites that didn't pay to create the content.

Fair Use

This has to do with how content is gathered, displayed, and monetized by aggregators, not how it is found and distributed. Fair use is a technical term for the standards one must meet in order to use copyrighted material without the permission of rights holders, as in excerpts, snippets, or reviews, and it turns out to be far more flexible than I long had thought. U.S. copyright law sets four main factors to consider in determining what is fair use: whether the quotation of the material is for commercial gain, the nature and scale of the work, the amount being used in relation to the whole, and the impact on the value of the material by its secondary use.

The definition of fair use was central in the lengthy negotiations among book publishers, the Authors Guild, and Google to settle litigation over Google's intention to digitize copyrighted books for search and distribution without paying for them. At the outset, in 2006, Google apparently believed that releasing only "snippets" of the books meant it would prevail in a court test. The publishers and authors argued that once Google had unrestricted access to the content, it would inevitably be widely used in full or large part.

Ultimately, the sides decided not to force the matter to resolution. Instead, in October 2008, Google agreed to pay $125 million to the plaintiffs and to establish a system to pay copyright holder, share advertising revenues that may result, and build a registry for all books that are available.

The book agreement—actually the settlement of several lawsuits—is nearly 150 pages, plus attachments, of excruciatingly complex detail. Debate over the terms ever since they were announced has been fierce and the court has already postponed final comments from interested parties until October 7. He will then look at the criticisms put forward by, among others, the Harvard librarian and lawyers funded by Microsoft who contend that Google is gaining what amounts to a monopoly in the digital book arena. Then, the judge will determine whether to approve the agreement as is, or send it back for further nego-

tiations to satisfy the objections of its critics. He cannot amend the terms himself.

How the logic of publisher-author-Google pact applies to the news business is not clear—except that Google has acknowledged that the right to scan and distribute information has value, which can be shared with the originators of that content. Google's licensing agreement with the AP and other wire services—in which it publishes some AP content on its own servers rather than merely linking to it—may be another illustration of the same idea: pay to play.

But what of the aggregation of links? The Google position is that a link with a sentence or two as a tease is fair use of the material, and the site that generated the content actually is a beneficiary of the traffic. With news, the argument becomes entangled in whether the aggregation enhances or detracts from the value of the original content, and also in determining what amounts to fair use when an aggregator surrounds those links with its own summaries, blogs, and other interpretative embellishments, as some aggregators do. The news organizations also argue that aggregators should pay for that right to aggregate when they sell advertising around the links and snippets.

It would take a mind-bending interpretation of fair use to work these issues out, especially if the case went to trial. Many news providers don't have the time that a case would take (years, probably). And Google, again, may not want to force a final determination of the matter, as in the books case. As the controversy over Google's role in news intensified in the spring, executives from The New York Times Company, The Washington Post Company, and presumably others, met with Google in search of formulas that might balance their respective interests. Every one involved has signed nondisclosure agreements. If progress has been made in these discussions, it has not become public.

Fair Compensation

All of this still leaves the considerable question of monetizing the reading of material on the free-to-access sites that newspapers and magazines offer, now that it seems that online advertising alone will not be enough to support those operations. There are many ideas around for micropayments or subscriptions, memberships or paid sections within a free site, out of which may come a viable business solution or solutions. Based on my own reporting, the answer could be in some combination of individual payments or cable and telephone fees. Americans routinely pay telecom providers (Verizon, Optimum, and AT&T are the ones in my house) to deliver information and entertainment by television, computer, and wireless devices. The goal would be to extend those payments to the originators of news content. Google, it seems to me, might serve as a kind of meter, helping determine what percentage should go to the content originators. Complicated? Yes, but that is the kind of challenge that computers and the engineers who master them are meant to meet.

One of the best statements on this subject came from Jonathan Rosenberg, president for product management at Google, who wrote on a company blog, "We need to make it easier for the experts, journalists, and editors that we actually trust to publish their work under an authorship model that is authenticated and extensible, and then to monetize it in a meaningful way." The book publishers and authors agreement with Google recognized that goal, acknowledging that all information is not equal and cannot be free and endure.

These fairness goals for the internet age are plainly arguable. However, this is not a debate that will end in a vote that determines the outcome by majority rule, which is why predicting where things will go next is so hard. Still, what is known, earnestly but correctly, as accountability journalism— news that orders and monitors the world—is indispensable, and paying for it is vital to society. We now know conclusively that digital delivery is going to be a (or perhaps the) main way people find out what is happening around them, so the burden of responsibility on those who frame the way news is presented is incalculable.

Google is in its adolescence as a company. Cycles in the digital era tend to be short, but Google and the enterprises and services it encompasses are at the pinnacle now. What the company will do with that power is unknown in large part because, like most big institutions, Google limits transparency and is defensive when it comes to criticism.

There is a message in history for Google's leaders: nothing in the realms of business, information, entertainment, or technology remains as it is. Brin and Page stand on the shoulders of Gates and Jobs who followed Watson, Sarnoff, and Paley, who came after Luce and Disney and succeeded Hearst, Edison, and Bell. The next breakthrough innovators are doubtless at work somewhere. Will they help meet society's fundamental demand for news that supports itself in a way that Google and the rest of the digital generation say they want to do, but have not yet done?

Google is an extraordinary company with a nonpareil record of creativity. What a wondrous thing it would be for newsgathering, in a time of mounting crisis, if Google turned out to be as much a source of solutions as it is a part of the problem.

Critical Thinking

1. Summarize Stewart Brand's well-known "Information wants to be free . . ." description in your own words. Is it accurate?

2. What are reasonable standards of "fair use" applied to information distributed on the internet?

PETER OSNOS, *CJR*'S vice-chairman, is the founder and editor-at-large of PublicAffairs Books and a senior fellow for media at The Century Foundation. His previous *CJR* piece was about the future of books.

Economic and Business Dimensions: Is the Internet a Maturing Market?

Christopher S. Yoo

If so, what does that imply?

Two concerns dominate the current debates over U.S. Internet policy. The first is the relatively low level of U.S. broadband adoption. Although the U.S. once ranked 4th among industrialized nations in the percentage of residents subscribing to broadband, it has currently slipped into 15th place. Concerns that the U.S. may be losing its leadership position in this key industry have spurred a series of governmental initiatives to address the problem. The stimulus package enacted during the initial days of the Obama administration dedicated $7.2 billion for new investments in broadband infrastructure. It also required the Federal Communications Commission to prepare a national broadband plan, which the agency released to much fanfare this past March. The plan is designed not just to ensure that broadband is available and affordable to all Americans, but also to devise ways to address the fact that a surprising number of households are not subscribing to broadband even when it is available.

The second is the debate over network neutrality. Network providers are experimenting with a variety of new business arrangements. Some are offering specialized services that guarantee higher levels of quality of service to those willing to pay for it. Others are entering into strategic partnerships that allocate more bandwidth to certain sources and applications.

Interestingly, management literature exists suggesting that both developments may simply reflect the ways the nature of competition and innovation can be expected to evolve as markets mature. If applicable to the Internet, this literature has the potential to provide new insights into how to craft broadband policy and what steps business managers might take to prepare for the future.

Demand-Side Considerations: Product Life Cycle Theory

The best-known theory of market maturation is known as the product life cycle. A central feature of every leading marketing textbook, product life cycle theory examines how the pattern of demand growth affects the nature of competition over time. Empirical research has confirmed that many, if not most, markets follow the pattern predicted by product life cycle theory.

The predominant version posits that new product markets pass through four distinct stages shown in the product life cycle. During the introduction stage, the product's novelty dictates that sales are small and grow relatively slowly. If a market for the new product develops, this initial stage gives way to the growth stage, during which sales grow rapidly. Over time, market saturation causes the product to enter the maturity stage, during which sales growth flattens. Eventually, the product enters the decline stage, as technologically superior substitutes emerge. The nature of competition changes as the market advances from one stage to the next.

Internet usage over the last two decades fits comfortably into this pattern. During the introduction stage of the broadband Internet during the mid-to-late 1990s firms focused on inducing early adopters to try the product, as the theory predicts. Early adopters tend to be technologically sophisticated, risk tolerant, and price insensitive, which describes the typical Internet user circa 15 years ago. This focus in turn caused firms to emphasize cutting-edge technological features and to deemphasize product quality and price, once again, as theory predicts.

As the market transitioned into the growth phase, firms began to target the mass market and to compete to attract new customers who are not yet being served. Price and quality took on greater importance. In order to keep production processes simple and to make the product easy for customers to understand, firms typically offered a single product designed to appeal to the broadest possible audience.

After enjoying an extended period of rapid growth, there are some indications that the market is on the cusp of entering the maturity phase. U.S. Internet penetration has leveled off at approximately 75 percent. When one focuses solely on broadband, data collected by the FCC suggests that the growth curve has passed the infection point making the transition from growth to maturity. As the market enters the maturity phase, revenue growth no longer depends on attracting customers who are not yet in the market. Instead, firms focus on finding ways to deliver greater value to customers who are already in the market.

According to this theory, there is nothing surprising about the prevalence of offering a more complex array of services and price points. These firms are trying to increase revenue in their primary market and set themselves up to offer new services that generate more revenue. That also explains why industry leaders such as Yahoo, Google, Apple, and Microsoft are becoming more aggressive about invading territory traditionally controlled by other leading firms. It is a natural outgrowth of maturity and the natural increase in rivalry that results when firms compete in a market that is no longer growing as fast as it once did.

Supply-Side Considerations: Dominant Design Theory

A parallel line of research in this framework explores the supply-side of market maturation. Called dominant design theory, it posits that when a technological breakthrough first occurs, uncertainty fosters lack of product standardization, which provides little incentive to invest in advanced production processes. At some point the basic product features and technological characteristics coalesce into a dominant design. Innovation becomes less driven by trial and error and instead becomes more systematic and incremental. Other scholars have extended this analysis, suggesting that technological guideposts or paradigms emerge that direct research along particular avenues or trajectories. These technological trajectories frame the way each field determines which problems are worth solving and which technological solutions are likely to be the most promising. This impetus toward certain trajectories becomes more pronounced if a technology is embedded in a web of interdependent technological processes. The presence of such a design hierarchy establishes a technical agenda that channels subsequent innovation along particular lines. It also obstructs innovations that are inconsistent with the existing architecture and can delay or prevent new architectures from evolving.

What does that have to do with the Internet? A growing number of technologists have noted the core architecture for the Internet, built around TCP/IP and its many extensions, is several decades old. They suggest the new demands being placed on the network are creating the need for fundamentally different design architecture. And as this theory would predict, they are finding that the standardization on a certain approach combined with the interconnected nature of the technologies comprising the architecture is limiting the Internet's ability to evolve to meet these new demands.

Significance for Internet Policy and Business Strategies

The implications are myriad. The transformation of the Internet from an experimental testbed into a mass-market platform has made major architectural change more difficult, just as design hierarchy theory would predict. The flattening of revenue growth inevitably gives network providers incentive to experiment with increasingly specialized equipment, both to

lower costs and to offer services targeted at particular subgroups of customers, just as product life cycle theory would predict. The desire to provide greater value to customers is creating greater interest in facilitating content providers' long-standing interest in monetizing content streams. At the same time, market maturation is causing firms to place greater emphasis on capturing a bigger fraction of the dollars that are available.

This theory also suggests that policymakers should be careful not to lock the Internet into any particular architecture or to reflexively regard deviations from the status quo as inherently anticompetitive. Such measures would reinforce the obstacles to architectural innovation that already exist. Instead, they should focus on creating regulatory structures that preserve industry participants' freedom to experiment with new solutions and to adapt to changing market conditions. Any other approach risks precluding the industry from following its natural evolutionary path and rendering the obstacles to architectural innovation that already exist all but insuperable.

Applying market maturation theory to the Internet comes with a number of limitations. Although the pattern of sales growth predicted by product life cycle theory is the most common, empirical research indicates that other patterns exist as well, which leads some to question the theory's generality. Others condemn these theories as self-fulfilling prophecies, as their widespread acceptance leads firms to manage their products in ways that cause these patterns to come true. Moreover, while key turning points are easy to identify in retrospect, they have proven quite challenging to anticipate far in advance.

Applying market maturation theory to the Internet comes with a number of limitations.

Even if it is not always possible to anticipate precisely how the nature of competition and innovation will change, that both will change over time is a given. The real question is not if the nature of competition and innovation will change, but rather how and when. Business managers and IT professionals must not take for granted that the competitive dynamics and the technology underlying the industry today will still be in place tomorrow. Instead, they should look for indications that the market may be reaching saturation and plan for how their strategy and those of their customers and competitors are likely to change as these phase transformations occur.

The real question is not if the nature of competition and innovation will change, but rather how and when.

Critical Thinking

1. What role should government play in regulating the Internet?

2. Is it worth it for you to pay more for television, magazines, newspapers, radio, and/or the Internet with fewer or no advertising messages? Why or why not?

CHRISTOPHER S. YOO (csyoo@law.upenn.edu) is Professor of Law, Communication, and Engineering and Director of the Center for Technology, Innovation, and Competition at the University of Pennsylvania. For a more extensive presentation of these ideas, see "Product Life Cycle Theory and the Maturation of the Internet," *Northwestern University Law Review*, 104:2 (forthcoming 2010).

From *Communications of the ACM*, vol. 53, no. 8, August 2010, pp. 24–26. Copyright © 2010 by Christopher S. Yoo. Reprinted by permission.

Ideastream: *The New* "Public Media"

In Cleveland, a partnership between a public radio station and public television station may be one model for the future of American public media.

M. J. ZUCKERMAN

A short walk from the Rock and Roll Hall of Fame and not far from "The Jake," home of the Cleveland Indians, there's a curious 95-year-old seven-story building—originally a fashionable furniture showroom—which, recently renovated, is the home of ideastream, a re-invention of public broadcasting that is generating a digital pulse of media excitement in the surrounding communities while, nationally, attracting curiosity and some downright envious stares.

An engagingly open structure, with more than 80 feet of windows on the avenue enticing passersby to peer in on live broadcast operations and dance studio rehearsals, the building is the physical manifestation of an elegantly simple concept. This is the vision of two media veterans who placed the mission ahead of all other interests to create an organization whose work is rippling outward into the education community, rejuvenating real estate development, bringing at least a thousand jobs to downtown, increasing public access to government and the arts, providing a center for performing artists to train and exchange ideas, giving rise to a hip tech neighborhood and convening public debate about American ideals.

And those are just the bonuses, the add-on benefits. Originally, when this all began about 10 years ago, the goal was to define a sustaining purpose for public broadcasting in Cleveland. The underlying concept was to merge the resources of public television and public radio. And then things kept percolating. By most accounts, ideastream has not only succeeded in defining a sustaining purpose for public broadcasting in Cleveland, but also demonstrated enduring potential as a hybrid: public media.

Along the way, ideastream's founders struck upon what more than a few leaders in the industry see as one of the most robust models for the future: A multiple media public service organization operating on broadband and built on two critical principles: 1) a commitment to the mission of "strengthening our communities," which is realized by 2) placing the values of partnership ahead of any desire for control.

If this sounds simple, it isn't. Even if you are deeply versed in the pervasive challenges facing public radio and public television, there is likely to be an "Aha!" moment as you come to understand that Jerry Wareham and Kit Jensen—respectively, the CEO and COO of ideastream—have established a *raison d'etre* for public television and public radio that transcends traditional notions of broadcast and simultaneously offers a model that could, in time, remedy what some have called "the flawed business model" of public broadcasting.

Wareham, formerly CEO of television station WVIZ, acknowledges that his "midwestern modesty" is an essential asset, keeping ideastream's partnerships free of control issues and, yet, it is also a quality that innately limits his ability to openly tout the accomplishments he has realized in concert with Jensen. He is the genial host and deal maker, she is the firewall and executor of planning.

Jensen, the former CEO at radio station WCPN, is a serious woman who chooses her words carefully and whose frontier, can-do spirit (she spent nearly 20 years in Alaska, building the state's first National Public Radio station, which for years broadcast the only statewide news content) has been instrumental in shaping ideastream. Jensen recalls arriving in Alaska in 1968 as a period ripe with potential, a time when the federal government was anxious to see Alaska's social, cultural and economic infrastructure developed in support of the oil pipeline to Prudhoe Bay. But she says it took "intentionality" to make the government's interests dovetail with the community's need for honest, broadcast information.

"I had this incredible opportunity to be there and be part of it, so my background is predisposed to possibilities and a little broader view of what broadcast could be and mean to a community," she says. "It was an exciting, and heady time."

She speaks similarly of her work with Wareham in creating ideastream and later overseeing the renovations of the building at 1375 Euclid Avenue, now known as the Idea Center. Though Jensen sees the development of ideastream as mostly the product of "really hard work," she also says, "I think a lot of it is making your own luck. Seeing things as they might be and asking: Why not? I think it's a matter of will, willing it to be and using every asset you can find to bring it about."

Initially, what Wareham and Jensen sought to accomplish, the merger of WVIZ and WCPN, was by itself no small management task. While each organization had outgrown its facilities and recognized the benefits of convergence, both in terms of technology and reducing costs through shared infrastructure and operations, they faced an uphill struggle in making their boards and staffs understand the value of surrendering separate, time-tested identities as traditional programmers and broadcasters to become a single, multiple-media public service organization.

And, as they began to wrap their minds around the challenges inherent in such a merger, the tougher, bedrock issues emerged: lingering 20th century questions facing public broadcasting, made more critical by the digital era's costly rules of engagement:

- Is public television still relevant in an era when 90 percent of American households are wired to receive 500 television channels, which in many cases deliver the type of content formerly available only from the Public Broadcasting System (PBS)?
- How are PBS, NPR, their affiliates and sister organizations to produce competitive, quality programming when the business model for financing public broadcasting—dependence upon the whims of federal, corporate and philanthropic sponsors, supplemented by mind-numbing on-air fund drives— is showing signs of new structural defects and losses in audience?

The answer, in Cleveland, was to create a multiple-media center that is not only about more or better-targeted programming but also about becoming a resource for community interaction, providing a variety of traditional broadcast and extraordinary broadband-related services.

David Giovannoni, whose market analysis of public radio over the past 20 years is widely credited with shaping today's success at NPR, insists that it's a mistake to lump radio and television together. They are separate entities with their own strengths and failures. "There is no such thing as 'public broadcasting,'" he says. "There is public radio and there is public television, and then, arguably, there is something you could call public media."

From the consumer's perspective the merger is seamless. WCPN is still public radio and WVIZ is still public television. *Morning Edition* is there when folks awake and *All Things Considered* brings them home at night; *Sesame Street* inspires children's learning and *The NewsHour* informs adults' ideas. But when you talk to those who have worked with ideastream, they will tell you, again and again, that together, the two stations are doing much more than they could ever have done separately to serve their communities.

The media and technology here runs the gamut: obviously there is television and radio and, certainly, Internet, but also broadband delivering on-demand, digitally stored lesson plans, live accounts from the state legislature and the state supreme court, hi-tech classrooms to help educators learn cutting-edge software to engage their students and a truly stunning state-of-the-art theater adaptable for live performance and/or broadcast. They have done away with separate TV and radio staffs; there is no "newsroom." Instead, they have merged into a single "content staff," charged with finding new ways to embrace and engage various communities— defined with a broad brush as regions, ethnic groups, political interests, technologies, educators, health matters, families, children, religions, and so on—with a digital presence. That's how you compete and remain relevant in a 500-channel environment.

Think of ideastream as a digital community center or a virtual YMCA, seeking to draw together the resources of "heritage institutions" (museums, theaters, colleges, libraries, medical centers, government agencies, etc.) and make them digitally available on-demand to patrons, clients and students. For these and other services they develop, ideastream and its partners receive grants or are paid an operating fee by school districts, government agencies or philanthropies. This is still a not-for-profit organization, but one financed, sometimes directly, by the communities it serves. They call it a "sustainable service model." Skeptics have called it "pay to play."

Ideastream is certainly not the only PBS or NPR affiliate attempting these kinds of initiatives. Wareham and Jensen rattle off the call letters of many affiliates in cities large and small that have inspired, influenced and informed ideastream's efforts. Many of the 355 PBS and 860 NPR stations are examining the benefits of mergers or partnerships, experimenting with new media, working with new ways to produce and distribute content, and becoming more interactive with their communities. Yet ideastream, for now, seems to be ahead of the crowd.

"What Jerry and Kit are doing in Cleveland may well be the model for what other stations should be doing," says David Liroff, a widely recognized visionary of public media. "And they are not alone in this. They just have focused more clearly as a locus and catalyst and convener of civic discussion. And what is truly radical about them is that they mark such a departure from the traditional expectations of what the traditional public television and public radio model should be."

Origins of Public Broadcasting

There seems little doubt that the original lofty goals set out for public broadcasting remain deeply woven into the character of the organization and the aspirations of its leaders. "On a sustaining basis no one is in the space that we're in," says Paula Kerger, President of the Public Broadcasting System.

"At the end of the day, the commercial marketplace simply is not fulfilling what public television originally set out to do, which was to use the power of media to entertain, educate and inspire. They [cable] sometimes entertain pretty well but they don't always hit that educate and inspire part."

While several of the 500 channels—"the vast wasteland" as former FCC Commissioner Newton Minow famously labeled television in 1961—have sought to produce high-minded programming, it rarely survives Wall Street's demands for ever-increasing profits, which require large and loyal audiences, typically built on a formulaic "lowest common denominator" of public interests. Thus, A&E has lowered its once PBS-like standards and now provides prime-time staples such as *CSI Miami* while Bravo touts its lineup as: "Fashion, Comedy, Celebrity and Real Estate."

Although commercial attempts at playing in the PBS marketplace have frequently fallen short, PBS itself, while true to its calling, struggles to maintain its viewership, with the commensurate loss of pledges those viewers provide. Add to that erosion in the financial support it previously enjoyed from business, foundations, governments and universities.

The *New York Times* wasn't the first to question PBS' future this past February, when it wrote a biting analysis beneath the headline "Is PBS Still Necessary?" According to the article, "Lately, the audience for public TV has been shrinking faster than the audience for commercial networks. The average PBS show on prime time now scores about a 1.4 Nielsen rating, or roughly what the wrestling show 'Friday Night Smackdown' gets." Acknowledging the occasional "huge splash" from a Ken Burns special, the *Times* uses the term "mustiness" to describe PBS's prime-time lineup, noting, "*The Newshour, Nova, Nature, Masterpiece* [Theatre] are into their third or fourth decade, and they look it."

While PBS viewership has slipped from 5.1 million members in 1990 to 3.7 million in 2005, public radio scored dramatic gains in weekly audience, up from about 2 million in 1980 to nearly 30 million today. But NPR, too, is realizing significant losses, according to Giovannoni, whose market research is the gold standard of public radio.

There was a 6 percent decline in listeners to *All Things Considered* and *Morning Edition* between 2004 and 2005, Giovannoni's research found. His most recent report, *Audience 2010,* which "set out to identify what is causing public radio's loss of momentum" found that "our listeners are still listening to radio [but] increasingly not listening to us."

Losses in popularity translate into lost revenues. While listeners and viewers who remain loyal have been willing to pay more in annual subscriptions or membership fees—on the PBS side, an average of $55.04 per subscriber in 1990 rose to $99.84 in 2005—the loss in market share has taken its toll as corporate sponsors follow the audience. And because the federal side of the ledger is light in a good year, the bulk of funding comes from subscribers, corporate sponsors, foundations and state and local government, with the balance coming from colleges, universities, auctions and other activities. For 2005, the last year for which the Corporation for Public Broadcasting (CPB) has reported data, statistics reflect a one-year loss of 6.7 percent in business sponsorships, a 7.1 percent decrease in foundation support, a 3.9 percent cut by states, a 3.7 percent loss in federal grants and contracts, and a meager 0.3 percent rise in subscriber support.

Adding to the difficulty, each year since taking office, the Bush administration has sought to slash spending for public broadcasting operations, most recently seeking a $200 million slice of the $400 million Congress approved for the FY2009 budget. Each year the faithful have rallied, successfully preserving the 10-to-20 percent federal share of the PBS and NPR budgets.

This financial dilemma is as old as public radio and public broadcasting in the U.S.. In January 1967, the landmark Carnegie Commission on Educational Television, created by Carnegie Corporation of New York, completed a two-year study, providing the blueprint for creating public television—to which Congress added, over some objections, public radio—and enacted the Public Broadcasting Act of 1967, creating CPB as the oversight mechanism which, in turn, created PBS in 1969, and NPR in 1970, as the national content producers and parent organizations for stations throughout the nation. Congress rejected the Carnegie Commission's proposal for a 2-to-5 percent excise tax on the sale of television sets—modeled on the British system for funding the BBC—to guarantee the unfettered, financial health of public broadcasting.

Ten years later, a second Carnegie Commission, often called Carnegie II, issued *A Public Trust: The Report of the Carnegie Commission on the Future of Public Broadcasting,* which sought, once again, to secure financial independence for media technology and a more forward looking purpose for public broadcasting.

Carnegie II recognized that new technologies were affecting the media and reinforcing the deeper questions, raised by visionaries such as Marshall McLuhan, regarding media's influence on society, cultural values and democracy. Said the report, "This institution [public broadcasting], singularly positioned within the public debate, the creative and journalistic communities, and a technological horizon of uncertain consequences, is an absolutely indispensable tool for our people and our democracy." Thus, Carnegie II sought to keep the door propped open to future technologies through a strong, independent financing mechanism, noting, "We conclude that it is unwise for us to attempt to chart the future course of public broadcasting as it continues to interact with new technologies. We are convinced, however, that it is essential for public broadcasting to have both the money and flexibility necessary to enable it to chart its own course as it responds to the future."

That idea, too, went nowhere. Not surprising, suggests Liroff, a 28-year veteran of WGBH in Boston and currently Senior Vice President, System Development and Media Strategy at CPB. He says, "It was, to paraphrase McLuhan, as though we were speeding into the future at 90 miles per hour with our eyes firmly fixed on the rearview mirror. The idea of public broadcasting pre-Internet, pre- any of these technologies, was going to be a manifestation of the broadcasting system they knew at the time, dominated, of course, by commercial broadcast." He continues, "This question of what is the role of public broadcasting in the media environment is as relevant today as it was back then except that the answers have to be very different. This is hardly the environment in which this system [of media distribution] was first envisioned."

Increasingly, there is appeal for public broadcasting to expand its traditional role, to grow their portfolios as ideastream has done in order "to provide new services in new, non-broadcast ways," explains Richard Somerset-Ward, an expert on public media and senior fellow at the Benton Foundation, which promotes digital media in communications. "This includes distributing other people's content as well as its own; to open up the possibility of new revenue streams and to become, in general, a community enabler, a go-to organization at the heart of the community, one whose identity is bound up in that of the community," he says.

Somerset-Ward and others argue that public broadcasting has followed a flawed trickle-up business model: local public broadcasting stations must raise funds which they pay to NPR or PBS to produce programming. This has created enormous challenges, primarily for television where production costs are huge and viewership is decaying.

"The problem with the PBS stations is that they've never been able to contribute enough for PBS to not be almost totally dependent upon sponsorships, which they have been unable to keep up," says Somerset-Ward. "What you need to do is to increase the amount of funding the stations put in and that means optimizing the health of the stations. That doesn't mean an entirely new business plan [for the stations], just augmenting the present one. And the way is open to do that because of digital and all that implies. And Cleveland is the best example of how that can be done."

However that requires an attitude adjustment on the part of broadcasters accustomed to an "I-produce, you-view" model, in which content is tightly control by producers and "pushed" to consumers, says Liroff.

Larry Grossman, the former PBS president, highly regarded as a visionary in public broadcasting, began talking in the 1980s about the need to create "a grand alliance" of "heritage institutions," bringing together public broadcasters, universities, libraries and museums. Today, Grossman remains committed to a top-down approach in which PBS and NPR lead and the stations follow. What is lacking, he says, "is a blueprint and anybody articulating the dream: what is the role of public broadcasting, what should it be going forward?"

Yet, Grossman's vision in the 1980s remains vital today. Explains Liroff, "What Grossman saw more clearly than the rest of us is that public broadcasters and universities and

libraries and all the rest are all in the same business and the old business model that makes them look so different is being compromised—in the best sense of that word—in terms of their separate identities by digital technologies, which they all share. So it is just as likely . . . that digital technologies allow these heritage institutions, among others, to begin to extend their services . . . on the Internet in ways, which at least in form, will be indistinguishable one from the other."

Or, put another way, Internet consumers tend to be agnostic about the sources of data; they don't necessarily know or care which museum or library provided the recording of, say, Robert Frost reading "The Road Not Taken"—just that they can access it. Add to that the current steep declines in the cost of digital storage and you have "extraordinary consequences for any individual's ability to call up what they want when they want it," says Liroff.

What all this means is that broadcasters and journalists, who have been trained by competition and regulators, most notably the FCC, to fiercely protect and keep tight reign over their turf, to serve as gatekeepers, must learn to loosen the controls, become more interactive and accepting of "pull" technologies.

But that raises an important question: if traditional broadcasters are expanding their roles to serve as content developers and data distributors on platforms other than broadcast, does the mean that five or ten years from now their primary function could be something other than delivering programming by radio and television?

That seems a distinct possibility, say many observers, including Liroff, Grossman and Somerset-Ward. Yet industry leaders, including Wareham, Kerger and others, are quick to disagree.

"Everyone is quick to write off traditional broadcasting, but it's been around a long time and survived all sorts of predictions of early demise," says Ken Stern, former CEO of NPR. "So I don't think that's going to change."

Stern resigned his post as CEO this March after only 18 months, reportedly in a dispute with his board over NPR's digital future, which he saw combining a strong video presence on the web with Public Radio's traditional radio journalism. "I absolutely agree that the audience is being fragmented and it's important for public broadcasters to meet the audience where it is, so things like podcasting and moving to multiple platforms is the reality," he says. "But the need is to meet the audience across many platforms and not to give up the broadcast platform."

Creating Ideastream

Wareham and Jensen are absolutely sure that they can't recall the first time they discussed merging WCPN and WVIZ. That's probably because they tried dating for a while before contemplating marriage—that is, the broadcast operations, not Wareham and Jensen.

The Idea Center

It was here, at 1375 Euclid Avenue, back in the 1950s, in the studios of WJW, that disc jockey Alan Freed coined the phrase "Rock & Roll." Well, Cleveland still rocks!

All the proof you need is a visit to The Idea Center, home of ideastream, where you will experience a symbiosis of community-based arts and media raised to the highest level of quality. For example: one afternoon last December, Alice Walker and Marsha Norman sat facing each other on the stage of the black box theatre that occupies a three-story space in the center of the building.

This was an event that served multiple purposes. Walker, author of *The Color Purple,* was in Cleveland to promote the Oprah Winfrey musical based on her book, due to open in the spring of 2008. Norman, author of the play *'night Mother',* wrote the libretto for the Winfrey musical.

Walker made a little news by saying this would be her final appearance on behalf of the book, the movie or the musical. But the real show was listening to these two sophisticated ladies light up a corner of downtown Cleveland.

Filling the 300-seat bleachers rising up two stories in front of the floor-level stage were college and high school students as well as several local arts dignitaries, who took turns lining up at the microphones to ask questions. Meanwhile, at a half-dozen schools throughout northeast Ohio, another hundred-plus students watched the event live via broadband and they, too, lined up for a chance to interact

with the two Pulitzer Prize-winning writers. Currently, ideastream is linked via broadband to 115 public schools and 190 private schools, reaching a potential audience of 500,000 students.

On any given day, the black box theater does double duty, serving primarily as a theater for the performing arts sponsored by the Playhouse Square Foundation and also as a live TV studio for WVIZ and PBS. So, on this occasion, the two-hour event was also taped for local broadcast in the spring, when *The Color Purple* is presented at one of the major theatrical stages at Playhouse Square and is being offered to PBS affiliates as one in a series of artist appearances at the Idea Center.

These presentations, and the resulting TV productions, are called "Master Moments," where famous performers speak candidly about their work. Some other recent visitors to the "Master Moments" stage include composer Marvin Hamlisch, actress Chita Rivera and composer/lyricist Adam Guettel.

Many of the student-questions Walker fielded related to fame—How has it changed her life? Does it make writing easier or more difficult?—and with each answer she seemed to become more succinct and focused until, towards the end of the two-hour session, she offered in reply a poem she said she wrote some time ago:

Expect nothing, Virgules Live frugally Virgules On surprise.

In 1997, the stations joined forces to do a series of stories on "urban sprawl," and despite a rough start it pointed the way towards greater cooperation. "It was a really miserable experience," says Wareham, laughing. "The computer systems didn't talk to one another. The radio people thought the TV people were shallow. The TV people thought the radio people were weird. But a funny thing happened. We started getting these phone calls from viewers and listeners: 'Didn't I see or hear something about how to get involved in my community?' And, in spite of ourselves, we had made an impact and that got the attention of our boards." They continued to look for joint projects and, with Wareham and Jensen in the lead, by the fall of 1999 the planning committees of the two boards were in meetings discussing merger.

While Cleveland's economy was and continues to be distressed, the financial motivations for merger related to increased efficiencies realized in staffing, marketing, fundraising and grant seeking. Both were also desperate to replace dilapidated facilities.

"But this did not start out with something being broken. Both broadcast stations were in good shape. Except for their physical location," says Susan Eagan, then with the Cleveland Foundation, which served as a neutral moderator to the discussions. "It was mostly Kit and Jerry looking out ahead and seeing a lot of unrealized opportunities . . . and knowing

that if public broadcasting was not repositioned and aligned with what was going on in the larger marketplace, at some point down the road there could be some significant issues."

Wareham and Jensen argued that the emerging reality, the shift in the marketplace, meant, "Access to programming through broadcast distribution is becoming relatively less valuable than content creation, packaging, marketing and control of intellectual property." In other words, having control of the media delivery system is no longer sufficient to remain a player in the community; content development is of greater importance.

While much of this may seem self-evident today, it wasn't all so clear in 1999 to members of the two boards. To make their case, Wareham and Jensen turned first to Chicago and then to Cinderella.

Network Chicago, a multiple media public service organization operated by Chicago's WTTW was a model very similar to what Wareham and Jensen wanted to create in Cleveland. A 1999 promotional video, which they brought to a meeting of the Cleveland boards, explains, "We can create alliances with cultural, educational and business institutions . . . We can leap beyond the television screen and carry our quality content to radio, print, and the Internet . . . [create] strategic alliances . . . driven by our values." (Unfortunately for WTTW, Network Chicago's business model relied heavily on advertising in a print publication, which did not succeed.)

But the "Aha!" moment in the negotiations, the inspiration that enabled people to understand how this worked, they say, came when Jensen posed the question, *What is Cinderella?* To illustrate the point, she passed around several props including a Disney DVD, an illustrated story book, a Cinderella Barbie, and a volume of the original French fairy tale. Which one of these various media forms is Cinderella? "The right answer was really intellectual property," she says. "We needed an object to illustrate that platforms do not define content, content just exists. Cinderella had presented itself in all these different media in all these periods of time. And now we were facing the need to reinvent how we present our stories. This really worked for people."

From that point forward, parties to the talks say, there was only one essential sticking point: who's in charge? And this provided a defining moment in ideastream's reinvention of public broadcasting.

"When it came to the CEO question it all fell apart because people had their loyalties," says Eagan. The WVIZ board pressed for Wareham; the radio side wanted Jensen. But what happened next was iconic in terms of the ideastream partnership model: Wareham and Jensen wrote a memo saying, if the boards agreed, they would resolve the leadership issue on their own. But until the discussions moved off this point neither of them would have anything further to do with the proposed merger. They took their egos off the table.

"That was a very, very critical moment," says Eagan. "And it set a standard that said, this is not about us, this is what the community is entrusting to us."

The boards bought it. Weeks later, on a Sunday, Wareham and Jensen met over coffee. Each made a long list of what they liked most and least about their jobs. They exchanged documents. They agreed he would be CEO and she COO. The same procedure was followed with other managers at the two stations.

Somerset-Ward and others credit this enduring, almost stubborn, spirit of cooperation as the primary reason for ideastream's success, stemming from the Wareham-Jensen leadership model. "They don't take credit for anything and that, of course, is one of the main reasons why it works," he says. "Everywhere else, public broadcasting stations that I know of, would leap at the opportunity to grab credit. Jerry and Kit understood from the beginning that you couldn't do that, not if you want to be a partner. That is why they have been successful."

On July 1, 2001 ideastream became a reality.

The Listening Project

Wareham is fond of noting how clearly the current mission and approach of ideastream mirrors a key statement of the 1967 Carnegie Commission report, which contends that the underlying purpose of public media is not about technology or distribution: "It is not the location of the studio or transmitter that is most relevant. Rather, what is critical is the degree to which those operating the facilities relate to those they seek to serve."

Toward that goal, Jensen created The Listening Project, which has informed ideastream's programming, content and partnerships since its inception. Every year since 2001, ideastream goes out into the communities it serves, drawing leaders and citizens into a discussion of what matters most to them, how they see their lives, what assets they see in their communities and what public services they see a need for. Ideastream was overwhelmed when nearly 10,000 people took part in 2001. Since then, the number has been held to a more manageable level—1,410 in 2007—who respond to on-air, in-print and online solicitations to fill out a questionnaire. There are also live town meeting discussions open to the public.

This is not the usual market research approach: what do you think of our product and how can we make you use it more? Instead, the key proposition is how to connect to communities in ways that are deemed useful by those in the communities.

Four standard questions are asked each year are: 1) What are the most important assets of the community? 2) What are the most important challenges? 3) Who strengthens those assets and challenges? 4) What could multimedia do to strengthen those assets and [address those] challenges?

What they have heard clearly is that citizens want public media to look into problems and then stay on the topic long enough to lead the way towards some resolution. That means, unlike the normal modus operandi of media, not merely shining a bright light on an issue. Such an approach, The Listening Project finds, only serves to increase public anxiety.

"What the community was really asking us to do was to do the partnership, but then hang in there and be consistent about addressing these challenges and assets," says Wareham. "They wanted us to create community connection and participation. They wanted us to facilitate the process of community members talking with one another." That has given rise to a community advisory board and two new programs, *Sound of Ideas* a daily radio show and *Ideas* a weekly television program, which extend the community dialogue.

In 2001, Doug Clifton, the editor of *The Cleveland Plain Dealer,* asked ideastream to join the newspaper in a project ideal for the new organization. Clifton wanted to do a series of stories, editorials, town meetings and panel discussions examining the departure from Cleveland and the surrounding area of Fortune 500 companies. Wareham and Jensen jumped at the opportunity.

During the next few years, the organizations shared resources and promoted one another's efforts in what was called "the Quiet Crisis," which rapidly became the shorthand by which everyone in the region referred to the economic downturn affecting northeastern Ohio. "It was an effort to document the depth of the decline, assess what the future might hold and look at some solutions," says Clifton. "Although the *Plain Dealer* penetrated the home market very deeply some people would turn to public radio and public TV and that was the audience we were looking for."

Both organizations saw the effort as a success. "The sum of it was greater than its individual parts because it brought together three of the serious institutions in the region who were speaking with one voice," Clifton says.

In addition to anecdotal evidence of success, ideastream can point to:

- Combined 2007 radio and television fund raising campaigns that brought in $1,999,653, up from $1,419,530 in FY 2006, $1,425,575 in FY 2005, $1,632,609 in FY 2004 and $1,490,434 in FY 2003.
- Weekly cumulative audience for the spring Arbitron ratings found WCPN audience increased 32 percent between 2001 and 2005. During the same period, the national audience increased 11.5 percent.
- Weekly cumulative audience for the February Nielsen ratings period found the WVIZ audience declined 6.25 percent between 2001 and 2005 compared with a 13.5 percent downturn regionally.
- In the past five years, public radio and public television stations throughout the U.S. have sought guidance from ideastream; they have taken their story on the road to public broadcast operations in at least nine states.

Partnerships: Inside ideastream
Playhouse Square Foundation Provides a Home

Among the partnerships fostered by ideastream, the most evident is The Idea Center, at 1375 Euclid Avenue, from which all else emanates.

One of Wareham's and Jensen's earliest ambitions for the WVIZ-WCPN merger was to combine their infrastructure operations and develop a new headquarters. After contemplating a number of locations and partnerships, they became enamored with a proposal from Art Falco, Executive Director of Cleveland's Playhouse Square Foundation, which, with 10,000 seats, is the second largest center for the performing arts in the U.S., after New York's Lincoln Center.

Over the past 20 years, Playhouse Square has invested $55 million to obtain and renovate almost one million square feet of commercial real estate in downtown Cleveland in an effort to restore the once-thriving theater district, says Falco. According to one economic impact study, the commercial and theatrical programs enabled by Playhouse Square generate $43 million a year for the local economy.

The building on Euclid Avenue was seedy, run down, and only about 10 percent occupied when the mortgage holder agreed to donate it to the foundation, which hoped to turn it

into auxiliary work space for its performing arts operations. "We needed to create an arts education space," says Falco. "We had these wonderful theaters but we didn't have classrooms and we didn't have a dance studio, we didn't have a . . . theater, we didn't have gallery space."

Knowing that ideastream was in the market, he approached Wareham and Jensen and after some design work the two organizations realized they could realize some big savings by sharing their most costly facility needs: Falco wanted a "black box theater" (unadorned performance space) and ideastream needed a second television studio, but neither needed to have access to it on a daily basis. "We knew that we could build a great education and arts center and they could built a great tech and broadcast facility, but we knew it wouldn't be as good as it would be if we did it together," says Falco.

By sharing their space needs, the two groups reduced their total footprint from 120,000 square feet down to 90,000, and saved $7 million. It also meant that a greater portion of the four upper floors would be available to rent, creating revenue flow to defray their annual operating costs. "It has turned out to be a building that not only served our purposes, but has been characterized as a 'cool' building, where other commercial tenants who have connections with technology and architecture and design want to be located," says Falco. "It's surpassed my expectations."

As has proven true with many of its partnerships, the ideastream-Playhouse Square partnership is a wondrous symbiosis. Their combined capital campaign exceeded its goal, bringing in $30 million. They began moving into the facility in fall of 2005 with the last wave in February 2006. The upper floors are 90 percent occupied, well ahead of schedule.

OneCommunity Provides Reach

The grand symbiotic relationship ideastream has embarked upon, which has drawn national attention—including a Harvard Business School study—and opened vast opportunities for Cleveland, is with OneCommunity.

OneCommunity—formerly OneCleveland—was the vision of Lev Gonick, who became CIO and Vice President, Information Services at Case Western Reserve University in 2001, just as ideastream came into being and the Cleveland community was coming to know about the Quiet Crisis. Essentially, what Gonick sought was to build a regional broadband network at relatively little cost to serve the educational, health and non-profit communities of northeast Ohio. What he didn't have in mind, until he was approached by Wareham, was someone to provide content to that network and, perhaps more importantly, someone with the community connections to bring together the nonprofit community in Cleveland in support of Gonick's vision.

Toward the end of the 20th century, an estimated $3 trillion-plus was sunk into the streets of the U.S. in the form of fiber optic cable in anticipation of the explosion in broadband digital service, which halted abruptly when the e-commerce bubble burst. Gonick understood that this fortune in so-called "dark fiber" (unused cable), was everywhere in the country. In 2003, Gonick convinced City Signal Corp. to donate several strands of dark fiber to his nonprofit organization, for which the corporation got a substantial tax write-off. In September of that year, OneCleveland was incorporated and Scot Rourke, a former venture capitalist and Cleveland native, became its first executive.

If Gonick is the visionary, Rourke is the master builder. Rourke's plan for the nonprofit was to expand the broadband connection well beyond the city of Cleveland. What he proposed was that the corporations donating some portion of their dark fiber would not only get a healthy tax write-off, but also, said Rourke, "We are going to build the market for you. We will expose the community to the value of [broadband], we'll do the missionary work and build a market demand for the rest of your fiber."

"Scot has a wonderful concept," says Wareham. "He refers to 'Liberating content held captive by various community institutions, universities, foundations, and nonprofit organizations.'" Adds Rourke: "It's not that they are trying to imprison it, it's that they don't know how to let it out."

Some of the programs enabled by the ideastream-OneCommunity partnership:

Distance Learning enables schools, which pay an annual fee, to have interactive access to live shows and instructional classes presented at the Idea Center.

Voices and Choices enables anyone interested in the economic issues of the region to log into a dedicated website, study the issues, make choices and contribute to an ongoing dialogue, including community town meetings.

One Classroom is the outgrowth of a $2 million grant from the Cleveland Clinic connecting 1,500 area schools to the OneCommunity network, making rich media content created by ideastream, including lesson plans and other educational content, available on-demand. In time, this is expected to include digitized content from the many museums and cultural institutions in the region.

Wireless Mesh Network is a work in progress, building on ideastream's FCC licenses to develop a citywide wi-fi network with OneCommunity, Case Western Reserve University, the city of Cleveland and area schools.

Rural Health Network, when completed, would create a broadband network for participating medical institutions in Northeastern Ohio to exchange medical data ranging from paper records and MRIs to televised medical exams.

Somerset-Ward says of ideastream and its partnerships: "They are becoming much more than just community broadcasters, they are becoming community enablers. And they are doing that by forming partnerships with community institutions. Jerry and ideastream are in a class of their own . . . But it's a model of what communities can do when institutions like schools, universities, and health authorities create partnerships."

Harsh Realities

Perhaps the toughest part of using ideastream as a model is broadband access. Rourke, however, insists that should not be a problem. Dark fiber exists throughout the nation and large telecommunication companies are anxious to build a market for broadband by getting the attention of consumers—and one way to do that is to donate a couple of strands of fiber to a local nonprofit, with the added benefit of a tax break. "We know we can repeat this pretty much anywhere in the United States by promising that we are going to create the market and we aren't going to touch the residential customer," says Rourke.

It's a tough challenge for people to cede control in terms of the traditional gatekeeper role played by broadcasters and journalists.

Some observers say that an equally tough challenge is finding people willing to cede control, both in terms of the traditional gatekeeper role played by broadcasters/journalists and a willingness to enter into partnerships in which the traditional objectivity of the broadcaster/journalist might be questioned. Other skeptics have challenged ideastream's partnerships with regional institutions that are sometimes subjects of media scrutiny, such as the Cleveland Clinic, the second-largest employer in the state, which has provided grants to OneCommunity and ideastream.

Unquestionably, partnerships can create the appearance of conflicts of interest for journalists whose stock in trade is perceived objectivity. But the same can be said with respect to advertisers: does The *New York Times,* for example, have a problem covering a scandal at General Motors because it accepts ads from GM?

David Molpus, a veteran reporter with NPR and Executive Editor at ideastream since March 2006, says that there are some legitimate issues to be addressed when working with another organization on content creation. "What are the rules of the game? We've started to work that out and codify it," he explains. "We obviously see that there is one level of cooperation with another news organization like the *Plain Dealer.* But then there are degrees of variation: What could you do with the university? What could you do with the city library? What could you do with other nonprofits? What could you do with a government agency?"

There was an early dust-up over a perceived conflict of interest, concerning a grant provided to ideastream to do stories about affordable housing by an organization that also provided affordable housing. "There was concern in the newsroom, at that time, that this organization was setting some agenda," says Mark Smukler, ideastream's Senior

Director of Content. "But they never did get involved, there was no direct conversation, no proposals, no story ideas. At one point they did place a call to the reporter that was working on it and I told them not do that and they said fine and that was the end of it."

And, as with any merger or change in corporate identity, there were myriad management issues, including heightened staff distress and brain drain. "I have a great deal of admiration for the model and for the people who put it in place," says Mark Fuerst of the Integrated Media Association. "Merging any two organizations is a particularly hard undertaking. There are fears, anxieties and big concessions that have to be made. Kit and Jerry deserve great credit for what they've done."

Neither Wareham nor Jensen is recommending others follow ideastream's lead. "I don't know if our model can be or should be replicated elsewhere," says Jensen. "But the key has to be to work within the resources that the communities provide and with full recognition of the communities' needs."

Critical Thinking

1. Describe the traditional PBS business model.
2. Ideastream-One Community has won critical acclaim for its core value of connecting with the community. Is it a viable business model for wide implementation?

M. J. ZUCKERMAN is a veteran freelance journalist, author and lecturer, currently on the adjunct staff of the George Washington University School of Media and Public Affairs.

Too Graphic?

American newspapers, often squeamish when it comes to running disturbing images, overcame their inhibitions after the Haitian earthquake. Journalists say powerful, graphic photographs made clear the depth of the tragedy and fostered support for rebuilding the devastated island nation. But to some, the deluge of images of naked corpses and severed body parts was insensitive and dehumanizing.

ARIELLE EMMETT

One by one the photos trickled in; then they came in torrents. On a piece of cardboard draped over a makeshift stretcher, the corpse of a Haitian man lay caked in dust like a powdered doll, a woman's dark legs in capri pants striding past him. In another image, a young man was digging his way out of a collapsed school building after the quake. As he picked his way through the rubble with hand tools, trying to rescue a teacher trapped inside, he looked up at the camera, seemingly unaware that he was flanked by a schoolgirl kneeling lifeless at her desk, her head and neck pinned by blocks of collapsed concrete.

The photos displayed by dozens of U.S. newspapers and websites showed tiny Haitian orphans crawling and playing in tent cities. There were hundreds and then thousands of photos of dazed, poorly bandaged victims; of nude or partially nude bodies falling out of pushcarts; of men in surgical masks dragging by legs and arms the bloated dead to parking lot morgues. The cinderblock houses and government palaces had been leveled by a seismic blast; there were images of body parts and screaming people, collapsed grocery stores and looters shot in the act.

It was hell, a 7.0 magnitude earthquake that struck Haiti on January 12, killing an estimated 230,000 people, leaving perhaps 3 million injured or homeless.

American news photographers with digital cameras and satellite phones rushed to the scene. This was not like Afghanistan or Iraq, with countless rules of embedding and the continual threats of bullets and roadside bombs. And editors generally loath to publish graphic and disturbing images saw justification for doing so in the case of the catastrophe in Haiti. This time, photographers and videographers went all out, loading their digital cameras with as much grief, hope and horror as they could bear.

"One of the reasons the pictures were more graphic in Haiti was that the Haitian people wanted the journalists to photograph the dead bodies and tell their stories. They wanted the world to see, to know how horrible it was," says Michele McNally, assistant managing editor for photography at the New York Times, which initially sent five photographers, including Pulitzer Prize-winner Damon Winter, to cover the disaster.

But Valérie Payen-Jean Baptiste, a Haitian elementary school principal who lost every possession, her home and school, and nearly her family in the quake, was sickened by the images. "I'm tired of it; the photos are too much," she says. "I know that [news outlets] took pictures, and that enabled people to raise money. But what I see is that people in Haiti are really upset. Some view the photos as an insult, a disaster, since we have already suffered so much."

"I'm not criticizing journalists [who] talk about the facts of the earthquake," she wrote in a follow-up e-mail. "But my critique is about the tone of unnecessary pictures and videos that show pieces of bodies, dying people, the nudity of people, or the misery/tragedy of people in line for food and water. Seriously, is this cruelty really necessary to mobilize massive humanitarian action?"

Photojournalists and their editors thought publishing the photos was an essential aspect of covering the news. "At the Herald, and at most publications, I suspect, we try to strike a balance, delivering not only what readers want to see but also what they need to see. We must act with sensitivity but, more importantly, our mission is to create a complete and accurate visual report. In this story in particular, images of death were inescapable. Death was everywhere," says David Walters, the Miami Herald's deputy editor-photos and video. He says the more graphic images made up "only a small portion of what we publish."

Walters works with Patrick Farrell, who won a Pulitzer for his stunningly poignant black-and-white images of the Haitian survivors of Hurricane Ike and other storms in 2008. Farrell once again was dispatched to Port-au-Prince right after the earthquake to document fresh heartache. "I thought [the quake] was the worst thing I'd ever seen. I was thinking if it gets worse than this, it's the end of the world," he says. "You can't tune it out; until you're looking at your pictures on the computer, you're thinking this is a movie, it isn't real."

And he adds emphatically, the Haitian photographs are essential. "I'd say there were not enough images of Haiti; I would say you can never have enough," Farrell says. "People need to know that the suffering continues; they're suffering just living a normal life. They get slammed with four storms, and now this. It's cruel and unlucky."

From the Miami Herald to the Palm Beach Post, the Birmingham News to the San Jose Mercury News, the Los Angeles Times to the Lincoln Journal Star, the New York Times and more, the verdict was the same. Unvarnished stories and images of Haiti's horrific loss and the rare, miraculous rescue of victims dominated A sections and front page real estate for several days—in some cases, a week to 10 days and more. Many journalistic boundaries were crossed on television. CNN's Sanjay Gupta, a neurosurgeon, was photographed performing brain surgery on an injured Haitian girl; Anderson Cooper of the same network interrupted his on-the-scene newscast to sweep up a boy in the midst of a violent looting incident. Other newscasters were filmed giving water to the trapped and weeping.

The more images of unimaginable suffering were published, the more international aid poured in.

Photo coverage of the quake touched off an intense debate about the role of the explicit photo—the iconic, bloody shot—in a media world of surprisingly delicate sensibilities. Did news outlets publish images that were too graphic, and too many of them? And what of stark depictions of other disasters, natural or man-made? Or U.S. military casualties? What about victims of terrorism or crimes of passion? Should all of them get the same treatment?

Readers and newspaper ombudsmen in January engaged in spirited exchanges about whether the media had gone too far. And if the public was surprised by the tone and volume of the photography, that shouldn't come as a shock. Because in recent years, for a variety of reasons, powerful, iconic images of national and international events have been harder to find in many American newspapers.

Many dailies have taken a hyperlocal approach to news coverage. News managers say that rather than publish national and international news that is widely available on the Internet, news organizations should heavily emphasize material that they are best suited to dominate: local news. Generally, newspapers with heavily local orientations avoid large-format foreign news photos and packages on their front pages and inside their A sections.

Another factor: Editors, troubled by sinking circulations, are wary of alienating their remaining readers by publishing images they may find troubling. In particular, many news outlets are reluctant to spotlight photos of dead or wounded U.S. troops or foreign civilian casualties.

Yet that doesn't mean compelling photography isn't widely available. News organizations publish powerful photographs by professional photojournalists and citizen journalists alike on their websites. The computer is considered a more private viewing arena than the newspaper. Online images may be edgier and more graphic than what appears in print, and they are viewed by millions of people who flock to photo galleries and slide shows.

"The Internet has become the saving grace of photojournalism," says Donald Winslow, editor of News Photographer magazine, a monthly publication of the National Press Photographers Association. "What you see in the daily newspaper today is the lowest common denominator of what a photographer is willing to print."

Tim Rasmussen, assistant managing editor for photography at the Denver Post, says the unlimited space online has greatly deepened photojournalism's ability to tell the story. "We put far more compelling, important news photos for the U.S. and the world on our website now than we ever put in the newspaper," he says. "We've built a good online audience for our photography with high-end photo blogs and galleries. . . . There is more emphasis online on national and international news than in the newspaper."

Despite the abundance of material on the Web, the timidity of many news organizations is a source of concern for some journalists. "The truth is that there is a lot of visual censorship that goes on," Washington Post picture editor Bonnie Jo Mount was quoted as saying in a column by Post Ombudsman Andrew Alexander. "We're in a culture that censors visuals very heavily. I think that sometimes works to our detriment because we don't run visuals that people need to see."

Haiti, though, was an exception. The country's rich culture and frequent natural disasters have spurred graphic coverage before—particularly photos of naked children who had been killed during the tropical storms of 2008. "In the past I've objected to this graphic coverage, particularly in regards to children," says Leonie Hermantin, a deputy director of Lambi Fund of Haiti, a Washington D.C.-based nonprofit that focuses on Haiti's economic development. "But the earthquake was of such apocalyptic, horrible dimensions that, in this case, it's OK to show what those who remain alive have to deal with. This is what children are seeing on a daily basis. The images afford an opportunity to be there vicariously, and at that level I do not object."

But, she adds, some images did go too far and showed no respect for the dead. "There has always been a sense among photographers that everything goes in Haiti," she says. "You can take whatever shot you want, because the people are poor and the government never reacts with outrage when these images are displayed." Hermantin does not fault the photojournalists, though. The news and photo editors who decide what gets published "should think they are not dealing with animals, but with people who care very much about dying with dignity. People from Haiti want to be buried clothed."

Hermantin and Farrell agree that Haiti's nightmare was beyond anyone's imagining. "You could write a million times that there are 100,000 people dead in the streets," Farrell says. "But if you don't see it for yourself, or in pictures, you won't believe it. It just won't register."

But it did register. It registered with billions, and for some the light it cast on the country and its multiple catastrophes was unnatural. Payen-Jean Baptiste, the Haitian elementary school principal who was trapped with her husband and two small daughters in a car during the earthquake, says she and her extended family needed no more graphic reminders of falling buildings or crushed bodies. "We lived through it," she says. "I have nightmares, and I am fighting these images. I just can't imagine what this is like for my two little girls, who are also dealing with nightmares. Two or three days after the quake, my four-year-old fell down because she was running, and she started crying nervously, thinking that she will die. So I can't understand the purpose of publishing such pictures or watching such horrifying things on TV for entertainment."

Payen-Jean Baptiste doubts that media coverage of the disaster will provide any more than a temporary Band-Aid. "As for helping Haiti," she says, "Haiti has been 'helped' by nations for 25 years. . . . The country is becoming poorer and poorer all the time. Thanks to the media, who will be motivated to go to Haiti in the next decade after seeing how 'ugly,' 'poor' or 'insecure' it can be?"

Many American news consumers wondered the same thing. Christa Robbins of Chicago wrote a letter to the New York Times protesting the graphic images of corpses and destruction published by the paper. The letter was quoted in a column by Times Public Editor Clark Hoyt. Robbins wrote, "I feel that the people who have suffered the most are being spectacularized by your blood-and-gore photographs, which do not at all inform me of the relief efforts, the political stability of the region or the extent of damage to families or infrastructure."

Robbins and other readers suggested that Haiti was considered fair game because it was *other*—black, poor and foreign. "If this had happened in California, I cannot imagine a similar depiction of half-clothed bodies splayed out for the camera," Robbins wrote. "What are you thinking?" A Washington Post reader wrote to Ombudsman Alexander: "I wonder if the editors of the Washington Post would run pictures of charred smoldering bodies or of a young girl crushed to death if those bodies had been of a 12-year-old girl from Chevy Chase or a 45-year-old father of three from Cleveland Park," referring to two largely white, well-off local communities.

At the same time, some readers defended the use of graphic images. One of them, Mary Louise Thomas of Palatka, Florida, wrote to Hoyt that a photo of a dead baby lying on her dead mother impelled her to cry for an hour. "But run from it? Never," Hoyt quoting her as saying. She added that those repelled by such images "should really try staring truth in the face occasionally and try to understand it."

While Alexander and Hoyt defended their papers' Haitian imagery, arguing it underscored the gravity and urgency of the situation, both also acknowledged that there are multiple standards for choosing photographs. One standard—proximity to readership—prevents most newspapers from publishing pictures of dead bodies with local stories because of the "likelihood that readers may be connected to the deceased," Alexander wrote.

The sheer magnitude of a disaster also influences editors' willingness to publish images of pain, according to Hoyt. During the 2004 Indian Ocean tsunami, for example, "The Times ran a dramatic front-page photo of a woman overcome with grief amid rows of dead children, including her own," he wrote. Though some readers protested, Hoyt continued, "the newspaper's first public editor, Daniel Okrent, concluded the paper was right to publish the picture. It told the story of the tsunami, he said."

National newspapers like the Times, however, do not have the same strictures as many local and regional dailies, which readily invoke reader demographics to help winnow out certain disturbing images. "It's weird what offends people, what actually bothers people over breakfast," says Torry Bruno, associate managing editor for photography at the Chicago Tribune. At his newspaper, he says, decisions about graphic photos depend on the circumstances: "In each case, we have long, thoughtful conversations about whether or not publishing is the right thing to do," he says. After the quake, for example, "We published an image of an arm coming out of some rubble with a weeping person behind it," Bruno recalls. It was a decision that Tribune editors felt was warranted, given the depth of the catastrophe.

Haiti aside, there is widespread agreement among those who practice and monitor photojournalism that America's newsrooms have become far more cautious when it comes to choosing photographs. "The kind of enlightened editor I used to have at the Palm Beach Post doesn't exist anymore," says Winslow, the NPPA photojournalist. News editors "today don't want to offend readers, and they don't want to piss people off, and they don't want to take the phone calls [from irate readers] the next day."

Kenny Irby, visual journalism group leader and director of diversity at the Poynter Institute, says the shift in newspaper photojournalism is a byproduct of economic flux. "There is a declining commitment to quality photojournalism today in mainstream media," he says. "But it's not part of a sinister plan. It's the reality of an industry . . . where print publications are all struggling. Photography is an expensive endeavor; it costs to deploy and support photographers in remote locations."

Another factor: "There is less training and less of the intellectual photo editor thinking about the assignment," says Michel du Cille, the Washington Post's director of photo/multimedia/video. At some, though not all, newspapers, he continues, "the editors are going for the gimmicky photograph over a storytelling photograph. Yes, that's happening around the country, and we are fighting it in the newsroom."

The transformation of American photojournalism didn't happen overnight. "I started to see the change in photo editing after I retired in 1990," says James Atherton, a former Washington Post photographer who took many iconic photographs of U.S. and world leaders, from President Truman to Martin Luther King Jr. to Pope John Paul II to Jimmy Carter. "Newspaper photos are less high quality than they used to be because they're [mostly] feature pictures, not breaking news pictures," he says.

Moreover, Atherton says, the U.S. military has often handcuffed the press by restricting access to citizen casualties in foreign wars in which U.S. troops are involved. An exception: an April 29, 2008, Associated Press photo of the death of a 2-year-old Iraqi child, Ali Hussein, who died in Baghdad during a U.S. bombing raid. The image of a suffocated child appeared on the front page of the Washington Post. Although the photograph was beautifully framed and shot—a potential icon—a survey of U.S. newspapers suggests that Ali Hussein's image was rarely used. The photograph, on the other hand, was commonly distributed and published in foreign media.

"It's taken a long time for us to suddenly realize that when we lose soldiers over there that civilians are dying too," Atherton says. "Civilians should be counted."

But even if news organizations wanted to publish such pictures, it's become increasingly difficult for their journalists to get access to them. During Vietnam, for example, "U.S. photojournalists had virtual carte blanche to photograph whatever they wanted," Winslow says. Journalist Malcolm Browne recorded the Buddhist monk Thich Quang Duc setting himself on fire on a Saigon street in 1963 to protest the corruption in the Diem regime. The image ended up on the front page of the Washington Post.

Photographer Eddie Adams produced the chilling, split-second capture of Gen. Nguyen Ngoc Loan executing a suspected Viet Cong prisoner in 1968. These images, along with Nick Ut's iconic 1972 photo of a young South Vietnamese girl fleeing after a napalm attack, were published and helped change the course of the war.

But the U.S. military altered rules of journalistic access after Vietnam. "The first [Persian] Gulf War had 100 percent photographic censorship; the military kept you on boats," Winslow recalls. "Then the military came up with the idea of 'embedding' in Iraq." Today, journalists who embed with U.S. troops in Afghanistan or Iraq are governed by military regulation limiting where they can go.

U.S. photojournalists went to Haiti to document the enormity of the battered island nation's misery.

For Haitian citizens who wanted their privacy respected, and who seek a long-term international commitment rather than charity, the graphic photography may have a tarnishing effect. "People in Haiti are strong," Payen-Jean Baptiste says. "There are people [here] fighting alone to recover and try to get back on their feet. They are used to dealing with such unfairness. But if there is a way we can stop humiliating them by taking away their dignity while they are suffering, that would be the best help forever we can bring to this nation."

The Miami Herald's Walters sees a broader issue. "Some people, both readers and journalists, find some of the images from Haiti to be gut-wrenching and undignified. These graphic, hard-hitting photos always spawn debate in our newsroom . . . careful debate. But the fact remains that the devastation in Haiti is gut-wrenching and in many instances, tragic circumstances *have* stripped away the dignity of victims who were so mercilessly affected by this disaster. That part of the story must be acknowledged in both words and pictures or the story is incomplete."

Critical Thinking

1. How would you define *ethical practice* in publishing graphic photographs of death? Where is the line between *graphic* and *too graphic?*

2. Should the rules differ online vs on television?

ARIELLE EMMETT, a former Temple University journalism professor, is studying for a PhD at the Philip Merrill College of Journalism at the University of Maryland. She wrote about journalism and social networking in AJR's December 2008/January 2009 issue.

Carnage.com

**Videos depicting the gruesome deaths of enemy soldiers—
and civilians—have taken the Internet by storm.**

JESSICA RAMIREZ

The video isn't quite clear. Three Iraqis stand in a field, unaware that a U.S. Apache helicopter is eyeing them from afar. Two of the men are handling what looks like a weapon, but there's no time to check. The Apache pilot gets an order: hit them. The 30mm bullets go clack-clack-clack. "Got [one]," says the pilot. "Good, hit the other one," says a voice on the radio. Clack-clack-clack. No. 2 goes down. The third man tries to hide behind a truck as bullets slam into the vehicle. After a few seconds a figure crawls into the open. "He's wounded," says the pilot. "Hit him [again]," says the voice. Clack-clack-clack. When the dust settles, the third man is dead.

Some 7,000 miles away, Nate J. sat in front of his computer, mesmerized by these images. It was 2006, and Nate, who owns a decal company, got his first taste of what soldiers and scholars call war porn. Although he's never been a soldier, Nate loves all things military. But this was better than anything he'd seen on the Military Channel. "I was just like 'Wow,'" he recalls. "'I have to find more.'"

That was easy enough. Although the recently released footage of U.S. Apache helicopters gunning down two Reuters journalists appalled many, similar war videos are plentiful on websites like GotWarPorn.com and YouTube. Nate, who asked NEWSWEEK not to use his last name because he's received death threats, has uploaded more than 800 to his own channel on LiveLeak.com and other sites.

When the Afghanistan and Iraq conflicts broke out, the military officially released some of the raw combat footage now on the Internet to build a stronger bond between the home front and the battlefield. Soldiers also took their own videos or pulled them from cameras on military systems like Predator drones. But almost as soon as these images became available, civilians and soldiers alike started splicing the clips together, often adding soundtracks and spreading them across the Web. Today there are thousands of war-porn videos, and they've been viewed millions of times. Like sexual porn, they come in degrees of violence, ranging from soft-core montages of rocket-propelled grenades blowing up buildings to snuff-film-like shots of an insurgent taking a bullet to the head. And even as the U.S. begins its march toward the end of two long conflicts, these compilations continue to attract viewers. With a videogame sensibility, they fetishize—and warp—the most brutal parts of these high-tech wars.

Historically, combat images have been captured and disseminated by a handful of professionals, such as the photographers Mathew Brady during the Civil War and Robert Capa during World War II. Now the immediacy of the Internet, coupled with the spread of cheap video technology, allows anyone to document war as they see it. "There's a new order," says James Der Derian, a professor at Brown University's Watson Institute for International Studies. "Unlike the photograph, the moving image creates a feeling that it more accurately depicts what it is representing, whether it does or not."

Academics date the origins of war porn to the scandalous images from Abu Ghraib Prison, in which Iraqi prisoners were stacked on top of each other to form naked pyramids, forced to simulate sexual acts, or otherwise abused. The snapshot of Pvt. Lynndie England holding a naked prisoner by a leash became an iconic representation of the war. The acts were born of an aimless power and a pornographic sensibility, argued the French social theorist Jean Baudrillard, who defined this form of "war porn" in a 2004 essay in the French newspaper *Libération*.

After Abu Ghraib the floodgates burst, with U.S. soldiers even trading war porn for real porn. Chris Wilson was running a user-generated porn site when he started getting requests for sexual material from soldiers in both war zones. But when paying via credit card proved problematic, Wilson let them swap war footage for access to the site's sexual content. The first images he received were fairly tame. But as the Iraq War took a turn for the worse in late 2004, the photos and footage got bloodier and included shots of headless corpses and body parts like intestines, brains, and what appeared to be limbs. By 2005, Wilson had an estimated 30,000 U.S. military personnel as members. "It was a view of war that had never been seen," he says.

The flood of images includes pictures of headless corpses and body parts like intestines, brains, and what appear to be limbs.

Eventually the Office of the State Attorney in Polk County, Fla., charged Wilson with 300 obscenity-related misdemeanor counts and one felony count. A Pentagon investigation into the war footage on his site led to no charges against him or military members. (The Department of Defense says it is against its policy to show "recognizable photos of wounded or captured enemy." The Marines, Air Force, and Navy haven't prosecuted anyone for such posts; the Army says it has no way to track this.) Wilson did plead no contest to five of the misdemeanor charges; he served no time, but his site was shut down. He believes that decision had more to do with the war porn than the sexual content. "If you're curious, and you're an adult, and you live in a free country, there should be no reason why you can't look at this stuff," he says. "I don't think there's any harm in it."

Critics disagree. The videos, after all, depict attacks only on enemy combatants and civilians—never American troops. (In many ways they're strikingly similar to jihadist propaganda.) Aside from providing a one-sided perspective of conflict, war porn soft-pedals the horrors of battle. "People watching it on their iPhone or on their home computer don't generally do it for the information; they do it because it's entertainment," says P. W. Singer, author of *Wired for War*. "That's the porn part of it.

The soldiers use the word because they know there's something wrong with it."

What gets lost in the highlight reels of explosions and bodies is the moral complexity of war, says Bryant Paul, an expert on the psychological and sexual effects of media. He points to a video of American soldiers making fun of a dog eating a dead Iraqi. "The behavior may be a coping mechanism for war, because they might have to normalize what is not normal in order to survive," he says. "But the people who watch this stuff can't know that, so they can't understand the entirety of what they're seeing."

Yet these images will perpetuate a particular version of these wars, says Paul. It is a version that does not treat the enemy as human, or life as valuable. It is a version that does not recognize the pain of some of the U.S. soldiers who pull the trigger. And as realistic as these videos might seem, they do not show war for what it actually is: terrifyingly real.

Critical Thinking

1. Define *war porn*, in your words.

2. Should there be restrictions on, or consequences for, posting war porn online?

Distorted Picture

Thanks to Photoshop, it's awfully easy to manipulate photographs, as a number of recent scandals make painfully clear. Misuse of the technology poses a serious threat to photojournalism's credibility.

SHERRY RICCHIARDI

If photo sleuths in Ohio hadn't noticed a pair of missing legs, Allan Detrich still would be cruising to assignments in his sleek blue truck, building his reputation as a photographer extraordinaire at the Toledo Blade. In April, the veteran shooter was forced out of the newsroom in disgrace, igniting a scandal that swept the photojournalism community. Coworkers were mystified about why a highly talented, hard worker who had garnered a slew of awards would cheat.

Detrich says that for a time, he felt like the most "reviled journalist in the country." Internet forums buzzed about his misdeeds, and photographers attacked him for sullying the profession. Some even sent hateful e-mail messages. "I wasn't the first to tamper with news photos and, unfortunately, I probably won't be the last," he says. "I screwed up. I got caught."

In his case, he says, he was seduced by software that made altering images so easy that "anyone can do it."

With new technology, faking or doctoring photographs has never been simpler, faster or more difficult to detect. Skilled operators truly are like magicians, except they use tools like Photoshop, the leading digital imaging software, to create their illusions.

Detrich, who had worked for the Blade since 1989, manipulated most of the images while alone in his truck, using a cell phone or WiFi for quick and easy transmission to the photo desk. There was little reason for him to return to the newsroom to process images. Until April 5, no one challenged the veracity of his photographs.

The photographer's downfall underscores a disturbing reality: With readily accessible, relatively inexpensive imaging tools (Photoshop sells for around $650) and a low learning curve, the axiom "seeing is believing" never has been more at risk. That has led to doomsday predictions about documentary photojournalism in this country.

"The public is losing faith in us. Without credibility, we have nothing; we cannot survive," says John Long, chairman of the ethics and standards committee of the National Press Photographers Association. Long pushes for stricter newsroom standards with missionary zeal and believes all journalists are tarnished when someone like Detrich falls from grace.

On June 2, Long, who built a distinguished career in photography at the Hartford Courant before retiring earlier this year, preached to an audience at NPPA's photo summit in Portland, Oregon. If the self-described purist had his way, news photographers would take a vow of abstinence in regard to photo altering; editors would enforce zero-tolerance policies. "The problem is far greater than we fear," Long told the group that afternoon.

There are no statistics on the number of rule-breakers, but indicators within the profession do not bode well for the cherished precept of visual accuracy.

During an NPPA ethics session in Portland, a group of some 50 photographers and photo managers were asked for a show of hands if they believed they had ever worked with peers who routinely crossed ethical boundaries. Nearly every arm flew into the air. "That was a scary thing to see," says Long, who was on the panel. Ethical breaches were the topic of conversation at coffee breaks and during presentations at the photo summit.

Many of the offending photos and illustrations discussed in Portland appear in a rogues' gallery posted by computer scientist Hany Farid (www.cs.dartmouth.edu/farid/research/tampering).

Among the dozens he highlights are Time and Newsweek covers, a Pulitzer Prize-winning photo, images in the Charlotte Observer and Newsday, and a famous portrait of Abraham Lincoln that was discovered to be less than accurate.

The Dartmouth College professor uses the term "digital forensics" to describe pioneering methods to detect image altering. Although not a cure-all, these tools could provide help in the future, says Farid. He predicts that scandals over photo forgeries are "absolutely going to get worse." That notion is underlined by the attention being paid to the problem by media organizations and at conferences.

In August, visual communications expert David Perlmutter will serve on a panel titled "Seeing is Not Believing: Representations and Misrepresentations" at the Association for Education in Journalism and Mass Communication gathering in Washington, D.C. Perlmutter poses the question: "Is the craft I love being murdered, committing suicide or both?"

The Toledo Blade's descent into photo hell began with a telephone call.

On April 4, Ron Royhab, the paper's executive editor, returned home to find a message requesting he phone back, no matter how late. He punched in the number and listened in stunned silence to the voice on the other end. There were suspicions that a photographer had altered a news photo that had run prominently on the Blade's front page four days earlier. The caller was Donald R. Winslow, editor of News Photographer magazine, an NPPA publication.

"I was speechless; I couldn't collect my thoughts. I felt like someone had punched me in the stomach," recalls Royhab. "I got off the phone and thought, 'Not at my newspaper. It can't be!'"

By noon the next day, Detrich, 44, was being questioned in the newsroom. He admitted altering the photograph but said it was for his personal use, a copy he intended to hang on an office wall. He claimed he had mistakenly transmitted the wrong version on deadline. He told Photo District News, "that's not something I would do."

The paper's editors decided to review all of the photos that Detrich, twice named Ohio Photographer of the Year and a Pulitzer Prize finalist in 1998, had submitted for publication this year. They didn't like what they found. By April 7, he had resigned. If he had not, he would have been fired, says Royhab.

The episode began on March 30, when Bluffton University's baseball team played for the first time since five of its athletes had been killed in a bus accident earlier that month. Photographers jostled for position as players knelt in front of banners bearing the names and uniform numbers of the dead.

When similar photos appeared in Cleveland's Plain Dealer, the Dayton Daily News and Ohio's Lima News the following day, a pair of legs clad in blue jeans was visible from behind one of the banners hanging from a fence. In Detrich's version, there was only grass under the banner, although he shot from roughly the same angle. Ohio photographers brought the mysterious disappearance to Winslow's attention.

A review of Detrich's original digital files revealed that he had habitually erased unwanted elements in photos, including people, tree limbs, utility poles, electrical wires, light switches and cabinet knobs. In some instances, he added tree branches or shrubbery. In one sports shot he added a hockey puck; in another he inserted a basketball.

Detrich submitted 947 photographs for publication from January through March of 2007. Editors found that 79 clearly had been doctored. The paper apologized to readers and Detrich posted a mea culpa on his website (www.detrichpix.typepad.com/allandetrich_picturethis). The investigation found that Detrich had altered photos as far back as 2002. The Blade noted that no evidence of tampering was discovered on Detrich's award-winning photos, and there were no alterations in earlier years, when he was shooting on film and editing and processing in the newsroom.

In the May issue of News Photographer, Winslow ran a report on the situation at the Blade and labeled Detrich a "serial digital manipulator," the most prolific to surface in newspaper history.

As for the legs, it turned out they belonged to freelancer Madalyn Ruggiero, who was shooting in Bluffton for the Chicago Tribune and had positioned herself behind the fence in search of a different angle.

Brian Walski had covered war in the Balkans, famine in Africa and conflict in Kashmir before he made a fateful decision while on assignment in Iraq for the Los Angeles Times. The Chicago native was fired via satellite phone on April 1, 2003, after it was discovered he used his computer to combine two images, taken seconds apart, into a composite that ran on page one of the Times on March 31. The subject was a British soldier helping Iraqi civilians find cover outside Basra.

After the photos appeared, an employee at the Hartford Courant noticed that several Iraqis in the background appeared twice (see Drop Cap, May 2003). The Courant, which like the Times is owned by the Tribune Co., had also published the picture.

In an e-mail to the newspaper's photo staff, Walski, who had been with the Times since 1998 and had won Photographer of the Year honors in California, wrote: "This was after an extremely long, hot and stressful day but I offer no excuses here. . . . I have always maintained the highest ethical standards throughout my career and cannot truly explain my complete breakdown in judgment at this time. That will only come in the many sleepless nights that are ahead."

Colin Crawford, the L.A. Times' assistant managing editor for photography, calls Walski "incredibly experienced and talented" and says there was no hint of wrongdoing before the lapse. A review of his work found no other evidence of tampering.

"It's hard for me to get into the head of someone who is risking his life every day," says Crawford, who acknowledges the pressures Walski was under on the battlefield. Still, "I can't imagine in my wildest dreams why he would ever do it." After leaving the Times, Walski started Colorado Visions, a commercial photo business.

In another war-zone episode, Adnan Hajj, a Lebanese freelancer on assignment for Reuters, was fired for doctoring images during the August 2006 conflict between Israel and Hezbollah in Lebanon. In one photo, Hajj darkened and cloned plumes of smoke rising from buildings the Israelis bombed in Beirut, amplifying the devastation. In another, he altered the image of an Israeli F-16 fighter jet to make it appear that it was firing several missiles instead of a single flare, as the original photo of the plane shows.

This time, bloggers acted as sheriff. According to news reports, Charles Johnson, who runs a blog called Little Green Footballs (www.littlegreenfootballs.com/weblog) sounded the alarm about the Beirut photo. Another conservative political blog, The Java Report (www.mypetjawa.mu.nu), drew attention to the phony missiles.

Bloggers also played a role in uncovering a USA Today misstep. (Disclosure: My husband, Frank Folwell, is a deputy managing editor who oversees photography and graphics for USA Today.) On October 26, 2005, WorldNetDaily.com reported that the newspaper pulled a photograph of Condoleezza Rice from its website after a blog called The Pen (www.fromthepen.com)

Back in Action

In early May, the message board for SportsShooter.com lit up after the headline "Detrich Rises From the Dead" appeared. Photographer Allan Detrich, who resigned from the Toledo Blade in April after an investigation showed he had doctored more than 79 images, was back.

The avid storm chaser had covered a tornado that leveled Greensburg, Kansas, on May 4, killing 12. Several news outlets interviewed Detrich, including Fox News Channel and CNN, and his pictures were shown on the air. The president of Polaris Images, a New York photo agency, saw the broadcasts and offered to distribute the Greensburg photos.

Some on SportsShooter.com were outraged by the turn of luck for a photographer ostracized one month earlier. Others took a more practical view. "Sad but true, it seems like the only people upset about this are the photographers. [They] liken what he did to a deadly sin, while the average person sees it as a simple mistake that should be forgiven," said a respondent from Cedar Park, Texas. That is what Detrich is counting on.

After he left the newspaper, he found it difficult to go out of the house, "I felt everybody would be looking at me, saying, 'That's the guy.'" Now he has moved on.

"I have apologized and admitted I was wrong. I'm being up-front with people if they ask about it. I can't do more than that," Detrich says. "I'm not going to sit back and sulk for the rest of my life. I am going to let my images speak for themselves."

—S.R.

revealed it had been manipulated, giving the secretary of state a menacing stare. The blog used the original version of the Associated Press photo to show the image had been doctored.

The altered photo circulated on other blogs, drawing a firestorm of public protest. USA Today explained in an editor's note that "after sharpening the photo for clarity," a portion of Rice's face was brightened, "giving her eyes an unnatural appearance." The distortion violated the paper's editorial standards, the note said.

One of the most ballyhooed examples of photo manipulation was Time magazine's June 27, 1994, cover. Time darkened the skin and added a five o'clock shadow to a mug shot of O.J. Simpson, making him look more sinister. On its December 1, 1997, cover, Newsweek glamorized Bobbi McCaughey, the Iowa mother of septuplets, by straightening her teeth. The magazine superimposed Martha Stewart's head on a model's body for the March 7, 2005, cover, when Stewart was released from prison.

The credit explaining the super-imposed photo of Stewart appeared inside the magazine. Since then, Newsweek's attribution policy has changed. When a photo illustration runs on the front of the magazine, the credit also appears on the cover, says Simon Barnett, Newsweek's director of photography. That provides "an additional layer of information, so if anyone is in any doubt whatsoever, it's there to confirm what they see as being an illustration," he wrote in an e-mail interview.

As for news photos, "We do nothing beyond what has traditionally been done in the photographic darkroom," says Barnett, who took over as photo director in July 2003.

Barnett says the advent of Photoshop has increased the push to create flawless magazine covers. "As digital technology has evolved, art directors at major magazines have forgotten how and when to say 'enough.' This tweaking and buffing and polishing down to the last pixel has frequently had the consequence of changing the photograph into something that at a minimum is plastic, and at worst inaccurate," says Barnett, who counts himself among a minority that appreciates the natural imperfections that real photography brings. "It adds to authenticity," he says.

Time's readers are accustomed to finding the credit for covers on the table of contents, says spokesman Daniel Kile. If the photograph has been altered, the image is clearly labeled a "photo-illustration." That was the case on March 15, when Time illustrated a story, "How the Right Went Wrong," on the cover with a photo of Ronald Reagan crying. The inside credits noted: "Photograph by David Hume Kennerly. Tear by Tim O'Brien." (See "Finding a Niche," April/May.)

But no matter how pure the intention, NPPA's John Long doesn't buy attribution as a substitute for authenticity. "No amount of captioning can ever cover for a visual lie or distortion. If it looks real in a news context, then it better be real," says Long, who maintains there should be the same respect for visual accuracy that there is for the written word in journalism.

Long points out that some photos are doctored with the sole intent of doing harm. In February 2004, a photograph showing Democratic presidential candidate John Kerry with actress Jane Fonda at a 1971 anti-Vietnam war rally swept the Internet. Two photos, taken a year part, were merged into one and carried a phony AP credit line.

Ken Light, who took the original Kerry photograph sans Fonda, raised a key question in a March 11, 2004, New York Times article about faked images: "What if that photo had floated around two days before the general election and there wasn't time to say it's not true?" The story noted that image tampering did not begin in 1989, with John Knoll's creation of Photoshop.

On the cusp of the digital revolution in 1991, ethicist Paul Lester documented the history of forgeries in a book, "Photojournalism: An Ethical Approach." He noted that Hippolyte Bayard made the first known counterfeit photograph more than 160 years ago, and during the Civil War soldiers were instructed to play dead and corpses were moved for dramatic impact. In World War I, photos were forged for propaganda purposes, including one of Kaiser Wilhelm cutting off the hands of babies.

Lester included a classic example from 1982 often cited as the beginning of the steep challenge for photojournalism in the digital age. When National Geographic employed what was considered computer wizardry to squeeze together Egypt's pyramids of Giza for the perfect cover shot, tremors shot through the photo community. Many bemoaned the onset of an era when tampering with photos would be effortless.

In his book, Lester quoted Tom Kennedy, photo director at the Geographic from 1987 to 1997, who laid down new rules for the magazine. Technology no longer would be used to manipulate elements in a photo simply to achieve a more compelling graphic effect, Kennedy said. As for the pyramids, "We regarded that afterwards as a mistake, and we wouldn't repeat that mistake today."

Writing for the New York Times in 1990, acclaimed photo critic Andy Grundberg predicted, "In the future, readers of newspapers and magazines will probably view news pictures more as illustrations than as reportage, since they will be aware that they can no longer distinguish between a genuine image and one that has been manipulated." History has given weight to his prophecy as photo managers search for answers.

"Fundamentally, there is only so much you can do. You hope and pray and respect your staff. . . . You trust that they're not going to do this kind of thing," says the L.A. Times' Crawford, who, like many others interviewed for this story, sees setting clear, strict policies as critical for quality control. He believes that, despite the Walski incident, the Times has had a solid system in place. "You do the best you can, talking to your staff and making sure they understand what your ethics are," he says.

Since the Detrich episode, the Toledo Blade is spot-checking more photos and scheduling more one-on-one time with photographers to go over their work. "With the ability to send electronically, it is easy to feel isolated from the rest of the photo department, so we will try harder to establish a sense of team," says Luann Sharp, the Blade's assistant managing editor for administration.

Santiago Lyon, the AP's director of photography, oversees the wire service's vast army of 300 shooters plus 700 others operating on a freelance or contract basis. The AP handles about three-quarters of a million images a year, leaving ample potential for error.

Lyon has turned to the Poynter Institute, NPPA, the White House News Photographers Association and other media groups for guidance as he updates and fine-tunes the wire service's standards.

"We're looking at their ethical guidelines and our own and coming up with wordage and phraseology more in tune with the changing world out there," says Lyon, who attended Photoshop training sessions for about 200 AP photographers and photo editors throughout the U.S. in 2006. At each stop, he hammered home the guidelines for responsible use of imaging tools and repeatedly stressed that "credibility is the most important thing we have at the AP and journalism in general."

Lyon says a handful of photographers have been fired for tampering with pictures over the years. He views the core of experienced photo editors at AP's editing hubs around the globe as a first line of defense for detecting phony images.

There are certain clues photo monitors look for. According to experts, the most common signs are differences in color or shadows, variations in graininess or pixilation, blurred images or elements in the photo that are too bright or much sharper than the rest.

Dartmouth College professor Farid is developing computer algorithms, or mathematical formulas, that can detect altered images. Lyon and Farid have met to discuss possibilities for the future, and Lyon has had the professor analyze old photos the AP had on file and knew had been altered to test the reliability of the detection software. It worked in all but one case, Lyon says.

But for now, the method is too cumbersome, given that the AP receives between 2,000 and 3,000 pictures each day. "To work for us, that type of process would have to be instantaneous, or close to it," says Lyon.

Farid doesn't promote his detection software as a magic formula. "The technology is getting better and better. It's getting easier to manipulate, and it is affordable. Everybody has it. At least we might slow [the forger] down, make it more challenging, more difficult," says the computer scientist, who likens the scramble for improved safeguards to an arms race.

"I guarantee you there will be people out there developing anti-forgery detection software or software that makes better forgeries," says Farid.

Beyond stopping cheaters, there also is the thorny issue of defining the limits of what is and is not acceptable. Photo editors commonly say that the only appropriate techniques with Photoshop are those analogous to what was acceptable in the traditional darkroom. That might ring hollow to a generation of photographers who have always processed images on computers and transmitted them to the photo desk from the nearest Starbucks. Still, one rule is clear: Removing visual content from a photo or adding it crosses the divide.

Lyon warns that using words to describe visual nuances in guidelines is very complicated. "How do you define the correct use of tonal differences—lightening or darkening aspects of a picture in a way that accurately reflects what the photographer saw?"

In an attempt to clarify standards, Kenny F. Irby, the Poynter Institute's photo expert, confessed in a September 2003 report that he had "dodged" (to lighten) and "burned" (to darken) elements in his pictures throughout his career. He maintained there was nothing sinful about his actions because he did not take those techniques to extremes.

Irby listed notables such as Gordon Parks and W. Eugene Smith among the many great photojournalists who employed the same techniques. When, then, do photographers slip into the abyss?

On August 15, 2003, Patrick Schneider of the Charlotte Observer was suspended for three days without pay for excessive adjustments in Photoshop. The North Carolina Press Photographers Association stripped Schneider of the awards he had won for the photos in question. Its investigation found that details such as parking lots, fences and people had been removed from pictures.

At the time, Schneider told Irby, "I used the tools that for decades have been used in the darkroom, and now, in Photoshop, I do them with more precision. My goal is to bring more impact to my images, to stop the readers and draw their attention."

The award-winning photographer was fired in July 2006 for an image of a firefighter on a ladder, silhouetted against a vivid sunlit sky. The Observer explained in an editor's note that in the original, the sky was brownish-gray. Enhanced with photo-editing software, the sky became a deep red, and the sun took on a more distinct halo. In the judgment of his bosses, Schneider had violated the paper's rules.

While the photo establishment buzzes over scandals like those of Schneider and Detrich, others ask, "So what?"

The Toledo Blade's Royhab was surprised when some readers questioned the ruckus raised over Detrich's misdeeds and asked what was wrong with changing the content of a photograph in a newspaper. "The answer is simple: It is dishonest," Royhab wrote in an April 15 column.

On SportsShooter.com, a website run by USA Today photographer Robert Hanashiro, some attacked Detrich for his duplicity while others defended his right to stay in journalism. That did not sit well with Bob DeMay, chairman of the board of the Ohio News Photographers Association and an acquaintance of Detrich's.

"I find it very scary that some people didn't find fault at all," says DeMay, photo editor at the Akron Beacon Journal. "There used to be an old saying, 'Pictures don't lie.' Well, they do now. Once that seed of doubt is put in somebody's mind, it's frightening."

Like many others, DeMay sees the troubled state of newspapers playing into the equation. Pushed to the limits by layoffs and hiring freezes, many photo departments have fewer bodies to do more work. Three photo staffers at the Beacon Journal were laid off last year, taking a toll on quality, says DeMay. As travel budgets are slashed, there is more reliance on freelancers who file photos from a distance, without the backstop of newsroom accountability or ethics codes. And the competition for newspaper space has never been fiercer, increasing the pressure for dramatic images.

There also has been a cultural change in how photo departments operate. In the past, photographers often worked together in the darkroom; there was more collaboration and more oversight from photo desks. Today, it is common to transmit images from the field via laptop computers, with only occasional newsroom visits.

Opportunities for misdeeds are boundless, warns Larry Gross, coeditor of the book "Image Ethics in the Digital Age." Once photographers step over the line, there is very little they can't do, and, if they are skilled enough, they may leave little or no trace, says Gross. Years ago, editors could ask for the photo negative to make comparisons, but digital images can be changed so that there's no original left, no way to track back to an initial state. Adding to the angst of photo watchdogs, new and better versions of Photoshop are on the horizon, which is likely to widen the scope of fakeries.

NPPA's Winslow wonders if the ethics quandary in photojournalism is akin to the problem professional baseball has with steroids. "Are there lots of people doing what Detrich did without editors and managers realizing the extent of the problem?" he asked in his May article. "Or do they suspect, but do nothing about it?"

Not everyone sees a dim future. Author David Perlmutter believes that, by some standards, this is the golden age of photojournalistic ethics.

"If you are caught faking a picture today, you are fired. Fifty years ago, it was just part of the business. Now most people have gone to journalism school and learned ethics. Newsrooms are taking these things more seriously. Standards are higher than ever," Perlmutter says. "On the other hand, it has become so much easier to get away with the crime."

Critical Thinking

1. Is it OK, from your perspective, to digitally alter your wedding photos? Your family holiday card photo? Photos for the high school yearbook? What decision-making rules apply?

2. How would you define *ethical practice* for mass media regarding digital alteration of photographs?

Senior contributing writer **SHERRY RICCHIARDI** (sricchia@iupui .edu) has written about coverage of the war in Iraq and the Virginia Tech massacre in recent issues of *AJR*.

The Quality-Control Quandary

As newspapers shed copy editors and post more and more unedited stories online, what's the impact on their content?

CARL SESSIONS STEPP

Sunrise approaches on a Friday morning, and the St. Louis Post-Dispatch website is being updated early—from Mandy St. Amand's bathroom.

St. Amand, the Post-Dispatch continuous news editor, has balanced her laptop on the toilet lid and, while drying her hair and prepping for the office, is reworking homepage headlines.

Not surprisingly, no copy editor is handy at 5:30 A.M., so St. Amand's work goes online unchecked by a colleague. She estimates that between 40 and 50 Post-Dispatch staffers can post directly to the site, often remotely and without a second read—a growing, troubling trend in these days of never-ending news cycles and ever-dwindling editing corps.

A similar if less dramatic effect follows on the print side, where buyouts and layoffs over several years have cut the number of Post-Dispatch copy editors from more than 40 to about 21. The inevitable result, not only at the Post-Dispatch but at newsrooms nationwide, is that fewer editors scrutinize copy, and they often spend less time per item than they would have just a few years ago.

Together, these developments raise unprecedented questions about the value—and the future—of editing itself. Already at many news organizations, journalists and readers alike have noticed flabbier writing, flatter headlines, more typos. How far can you cut editing without crippling credibility? How do you balance immediacy and accuracy? How much does fine-tuning matter to the work-in-progress online ethos?

"When you think about the assembly line that was a newsroom, it's changed," says Post-Dispatch Editor Arnie Robbins. "In the world we live in now, readers expect immediacy, and we have to deliver. But we also have to be careful."

At ground level, these concerns fuel another trend: developing ways to maintain reasonable quality control now that the end-of-the-line copy desk can no longer process everything. Interviews and visits by AJR make clear that newsrooms are lurching toward new ways, from "buddy editing" (where you ask the nearest person to read behind you) to "back editing" (where copy is edited after posting) to "previewing" (where copy goes to a holding directory for an editor to check before live posting).

For now, though, progress is slow, and the risks seem scary.

Bill McClellan, a Post-Dispatch columnist since 1983, has one of the news organization's most familiar bylines. But he recently experienced a "brain cramp" and called Missouri a blue state, even though it has gone Democratic only twice in the past eight presidential races. The error zipped past editors and ended up in print.

McClellan won't blame the copy desk, which he says is "astoundingly good," and regularly calls to check things like song lyrics he's tangled. "Nine times out of 10 the copy desk catches things," he says, "and the red-blue error was the tenth."

But, he adds, "You never do more with less. You do less with less. You have fewer copy editors, more mistakes get through."

Reporter Adam Jadhav remembers writing that a woman had lost her right arm in a car crash. Six paragraphs later, he called it her left arm. Like McClellan, Jadhav takes full responsibility for his errors. Still, he says, "I'd like to think that a reasonably worked copy desk could catch them."

"Obviously in the future there are probably going to be fewer and fewer reads," Editor Robbins says. "There is concern there, and there is some risk there. However, I think it is manageable."

Can good editing endure amid all the changes?

Mandy St. Amand, by now operating from the newsroom rather than the bathroom, thinks about the question. "I really wish I had a wise-sounding, beard-stroking answer," she says. "But I don't."

Post-Dispatch Managing Editor Pam Maples is leading a newsroom tour, pointing out physical and operational alterations aimed toward Journalism 2.0.

In the center, a glass office has been dismantled, creating space for a 9:30 A.M. stand-up news huddle—earlier, faster-paced and more Web-oriented than before. A homepage editor presides. For the first agenda item, she turns to a dry-erase board where the phrase "top mods" appears in all caps. What should fill the modules atop the website?

The newsroom now has two early-morning reporters, often hustling on traffic and weather stories. Their goal is to start the process of moving at least 20 items a day through the top Web positions. The nine editors also discuss tomorrow's printed paper, but they project urgency to get moving online.

"Anything that happens, our assumption is it goes online," Maples says. "It puts a demand on editors and how they manage their people and how they think. Deadline is always."

Maples and Robbins have graciously let AJR into their newsroom at a bad time: the week after the paper laid off 14 people in the newsroom, including several editors. Four other rounds of layoffs or buyouts have taken place since 2005. A news staff of about 340 five years ago is about 210 today, Robbins calculates. Some 40 pages of space per week have been lost in the newspaper, which is introducing a narrower page width that could cost another 5 percent of newshole.

These challenges are not unique to St. Louis, but the Post-Dispatch seems a symbolic place to examine their impact on editing. It is a 241,000-circulation, middle-American, blue-collar institution, founded in 1878 by Joseph Pulitzer, the editing giant famous for preaching "accuracy, accuracy, accuracy."

Even today, four years after the Pulitzer family sold the paper to Lee Enterprises (see "Lee *Who?*" June/July 2005), a visitor is reverently shown a vacant but still furnished office, last occupied by a Pulitzer family member, where portraits of multiple generations of the family peer down. As you enter the paper's downtown lobby, the founder's words thunder from the front wall: "Always remain devoted to the public welfare."

The ghost of Joseph Pulitzer, it seems, haunts the Post-Dispatch, and perhaps newspaper journalism itself. Can "accuracy, accuracy, accuracy" survive "cuts, cuts, cuts"?

Post-Dispatch staffers warm to the challenge.

"We have a brand," says Deputy Metro Editor Alan Achkar. "People expect from the St. Louis Post-Dispatch a level of quality and accuracy. If we don't have good, responsible journalism that people can bank on, we don't have anything."

But maintaining quality takes more and more effort.

"For the Internet, speed is king," Achkar says. "You often worry that we're just slapping stuff online without properly vetting it. . . . It's added work. Sometimes you feel that no one wants to acknowledge that putting out a newspaper—even a thinner one—is a monumental task."

Top editors acknowledge that, by policy, cutbacks have fallen disproportionately on editors. Saving reporting jobs is the priority.

"People on the street, you try to protect as much as possible," Robbins says. "That's not to minimize the importance of editing and design at all. But ultimately you have to make tough decisions. Reporters on the street do separate us from other places."

So, the assigning editors and copy editors who are left adapt.

These days, says Frank Reust, a Post-Dispatch copy editor for 10 years, editors find themselves hovering somewhere between "comfortably rushed" and "always having to railroad stuff."

That means more rapid copy editing and sometimes, especially for wire stories, fewer reads. For online copy, says designer and Web producer Joan McKenna, "we are forgiven for mistakes. Speed is much more important than anything else."

The fallout so far seems noticeable but not calamitous. More than one reporter mentioned increased reaction from readers pointing out errors, mostly small. For example, a sportswriter's post confusing the names of two St. Louis Rams coaching prospects was flagged in the comments section and fixed within minutes.

Editors also express some larger concerns.

For instance, Reust sees less creative time applied to the "accuracy and tone" of headlines. He also worries that writers and editors brainstorm less. "The general time devoted to good writing is almost nonexistent now," he says.

Jean Buchanan, the paper's assistant managing editor for projects, sees that too. Writers sometimes can't get an editor's attention when they need it, and less time goes into those vital ingredients of enterprise and investigations, "rooting around for potential stories, requesting information that might lead to a story, meeting with small groups of reporters talking about what they are seeing."

Reid Laymance, the assistant managing editor for sports, spends more time on hands-on editing and less on planning. His editors have less time to develop "extras" like charts or breakout boxes. Down a copy editor since he took over last spring, "we're not as much editors as we used to be," he says. "Our guys have become processors. Getting the game in by 8 o'clock, making sure the headline fits, that's all we have time for."

Director of Photography Larry Coyne offers a good news/bad news example. With today's digital cameras, it isn't uncommon for photographers to shoot a thousand exposures on an assignment, many times more than they previously would have. Online galleries allow far more photos to run. But Coyne has three-and-a-half photo editors today instead of the five-and-a-half of about three years ago, so collaboration and editing can suffer. "There is more emphasis on quantity and getting them out," he says, "and less on feedback with photographers."

In fairness, it must be emphasized that not one of these editors comes across as whiny or bitter. They seem candid about their plight but determined to succeed. "Every time there's a reduction in staff," copy editor Reust says, "there is a period where you feel the load is just too much to handle. Then two months down the road you're thinking, 'We can handle things.'"

Patrick Gauen, the self-described "cops and courts editor" and a veteran police reporter, looks back over his 24 years at the paper and says, "A lot of what is changing—the platform stuff—really doesn't matter to me. It gets to the public one way or the other. . . . I feel like I still have the time I need. Our adequacy of editing is still good."

> **"There are so many balls in the air at once and some of them are going to drop. You try to understand which ones are breakable and try not to let those go."**
>
> —Patrick Gauen

He lives by something he once heard: "There are so many balls in the air at once and some of them are going to drop. You try to understand which ones are breakable and try not to let those go."

General assignment reporter David Hunn echoes that balanced sentiment. "The most serious stories I write" get attentive editing, he says, but the rush to post online is "kind of like the Wild West. . . . If anything is clear to me right now, it's that we are feeling our way as we go—and as a whole doing a pretty good job of it."

Editors being editors, though, they tend to see themselves in a code orange world, their equivalent of an earthquake zone or hurricane corridor, bracing for the Big One.

"What will wake us up," says Enterprise Editor Todd Stone, "is going to be the first big lawsuit where somebody really gets creamed. It's going to happen. And I'd bet you about 10 bucks it will be because of a lack of editing vigilance."

At the Washington Post, another paper that has lost editors, A-section copy desk chief Bill Walsh has the same worry.

"I keep fearing a disaster of some kind. I think it is only a matter of time," says Walsh, a nationally known blogger and author. "Doing more with less is always going to mean a compromise in quality. Three sets of eyes are always better than two."

Last year, the Post's ombudsman at the time, Deborah Howell, made a public pitch for editing. Reporting that the Post had lost 40 percent of its copy editors since 2005, Howell wrote that they are "the last stop before disaster."

On Walsh's combined national-foreign copy desk, seven editors now work where 12 once did. Where a typical piece of copy formerly got careful reading from an assigning editor, copy editor, slot editor and an editor looking at page proofs, today there tends to be one less layer, with the slot editor just taking a "glance," Walsh says.

Front-page and other sensitive stories still get extra edits, but Walsh acknowledges, "We're probably spending on average less time with stories, although that is not universally the case. I can't say we are doing as good a job with a rim read and a half-assed slot read as we were with more people looking at every story."

To help compensate, Walsh adds, the Post has succeeded in improving flow so copy reaches his desk earlier. It is also stressing that assigning desks must polish stories as much as possible before moving them.

Forty miles up I-95, the Baltimore Sun offers its version of the same tale.

The Sun, too, features its founder's words on the lobby wall, A.S. Abell's 1837 exhortation to serve "the common good."

But like other newsrooms, the Sun has fewer editors' eyes trained on that common good. John E. McIntyre, the director of the copy desk since 1995, counted about 54 copy editors several years ago, 48 about a year ago and 34 as of January, for news, features and sports.

However, McIntyre points out a "grim advantage" for the Sun and other papers. For print, at least, there is less copy to edit. The paper, he says, has lost about a third of its staff in the past few years and almost that much newshole.

"The size of the paper has been cut back to the point at which we have just about enough copy editors to manage it," he says. "It's the only reason we are not slapping basically unread copy into print."

Still, McIntyre sees worrisome signs, like "minor errors in fact and slack writing," fewer minutes for making headlines shine and, of course, less attention to online postings.

"That scares the bejeezus out of me," says McIntyre, who writes a blog about language called You Don't Say (http://weblogs.baltimoresun.com/news/mcintyre/blog). "I would rather have people on the staff catch my errors than readers."

Like editors elsewhere, McIntyre pledges to maintain quality. "The Sun has a reputation for the accuracy and clarity of what it publishes, and we are going to find a way to uphold the paper's standards."

McIntyre, a charter member and former president of the American Copy Editors Society (ACES), believes in documenting to management the vital contributions editors make.

A man given to unusually natty dress for a newsroom, who sips tea from a real cup during an interview, he offers an earthy defense of the editor's role. It is, he says, "to save the paper's ass."

He keeps a file of great prepublication catches by editors. Not long ago, he says, a veteran reporter and an assigning editor let through a piece of libelous work. "Were it not for the copy editor," McIntyre declares, "the biggest decision on the afternoon after publication would have been how many zeroes to put on the settlement check."

ACES and its current president, Chris Wienandt, have boosted efforts to promote and defend editing.

"Everyone is trying to cut costs, and editors and copy editors are relatively invisible jobs," says Wienandt, the business copy chief of the Dallas Morning News. "There is still this perception that we are proofreading drones.

"But the work of the copy editor involves the most-read work in the paper—the headlines. Editors are guardians of credibility, and without credibility we really haven't got a leg to stand on. Imagine a manufacturing company that didn't have a quality-control department. They would be in hot water pretty quick if things started going out defective."

"Imagine a manufacturing company that didn't have a quality-control department. They would be in hot water pretty quick if things started going out defective."

—Chris Wienandt

Wienandt and other ACES board members have collaborated on several editorials on the organization's website (www.copydesk.org), scolding those like Tribune Co. owner Sam Zell, who complained that layers of editing delay publication.

If stories are posted too quickly, the ACES editorial countered, they are "more likely to contain errors . . . be unethical, or present an actual legal problem. . . . If credibility evaporates, so will sales."

ACES also attacked the idea of outsourcing editing. "You simply can't duplicate the collective wisdom of a locally based copy desk," another editorial argued. To diminish local editing would jeopardize quality and undermine "the key selling point to an industry that more than ever needs selling points."

What then is the future of editing?

Will Sullivan, the Post-Dispatch's 28-year-old interactive director, appreciates the concerns of veteran colleagues but also welcomes a future of new thinking and tools.

He envisions that editing will become "more of a barn-raising . . . an everyone-is-an-editor model," where "the concept of news is a wiki" and a story becomes "a kind of rolling document" moving through a continuous editing process.

Better training can spread editing skills to writers and producers, he says. New tools, from automated step-savers like spell-check to simplified photo-editing software, can add speed and quality. Merging staffs can promote efficiency, for example, by assigning the same section editor to manage features on the Web and in print.

During this time of transition, several practices seem increasingly common:

- bringing copy editors in earlier to help with online copy and to expedite flow
- using floating, "quick-hit" editors to handle stories as they break
- expecting writers and assigning desks to move copy earlier
- enforcing the perhaps neglected principle that writers should be better self-editors
- encouraging "buddy editing," where a writer or poster doesn't wait for the copy desk but asks a colleague for a second read
- using "preview" directories as a holding point for material about to go live online, so an editor can look over it first

- creating protocols for Web editing, such as posting a note whenever something new goes onto the Web, to trigger an editor's check
- systematizing "back editing," so that even after being posted, all copy gets edited as soon as possible

Repeatedly, Post-Dispatch editors and reporters underline the importance of constant coaching and communicating to help solve problems early rather than dump them on editors late.

"The shift in responsibility has moved to the front end with the reporter and the originating editor more than ever," says Adam Goodman, deputy managing editor for metro and business news. "You can't rely on somebody catching things down the road as much as we used to. . . . It needs to be camera-ready when the reporter sends it."

Deputy Managing Editor for News Steve Parker tracks every published correction. ("It's kind of like being a prison guard," he jokes.) From 2002 to 2005, the annual number sat in the 800s. Then it began drifting downward, to 771 in 2006, 636 in 2007, and 546 last year.

Partly, Parker acknowledges, the drop reflects a declining newshole and volume of copy. But in 2006, the paper also developed a set of "verification guidelines" to reduce errors and spread accountability. They range from the basics ("Ask the subject to spell his/her name. . . . Just before ending the interview, recheck the spelling") to avoiding hoaxes ("Remember that IDs can be faked") to double-checking graphics ("A finished copy . . . must be provided to the reporter or originating editor before it is published").

In addition, Managing Editor Maples says, it becomes essential to recognize when you truly must take your time.

She cites high-profile breaking stories where the newsroom delayed or withheld postings while discussing thorny issues. When area police made a surprise discovery of two missing teenage boys, one of whom had been gone for four-and-a-half years, the Post-Dispatch held an early report because it was based on only one source. A television news operation broke the story, beating the paper by a few minutes. The Post-Dispatch also withheld other information because a reporter's online research was putting it in doubt. It turned out to be incorrect, but other outlets used it.

Last year, a Post-Dispatch stringer witnessed a shooting at a Kirkwood, Missouri, city council meeting. The stringer saw two people get shot, by someone whose voice she recognized, before she took cover under a chair. Reached on her cell phone, she identified both victims and the shooter. After a quick, intense debate involving key editors, the paper's website went with the names but not their conditions or other sensitive details.

By contrast, the paper last year apologized for a "journalistic breakdown" over a feel-good Easter story about a woman's past of "victimization . . . followed by recovery." Multiple details—including the woman's name, marriage, children and various dramatic incidents—were challenged after publication.

To Maples, the broad lesson is that "we have to keep talking about the balance between immediacy and standards . . . We can't slow down, but it should not be 'publish at all costs.'"

Reporters want the help. "If we have to wait six more minutes," says 24-year veteran reporter Tim O'Neil, "let's get it out correctly. The number of times I might grouse about being edited is outweighed by the times people have saved my tail."

Mandy St. Amand, the continuous news editor, once worked at the Associated Press and still believes, "Get it first, but first get it right."

But she recognizes, too, that changing times will test that venerable credo.

"I think there is a trade-off," she concludes. "The editing overall in terms of polishing has waned, but the sense of urgency and excitement has increased. I guess whether that's a fair trade-off will be decided by the readers."

Critical Thinking

1. To what degree do you assume fact-checking and accuracy in news stories you read online? In hard copy publications? Does it matter?

2. What are the implications of "the shift in responsibility [moving] to the front end with the reporter and the originating editor [unable to] rely on someone catching things down the road as much as we used to".

CARL SESSIONS STEPP (cstepp@jmail.umd.edu), AJR's senior contributing editor, teaches at the Philip Merrill College of Journalism at the University of Maryland.

What Would You Do?

The Journalism That Tweaks Reality, Then Reports What Happens

DANIEL WEISS

On a Friday morning last January, a group of Washington, D.C., commuters played an unwitting role in an experiment. As they emerged from the L'Enfant Plaza metro station, they passed a man playing a violin. Dressed in a long-sleeved T-shirt, baseball cap, and jeans, an open case for donations at his feet, he looked like an ordinary busker. In reality, he was Joshua Bell, an internationally renowned musician. The idea was to gauge whether Bell's virtuosic playing would entice the rushing commuters to stop and listen.

The experiment's mastermind was *Washington Post* staff writer Gene Weingarten, who had dreamed it up after seeing a talented keyboardist be completely ignored as he played outside another metro station. "I bet Yo-Yo Ma himself, if he were in disguise, couldn't get through to these deadheads," Weingarten says he thought at the time. Ma wasn't available to test the hypothesis, but Bell was.

For three-quarters of an hour, Bell played six pieces, including some of the most difficult and celebrated in the classical canon. Of 1,097 passersby, twenty-seven made donations totaling just over $30. Seven stopped for more than a minute. The remaining 1,070 breezed by, barely aware of the supremely talented violinist in their midst.

When Weingarten's account of the experiment ran in the *Post's* magazine three months later, readers followed the narrative with rapt attention that contrasted starkly with the indifference of the commuters. The article was discussed on blogs and other forums devoted to classical music, pop culture, politics, and social science. Weingarten said he received more feedback from readers than he had for any other article he had written in his thirty-five-year career. Many were taken with the chutzpah of disguising Joshua Bell as a mendicant just to see what would happen. Others were shocked that people could ignore a world-class musician. Still others argued that the results were insignificant: rerun the experiment outdoors on a sunny day, they said, and Bell would draw a massive crowd.

I was one of those rapt readers, but I wasn't quite sure what to make of the piece's appeal. Was it just a clever gimmick or was there something more profound going on? At the same time, the story felt familiar. Indeed, Weingarten's experiment was a recent entry in a journalistic genre with deep, quirky roots.

Working on a hunch that begs to be tested or simply struck with an idea for a good story, journalistic "experimenters," for lack of a better term, step out of their customary role as observers and play with reality to see what will happen. At their worst, these experiments are little more than variations on reality-TV operations that traffic in voyeurism and shame. At their best, they manage to deliver discussion-worthy insights into contemporary society and human nature. The very best, perhaps, serve up a bit of both. In any case, the growing number of journalists and news operations who do this sort of thing are heirs to a brand of social psychology practiced from the postwar years through the early seventies. During this period, considered by some the golden age of the discipline, experiments were bold and elaborately designed and frequently produced startling results. Many were conducted outside the laboratory and often placed subjects in stressful or disturbing situations.

These experiments also have roots in forms of investigative, immersion, and stunt journalism that have been practiced for more than a century. In 1887, while working on an exposé of asylum conditions, muckraker Nellie Bly demonstrated that one could feign insanity to gain admission to a madhouse—and when she began to insist that she was in fact perfectly sane, doctors interpreted her claims as delusions. In so doing, Bly anticipated psychologist David Rosenhan's classic 1972 experiment in which "pseudopatients" claiming to hear voices were admitted to psychiatric hospitals and then kept for an average of several weeks despite reverting to sane behavior.

It's difficult to pinpoint when the genre shifted, but by 1974, when New York City's WNBC-TV asked its viewers to call in and pick the perpetrator of a staged purse snatching from a lineup of suspects, the journalistic experiment had attained its modern form. The station was flooded with calls and, after fielding over 2,100, cut the experiment short. The results: respondents picked the correct assailant no more frequently than they would have by guessing.

Over the last decade, as best-sellers such as *The Tipping Point* and *Freakonomics* have lent social science a sheen of counterintuitive hipness and reality television has tapped into a cultural fascination with how people behave in contrived situations, journalistic experimentation has become increasingly common. In addition to *The Washington Post Magazine,* it has been featured in *The New York Times, Harper's,* and *Reader's Digest.* Its most regular home, however, has been on network-television newsmagazines.

ABC'S *Primetime* has staged a series of experiments in recent years under the rubric "What Would You Do?" which enact provocative scenarios while hidden cameras capture the reactions of the public. Chris Whipple, the producer who conceived the series, refers to it as a *"Candid Camera of ethics."* Starting with a nanny verbally abusing a child, the series has gone on to present similar scenarios: an eldercare attendant ruthlessly mocking an old man; a group of adolescents bullying a chubby kid; a man viciously berating his girlfriend, seeming on the verge of violence; etc.

The sequences tend to begin with the narrator pointing out that many pass right by the incident. Several witnesses are confronted and asked to explain why they didn't step in. One man, who gave the fighting couple a long look before continuing on his way, reveals that he is an off-duty cop and says he determined that no laws were being broken, so there was nothing for him to do. The focus shifts to those who did intervene, and the camera lingers over the confrontations, playing up the drama.

These experiments are, in a sense, the flip side of the reality-TV coin: rather than show how people act in manufactured situations when they *know* they're being watched, they show us how people act when they don't. And the experiments have clearly appealed to viewers. From the first minutes of its first hour, when its ratings doubled those of the previous week, "What Would You Do?" has been a success. After appearing periodically in 2005 and 2006, ABC ordered five new hours that were scheduled to air last November before the writers' strike put them on hold. It is, Whipple says, highly "watchable" television.

In the world of print, *Reader's Digest* has come closest to making such experiments a franchise. Over the last two years, the magazine has pitted cities around the world against each other in tests of helpfulness and courtesy, to determine which city is most hospitable. The first round used the following three gauges to separate the rude from the solicitous in thirty-five cities: the percentage of people who picked up papers dropped by an experimenter; the percentage who held the door for experimenters when entering buildings; and the percentage of clerks who said "Thank you" after a sale. When the scores were tallied, it was clear that *Reader's Digest* had hit the counterintuition jackpot: the winner was New York City. According to Simon Hemelryk, an editor with the UK edition of *Reader's Digest* who came up with the idea for the tests, the press response was "totally, totally mad." Hundreds of media outlets picked up the story. David Letterman presented a tongue-in-cheek, top-ten list of the "Signs New York City Is Becoming More Polite."

The notion that New Yorkers are more polite than commonly believed was also at the center of a 2004 experiment conducted by *The New York Times.* Reenacting an experiment originally performed by graduate students of social psychologist Stanley Milgram at the City University of New York in the early seventies, two *Times* reporters asked riders on crowded subway cars to relinquish their seats. Remarkably, thirteen of fifteen did

so. But the reporters found that crossing the unspoken social boundaries of the subway came at a cost: once seated, they grew tense, unable to make eye contact with their fellow passengers. Jennifer Medina, one of the reporters, says that she and Anthony Ramirez, her partner on the story, found the assignment ludicrous at first. "It was like, 'What? Really? You want me to do what?'" she says. "We made so much fun of it while we were doing it, but we got so much feedback. It was one of those stories that people really talked about." And papers around the world took notice: within weeks, reporters in London, Glasgow, Dublin, and Melbourne had repeated the experiment.

In these journalistic experiments, the prank always lurks just beneath the surface and is clearly part of the genre's appeal. During ABC *Primetime's* experiments, there always comes the moment when host John Quiñones enters and, with a soothing voice and congenial smile, ends the ruse. *These people are actors. You have been part of an experiment.* And in that moment, no matter how serious the scenario, there is always the hint of a practical joke revealed, a touch of "Smile, you're on *Candid Camera!"*

Sometimes the experiment is overwhelmed by the prank. Last year, *Radar Magazine* sent a reporter to snort confectioner's sugar in various New York City locales. The idea was to test anecdotal evidence from a *New York Times* article that cocaine use was growing more publicly acceptable. (The results: public snorting was actively discouraged at the New York Public Library's main reading room, but not at a Starbucks or *Vanity Fair* editor Graydon Carter's Waverly Inn.) Carter's own *Spy Magazine* pulled a classic prank/experiment in the late eighties when it sent checks of dwindling value to moguls in an attempt to determine who was the cheapest millionaire. (Donald Trump reportedly cashed one for just thirteen cents.) Even *Borat* was, in a sense, an extended experiment in the extremes to which a Kazakh "journalist" could push pliant Americans, and was anticipated by one of *Primetime's* "What Would You Do?" episodes in which a taxi driver goes off on racist or homophobic rants, baiting riders either to defy him or join in.

If Medina, the *Times* reporter, was made uneasy by the whiff of "stunt" in the subway experiment, she is not the only one. Even Weingarten, whose Joshua Bell experiment was a monumental success, looks at the genre slightly askance. Asked whether he plans to conduct similar experiments in the future, he replies: "If I can think of one this good, there's no reason I'd quail at it. But, you know, you also don't want to go off and be the stunt writer. I would need to feel as though the next thing I'm doing was of equal sociological importance. And this wasn't just a lark. We had something we wanted to examine, and it was the nature of the perception of beauty."

The appeal of the best journalistic experiments, indeed, runs much deeper than their entertainment value. Medina came to see her role in the subway experiment as that of a "street anthropologist or something, which is essentially what [reporters] are supposed to be doing every day." And Weingarten received over one hundred messages from people who said that his piece on the Bell experiment made them cry. (One testimonial from an online chat Weingarten had with readers: "I cried because I find it scary and depressing to think of how obliviously most people go through daily life, even smart and otherwise attentive people. Who knows what beautiful things I've missed by just hurrying along lost in my thoughts?") In essence, many readers imagined themselves as actors in the story. Weingarten set out to chronicle an experiment; he ended up writing a deeply effective profile of his own readers. "What Would You Do?" asks *Primetime*—and that, on some level, is the question that all such journalistic experiments ask. Would you walk by the famous violinist? Would you give up your seat on the subway? Would you protect a woman from an abusive boyfriend?

In that quirky, postwar "golden age" of the discipline that informs today's journalistic experimenters, researchers captured the public imagination with bold, elaborately choreographed experiments that frequently drove subjects to extreme behavior or confronted them with seemingly life-or-death situations.

Stanley Milgram, the designer of the subway-seat experiment, was one of the most creative social psychologists of that era. His infamous obedience experiment, first performed in 1961, in which subjects were instructed to shock a man in a separate room every time he gave an incorrect answer on a memory test, showed that normal people were capable of great cruelty. Sixty-five percent of the subjects went to the maximum—450 volts—despite the test-taker's cries of pain and pleas to be released due to a heart condition. By the end, the test-taker no longer responded at all, having presumably passed out or died. (In reality, the test-taker was an actor and his protests tape-recorded.) Even more unsettling was Stanford professor Philip Zimbardo's 1971 prison experiment, in which college students randomly assigned to play the role of guards in a mock prison terrorized those playing inmates. Slated to run for two weeks, it was terminated after six days, during which several "prisoners" came close to nervous breakdown.

Given the dramatic nature of these experiments, it's little wonder they've provided such inspiration to journalists. Bill Wasik, an editor at *Harper's*, started the flash mobs trend in 2003 as an homage to Milgram, whom he considers as much performance artist as scientist. Flash mobs were spontaneous gatherings in which participants showed up at a given location for a brief period and did something absurd, such as drop to their knees en masse before a giant Tyrannosaurus Rex at Toys "R" Us. In a piece published in *Harper's*, Wasik explained that he saw the mobs as a Milgram-esque test of hipster conformity. Like a hot new indie band, he hypothesized, the mobs would rapidly gain popularity before being discarded as too mainstream and, ultimately, co-opted by marketers, which is more or less what happened.

Wasik argues that the popular resonance of experiments by Milgram and others of the golden age derives from the compelling narratives they created. "It's like a demonstration whose value is more in the extremes that you can push people to and the extremes of the story that you can get out of what people do or don't do," he says. "Milgram could have done an authority experiment in which he got people to do all sorts of strange things that didn't seem to be simulating the death of the participant." Many contemporary social psychologists credit researchers from this fertile era with cleverly demonstrating how frequently human behavior defies expectations. But others, such as Joachim Krueger of Brown University, argue that the experiments were designed in ways that guaranteed unflattering results. "You could call it a 'gotcha psychology,'" he says.

Due in part to the rise of ethical concerns, contemporary social psychologists rarely do experiments that take place outside the laboratory or that involve deception or stressful situations. This has left journalistic experimenters as a sort of lost tribe of devotees of the golden-age social psychologists. Unlike investigative journalism, these experiments have largely flown under the ethical radar. This may be because of the fact that, while some journalistic experiments may be frivolous, they are on balance innocuous. However, as experimenters increasingly tackle sensitive topics, they have begun to draw some heat. In 2006, conservative bloggers accused *Dateline* of trying to manufacture a racist incident by bringing a group of Arab-looking men to a NASCAR race. And, last November, these same bloggers ripped an experiment by *Primetime* in which same-sex couples engaged in public displays of affection in Birmingham, Alabama, for attempting to provoke homophobic reactions. (As of press time, the same-sex segment had not yet aired, but according to the Fox affiliate in Birmingham, which broke the story, Birmingham police received several complaints from people disgusted by the sight of two men kissing in public.)

But what of the oft-cited "rule" that journalists should report the news rather than make it? Michael Kinsley, who conducted a 1985 experiment while at *The New Republic* to determine whether the Washington, D.C., elite actually read the books they act like they have, rejects the premise. "If you've got no other way to get a good story," he says, "and you're not being dishonest in what you write and publish, what's wrong with it?" Kinsley's experiment involved slipping notes deep into fashionable political books at several D.C. bookstores, offering $5 to anyone who called an intern at the magazine. In five months, not a single person claimed the reward.

Journalistic experiments have been criticized far more consistently for their scientific, rather than ethical, shortcomings. Robert Cialdini, an Arizona State University social psychologist, believes strongly in the value of communicating psychological insights via the media, but he has found that journalists don't always value the same material that he does. For a 1997 *Dateline* segment on conformity, he conducted an experiment showing that the number of people who donated to a New York City subway musician multiplied eightfold when others donated before them. A fascinating result, but even more fascinating to Cialdini was that people explained their donations by saying that they liked the song, they had some spare change, or they felt sorry for the musician. These explanations did not end up in the finished program. "To me, that was the most interesting thing, the fact that people are susceptible to these social cues but don't recognize it," says Cialdini. "I think that's my bone to pick with journalists—they're frequently interested in the phenomenon rather than the cause of the phenomenon."

Others are frustrated by the premium journalists place on appealing to a mass audience. Duncan Watts, a Columbia University sociologist, designed an experiment for *Primetime* to test Milgram's small-world theory—commonly known as "six degrees of separation"—that people divided by great social or geographical distance are actually connected by a relatively small number of links. In the experiment, two white Manhattan residents competed to connect with a black boxer from the Bedford-Stuyvesant neighborhood of Brooklyn using the fewest links, then the boxer had to connect with a Broadway dancer. All three connections were made using at most six links. Watts says that after the segment aired in late 2006, he received an e-mail from its producer, Thomas Berman, saying that its ratings had been poor. (An ABC spokeswoman insists that the network was satisfied with the ratings.) "One of the limitations of this model is that it's crowd-driven, it's about entertainment," says Watts. "It's a bit of a Faustian bargain."

Another quibble that some social psychologists have with these journalistic experiments is the use of the word "experiment" to describe them in the first place. To a dyed-in-the-wool researcher, an experiment involves comparing a control group with an experimental one, in which a single condition has been varied so that any changes in the outcome can be clearly attributed. Practically no journalistic "experiment" meets this standard, but many golden-age experiments didn't either, strictly speaking. In addition, practically every journalistic experiment includes a disclaimer that its results are decidedly unscientific.

Wendell Jamieson, city editor at *The New York Times* who assigned the subway-experiment story, chafes at calling the exercise an "experiment," pointing out that it was conducted in connection with another article about the original experiment. "It's just a fun way to take a different approach to a story," Jamieson says, comparing it to when he was at the New York *Daily News* and sent a reporter to Yankee Stadium during a subway series dressed in Mets regalia. "It's tabloid trick two-hundred and fifty-two." Bill Wasik, the *Harper's* editor who started flash mobs, points out that using the word "experiment" is a way for journalists to appropriate the "alpha position" of science, lending their endeavors a sort of added legitimacy. "The piece is wearing a lab coat," Wasik says of his own article, which repeatedly describes flash mobs as an experiment, "but it's not entirely scientific by any means."

Perhaps no media outlet has tried harder to achieve uniformity in conducting its experiments than *Reader's Digest*. Detailed instructions for how to conduct its "studies" are distributed to researchers in more than thirty cities around the world to ensure that their results will be comparable. For the courtesy tests, researchers were told how long dropped papers were to be left on the ground, how far to walk behind people entering buildings to see whether they would hold the door, and what sort of demeanor to adopt when speaking with clerks who were being tested to see whether they would say "Thank you." Nonetheless, despite all the careful planning, New York City's courtesy title may need to be affixed with an asterisk. Robert Levine, a social psychologist at California State University, Fresno, did a series of helpfulness experiments in the early nineties in which New York City placed dead last out of thirty-six United States cities. While this doesn't necessarily contradict the *Reader's Digest* result, in which New York was the only U.S. city tested among a global selection of cities, Levine points out that all the *Reader's Digest* New York tests were carried out at Starbucks, yielding a potentially skewed sample. What if Starbucks employees and customers are simply more courteous than New Yorkers as a whole? "I'm not saying they screwed up," says Levine, "but that was certainly a flag that was raised for me."

So maybe journalists can and should be more careful in how they design experiments, but that debate, in many ways, is beside the point. The best examples of the genre are undeniably good journalism, and the lesser lights, for the most part, amount to innocuous entertainment. Indeed, my hope is that some enterprising reporter is even now hatching a plan to find out whether Joshua Bell really would draw such a big crowd outdoors on a sunny day in D.C.

Critical Thinking

1. What's the difference between ABC's "What Would You Do?" story set-ups and social psychology studies by Stanley Milgram and Philip Zimbardo?

2. How would you define *ethical practice* for mass media regarding journalistic "experimenters"?

DANIEL WEISS is a freelance writer based in New York City.

The Lives of Others
What Does It Mean to 'Tell Someone's Story'?

JULIA DAHL

On March 22, *America's Most Wanted* told my story. I wasn't the fugitive, or the victim, and it shouldn't have been my story. It should have been Tyeisha's. But as the producer from *AMW* told me, "Girls die in ditches every day. The reason Tyeisha stands out is because she was profiled in *Seventeen* magazine." I met Tyeisha Martin at a Red Cross shelter in Henry County, Georgia, on a sunny September afternoon in 2005. She was barefoot, wearing a tank top and Capri jeans, waiting in line to get a tetanus shot. I was living in a small town nearby called McDonough, south of Atlanta. I'd moved there a year earlier from New York City with my boyfriend. We were both writers, still thinking we might be able to publish the novels we'd written in grad school. I knew I wanted to write for a living, but I'd left my job at a women's magazine certain I'd never go back. I didn't like what I'd been able to write in that world. Every time I put together an article, it felt like I was building a little lie. Whether it was culled from quotes e-mailed through a publicist, like the cover story I did on the movie star; or built upon crude stereotypes, like the "profile" of the three beauty queens who lived together in Trump Place; or the time I followed the rules of a dating book and neatly concluded that it's better to just be yourself if you want to meet a guy. My instincts as a writer were nowhere in these stories. They weren't little windows on the human condition, they didn't wrestle with questions about the world; they passed the time on the Stair-Master, at the dentist, by the pool.

I justified it plenty. I told myself that Joan Didion had started at *Vogue*. I told myself it meant something that I could make it in the glossies. That I was successful. The problem was that I didn't feel successful. I decamped to Georgia, in part, to get some perspective on all this. But still, I wanted to write. So when *Seventeen* called and asked me to do a story for its Drama section about a young girl in Tennessee who'd been drugged and raped by her cousin, I said yes. Hell, yes. I did stories like this for two years. I went to Birmingham, Alabama, to learn about twelve-year-old Jasmine Archie, who died, according to police reports, after her mother poured bleach down her throat and sat on her chest until she stopped breathing. I went to Wythe County, Virginia, and knocked on the door of the home where fourteen-year-old Nakisha Waddell had stabbed her mother forty-three times and buried her in the backyard. I wrote about

two teenage lesbians who murdered one's grandparents in Fayette County, Georgia. The stories were still formulaic, but instead of chasing publicists and trailing beauty queens, I got to read trial transcripts, track down family members, and hang out in county jails. Each story was an adventure, and, at least initially, the reporting felt like the kind of work I imagined a "journalist" would do.

Tyeisha was an accident. I was in Virginia reporting Nakisha's story when Hurricane Katrina hit, and my editor called to ask if I knew anybody in New Orleans. They wanted to profile a teenage evacuee. I said I might know someone—a girl I knew from the local coffee shop had been headed to Tulane—but I'd have to get back to her.

I promptly forgot about it. There was no easy way to find this girl, since I didn't even know her last name, and I was tired from the reporting trip. Sitting for hours with Nakisha's grandmother had been mentally exhausting. This was the second Drama piece I'd done, and I knew what *Seventeen* wanted was brief and uncomplicated. I wouldn't be able to tell how the old woman's hands shook, or how cigarette smoke was stitched into every fiber in her trailer. Or that hanging in the back hallway where Nakisha stuck a knife in her mother's throat was a plaque that read: "This house shall serve the Lord."

When I got home, I needed to get out of myself, so I went to the Red Cross shelter at the local church where my boyfriend's mom, a nurse, was helping tend to the hundreds of suddenly homeless people from New Orleans. That's when I saw Tyeisha, standing in the middle of a group of boys. Tall, bored, beautiful. I remembered the editor from *Seventeen* and I approached her. She agreed to be profiled. Over the next several days, as she waited for FEMA money in a Days Inn near Atlanta and tried to decide where to go next, Tyeisha told me about her life. She'd dropped out of school in the ninth grade and had a baby at seventeen (she was nineteen when we met). When Katrina hit, she had a GED, a job at a linen factory, and though she and her daughter, Daneisha, were living at her mother's house, Tyeisha dreamed of getting her own place.

On the evening of August 28, 2005, when residents were bracing for the storm, Tyeisha took her daughter to the little girl's father's apartment; he lived on the third floor and she thought two-year-old Daneisha would be safer there. Tyeisha spent the night with her sister, Quiana, and Quiana's boyfriend, Chuck. Before dawn, the water broke down their front door. Tyeisha was terrified as the water rose; she couldn't swim, and thought she was about to die. But Chuck and Quiana helped her, and the three of them climbed out a window and found a wooden door to float on. After several hours of paddling through the filthy water, they found a three-story house that had been abandoned, kicked in a window, and spent the night.

The next morning, the three refugees climbed up to the roof, and at the end of the day were lifted to safety by an Army helicopter. After several sweltering days in the gym at the University of New Orleans, they boarded a bus to Atlanta, where Quiana had friends. Through a series of fortunate coincidences, Tyeisha got in touch with her mother, who had Daneisha and was in Dallas. Her on-again, off-again boyfriend was in Texas, too. Tyeisha decided that's where she should be.

On Friday, September 16, 2005, I dropped Tyeisha off at the Atlanta Greyhound station. She bought a ticket to Dallas and set off for the fifteen-hour ride. Six months later, Tyeisha was dead. She was found in a ditch beside a rural road in Fort Bend County, Texas. She'd been shot in the back of the head.

I learned about Tyeisha's death from Quiana, who called me one night in March 2006 and whispered, "Tyeisha's gone." When she hung up, I went to my computer and found an article in the Texas paper: there was a sketch, and though her features were exaggerated, it was clearly Tyeisha. The article said the body they'd found had tattoos: *Daneisha, RIP Larry.* I remembered those tattoos. I'd asked about them as we sat on a bench outside the church. Larry was Tyeisha's father, who had died, she said, about a year before Katrina hit.

I called the number in the paper and asked to speak to the detective in charge. I explained that I hadn't seen or heard from Tyeisha in months, but I told him what I knew: that she'd survived Katrina, and that she'd apparently gone to Texas to be with her mother, daughter, and boyfriend. He asked me to fax him a copy of the article I wrote for *Seventeen.* He said they didn't have many leads. I gave him Quiana's number, and he promised to call me back. I called *Seventeen,* thinking that if the editors would allow me to write about her death, I could finance a trip to Texas. I could help find her killer. The impulse was a combination of personal outrage (I'd never known anyone who'd been murdered), curiosity, and ambition. I knew the victim and already had the family's trust. I began having visions of writing the *In Cold Blood* of the Katrina diaspora. But there was a new editor on the Drama section, and she didn't sound terribly excited about the idea. She said she'd talk to the editor-in-chief and get back to me.

Days passed. My editor called and said they might want to mention Tyeisha's death in the next issue, but that they didn't want a story about it. "It might be too morbid for the readers," she told me. In my three years covering crimes for *Seventeen,* I had written about four female murderers, about stabbings and suffocation and gunshots to the head. The editors I'd worked with talked a lot about what their readers "wanted." Those readers' attention spans were short, apparently, and their eyeballs had to be hijacked with big, red letters and shocking graphics. When my story about Nakisha ran, "She killed her mom" was

splashed in red letters across the first page; pictured below was a hunting knife "similar" to the one she'd used, and opposite was a grainy yearbook snapshot of Nakisha with stab marks Photoshopped all around her. I called to complain. My editor was polite, but said they knew what was needed to grab the readers' attention in this "media-saturated" environment.

Of course, I was as culpable as the editors at *Seventeen.* I did the reporting that revealed nuance and uncertainty, and then did what I was told and turned in simplistic, straightforward stories with immutable lines between cause and effect. So why didn't Tyeisha's unsolved death make the cut? It occurred to me that the story didn't fit the fiction of the magazine. The rigid code that dictated a certain number of pages be given to fashion, celebrities, and make-up also assured that lines didn't get crossed. Tyeisha's story had been one of triumph over tragedy. To have her escape Katrina and six months later be found by a roadside in rural Texas was just too complicated.

But I didn't push. I dashed off pitches to various other publications I thought might be interested in her story: *Texas Monthly,* the *Christian Science Monitor, The New York Times.* No one bit. So I let go. Quiana and I talked every few days, then every couple of weeks. The case went nowhere.

Six weeks later, I got a call from *America's Most Wanted.* Karen Daborowski, a producer, had read about Tyeisha in the *Houston Chronicle* and said they wanted to do a segment on her death. "Maybe we can find her killer," she said. I had not watched *America's Most Wanted* in years. In fact, had you asked me about the show the day before Karen called, I probably would have said it had been pulled by Fox a long time ago. But what I remembered as a mildly creepy combination of *Unsolved Mysteries* and *A Current Affair* had been airing nonstop every Saturday night since 1988. The show was still hosted by a man named John Walsh, who'd been thrust into the spotlight in 1981 when his son, Adam, was kidnapped and murdered. To date, it has helped catch a thousand fugitives.

So I agreed to the interview. But the interview turned into a request to travel with the producers and a crew to Texas. "We want the story to be about you," said Karen. "About your bond with Tyeisha and how you cared enough to find her killer." Calling my fleeting relationship with Tyeisha a bond was a stretch, but in my mind, Karen was asking how much I was willing to do to help Tyeisha. The story of her death deserved to be told, and if I couldn't convince *Seventeen* or any other publication of that, I figured I could get in front of a camera and help someone else tell it. I didn't think about what it meant, journalistically, to become an advocate for someone I'd written about. Having had no formal training in the craft I practiced, I navigated articles and the people involved by my gut, and I felt I owed Tyeisha this much. It also didn't occur to me that I'd become to Karen what Tyeisha had been to me: a subject. Just as I'd asked Tyeisha to relive Katrina beneath a magnolia tree so I could write an article about her for *Seventeen,* Karen was asking me to be a character in her own television report about Tyeisha.

On October 13, 2006, I met Karen and Sedgwick Tourison, another producer, at the American Airlines terminal at Baltimore's BWI. We landed in Dallas around noon and drove to a Whattaburger restaurant near the airport to meet Dave Barsotti and Tom Overstreet, the local camera and audio guys. We all said hello, then Dave dropped a mini-microphone down my blouse, tucked a battery pack into my pants, and told me to get in the driver's seat of the rented Jeep Cherokee. As I drove, Tom aimed his camera at me and Sedg prompted me to talk about what I was doing.

"I'm driving," I said, lamely.

"To . . . " steered Sedg.

"I'm driving to visit Tyeisha's mom, Cabrini, and her daughter Daneisha," I said.

We exited the freeway and made our way into Cabrini's apartment complex. As the crew unloaded the equipment, I wondered how I would greet Cabrini. The woman's daughter had been murdered not six months before, and here I was waltzing in with cameras and lights and four more strangers to poke at her pain. The point, obviously, was to find Tyeisha's killer. I hoped Cabrini knew that. Karen gave the word, and I walked down the outdoor hallway toward Tom, who had his camera positioned on his shoulder, and knocked on the door. Quiana opened it, looking gorgeous, just liked I remembered her. We hugged and I stepped toward Cabrini, who was wearing a T-shirt with a picture of Tyeisha on it. I wasn't sure if I should hug her or shake her hand, but she came toward me with her arms open, and I was glad. The crew flipped on the lights, wired everyone up, and we started talking on-camera, first about Katrina, then about what Cabrini remembered of Tyeisha's arrival in Texas. Tyeisha didn't want to stay in Dallas a day longer than she had to. "She was like, 'Mama, it's all old people around here,'" said Cabrini. So she took Daneisha and left for Houston, where her boyfriend lived. For the first time in her entire life, Tyeisha got her own apartment. Her own furniture. "She was so excited," said Cabrini. "She said, 'Mama, there's no rules. I can wake up when I want.' I said, 'Lord, I wouldn't want to live where there's no rules.'" In February, Tyeisha stopped calling. On March 9, 2006, six months to the day after I met her, her body was found in a grassy ditch at the bend of a county road.

We woke up early the next morning and met downstairs at the hotel for breakfast. Sedg laid out the day's schedule, which began with an hour of them filming me typing on my laptop in my room. Sedg wanted more shots of Quiana and me, so we picked her up and drove to a nearby park. Quiana was six years older than Tyeisha, and more articulate and outgoing. Life hasn't been easy for her. She is twenty-nine, and has four children. She had an emergency hysterectomy just a few months before Katrina hit. The storm washed away her home and separated her from her mother, sister, and children. She settled in Atlanta with her boyfriend, but they broke up. And then her sister was murdered.

When the cameras were ready, we said our lines. I asked her about the last time she talked to her sister, and she said it had been weeks and that she'd begun to worry. We repeated this sequence several times so they could film us from different angles. Quiana didn't seem to mind. I remembered what she said to me months ago, when she called and told me about the murder: "I don't want to see my sister on *Cold Case Files* in five years. I want somebody caught."

After we dropped off Quiana, Sedg and Karen told me they wanted some *Sex and the City* shots of me, so we stopped at an upscale strip mall to do more filming. Trailed by Tom and his camera, I dutifully walked into a boutique and gazed at racks of clothing I couldn't afford. Karen assured me that they needed shots like this to "set me up" as a former New York City magazine writer. They thought it important to play up the "fish out of water" angle: big-city girl gets caught up in a small-town murder. The whole thing was false, and I reminded Karen that I hadn't been on staff at a women's magazine since 2002. But in the language of reality television, three years of my life are boiled down to a shopping trip in order to facilitate a story arc.

That night we flew to Houston, and the next morning we showed up at the Fort Bend County sheriff's station. Inside, Detective Campbell—who Sedg had warned me was "all business"—opened his case file, and pulled out color photographs of the crime scene. There she was: lying in the grass, her skinny legs sticking out from under a yellow tarp. She had on the same blue jeans and belt she was wearing when I met her. The grass around her body was long and lush, green and damp. I wondered if it rained on her while she laid, eyes wide open, in the clover. She was found just a few feet off the road, and according to Campbell, had been shot there. There were minimal wounds other than the fatal bullet wound, which Campbell said suggested that she had been killed by someone she knew. Campbell told us that when he visited her apartment, "it was organized and homey. Like she was focused on raising a child." He showed us birth certificates and FEMA correspondence. She'd kept her papers in a shoebox. "She was doing all the things she should," he said. "She was setting up her future."

The big Texas sky was crowded with clouds in every shade of gray as we drove past fields of cows and ducks, past an old country homestead with a gated family cemetery in the front yard, past Trav's Roadhouse, to the bend in the road where Tyeisha was murdered. A house sat just a few hundred yards away, but Campbell interviewed the people there, and they didn't hear the gunshot. "The TV was probably on," he said. As Tom and Dave set up the shot, I stepped onto the grass, half expecting to feel some sort of ghostly presence. The sun shone through the clouds, but I tried to imagine the road at night. I tried to see her in her last moments. I tried to feel her fear. But I couldn't. All I could do was what I was doing, standing before the cameras to make sure she was not forgotten.

Months went by. And then a year. Occasionally, I would get a phone call from Karen, saying they were planning to air the show soon, but then she'd drop out of contact for a couple of months. At one point, it had apparently been slated to run as part of a special Hurricane Katrina hour in late 2007, but then she told me it was "so strong," they wanted it to anchor another episode. Tyeisha had been dead more than two years when the segment finally aired on March 22, 2008.

I was back in Georgia that weekend, visiting my boyfriend's family. We got take-out BBQ from a local rib shack and gathered in front of the TV. Before each commercial break, they teased my segment: "Coming up: a magazine writer leaves behind the glitzy New York fashion world in a quest for justice." I covered my face as they pasted my voice over clips of Sarah

Jessica Parker adjusting her skirt on the street and cringed at the reenactments. The "Julia" in the segment had a big apartment with leather couches, and the "Tyeisha" was much more conservative than the tattooed girl with messy, maroon-tinted hair extensions I'd met in Georgia. They flashed images of the real Tyeisha on the screen, but my face was the most prominent. The piece even ended with John Walsh giving me a "personal thanks" for being involved.

To me, the compelling story is still Tyeisha's. How, like thousands of her friends and neighbors in New Orleans, she was torn from her support system, separated from the people who looked out for her. She'd tried to rebuild a life for herself and her child in a new state and instead became the victim of a brutal murder. But no one else seemed particularly interested in that story. According to the Centers for Disease Control, homicide is the second leading cause of death for black women between ages fifteen and twenty-four, but even to *America's Most Wanted*, Tyeisha's tale was only worth telling in relation to me.

I suppose I knew that the press tends to illuminate the exceptions, the extremes. The plight of the family with septuplets instead of the more common burden of unexpected twins; the detained immigrant with the amputated penis instead of the thousands with untreated depression. The impulse is understandable, and certainly an oddball story can draw attention to a worthy issue, but what of the issues inside the more common stories? By their very nature, such issues—like mental illness in immigrant communities, or the high murder rate among young black women—are more intransigent, harder to untangle and fit into a facile narrative. I imagine that maybe Jill Leovy, a reporter at the

Los Angeles Times, was thinking this way when she created The Homicide Report, a blog on the paper's website that attempts to report on every single homicide in Los Angeles County; last year, there were 324. As the explanatory page puts it, "only the most unusual and statistically marginal homicide cases receive press coverage, while those cases at the very eye of the storm—those which best expose the true statistical dimensions of the problem of deadly violence—remain hidden."

It remains to be seen whether my appearance on *America's Most Wanted* will lead to the capture of Tyeisha's killer. Two months after the show aired, there are no promising leads, but I believe I did the right thing, as a human being and as a journalist, when I realize that had I walked out of that Georgia church ten minutes later, or turned left instead of going straight out the door, Tyeisha Martin—not yet twenty years old, mother, sister, daughter, hurricane survivor—would have died not only too soon, but in silence.

Critical Thinking

1. How would you define the rules of *ethical practice* in "drama" pieces that personalize victims of tragedy? Who, besides the subject of a news story, is affected by such judgments?

2. Julia Dahl writes, "I suppose I knew that the press tends to illuminate the exceptions, the extremes." Do you find this to be true? To what effect?

Julia Dahl is a writer who lives in Brooklyn.

A Porous Wall

As news organizations, in their struggle to survive, blur the line between editorial and advertising, does credibility take a hit?

NATALIE POMPILIO

The latest fissure in the wall between editorial and advertising came in April, when the Los Angeles Times ran a front-page advertisement that could easily have been confused for an actual news article. Placed prominently in the left-hand column below the fold, an ad for the police drama "Southland" carried NBC's peacock logo and was labeled "advertisement," but it was written in story form as if a reporter had accompanied the police officer who is the show's main character on a ride-along.

Many in the Times' newsroom balked, including Editor Russ Stanton. A circulated petition decried the ad as deceptive and said it made "a mockery of our integrity and our journalistic standards."

The newspaper's publisher responded that the ad netted a premium rate and was part of the effort to ensure the survival of his publication, which has cut hundreds of jobs in the last year and whose parent company, Tribune Co., has filed for bankruptcy.

Is this a sign of things to come or simply a misstep as newspapers seek to redefine themselves as economically viable?

"There's so much economic pressure, it seems everything is on the table," says Andy Schotz, chairman of the Society of Professional Journalists' ethics committee and a general assignment reporter for the Herald-Mail in Hagerstown, Maryland. But "we have to be vigilant about maintaining the integrity of the news side. A struggling economy is not a reason to loosen the standards."

There was a time when advertisements on the front page of a newspaper were anathema, when the separation between marketing and editorial was as vigorously defended as the separation between church and state. "We were all so pristine," recalls Geneva Overholser, director of the School of Journalism at the USC Annenberg School for Communication and former editor of the Des Moines Register. The attitude, she says, was "no one from advertising should ever darken the newsroom."

Those days seem to be gone, as remote as newsrooms thick with cigarette smoke and loud with the clatter of typewriter keys. Even Overholser says, "I long ago gave up the idea of front-page ads as sin."

Front-page and section-front advertisements are more common, with even the most respected publications putting prime news real estate up for sale (see "No Longer Taboo," June/July 2007). Sponsored content, online and in print, is growing. Advertisers are crossing lines with their marketing techniques, packaging selling points as news to increase their product's credibility while possibly hurting journalists'.

While many experts agree the beleaguered news industry has to change its ways in order to survive, the question is how to do so while maintaining credibility and standards.

"Now, when newspapers are desperately trying to figure out what their future is, it's time to figure out what the principles are," Overholser says. "The rule is you don't try to deceive or fool readers. That's deeply offensive and breaks the bond with readers. That's not about the wall breaking down. That's about principles. It's about credibility."

Bob Steele, the Poynter Institute's Nelson Poynter Scholar for Journalism Values, says the idea of a solid Berlin Wall-type structure between advertising and editorial is outdated. He's long seen it as more of a picket fence: Each side has clearly delineated roles and principles, but "you can talk over the picket fence. If there's a gate, you can go back and forth," he says.

Skip Foster, former editor and now publisher of the Star in Shelby, North Carolina, says a different game is afoot when marketing and advertising decisions directly affect the number of newsroom bodies left to cover the news. While the L.A. Times ad may have stirred up a controversy, he says, at least it took a chance with something new.

"If we're not goofing up occasionally, we're probably not testing that line as we should," he says. If "we don't start trying some crazy things and [won't] be willing to fail and look stupid, I don't think we're going to make it."

He believes it's time to question those who simply want to maintain the status quo when talk comes to the dividing line between news and ads: "Did we have the line in the right place in the first place?" he asks. "How movable is that line? Is the line in a different place online and a different place in print?"

This is not the first time print organizations have made short-term news decisions that may not be in the long-term interest of the publication, he says. Some papers, his included, used to mock the old TV adage "If it bleeds, it leads." Now he finds his front page playing to the idea. "And not feeling bad about it, either. If it's what people want and we can benefit from it, there aren't many win-wins out there," he says. "Having a long-term view is a lot harder when you don't know what the long term's going to be or if the long term includes your presence as a news organization."

The Star hasn't dabbled in much front-page advertising—"we're probably holding out for too high a price," Foster says—but he's willing to consider it. The "right" advertisements will be clearly labeled with some design oversight so it's not messing up the page, but otherwise it's " 'you know it when you see it' type stuff," he says.

"If somebody comes to us willing to pay the premium rate to do something that doesn't fit into my initial set of standards, I'll listen," he says. "We're not going to do anything that's masquerading as news, but the rest is gray."

The bottom line is not to deceive: One newspaper publisher, who didn't want to be quoted by name, so as not to alienate his marketing department, described how one major local business not only wanted to sponsor a column related to its industry but also have one of its own writers produce it. Why not, the business argued, as another nearby newspaper is already doing the same thing? The publisher declined the column—and the ad revenue.

Kelly McBride, ethics group leader at Poynter, says she constantly gets questions on this issue. "Every major metro market is debuting new products meant to generate more revenue, and there's questions about all of it," she says.

She's written about one TV station that put a fast-food company's cup in prominent places on its anchors' desks during newscasts, and she participated in a panel discussion with bloggers whose independence was marred by the many handouts they received. She recently took a call from someone who knew of a newspaper that has a nightlife column that is editorially driven in print but is an advertisement online.

"It's going to become increasingly murky what is independent journalistic judgment and what is influenced by an advertiser with an ulterior motive."

—Kelly McBride

"I see the business imperative to find new sources of revenue and new ways to make money. What worries me is the cost to credibility," she says. "You can't tell me that people are not confused. I believe the audience is savvy, but I also believe the more things we throw at them, the more confusing it gets. The ultimate result of all of this is in the audience's mind. It's

going to become increasingly murky what is independent journalistic judgment and what is influenced by an advertiser with an ulterior motive."

More than one person interviewed for this article noted the growing number of advertisements packaged as news copy and wondered if publications should accept them. Weekend newspaper inserts have featured an advertisement for the so-called "Amish fireplace," an electric heater. The full-page ad is designed to look like a news story, complete with bold headline, subheads, photos and a byline. The word "ADVERTISE-MENT" appears in small print at the center of the top of the page.

SPJ's Schotz notes that ad designers will "push as far as they can" unless pushed back. In one case, a reader called Schotz's newsroom about an ad, wondering if reporters knew whether its claims were true. "I put him in touch with our advertising department," Schotz says. "We're used to how a newspaper is put together and what is what, but many people aren't necessarily as sophisticated."

At his own newspaper in Hagerstown, Schotz dislikes the placement of so-called "sticky ads"—the removable promo stickers that are now appearing on front pages. When, after a long illness, a local politician died, his name was stripped across the front—but the sticky ad was stuck over the all-important verb in the headline—"DIES".

"You can't have two pieces of information in the same physical spot," Schotz says. "You can't have a news headline and an ad and expect they won't interfere with each other."

Sponsored content is another vexing issue facing journalists in the 21st century. For the last two years, Citizens Bank has sponsored a column in the Philadelphia Inquirer. The bank's trademark green outlines the column and its logo appears prominently on the front page of the business section. The column is written by veteran business reporter Mike Armstrong.

Inquirer Editor William K. Marimow says the sponsorship brings in "a significant amount of revenue" but his only real complaint about the advertising element of it is that it takes away from the newshole.

"It's probably symbolically annoying to some of us, but in my view it has no effect on what Mike Armstrong writes or doesn't write," Marimow says. "When Citizens Bank does something great, we're going to report it, and if they do something awful, we're going to report it."

Could other columns receive sponsorship? "As long as something does not intrude with the news, it's something I'll consider," Marimow says.

Armstrong says that while it may sometimes be awkward—"who else has a column that has an ad wrapped around it in this country?"—the sponsorship has no effect on what he writes. He still addresses banking issues, as do other reporters in the business section. In some ways, he says, the choice of sponsor may have made the project easier on him: Citizens Bank is owned by the Royal Bank of Scotland and doesn't make much news in Philadelphia.

"If they were a bailout bank, it would be a little uncomfortable," Armstrong says, "but I would need to be writing about it."

He doesn't even notice the ad anymore. "It's like wallpaper," he says. But readers notice it, and sometimes they are confused. "I've gotten calls from readers asking for the name of the branch manager in their neighborhoods," he says. "I say, 'I don't work for the bank.'"

In some ways, allowing the bank to put its logo on the business page is simply a placement issue, similar to the way a clothing store might ask that its ad go in the features section or a law firm might want its ad near the legal notices, says Robert Niles, editor of Online Journalism Review and a blogger for Knight Digital Media Center.

"If a sponsor wants to say, 'I want my ad to appear every day on page A2,' and it runs opposite someone else's column, we've given them placement," Niles says. "It's only a baby step to say, 'This column is presented by.' It's not 'produced by.' It's not 'created by.' It's just 'sponsored by.'"

"For the advertiser, control of the day-to-day coverage isn't as important as there being coverage of the thing that is important to them."

—Robert Niles

When Niles worked at the Rocky Mountain News, the online weather page was sponsored by the outdoor gear company REI. There's little doubt that REI wasn't able to control what temperatures were reported. "For the advertiser, control of the day-to-day coverage isn't as important as there being coverage of the thing that is important to them," Niles says. "They're smart enough to know that if they control the everyday coverage, the public will know and ignore it. It's no good to publish something that nobody reads."

Dallas Mavericks owner Mark Cuban said as much last year in a post on blogmaverick.com. In the December missive, Cuban proposed creating a "beat writer cooperative." Funded by major sports leagues, the cooperative would employ at least two writers in each sports market. The owners would benefit with increased, in-depth coverage of their teams. The newspapers would benefit because the writers would answer only to the editors they were writing for.

In an e-mail interview with AJR, Cuban explained that control of content wasn't what mattered.

"Newspaper coverage helps build awareness and commitment to a team. Whether it's positive or negative," he wrote. "The suggestion that there is a theme of control means that you believe that there cannot be any trust or contractual agreement between media and teams. That is just not the case. It would be incredibly easy to do a document of understanding saying, 'you write what you want to write. We won't have any

say in the matter. Even if we get mad at you over what you wrote, we won't interfere. On the flip side, since we are contributing financially to your survival and hoped for success, we expect that you cover the team at minimum, on a daily basis during our season, and at least x times per week in the off season.'"

Such an agreement could improve sports coverage, according to Cuban.

Reporters and columnists in today's climate are so worried about keeping their jobs that they might hold back negative coverage so as not to affect their access to their teams. A cooperative would "provide some level of stability to the business of sports reporting [and] it could actually open the door for better reporting. Regardless of whether that coverage is positive or negative," Cuban wrote.

"Either you trust your reporters to do their job and for editors and publishers to attempt to be impartial in the stories they choose, regardless of pressure from any outside source, or you don't."

—Mark Cuban

"Either you trust your reporters to do their job and for editors and publishers to attempt to be impartial in the stories they choose, regardless of pressure from any outside source," he concluded, "or you don't."

Given all the entanglements, transparency may be the best way for news organizations to stay credible. "Anything that is sponsored by anything needs to be clearly labeled," Overholser says. "To me, transparency is the last strong ethic standing."

Readers have to know an organization's ethics policies—and be reminded of them again and again and again. McBride says that if she were editor of the Inquirer, for example, she might end each Citizens Bank-sponsored column with a tagline like, "Our standards for editorial independence can be found here," with an accompanying link.

"Full disclosure is a bare minimum," McBride says. "You also need to write policy and best-practices issues for your public and let them comment upon it."

What's worrisome, she says, is the fact that not everyone will hold to the same high standards. And that, she adds, "will undermine everything that we do. Their stink will wash off on us."

Fred Brown, a former SPJ president and vice chair of the organization's ethics committee, believes one of the mistakes the L.A. Times made with its front-page ad was not discussing the placement with everyone involved and invested in the product's credibility.

"If you're going to have standards that apply to your particular media outlet, everyone should have a say in what those standards are," Brown says. "That discussion needs to happen in the newsroom. Let the marketers in on the discussion, too. The problem is, reporters don't understand the marketing side, and the marketers don't understand the reporting side. Their goal should be the same, but their methods are different."

Brown recently worked to revise SPJ's ethics handbook. Someone asked about including the L.A. Times case as an example. He didn't think that was such a good idea.

"If you're going to have a good ethics case study, there ought to be two sides to that," he says. "In this case, one side would be, 'We have to survive,' but that's not an ethics question."

Critical Thinking

1. How would you define the rules of *ethical practice* regarding separation of editorial and advertising content and personnel in news media?

2. How do you respond to product placement in news media? Do you notice it? Do you have objections to it? To what degree do you think it affects consumer behavior? Are your thoughts any different regarding product placement in entertainment media?

NATALIE POMPILIO (nataliepompilio@yahoo.com), a former reporter for the Philadelphia Inquirer and New Orleans' Times-Picayune, is a Philadelphia-based writer.

UNIT 4
A Word from Our Sponsor

Unit Selections

Learning Outcomes

The articles in this section will contribute to your being able to

- Describe differences between Google and YouTube business models.

- Discuss the challenges of applying traditional media marketing tools, such as Nielsen ratings and circulation figures, to establishing advertising practices and rates for the Internet or Twitter.

- Analyze the implications of tensions inherent in producing "free" media content.

- Describe the relationship between advertisers and mass media. Develop and support a reasoned prediction of how advertising dollars will be spent in ten years.

Student Website
www.mhhe.com/cls

Internet References

Advertising Age
www.age.com
Citizens Internet Empowerment Coalition (CIEC)
www.ciec.org
Educause
www.educause.edu
Media Literacy Clearing House
www.frankwbaker.com/default1.htm
Young Media Australia
www.youngmedia.org.au/mediachildren/03_advertising.htm

Advertising is the major source of profit for newspapers, magazines, radio, and television, and advertising tie-ins are a common element in motion picture deals. While media writers have the potential of reflecting their own agendas and social/political viewpoints as they produce media messages, they depend largely upon financial backing from advertisers who have other interests to protect. Advertisers use media as a means of presenting goods and services in a positive light. They are willing to pay generously for the opportunity to reach mass audiences, but unwilling to support media that do not deliver the right kind of audience for their advertisements.

Mass advertising developed along with mass media; in fact, commercial media have been described by some as a system existing primarily for the purpose of delivering audiences to advertisers. The price for selling commercial space is determined by statistical data on how many and what kinds of people are reached by the media in which the ad is to appear. In 2008–2009, a 30-second spot on *Grey's Anatomy* sold for $327,000 (down from $419,000 in 2007–2008), on *Sunday Night Football* $435,000 (up from $358,000). A 30-second spot during the 2010 Super Bowl ran $3.2 million, an all-time high (the cost has quadrupled since 1990) even in a tough economy. The American Association of Advertising Agencies and Association of National Advertisers statistics report 18 minutes of each hour (30%) during prime time television is devoted to commercials; half-hour programs may include as much as 12 minutes of ads.

Super Bowl ads still draw a lot of attention, but changes in how consumers use and interact with media have had significant effect on traditional advertiser–media relationships. Television rarely delivers the kind of mass–mass audience to advertisers upon which ad rate practices were built; according to a recent study by Marian Azzaro, professor of marketing at Roosevelt University in Chicago, advertisers would need to buy 42% more time on the three major networks than they did 10 years ago to reach the same number of consumers. VCRs, DVRs, and TiVo allow consumers to bypass traditional commercial messages. New media draw a lot of eyes, but counting consumers and assessing how they interact with advertising messages there is a new science. Daily Google searches in 2000 numbered 100 million; in 2010, 2 billion. Active blogs in 2000 numbered 12,000; in 2010, 141 million. Video game revenue increased from $7.98 billion in 2000 to $19.66 billion in 2010. CD sales revenue decreased from $943 million in 2000 to $427.9 million in 2010. iTunes downloads increased from 0 in 2000 to 10 billion in 2010.

As the number of media choices increases and audiences diffuse, advertising agencies have adjusted their media-buying focus from quantity to quality of potential consumers who will be exposed to a single ad. The current focus of many agencies is niche advertising, with interest in data split by age, gender, ethnic background, and income factors that determine how a given consumer might respond to a product pitch. The outgrowth of niching is seen in media products from the Food Network and Home & Garden Television, to magazines targeted to narrowly defined interests (e.g., *Golf*), to ads on the Web, in video games, over cell phones, on "airport TV," and in classrooms on Channel One. Google sold $21.1 billion in ads in 2008, compared to

© The McGraw-Hill Companies, Inc./John Flournoy, photographer

$16.4 billion in 2007 and $10.5 billion in 2006. Sometimes, product pitches creep directly into entertainment media, where they can strike below the level of consumer awareness. Market research finds viewers 25% more likely to shop at Sears after viewing "Extreme Makeover: Home Edition," which features Sears Kenmore appliances and Craftsman tools. Coke is on the judges' desk on "American Idol," Doritos and Mountain Dew presented to challenge winners on "Survivor." Products or logos may also be inserted into already filmed movies and television programs—not a new practice, but one attracting new attention, as technological advances make it easier to do so.

This section begins with articles about financial support and new media. Aside from addressing its title question, "How Can YouTube Survive?" lends insight into new media business models and marketing strategies in general: "The fact that most people over the age of 30 doubt that online businesses can survive by offering free services is irrelevant, because most people under the age of 30 are demanding the. . . . And while many see this as a selfish, unrealistic attitude, the onus is on businesses to get themselves out of this mess because the digital medium exercises unstoppable power." AdWords has been described as "data-fueled, auction-driven recipe for profitability" by which Google sells online advertising. Google generates enormous profits. YouTube does not.

"But Who's Counting" includes discussion of panel-based audience measurement services designed to provide headcount figures for Web views that parallel Nielsen ratings for television. "Brain Candy" offers a brief introduction to neuromarketing, a process of using MRI brain scanning technology to maximize physiological effects of movies and advertising.

"Multitasking Youth" reports on research about how young people consume offline and online media: "While young consumers' multitasking activity is not welcome news for marketers stuck in a mind-set of traditional approaches to advertising and media planning, this increasingly common approach to media consumption presents significant opportunities to companies seeking to engage their audiences in new and different ways."

"Tossed by a Gale" analyzes the relationship between "aggregators" and their content sources. Aggregators "make money by funneling readers past advertisements, which may be tailored to their presumed interests. They are cheap to run: Google news does not even employ an editor."

"Open for Business" takes a position that consumers will pay for niche-specific specialized information and the future of news media lies in "deciding what you can sell to those willing to pay . . . to underwrite the cost of producing original work that might remain free and be of interest to more than a select few."

"Nonprofit News" points out that "Done right, the journalism-funder relationship benefits both parties as well as the public they aim to serve. . . . Done wrong, the association raises concerns about editorial objectivity, and whether it has been compromised by the funder's agenda."

Finally, in "Arianna's Answer," Daniel Lyons lays out the success and problems HuffPo (The Huffington Post) has encountered in being a profitable news and information outlet.

From a media literacy standpoint, analyzing the truth and values communicated by advertisements themselves is only part of understanding advertising's impact. It is important to understand the gatekeeping role financial backers have in overall media content. Most advertising account executives admit their unwillingness to be associated with media that create negative publicity. All of them put a premium on reaching certain advertiser-desirable groups; media targeted to the interests of those audiences proliferate, while those attractive to other audiences do not. As William Powers wrote in *The Atlantic Monthly* ("The Massless Media," January/February 2005), "Although much changes in the media over time, there are some eternal truths. Most outlets crave two things, money and impact, and the easiest path to both is the old fashioned one: grow your audience. Ambitious niches will always seek to become larger, and in so doing attract a more diverse audience."

How Can YouTube Survive?

It's wildly popular—and thought to be losing hundreds of millions of dollars a year. Now questions are being asked about the future of YouTube. Rhodri Marsden investigates a mystery of digital-age "freeconomics."

RHODRI MARSDEN

I t must surely rank as the most mundane business launch in history. Jawed Karim, one of the founders of YouTube, shuffles timidly in front of a video camera while standing in front of a group of elephants at San Diego zoo, with precious little idea of what he was starting. "The cool thing about these guys," he says, nervously gesturing behind him, "is that they have really long trunks. And that's pretty much all there is to say."

This 19-second video clip, uploaded to the brand-new website later that day, 23 April 2005, may have been insubstantial, but it certainly wasn't inconsequential. Within 18 months, Karim and his partners Steve Chen and Chad Hurley had sold YouTube to Google for $1.76bn, and in doing so became one of a select band of online entrepreneurs who managed to grab our attention—and keep it.

Innumerable jaded web entrepreneurs will tell you how easy it is to get thousands of people to glance at a site, but how tortuous it is to get people to stick around or even come back again the following day. Not only do you have to fulfil a desire that people didn't even realise that they had, but it has to be done with such style and panache that your service becomes indispensable. While the internet may have dismantled many of the traditional barriers to reaching us, the general public, if your idea is anything less than sensational, we will flatly ignore it.

But YouTube was sensational. Prior to its launch, creating a videoclip for someone else to watch online was an arcane and deeply frustrating procedure of digitisation, encoding and embedding that was way more trouble than it was worth—not least because incompatible technologies meant that many people wouldn't be able to watch it. But from humble beginnings in a room above a pizzeria in San Mateo, California, Hurley, Chen and Karim made the process simple, they made it relatively quick, and above all else, they made it free.

By mid-2006, the site was fizzing with activity as we started using our YouTube channel as a jukebox, a blogging service, a promotional tool for our bands, a home video vault, a repository of famous film and television moments—sometimes with the blessing of the copyright owners, more often without it—and just occasionally, it provided an unexpected route to stardom. YouTube entered the lexicon and became synonymous with online video; the former Secretary of State for Local Government, Hazel Blears, dropped the phrase "YouTube if you want to" into an attack on Gordon Brown's style of Government.

Blears making a feeble joke about YouTube is just one small measure of its phenomenal success. But while its staggering popularity is without question—some 345 million visitors worldwide descend upon the website every month—it is haemorrhaging cash. The question of exactly how unprofitable it is continues to be the source of fierce debate online; back in April, analysts at Credit Suisse estimated that its operating losses for this year would reach $470m, while San Francisco-based IT consultants RampRate were more optimistic, but still put the figure at just over $174m. Google isn't rushing to put an end to speculation over the scale of the debt. One thing is abundantly clear from both studies: Google isn't making money by letting everyone and their aunt share videos with each other for free. And the news last week that founder Steve Chen was leaving YouTube to work on other projects at Google kicked off another flurry of rumours as to its possible fate.

M usic, television, sport, gaming: the flow of free entertainment to our computer screens seems almost the result of a magical process, and there's been little need for us to consider the costs that might have been incurred by those making it all happen. It's broadly accepted that YouTube will receive around $240m of revenue from advertising this year, but that sum doesn't even cover their general overheads and the cost of acquiring premium video content (such as TV shows) from copyright holders. In addition, there are the huge fixed costs from the supply side—data centres, hardware, software and bandwidth—that have to cope with the 20 hours of video clips that we upload to YouTube every minute of every day. Again, no-one knows the true total of these costs—the Credit Suisse and RampRate reports put it between $83m and $380m this year—but Google's Chief Financial Officer, Patrick Pichette, would only reveal one thing: "We know our cost position, but nobody else does." Or, in other words, we're not telling you.

This typifies the slightly secretive but ultimately sanguine position of Google even as phrases like "financial folly" are bandied about to describe the YouTube business model. With Google's overall profits reaching some $1.42bn for the first quarter of this year alone, the king of online search is certainly in a position to support a loss-making venture that also happens to be the third-most-popular website on the internet. (Google, naturally, is the first.) But Keith McMahon, senior analyst for the Telco 2.0 Initiative, a research group that studies business models in the digital economy, believes that YouTube is not the albatross around Google's neck that it's widely imagined to be. He sees the search company as deriving massive indirect benefits from operating YouTube and believes that estimates of its losses obscure the true picture.

"There are many urban myths surrounding the way that companies extract value from the internet," he says. "Google's spin-off benefits from owning YouTube include the accumulation of our data and strengthening of their network design—and the more time people spend watching online video, the more advertisers will pour into marketing on the internet as a whole. There's no doubt that Google can afford YouTube."

McMahon also believes that by keeping quiet about YouTube's hidden benefits and by allowing the misconception of it as a deeply unprofitable business to circulate, things work very nicely in Google's favour when it comes to negotiating with copyright holders in the world of TV, movies and music. Copyright holders can't demand money that isn't there, and it would certainly take no more than a hint of profitability at YouTube for lawyers to descend, threatening court cases and demanding higher royalties. In the new, topsy-turvy world of online economics, it seems astonishing that losses on paper have actually made YouTube a more powerful online force.

But while Google's pockets may be deep enough to operate a phenomenally popular online service at no cost to its users, what about the countless other internet startups whose operations scarcely extend across a dingy office, let alone several continents? With the free model slowly establishing itself, how can businesses sustain their activities? Sadly, the most common answer is: they can't. The traditional way to generate revenue and offset losses has been to sell some form of advertising space on the website. But an increasing number of industry commentators believe that the internet advertising model is broken—and what better proof than YouTube itself, whose advertising revenues don't even cover their overheads, and who might be dead in the water if it wasn't for their multinational sugar daddy?

In a piece this year for the insider's technology blog, TechCrunch, entitled "Why Advertising Is Failing On The Internet," Eric Clemons, Professor of Operations and Information Management at the University of Pennsylvania, argued that the way that we're using the internet has shattered the whole concept of advertising. We need no encouragement to share our opinions online regarding products and services and offer them star ratings; as a result, we're much more likely to look for personal recommendations from other customers than wait for a gaudy advert to beckon us wildly in the direction of a company website or online store. He claims we don't trust online advertising, we don't need online advertising, but above all we don't want online advertising.

There's certainly a huge weight of evidence to support the latter theory; extensions for web browsers that block advertisements from displaying on the screen have proved to be incredibly popular, and we seem increasingly resentful of attempts by companies to compromise our free online experience by pushing marketing messages in our direction. Spotify, the online jukebox launched this year, has won countless plaudits for its innovative, free and legal approach to online music, but you don't need to look far online before finding users who bitterly complain about the brief audio adverts that play every 20 minutes, interrupting the flow of the new Kasabian album. One comment on a story about the possible expansion of YouTube's advertising is typical: "If advertising is made one iota more intrusive, I shall use other video sites instead."

Small wonder that YouTube only dare feature advertising in less than 5 percent of the videos on the website, along with a few subtle ads in the sidebar of their search results. But while Google continues to finesse its YouTube model, with click-to-buy links and sponsored competitions, it's contended by Professor Clemons that no matter how innovative the advertising industry might become, "commercial messages, pushed through whatever medium, in order to reach a potential customer who is in the middle of doing something else, will fail."

If this is true, it obviously has implications for Google, even though they're sitting very pretty at the moment as the overwhelmingly dominant force in online advertising. But other companies dependent on ad revenue aren't so fortunate. Joost, another ad-funded online video service, announced last week that it would be reinventing itself as a provider of white-label—generic—video for other businesses, and would be cutting jobs in the process.

"In these tough economic times," said its chairman Mike Volpi, "it's been increasingly challenging to operate as an independent, ad-supported online video platform."

But even taking the effects of the recession into account, Keith McMahon is unsurprised. "All those startups have burned through their initial venture capital money, and they've seen that the business model that they were originally planning for—this landgrab for advertising—just isn't there any more." As a leader in The Economist entitled "The end of the free lunch" put it earlier this year, "Reality is asserting itself once more . . . Silicon Valley seems to be entering another 'nuclear winter'."

We are uninterested, verging on contemptuous, of the marketing strategies that were supposed to pay for us to enjoy online services for free. We've become totally unwilling to pay for them directly, either; we simply figure that someone, somehow, will pick up the tab. Rupert Murdoch recently announced plans to "fix" the current newspaper business model by charging for access to News Corporation's newspaper websites, stating that "the current days of the internet will soon be over," but Chris Anderson, the editor of Wired magazine, spends 288 pages in his new book "Free: The Future of a Radical Price" explaining why this is ultimately impossible. He contends that information wants to be free, and that there's an unstoppable downward pressure on the price of anything "made of ideas," adding that the most worrying long-term problem for internet businesses is that the Google Generation are now growing up simply assuming that everything digital is free. They've internalised the economics of the free model "in the same way that we internalise Newtonian mechanics when we learn to catch a ball."

In other words, the fact that most people over the age of 30 doubt that online businesses can survive by offering free services is irrelevant, because most people under the age of 30 are demanding them. On messageboards and forums across the internet you can see them calling for record companies, film studios, newspapers and television channels to come up with a solution that will extend their entertainment utopia, and quick; if they don't, well, they'll find a way around it. And while many see this as a selfish, unrealistic attitude, the onus is on businesses to get themselves out of this mess because the digital medium exercises unstoppable power. However much Rupert Murdoch and others may wish to control it, it's Anderson's contention that the beast is way, way too slippery.

Anderson, along with other digital visionaries, tends to display a sunny optimism that new business models will inevitably step into the breach, while leaving speculation about what those models might actually be to others. But while Anderson says it's "head spinning—and exhilarating—to watch an industry reinvent itself in the face of a new medium," those working in the online economy aren't quite so thrilled. The news regarding YouTube's losses have caused such consternation because people simply can't believe that the third-most-popular website on the web is unable to stand alone and turn a profit. And suddenly, the magical web, whose supposed capacity to revolutionise business has attracted and continues to attract waves of ambitious entrepreneurs, may slowly be revealing itself as an arena in which only a few large companies can survive.

This was illustrated by a tale recounted by the publisher of the Dallas Morning News, James Moroney, who recently told the US Congress about Amazon's proposal for licensing his newspaper's content to be read on Amazon's e-reading device, the Kindle: he was informed that 70 percent of revenue would go to Amazon, with only 30 percent to the Morning News for providing the content. It seems both unhealthy and deeply disappointing that Amazon, Microsoft, Google and the like are beginning to wield so much power; it's even something over which even Google CEO Eric Schmidt has expressed concern.

But Keith McMahon says that we shouldn't be surprised. "Remember in the 1980s when the home computer boom started? The country was full of young kids coding games and selling them on cassette," he says. "But from that rose a gaming industry that's controlled by a small number of very wealthy organisations. Cottage industries that can't survive on their own will either fail, or get swallowed up."

McMahon's message to online businesses is essentially one that's remained the same ever since humans first started making transactions: business is business. For all the cries of foul by entrepreneurs or copyright holders in the face of "unfair" behaviour by multinational corporations or websites such as The Pirate Bay, if you can't find the money to make your business work, that's the end of your business. Because ultimately, the market can't be fought.

YouTube's lack of profitability other than as part of a colossal global multinational may signal the end of a dream that has somehow managed to extend past the bursting of the dotcom bubble back in 2001, and the options for new online ventures seem to be as follows: either produce something that people are willing to pay for, or come up with an idea for a free service that's so ingenious that a benevolent multinational is willing to take it off your hands. But remember: that trick of making a home video of yourself in front of a few elephants has already been done.

Critical Thinking

1. The article quotes Professor Eric Clemons: "commercial messages, pushed through whatever medium, in order to reach a potential customer who is in the middle of doing something else, will fail." Agree or disagree?

2. Without an influx of advertiser dollars, can YouTube survive? How? Should YouTube survive?

From *The Independent* by Rhodri Marsden, July 7, 2009. Copyright © 2009 by Independent Print LTD. Reprinted by permission. www.independent.co.uk

But Who's Counting?

No one really knows how many people visit websites. A San Francisco startup and Google are both working to change that.

Jason Pontin

In August 2006, when Roger McNamee invested in Forbes, he did so in part because its Web audience was thought to be huge. McNamee is a founder of Elevation Partners, a Silicon Valley private-equity firm that counts Bono of the rock band U2 as one of its managing partners; it specializes in big, bold investments in media and technology. Onstage at EmTech, Technology Review's annual conference, he said, "Look: I'm not investing in Forbes for its dead-trees business."

At the time, Jim Spanfeller, the chief executive of Forbes.com, claimed that more than 15 million readers around the globe had visited his site in February, making Forbes the world's leading business site. He supported his boast with research from ComScore Media Metrix, one of the two leading suppliers of third-party traffic data for the Web. The numbers seemed safe enough: Forbes.com's internal server logs showed even greater Web traffic. It was embarrassing, therefore, when ComScore announced that it had changed the methods it used to estimate worldwide audiences, and that little more than seven million people had visited Forbes.com in July. That placed Forbes's online audience below those of Dow Jones (whose sites include WSJ.com) and CNN Money (whose sites include Fortune). Bitchy press accounts suggested that McNamee had been overcharged—if not actually robbed—for his investment, which was variously reported at between $250 million and $300 million.

More than two years later, McNamee claims he always knew there were broad discrepancies between what the internal server logs of Forbes.com showed and what third parties reported. "To be a headache, it would have to be surprising," he says. Instead, he suggests, he invested with no very precise idea of Forbes.com's audience: "I looked at every indicator that was out there. They were all bad. In the end, I had to think about it differently. I invested in Forbes because I thought the market was underserved, and because they had made fewer mistakes than anyone else." (To this day, McNamee declines to say how much he paid for how large an equity stake.)

People still can't agree on how many readers visit Forbes.com. "According to ComScore, we have six to seven million visitors [per month]; our own logs say 18 to 20 million," says Spanfeller. But while the difference between third-party and internal measurements is, for a variety of reasons, particularly striking in the case of Forbes, confusion about the size of online audiences is universal.

No one really knows how many people visit websites. No established third-party supplier of audience measurement data is trusted. Internal Web logs exaggerate audiences. This matters to more people than investors, like McNamee, who worry that they have no way to evaluate new-media businesses. The issues involved are technical, and occluded by ugly jargon, but they concern anyone anxious about the future of media as print and broadcast television and radio shrink in importance.

Happily, a California startup and Google are working to measure Web audiences in new and better ways.

The Price of Journalism

Why care about something as arcane as dodgy audience measurement? Here's why: where content is free, as it is on most websites, the only thing that will pay for quality journalism—or, really, anything valuable at all—is advertising. For most new-media businesses, "display" or banner advertising is the main source of operating revenues. But the general inability to agree on audience numbers is stunting the growth of display advertising.

Every year, advertisers spend billions of dollars online; eMarketer, a research firm, predicts $25.7 billion in 2009 in the United States alone. Marketers study Web audiences to help them decide which sites to spend money on: they try to divine the number of people who visit a site every month, demographic details about those visitors, the length of time they stay on the site, the number of pages they view, and the relationship, if any, between the ads they see and the way they behave. The people who actually buy ads—media buyers and planners at advertising agencies—use this information to choose appropriate sites for campaigns. Finally, publishers use the data to set advertising rates.

However, the correlation between the size of Web audiences and their value to advertisers is not direct. In print, the relationship between audience size and advertising spending is simple, because the prices of ads derive largely from a publisher's audited statement of circulation; media planners buy the total audience. Online, it's more complicated because the currency of display advertising is ad impressions, or the number of times a specific ad is served to a particular part of a website. "Audience numbers don't affect my buying decisions very much," explains David L. Smith, the chief executive and founder of Mediasmith, an interactive-media planning and buying agency whose clients include the National Geographic Channel and Sega. "If we were buying the total audience of a site, it would be different. But most of the time we buy packages of impressions."

Jim Spanfeller, who is a past chair and current board member of the Interactive Advertising Bureau (IAB), the industry association that represents sellers of online advertising, agrees with Smith that unreliable audience measurement doesn't directly affect ad spending, at least at larger sites: "If you're an established site like Forbes.com, you're selling on an ad-impression basis. The problem arises when an agency is thinking about moving money from one medium, like print or television, onto the Web." Then, Spanfeller says, media planners can't show their clients whether Web audiences replicate or complement the audiences that advertisers are reaching through traditional media. "We need believable numbers so that we can do cross-media comparisons," he says. Additionally, bad audience measurement "hurts smaller sites with more targeted audiences that don't have a lot of impressions"—the class of sites that Spanfeller, like many digerati, says occupies "the long tail."

Thus, the real consequence of the audience measurement problem is a chilling effect on the transfer of advertising from older media to new. Meanwhile, another form of online advertising is growing quickly—but it's not the ads publishers sell. The numbers clarify. Spending on "keyword" or search advertising (the sponsored links that appear near search results on Google.com and other search sites) grew 21 percent in 2008, mostly at the expense of print, local television and radio, and Yellow Pages advertising; it now constitutes 45 percent of all online advertising. That's because the effectiveness of keywords is unambiguous: advertisers pay directly for click-throughs or purchases. There's no need to appeal to anything so disputed as the size or composition of Web audiences. This growth in keyword advertising has mainly benefited the search firms. By comparison, the display advertising that media companies sell grew only 4 percent the same year.

Four percent growth might sound all right to some, but it occurs at the same time that advertising revenues in print are falling rapidly. For instance, ad spending in newspapers will decline from $50.8 billion in 2007 to $45 billion by 2012, according to Borrell Associates, a research firm. Even Forbes is sweating. As a private company, it does not disclose its revenues, but the number of ad pages in its magazine has been shrinking since 2000. At the same time, the company's online advertising revenues are reported to be between $55 million and $70 million, a figure Spanfeller did not dispute. That's not so much for a publication with an audience of 20 (or even seven!) million. In the glory days of print advertising, publications with much smaller audiences earned as much or more: Red Herring, which I once edited, earned more than $50 million in print advertising revenue in 2000, and its circulation was only 350,000 readers, according to Ted Gramkow, the magazine's former publisher.

Display advertising was meant to fund the great shift of readers to new media. It's not happening. For more than 100 years, advertising paid publishers and underwrote their production of great journalism; now, those ad monies are being funneled to search firms that create nothing but code. As Roger McNamee says: "Getting this right is absolutely necessary for publishers to be able to continue to do interesting things."

Panel Discussion

What's wrong with existing methods of measuring Web audiences? Lots.

ComScore and Nielsen Online, a division of the Nielsen Company, are the established leaders in the field of audience measurement and the sale, to advertisers, agencies, and publishers, of the data that audience measurement produces.

These third-party audience measurement firms exist because the internal logs of publishers are notoriously unreliable in quantifying user activity on a given site. "When publishers use their log files, there are many limitations," David Smith says. He says that the limitations of using these internal logs (a practice sometimes called "census measurement") include, in ascending order of impact, overcounting individuals with multiple computers or Web browsers; counting "mechanical visits" by Web "bots" and "spiders" (for example, when Google crawls the Web to estimate the popularity of sites) as visits by real people; and overcounting individuals who periodically flush out the "cookies" of code that sites stash on browsers so that returning visitors can be recognized.

To create more-accurate audience numbers, ComScore and Nielsen Online rely on a methodology inherited from television audience research: the panel. Nielsen, for instance, has recruited nearly 30,000 panelists for its flagship product, called Netview. Panelists agree to have their Web browsing monitored through interviews and through "meters," or spyware, installed on their personal computers.

But what worked with television doesn't work nearly so well with the Web. "Panels are always problematical," says Spanfeller, "but on the Web they're super-problematical.

Panels undercount by one-third to one-half." In short, publishers simply can't accept that their audiences are as small as panel-based measurements suggest they are.

Among the problems with panel-based audience research, according to both Spanfeller and Smith, is that it tends to undercount people who look at sites at work, because most companies' information technology managers won't install strange spyware on their computers. Sometimes, panelists lie to interviewers. Also, both say, there is a straightforward "sampling error" (what statisticians consider the misprisions that derive from sampling too small a portion of a general population): with as few as 30,000 panelists, the audiences of smaller sites are often grossly underestimated or missed entirely.

A final problem with panel-based measurements is that at the moment, neither Nielsen nor ComScore has itself been audited by an independent party. Who knows, both Spanfeller and Smith asked darkly, how valid the firms' reporting methods really are?

Nielsen defends its panels. "I guarantee you, if our numbers were higher than the publishers' server data, we wouldn't be having this argument," says Manish Bhatia, the president of global services at Nielsen Online. Bhatia notes that Nielsen does sell products, such as SiteCensus, that install software tags on publishers' websites and measure server logs. "In combination with panels, they're useful," he says. "But panels are more reliable, they provide demographic information, and they tell you what people do after they've seen an online ad."

For its part, ComScore also concedes that server logs have their place: they disclose which Web pages a publisher served, and when. But like Nielsen, the company insists that only panels provide an accurate measurement of audiences and their demographic makeup. "Servers don't measure people," says Andrew Lipsman, director of industry analysis at ComScore.

Why are Nielsen and ComScore so wedded to panels? According to David Smith, "The incumbents have a huge amount of money invested in their methodologies—and getting them to admit they have a problem isn't easy."

Roger McNamee is more blunt. "I understand why Nielsen is so bad," he says. "But why isn't there anything better? There's a huge market opportunity for any venture capitalist who is willing to fund a system that audits actual traffic."

"What we need is a third-party Omniture," says Spanfeller, referring to the website analytics software that many publishers (including Technology Review) use to log their own traffic.

Measure for Measure

Recently, I visited Quantcast, a San Francisco-based startup that is hoping to provide just such a service. Founded in 2005 and funded with $26 million, mainly from Polaris Ventures and Founders Fund, the company wants its service, which launched in 2006, to overthrow traditional panel-based Web audience measurement.

Konrad Feldman, the company's youthful, redheaded, British-born chief executive and cofounder, met me at the company's headquarters overlooking the Yerba Buena Gardens and the Moscone Center. In a large conference room with a cement floor, decorated according to the precepts of venture-capitalist high minimalism, he asked whether Technology Review was "quantified"—that is, whether its online visitors were tracked by the startup's software tags. After we confirmed that our site had been quantified for some time, he opened his laptop and searched for our URL at Quantcast .com.

An elegant dashboard of audience information was swiftly served: TechnologyReview.com, it said, had 342,000 "global people" and 205,000 "U.S. people." These numbers, which measured monthly visitors to our site, were not so low as those reported by traditional third-party audience measurement firms, but they seemed suspicious: throughout 2008, Omniture reported around 650,000 unique visitors to TechnologyReview.com every month. But we also learned that 32 percent of TechnologyReview.com's readers earned more than $100,000 a year and that 24 percent had postgraduate degrees, which seemed about right. (A peek at Forbes .com, which is not quantified but whose numbers the startup had extrapolated, showed that the business site had 4.9 million "U.S. people," who were richer than TechnologyReview .com's readers, although not as highly educated. Because Forbes was not quantified, Quantcast didn't supply Forbes .com's total worldwide audience.)

Quantcast's service, like that of existing audience measurement firms, begins with panels—or, more precisely, panel-like data in the form of "reference samples," provided to the company by third parties such as market research firms, Internet service providers, and toolbar companies, among other sources. These statistical methods create a basic model of U.S. Web traffic. But when publishers install Quantcast's tags on their servers, Quantcast gets more details; the startup adjusts for spiders and bots, people with multiple computers, and cookie flushers. The two methodologies are combined using something Quantcast calls its "mass inference algorithm," created with the aid of two Stanford University mathematicians and refined by the seven mathematically minded PhDs who work at the company. This algorithmic analysis of panel research and server-based measurement is unique in Web audience measurement (although Nielsen more coarsely combines the two methodologies with a service called VideoCensus, which tracks online video viewing). The resulting audience information, says Feldman, is much more reliable than anything offered by ComScore or Nielsen.

"Publishers and advertisers have used panel-based research for nearly 75 years," says Feldman. "So there's obviously an established way of doing things. But equally, there's a pretty clear recognition in the marketplace that something has got to change."

Because Quantcast's audience information is free (where ComScore's and Nielsen's measurements are not), the company hopes to make money by charging publishers who enroll in Media Planner, a service launched last May that helps media planners spend their clients' cash. Although Media Planner is wholly free for now, Quantcast wants to expand the service so that it can finely describe demographic subsets within websites' audiences, a utility for which the company believes the sites themselves will pay. Feldman explains this tricky idea: "You have a sales force at TechnologyReview .com, and they can't possibly speak to everyone who might value your audience. But if you can expose that audience to buyers, then you can create a way whereby buyers can discover the parts of your audience they find particularly valuable." Feldman says that Media Planner allows media buyers to find appropriate audiences, "but it's the publishers that should pay, as they're the ones getting higher rates for their audience segments." More ambitiously, Feldman hopes Quantcast's audience data, in combination with ad impressions, will create a new currency for advertisers, advertising agencies, and publishers that will make display ads more effective and therefore more valuable.

Feldman and his cofounder, Paul Sutter, the company's president, do not approach the problem of audience measurement as veterans of media. Feldman, a computer scientist, was the cofounder of Searchspace (now Fortent), which developed software to help financial-services firms detect money laundering and the financing of terrorists. Sutter founded the network optimization company Orbital Data (later acquired by Citrix) as an expert on high-performance computer architectures, a background that has proved useful as Quantcast processes the thousands of terabytes of data it has collected.

When the founders first conceived the company, Sutter says, "we just asked the most simple, kindergarten questions, and it soon became clear that the language that media buyers and planners were speaking was nothing like the language of Internet advertising, with its cost-per-clicks and so forth. Media planners liked to talk about audiences, demographics, and lifestyles. So the answer was quantcasting, which means just reaching the people you want to reach." Today, the company claims that 85,000 broadly defined "publishers" have elected to be directly measured by Quantcast, including the Disney-ABC Television Group, NBC, CBS, MTV Networks, Fox, BusinessWeek, and Time's SI.com and CNNMoney .com.

Quantcast is not the only company with the bright idea of replacing panel-based audience measurement. Last June, Google announced a new service, Google Ad Planner, which uses the company's detailed knowledge of Web traffic to provide interested parties with a more accurate understanding of Web audiences. Wayne Lin, Ad Planner's product manager, demonstrated the service to me when I visited the Google-Plex in Mountain View, CA. Because Google owns Double-Click, one of the two dominant systems for serving ads, Web

audience data can be combined with the ad-serving system so that media planners know which sites are best suited for which ads. The combination should be powerfully attractive for media planners and marketers, says Lin.

How do media planners regard the two new audience measurement services? "We use Quantcast now at Mediasmith, but they are not complete enough yet to be a total solution," says David Smith, who briefly advised the startup during its formation. The difficulty, according to Smith, is that the site's audience information won't be really useful—let alone a new currency—until more publishers elect to be quantified. Jim Spanfeller agrees. "They're to be commended for working hard on the problem," he says. "But it's very much a chicken-and-egg thing."

As for Google's Ad Planner, Smith says, "the agencies will never stand for it." Smith, like everyone I spoke to, argued that media planners will resist Google's audience information because no one wants one company to be so dominant in online advertising: were Ad Planner to be widely adopted, Google would be selling keywords through its search advertising network, AdWords; selling banner advertising through its display advertising network, AdSense; serving those ads through DoubleClick; and advising media planners on where to spend their advertising dollars.

Ad Planner also lacks a number of important features that an advertising agency might expect from an audience measurement service. According to Smith, it offers neither very detailed demographics nor a full explanation of its methodologies. Patrick Viera, TechnologyReview.com's own digital strategist and West Coast advertising manager, said disdainfully when I asked his opinion: "Yeah, I looked at it. It doesn't do anything you want. It's just a tool for selling AdSense."

Still, says Smith, there's demand for something new. "Publishers have to use third-party measurements, but third parties [such as ComScore and Nielsen] may underestimate audiences, and the truth is probably somewhere in between. That's why new companies like Quantcast have a chance."

Growing Pains

But neither Quantcast nor Google nor improved products from ComScore and Nielsen Online could, by themselves or in combination, fix display advertising and thereby ensure the future health of media.

Whatever audience measurement tools are adopted, they will themselves have to be validated by an independent party. Quantcast, ComScore, and Nielsen Online (but not Google) are all in the process of being audited by the Media Rating Council (MRC), which was established by the U.S. Congress in the 1960s to audit and accredit the ratings of broadcasters. Accreditation will smooth disputes about the different audience measurement methodologies, according to George Ivie, the chief executive of the MRC: "It will help bring the numbers closer together; and it will explain and make transparent the differences between the census and panel systems."

In addition to the disagreements about the size of Web audiences, though, online advertising suffers from deep structural problems that must be addressed before media planners and their advertising clients will spend really large sums. These are various and dauntingly technical, but according to David Smith, they all involve, in one way or another, the absence of commonly accepted, automated means to create, sell, serve, and track the performance of online ads.

Fixing all that will take years, as will the adoption of undisputed audience measurement methods. "This industry is only 13 years old," says Smith. "It grew rapidly with few standards for six years. Then it collapsed, with very little research and development for four years, and has just been getting back to the right kind of R&D and standards in the past three."

Still, by any estimate, the general confusion about Web audiences is the reason why the online medium has matured in so ungainly a fashion. "It's an amazing topic," wrote Roger McNamee in a conversation using the messaging service of the social network Facebook. "You could see it coming a mile away. Unfortunately, the remedy is not yet obvious."

Critical Thinking

1. What is the difference between data provided by server logs vs. audience panels?

2. Compare and contrast the way you personally interact with television ads vs. Internet ads. If a company wants to draw your attention to a new product, where should it spend its advertising dollars?

JASON PONTIN is the Editor in Chief and Publisher of *Technology Review*.

Brain Candy

SCOTT BROWN

Do I really want Jerry Bruckheimer to jailbreak my amygdalae? Yes. Yes I do.

Here's a typical "date night" with me and Hollywood: I don't know what I want to see. Neither does Hollywood. But it bangs on my eyeballs and eardrums like Stanley Kowalski anyway. Sometimes I come away from the multiplex reasonably satisfied; other times I'm bummed beyond measure. It's like some endless, brutal visit to the optometrist: This explosion or that explosion? This superintelligent shark or that zombie anaconda? It's all so clumsy, so imprecise. Which is why I'm thrilled to learn that Hollywood has found a way to improve its hit rate. Not with better filmmaking—God forbid, we don't want artistry gumming up our popcorn flicks—but with science. Get ready for the optimized moviegoing experience, where every instant is calculated to tickle your neural G-spot—all thanks to functional magnetic resonance imaging, soon to be every director's new best friend.

That's the dream of MindSign Neuromarketing, a fledgling San Diego firm with an ambitious, slightly Orwellian charter: to usher in the age of "neurocinema," the real-time monitoring of the brain's reaction to movies, using ever-improving fMRI technology. The company uses the scanning technique to track bloodflow to specific areas (especially the amygdalae, those darling little almonds of primal emotion) while a test subject watches a movie. Right now the metrics are pretty crude, but in theory, studios could use fMRI to fine-tune a movie's thrills, chills, and spills with clickwheel ease, keeping your brain perpetually at the redline. MindSign cofounder Philip Carlsen said in an NPR interview that he foresees a future where directors send their dailies (raw footage fresh from the set) to the MRI lab for optimization. "You can actually make your movie more activating," he said, "based on subjects' brains."

MindSign has already helped advertisers dial in their commercials' second-by-second noggin delight and has even assisted studios in refining movie trailers and TV spots: One of its "videographs," mapped over a trailer for *Pirates of the Caribbean: At World's End,* clearly shows viewers' brains lighting up whenever a monkey appears onscreen. (Of course, if there's one thing we don't need a computer to tell us, it's that monkeys are funny.) Now the company wants to replace that ancient analog heuristic, the dreaded focus group. Carlsen claims that focus group members not only misrepresent the likes and dislikes of the broader population—they can't even articulate their own preferences. Often, they'll tell a human researcher one thing while the fMRI reveals they're feeling the opposite.

Neurocinema helpfully speeds up a process Hollywood began years ago, namely the elimination of all subjectivity in favor of sheer push-button sensation. By quantifying which set pieces, character moments, and other modular film packets really lather up my gray matter, the adfotainment-industrial complex can quickly and efficiently deliver what I actually want. Movies won't be "made," they'll be generated. Michael Bay, with access to my innermost circuitry, can really get in there and noogie the ol' pleasure center. And here's the best part: Once the biz knows what I want, it can give me more of the same. I'll soon be reporting levels of consumer satisfaction previously known only to drug abusers. My moviegoing life will, literally and figuratively, be all about the next hit.

"But now movies will be more formulaic than ever!" purists whine. Au contraire, aesthete scum. "Formula" is for suckers. It implies narrative—peaks and valleys. What MindSign seems to be offering is a new model—not formulaic, but fractal. Forget ups and downs, suspense and release. What if every moment were a spike, every scene "trailer-able"? In fact, movies will become essentially a series of trailers, which, incidentally, are far better-loved than the oft-crummy features they encapsulate. Movie houses will become crack dens with cup holders, and I'll lie there mainlining pure viewing pleasure for hours. Why not? I can't decide what I want to watch anyway. Luckily, Hollywood is there to make those tough choices for me. And to show me the zombie shark I never even knew I was dying to see.

Critical Thinking

1. What's your take on the intent of "neuromarketing"? Good for the product? For the consumer?

Multitasking Youth

To engage youth consumers, you must understand the paradox of their media consumption.

ANDREW J. ROHM, FAREENA SULTAN, AND FLEURA BARDHI

The ways in which consumers attend to and process information from commercial media has begun to change. Advertisers can no longer depend on consumers to attend to commercial media (TV, magazines and radio) in the same ways that previous generations did when there were minimal media alternatives. Today's technology-and information-rich environment enables individuals to consume large amounts of media as we view, read and surf across offline and online media—simultaneously. While watching the latest episode of Grey's Anatomy on television, we also might surf the Internet for deals on hotels for that much-needed vacation, check out various blogs for the latest in celebrity gossip and flip through Vanity Fair magazine all at the same time. In this way, we are more apt to consume media in a feeding frenzy that is fueled by the myriad media vehicles available to us 24/7.

We define media multitasking as the practice of participating in multiple exposures to two or more commercial media at a single point in time. Media multitasking has attracted the attention of advertisers and marketers because of the increasing challenges of engaging young consumers. Media multitasking is a particularly entrenched practice among Generation Y (Gen Y) consumers. Also known as "the Millennials," they are a specific cohort of individuals born from 1983 to 1997. Research demonstrates that the more media individuals consume, the more likely they will access several media types at once. For example, Nielsen Media estimates that almost one-third of all household Internet activity takes place while watching television. A 2006 Kaiser Family Foundation study illustrated a time-compression phenomenon where young consumers were able to compress eight hours of media consumption into 20 percent less time. How? By multitasking and overlapping their media consumption.

The implications of multitasking behavior on how consumers function in the marketplace are significant. For advertisers, Gen Y overlaps the 18-year-old to 34-year-old demographic coveted by marketers. Often referred to as the "digital generation," because they have grown up with the Internet and are the most active consumer group online, Gen Y represents more

than 70 million consumers in the U.S. and their spending power totals approximately \$200 billion. While young consumers' multitasking activity is not welcome news for marketers stuck in a mind-set of traditional approaches to advertising and media planning, this increasingly common approach to media consumption presents significant opportunities to companies seeking to engage their audiences in new and different ways.

In this article, we report on research we conducted with Gen Ys on their media consumption practices and experiences. Specifically, our research was guided by three questions:

1. How do Gen Y consumers multitask with media? What are their experiences related to media multitasking, and how has multitasking shaped Gen Y's media consumption?

2. What are the personal outcomes (benefits and challenges) of media multitasking among Gen Ys? How do Gen Y consumers cope with these challenges?

3. What are the implications of media multitasking behavior on the development of marketing communications strategy?

The purpose of this article is to highlight this multitasking phenomenon related to media consumption and what it means

---

Executive Briefing

Today's youth are media multitaskers who can watch TV, surf the Internet and read at the same time. This has a significant impact on the consumer marketplace. And while this can give them feelings of control, efficiency, engagement and assimilation, the paradox is that inefficiency, chaos, disengagement and enslavement also can occur. The authors propose that task-specific campaigns can help the positives outweigh the negatives in this paradox.

for marketers. Our findings are at the same time comforting and disturbing. On one hand, study participants reported feelings of empowerment, control, productivity and efficiency as a result of their self-described "mastery" of media access and multitasking. On the other hand, our study illustrates feelings of enslavement, chaos, disengagement and inefficiency on the part of participants with respect to their media consumption practices.

Media Multitasking

Today's media universe, consisting of both online and offline media, is as diverse as it is fragmented. Exhibit 1, a collage developed by one of the participants in our study depicting a "portfolio" of media vehicles and technologies, illustrates how media multitasking involves multiple communication technologies such as a TV, a magazine and a computer. Multi-tasking can also take place around a single technology, such as a laptop, on which one can simultaneously shop, read the New York Times and instant message with friends. This multitasking capability has been extended to mobile devices: Apple's iPhone and the Blackberry Storm both have facilitated single-platform multitasking. These devices are of growing interest to advertisers because of the location-based features that distinguish them from other media. In this way, the "three screens" (TV, personal computer and mobile phones) all facilitate media multitasking behavior.

Interestingly, research on multitasking outcomes is mixed. Studies on multitasking in the workplace have shown that employees benefit from the increases in work efficiency resulting from multitasking activity. A dominant conclusion in cognitive psychology research, however, is that multitasking behaviors inhibit or diminish task performance. In our study, we found that some level of multitasking can be beneficial for individuals in terms of their processing of media and commercial information.

The Multitasking experience

We found that media multitasking is a normal, even ritualistic, activity among our study participants. They reported spending between 3 and 10 hours a day with media in a multitasking mode. Multitasking was portrayed as an integral practice within their daily routines of socializing with friends, accessing news, doing research and being entertained. Our findings suggest that young, media-savvy consumers craft what we call "personalized media portfolios"—a combination of old and new media through which they multitask. These media portfolios, consisting of online as well as offline media (primarily television) illustrate the way in which commercial media are increasingly consumed, simultaneously within established media portfolios that are consistent over time.

One important take-away from our research concerning the concept of media portfolios is that each media platform possesses relative strengths. The collage shown in Exhibit 1 illustrates the union of traditional media (such as TV and print) that provide significant audience reach with new digital media that provide richer levels of personalization and interactivity. This illustrates how traditional media can be used to drive traffic and usage of these new media platforms, whereas digital media can supplement and add richness to the offline experience.

The Good and the Bad

We also uncovered a "love-hate relationship" related to our participants' media consumption. As shown in the exhibit we found four positive and four negative consequences relating to commercial media consumption.

Positive Consequences

1. **Control.** We found that study participants multitasked as a way of exerting greater control over their media consumption. Multitasking enabled them to filter and decide which media-related information and messages to process. We found that it also made them feel a part of the marketing communication process. What this means to managers is that consumers will increasingly seek control as active participants within brand-consumer communications, rather than as passive recipients of commercial messages. Advertisers should seek to tap into consumers' desire for control over their media environment by delivering themes, stories and games (or other "tasks") that are of interest to them and that can be accessed simultaneously across different media.

2. **Efficiency.** We found that multitasking can enable individuals to become more efficient in their media consumption, resulting in "greater convenience," "time savings," "constant connectivity" and "greater access to information." It is also an integral part of individuals' pursuits of instant gratification, enabling them to participate simultaneously in multiple worlds outside their private spaces. It is important for marketers to recognize the in-and-out nature of consumers' access and attention to media. Brand and advertising content that does not provide an immediate "hook" or some form of instant gratification will risk being bypassed or ignored by these consumers.

3. **Engagement.** In addition to fostering greater control and efficiency, media multitasking also was seen as a fun and enjoyable activity. Compared to passive media, such as TV, media consumption while multitasking was viewed as more engaging because it involves the viewer more actively in the communications process. What this means to advertising and media strategy is that different media platforms that work together to enable convergence on a single topic, objective or "mission" may be an effective strategy for fostering consumer engagement.

4. **Assimilation.** Media multitasking enables individuals to connect with friends and family, as well as with their surrounding culture. Collages illustrated that a benefit of media multitasking was the connectedness it enabled.

Study participants were motivated to use media in order to strengthen their social networks and generate social capital.

Negative Consequences

1. **Inefficiency.** While media multitasking provided a greater sense of control, efficiency, engagement and assimilation, it also led to feelings of inefficiency. It was described as distracting, leading to procrastination and reduced attention. Participants reported that they paid less attention to important tasks and needed much more time to decode media content during multitasking, since they were continuously dividing their attention among various media and secondary tasks.
2. **Chaos.** Multitasking also led to feelings of disorder and upheaval. Moreover, participants were not only aware of

their inability to process effectively during multitasking; they also expressed negative emotions, such as stress and guilt, associated with the chaotic experience of multitasking.

3. **Disengagement.** Media multitasking led participants to feel less engaged with commercial media, because the multitasking process challenged their ability to process and decode advertising messages. Disengagement was related to whether their media consumption was strategic or passive in nature. In a passive mode, media multitasking fulfilled the participants' need for constant stimulation and was therefore more suitable for peripheral or surface-level processing of advertising content. Strategic, task-oriented multitasking, however, helped participants to integrate multiple sources of information in a complementary and constructive fashion.
4. **Enslavement.** Media consumption was also seen as addictive. Participants spoke of their dependency on

Exhibit 1 The Good and the Bad

Positive consequences		Negative consequences	
Factor	**Illustrative quote**	**Factor**	**Illustrative quote**
1. Control Multitasking enables consumers to filter and process communication content.	"When multitasking I feel like I am the operator of a mission impossible and in control. I have all the information at my reach . . . I feel like I have a handle on all of the different media." (Alex, 20 years old)	**1. Chaos** Media multitasking can lead to an experience of disorder and upheaval.	"Multitasking is stressful because you are doing so many things, but at the same time, you are efficient. There's so much going on at once that you are not taking it all in. It's pretty chaotic. You become bombarded with information and ads. You have to be efficient in order to manage it all." (Bill, 22 years old)
2. Efficiency Media multitasking enables consumers to carry out tasks and process content.	"Multitasking is exciting and fast paced. For instance, I got the TV on mute, and I'm listening to my favorite band, and I turn around and the TV catches my eye and I see my favorite band is coming to the area and then I go online to check for tickets. Instant gratification!" (Amanda, 23 years old)	**2. Inefficiency** Media multitasking can lead to distractions and procrastination.	"When I'm watching TV and talking on the phone, I don't pay attention to the phone call. After I hang up I'm still behind in the show or game or whatever. Although I'm doing two things, afterwards it's like neither of them happened. (David, 21 years old)
3. Engagement Media consumption through multitasking constitutes a hedonic experience.	All pictures convey emotions of happiness or up-beat feelings. Noise and eyes illustrate consumption between mediums. This might seem counterintuitive (with the word noise), but my eyes and ears almost need the different mediums to stay intrigued." (Steve, 22 years old)	**3. Disengagement** Media multitasking can reduce consumers' involvement with particular messages.	"Dazed; confused; not paying attention to anything really. When I'm watching TV, I'm always doing something else. So I don't really pay attention to the TV. But at the same time I'm also not really paying attention to the other thing I'm doing." (Rich, 21 years old)
4. Assimilation Media multitasking enables individuals to connect with friends, family and cultural influences.	"One major advantage of media multitasking for me is the feeling of being 'connected.' If I am watching the news on TV while talking on my cell phone and checking out Myspace. com, I feel in synch with what is happening in today's world." (Tom, 22 years old)	**4. Enslavement** Media multitasking can be an addictive experience.	"I think I am probably A.D.D. undiagnosed. The cell phone buzzes and you get that text message and you just want to jump into it. And then you get an IM and you jump away from whatever you are doing." (Brandon, 20 years old)

media and technology, as well as their need to multitask to manage the vast array of media content available and stay "in touch" and "in the know." Participants expressed having a form of "attention deficit disorder," characterized by short attention spans and a need for ongoing stimulation from various media.

Media overload

. . . [W]e found four strategies that participants employed for coping with their multitasking and media consumption behaviors:

1. **Restrict number of media platforms.** This strategy involves restricting the number of media used at one single point in time. For example, a situation where one is watching TV, reading a magazine, shopping online and listening to the radio involves four different media. Switching among these four media requires more cognitive resources than switching within one device. What this means to marketers is that marketing communications and advertising efforts should attempt to leverage the specific media their particular target audience accesses most readily.

2. **Restrict number of media topics.** This strategy involved restricting the number of topics across various media platforms. Participants sought to complement and add depth to their media experience by focusing on one topic area, yet also by accessing information on this topic across multiple media—for instance, by searching for results of a sporting event online while watching the same event on television. The implication for marketing communications strategy is that advertising campaigns can be developed to focus on a specific topic or task.

3. **Create media hierarchies.** The third coping strategy was to create media hierarchies. Traditional media were often consumed as background media; new digital media were primarily consumed in the foreground. Participants often watched television with the sound off, yet it remained a central part of their media hierarchy. Participants also expressed that they paid less attention to background media and used them to fill the voids in their social environment. They strategically created media hierarchies as a way to enhance the processing of interesting content. Consumption of background media helped to enhance consumer engagement, and hence increased motivation to process media content. What this means to marketers is that foreground and background media serve different roles: digital, and particularly interactive media, are the most effective for delivering primary messages and content, while background media helps to stimulate initial engagement and maintain consumers' motivation to remain involved with advertising messages.

4. **Create media synergies.** The fourth coping strategy was to create synergies. Participants paired media strategically to reduce complexity. Recognizing the strengths and limitations of one medium over another,

they developed combinations of media that worked together in synergy, such as by complementing resource-dependent media (media requiring greater cognitive resources) with resource-independent media. As a segmentation strategy, marketers should recognize the formation of media hierarchies and develop strategies of their own, based on media synergies.

Five lessons for Managers

Our study shows that media multitasking is a prevalent and growing phenomenon among younger consumers. Because it is important for managers to consider the multitasking experience from the perspective of this consumer segment, we frame our findings with five lessons for marketers interested in reaching these media-savvy consumers:

1. **Gen Y processes information differently.** Managers must recognize that young consumers attend to and process communications differently than have previous generations.

2. **Leverage the behavior.** Our findings show that there are positive consequences resulting from the multitasking experience. Some level of media intensity and multitasking can be beneficial to attention and comprehension, but at the same time multitasking can be detrimental to consumers' ability and motivation to process content.

3. **Develop media strategies to address multitasking.** One strategy to counter the challenges and leverage the positive consequences associated with multitasking is to develop marketing communications that enable consumers to actively manage and control their media consumption. It will be increasingly important for managers to package commercial content and programming across multiple platforms. We refer to this as the "American Idol model," by which consumers become engaged with a single topic (e.g., choosing the number one amateur singer in America) via multiple media (TV, the Internet, and mobile marketing). This leads to lesson number four.

4. **Segment markets by media portfolios.** Running counter to existing assumptions about the reduced role of traditional media among young consumers is that while they concentrate their attention on foreground media (typically digital), they then use what they derive from the foreground media to elaborate on the content conveyed by traditional media. Although we found that TV often took on a background role, we also found that because Gen Y has grown up in a culture defined by television programming, as well as a culture where social interactions and entertainment tends to evolve around this medium, TV remained a central part of their media portfolios.

5. **Promote consumer control, rather than chaos.** Finally, advertising and brand managers must develop strategies that focus on a central, ongoing theme with

specific and engaging tasks that foster perceptions of consumer control—rather than perceptions of chaos. Further, when targeting consumer groups such as Gen Y, planners should develop message content in multi-platform campaigns that simultaneously employ both foreground and background media. Following a segmentation approach, campaigns could be structured around media portfolios that are identified as optimal in reaching specific target audiences.

Advertising and brand managers must develop strategies that focus on a central, ongoing theme with specific and engaging tasks that foster perceptions of consumer control.

To address challenges to attention and comprehension that participants expressed regarding their media consumption, we propose that task-specific campaigns can foster greater consumer engagement, greater perceived control within the brand-consumer communication process and more effective message decoding and comprehension. Such strategies would satisfy the consumer's desire for control, while helping to align the consumer's coping strategies with those of marketing and advertising. Marketers would thus take an active role in facilitating consumers' multitasking by reducing the intensity of concentration required by a message or interaction, or by utilizing other strategies that facilitate decoding and comprehension.

Critical Thinking

1. What are the personal outcomes (benefits and challenges) of media multitasking?
2. What are the implications of media multitasking on marketing communications strategies?

ANDREW ROHM is the Denise and Robert DiCenso Associate Professor of Marketing at the College of Business Administration at Northeastern University in Boston. He may be reached at a.rohm@neu.edu. **FAREENA SULTAN** is a professor of marketing and the Robert Morrison Fellow at the College of Business Administration at Northeastern University. She may be reached at f.sultan@neu.edu. **FLEURA BARDHI** is an assistant professor of marketing at the College of Business Administration at Northeastern University. She may be reached at f.bardhi@neu.edu.

Tossed by a Gale

It isn't just newspapers: much of the established news industry is being blown away. Yet news is thriving.

THE ECONOMIST

Perhaps the surest sign that newspapers are doomed is that politicians, so often their targets, are beginning to feel sorry for them. On May 9th Barack Obama ended an otherwise comic speech with an earnest defence of an embattled business. House and Senate committees have held hearings in the past month. John Kerry, the junior senator from Massachusetts, called the newspaper "an endangered species".

Indeed it is. According to the American Society of News Editors, employment in the country's newsrooms has fallen by 15% in the past two years. Paul Zwillenberg of OC&C, a firm of consultants, reckons that almost 70 British local newspapers have shut since the beginning of 2008. The *Independent* and the *London Evening Standard* depend on the largesse of foreign investors. The strain is not confined to English-speaking countries: French newspapers have avoided the same fate only by securing an increase in their already hefty government subsidies.

Broadcast television news is struggling too. Audiences have split and eroded: the share of Americans who watch the early evening news on the old "big three" broadcast networks (ABC, CBS and NBC) has fallen from about 30% in the early 1990s to about 16%. Local-news outfits are ailing as car dealers and shops trim their advertising. ITV, Britain's biggest commercial broadcaster, is pleading to be excused from its obligation to produce local news.

All this has provoked much hand-wringing. Yet the plight of the news business does not presage the end of news. As large branches of the industry wither, new shoots are rising. The result is a business that is smaller and less profitable, but also more efficient and innovative.

The clearest picture of how news consumption is changing comes from surveys by the Pew Research Centre. Since 1994 the share of Americans saying they had listened to a radio news broadcast the previous day has fallen from 47% to 35%. The share reading a newspaper has dropped from 58% to 34%. Meanwhile cable and internet audiences have grown. In 2008, for the first time, more people said they got their national and international news from the internet than from newspapers.

Deeper but Not Broader

It is not only a matter of people switching from one medium to another. Nearly everybody who obtains news from the internet also commonly watches it on television or reads a newspaper. Only 5% of Americans regularly get their news from the internet alone. Technology has enabled well-informed people to become even better informed but has not broadened the audience for news. The Pew Centre's most alarming finding, for anybody who works in the trade, is that the share of 18- to 24-year-olds who got no news at all the previous day has risen from 25% to 34% in the past ten years.

Those who do seek news obtain it in a different way. Rather than plodding through a morning paper and an evening broadcast, they increasingly seek the kind of information they want, when they want. Few pay. Robert Thomson, editor-in-chief of the *Wall Street Journal,* says many have come to view online news as "an all-you-can-eat buffet for which you pay a cable company the only charge."

The main victim of this trend is not so much the newspaper (although it is certainly declining) as the conventional news package. Open almost any leading metropolitan newspaper, or look at its website, and you will find the same things. There will be a mixture of local, national, international, business and sports news. There will be weather forecasts. There will be display and classified advertisements. There will be leaders, letters from readers, and probably a crossword.

This package, which was emulated first by broadcasters and then by internet pioneers such as AOL.com and MSN.com, works rather like an old-fashioned department store. It provides a fair selection of useful information of dependable quality in a single place. And the fate of the news package is similar to that of the department store. Some customers have been lured away by discount chains; others have been drawn to boutiques.

The Wal-Marts of the news world are online portals like Yahoo! and Google News, which collect tens of thousands of stories. Some are licensed from wire services like Reuters and the Associated Press. But most consist simply of a headline, a sentence and a link to a newspaper or television website where the full story can be read. The aggregators make money by funnelling readers past advertisements, which may be tailored to their presumed interests. They are cheap to run: Google News does not even employ an editor.

Although they are convenient, these news warehouses can feel impersonal. So another kind of aggregator has emerged, which offers a selection of news and commentary. Some are eclectic, like the *Daily Beast* and the *Drudge Report*—the grandfather of the boutique aggregators. Others are more specific, like *Perlentaucher,* a German cultural website. The most successful of the lot, and the template for many newly unemployed journalists who have tried to launch websites of their own, is the *Huffington Post.*

HuffPo, as it is broadly known, employs just four reporters among a total staff of about 60. Much of its news is second-hand. But it boasts an unpaid army of some 3,000 mostly left-wing bloggers. The website feels like a cross between a university common room and a Beverly Hills restaurant (your attitude to *HuffPo* will depend largely on whether you find this prospect appealing). Arianna Huffington, who runs it, calls it a "community around news". It now has 4.2m unique monthly visitors, according to comScore, an internet market-research company—almost twice as many as the *New York Post.*

Old-fashioned news folk increasingly complain that aggregators are "parasites" that profit from their work. They are, in a sense; but parasites can be useful. As the quality of journalism becomes more erratic, the job of sifting stories is increasingly vital. And aggregators drive readers, hence advertising, to original-news websites. Hitwise, another market-research firm, estimates that in March 22% of referrals to news sites came from search engines like Google, whereas 21% came from other news sites. "Reporters send us their stories all the time," notes Tina Brown, a magazine veteran who runs the *Daily Beast.*

The rise of the aggregators reveals an uncomfortable fact about the news business. The standard system of reporting, in which a journalist files a story that is broadcast or printed once and then put on a single proprietary website, is inefficient. The marginal cost of distributing the story more widely is close to nil, but the marginal benefit can be considerable. Interest in a story about Iraq in, say, the *Los Angeles Times* extends far beyond that city. Before the aggregators appeared, a reader in Seville or even San Francisco probably would not have known it existed.

The inherent benefit of spreading stories around helps explain why some established news outfits are coming to resemble aggregators. The Associated Press has a popular iPhone application which combines national stories with local ones from 1,100 partner news outlets. News Corporation set up a website, *Fox Nation,* which mixes news stories with right-wing commentary. It is intended to become a conservative

Huffington Post. Indeed, one of the great successes in both British and American news publishing is the *Week,* in effect an aggregator that is printed on paper.

With their stories roaming widely, English-language news outlets in particular are taking on broader identities. The *Guardian*'s website, visited by twice as many people outside Britain as inside, aims to become the international voice of liberal opinion. The *Daily Mail* has built a reputation for celebrity news. New contests are being joined. The BBC, which has set up a wire service and sells advertisements on its foreign websites, now competes with the Associated Press, which has moved beyond the business of supplying stories to American newspapers.

Up Go the Walls

General news is likely to remain free on the internet. The crush of similar stories is too great, the temptation of piracy is too strong and the aggregators are too good at sniffing out decent free reports. Yet it has become clear that online advertising alone cannot support good original journalism.

Until recently many print news executives believed that advertising revenues would follow their readers from print to the web. Between 2004 and 2007 online advertising revenues doubled from $1.5 billion to $3.2 billion, according to the Newspaper Association of America. But in the second quarter of 2008 they began to fall, just as the loss of print and classified advertisements accelerated. Worryingly, this cannot be blamed entirely on the recession. Online advertising money has moved to search—ie, Google—and excess supply has depressed prices of display advertisements. As a result, executives are looking hungrily at the few online outfits that dare ask readers for money.

One is the *Financial Times* (part-owner of *The Economist*) which demands registration of anybody wishing to view more than three articles per month and payment from anybody wanting to see more than ten. About 1m people are registered, of whom 109,000 pay. By going easy on casual readers, the *Financial Times* keeps a foot in what John Ridding, the company's chief executive, calls the "giant wave machines" of the internet, such as Google and Yahoo!, which drive traffic to the site. Registered readers are served targeted advertisements, which are more lucrative. It is an attempt to fuse a subscription model with one supported by advertising.

The *Wall Street Journal* takes a shrewd route to a similar destination. Rather than charging certain types of user, it charges for certain types of news. Earlier this week, it offered for nothing a story about swine flu, a review of the new "Star Trek" film and a report on looming cuts at car dealerships. It charged for pieces on Cigna Corporation's pension plan, Lockheed Martin's quarterly lobbying expenditures and a lawsuit against a bottling company which alleges that a board meeting was held improperly. In short, the fun articles are free. The dry, obscure stuff costs money.

The thinking is that broadly appealing articles draw readers to the website, where they can be tempted by advertisers and by the *Journal*'s more selective wares. Most people do not care about pensions in a Philadelphia health-insurance company. But those who are interested in such information are very interested, so much so that they will probably pay a monthly subscription for it. Just over 1m do—even though the specialised articles can be read for nothing via Google. And those who cross the main pay wall may be persuaded to purchase more premium content. The paper is also exploring a "micro-payments" model for individual articles.

Financial news is not the only kind for which people appear prepared to pay. ESPN, a cable sports channel, has erected several pay walls on its website. They protect information that only the most rabid fan would want to know, adhering to the *Wall Street Journal*'s dictum that people's willingness to pay for a story is inversely correlated with the size of its potential audience. The number of profitable news niches may grow as rivals close bureaus or go out of business altogether.

Newspapers and magazines are more likely to be rescued by a careful combination of free and paid-for content than by new technology. Portable news readers such as the Kindle DX, which some have hailed as potential saviours, will help only to the extent that they lure readers from the web, where news is mostly free. At the moment they seem to be doing something else. Ken Doctor of Outsell, a research firm, reckons that the Kindle appeals to baby-boomers who would otherwise read a paper magazine or newspaper. The young prefer their iPhones and their aggregators. Indeed, the top four magazines on Kindle, according to Amazon's website, are the *New Yorker, Newsweek, Time* and *Reader's Digest*. Not much of a youth market there.

King Comment

On cable television, a different kind of niche product is cleaning up. The right-wing Fox News Channel has become by far the most popular specialist provider of news. This is not surprising. The channel's newscasts and opinion shows are well-produced, and the crumbling of the Republican Party has left conservatives seeking a voice. Rather more surprising is that the left-wing MSNBC now draws more prime-time viewers aged 25 to 54 than the much more established CNN.

Fox and MSNBC provide a mixture of news, interviews and occasionally furious commentary. Phil Griffin, the chief executive of MSNBC, calls it "news-plus". The aim is to complement and give meaning to the mass of disconnected information that viewers pick up during the day. Viewers know what they are getting; indeed, they rate cable shows as more reliable than newspapers. Against the common charge of partisanship, Mr Griffin offers what could be the slogan of the cable news industry: "We're not trying to be all things to all people."

Hot talk may be popular at the moment because Americans are politically polarised. The calmer CNN won the battle for cable viewers on election night and may well do so again in 2012. Yet, as in so much of the news business, a return to normal is improbable. The market for news is likely to remain unstable, favouring different providers at different points in political, economic and even sporting cycles.

Take *Real Clear Politics,* an American political website, which aggregates news, commentary and opinion polls. It became essential reading during last year's presidential race. At its peak, shortly before the election, it attracted 1.4m unique visitors a month, according to comScore. Since then its popularity has plunged by 75%. Rivals like *Fivethirtyeight.com* and *Talking Points Memo* have lost many readers too. For newspapers, magazines and television programmes, with their high fixed costs, such fluctuations would be ruinous.

Not so long ago, news was a highly profitable business. Regional newspapers cultivated cosy monopolies and routinely enjoyed annual profit margins of more than 20%. In America local television stations sometimes had margins approaching 50%. Yet news does not always have to be profitable in order to survive.

Even in their diminished state, large newspapers attract rich men who seek political or business clout, or who believe that there is money to be made after all. Tony O'Reilly, who ran Independent News & Media until this year, used to describe the *Independent* newspaper as a calling card. He tolerated its losses, although the company's shareholders have been less patient. Rupert Murdoch's fondness for printer's ink has sometimes baffled Wall Street analysts. Still, last month David Geffen, a media mogul, reportedly tried to buy a stake in the parent company of the *New York Times.*

Less glamorous outfits can also attract benefactors. San Diego has a small, scrappy news website that was paid for at first largely by a local businessman. The *Voice of San Diego* concentrates on nitty-gritty issues such as water, crime and health care—the sort of stories that local newspapers used to cover extensively. Indeed, America long ago proved that radio news can be supplied by non-profit organisations. In the absence of profitable alternatives, it may be that expensive, worthy journalism on subjects like the war in Iraq will increasingly be supported by charity.

The spread of digital cameras has also enabled ordinary people to file pictures and news reports directly. They are encouraged in this by established news outlets like CNN, which have come to view citizen journalists as a source of both content and page views. Citizens have proved excellent reporters of dramatic, obvious news, such as terrorist attacks and sightings of Britney Spears. Leonard Brody, the head of *Now-Public,* a large Canadian news-gatherer, believes that amateurs will eventually liberate journalists from the tedious business of reporting, leaving them free to concentrate on analysis. He means it kindly.

Just now journalists have less competition from crowds than from governments. In Britain local authorities have created newsletters that carry advertising. The annual budget for the websites of the (state-owned) BBC was recently raised to £145m ($220m). According to Mr Zwillenberg, the total online spending of the country's national newspapers is only £100m.

America's president has proved an especially prolific citizen journalist. People who let Barack Obama's campaign team have their e-mail address last year still receive the occasional missive. The White House posts videos on YouTube that are often more polished than those produced by the news networks. In case the intention to bypass the news filter were not clear, during his second press conference on March 24th the president did not take a single question from a leading daily newspaper. Clearly, he knows where the future lies.

The decline of once-great newspapers and news programmes is not without cost. It means the end of a certain kind of civic sensibility that was built on broad agreement about what is important and what is not. But it was once difficult to imagine city centres without the unifying presence of department stores. Many of them went, yet people carried on shopping.

Critical Thinking

1. Discuss the implications of this statement from the article: "Technology has enabled well-informed people to become even better informed but has not broadened the audience for news."

2. The article states, "Old-fashioned news folk increasingly complain that aggregators are 'parasites' that profit from their work; but parasites can be useful." How so?

Open for Business

If you want readers to buy news, what, exactly, will you sell? The case for a free/paid hybrid.

MICHAEL SHAPIRO

I n the dark winter and spring of 2009, as dispatches from the news business grew ever more grim, as Jim Romenesko's posts took on the feel of casualty reports, newsrooms across the land began to feel like the Emerald City when the Wicked Witch soars overhead, trailing smoke and sending everyone scurrying not for cover, but for an answer, to the Wizard. So it was that in the midst of this gloomy time help appeared, and not merely the illusion of a wizardly hand. It came from Walter Isaacson and from Steven Brill, who were quickly joined by a determined chorus that, no longer willing to stand idly by as its trade died, took up a call that was clear, direct, and seemingly unassailable in its logic: *make the readers pay.*

They envisioned a happy time in which people so loved, or at least appreciated, what journalists did that they would pay to listen, watch, and read online. Excited by the prospect of compensation commensurate with their best efforts, news people raced to find evidence to support this encouraging talk. Suddenly, Peter Kann, dismissed as hopelessly un-Webby when he placed *The Wall Street Journal* behind a paywall in 1996, was being touted in retirement as a man so prescient about revenue streams that Rupert Murdoch, who had taken over Dow Jones with thoughts of bringing that wall down, was now preaching the wisdom of charging for access. People pointed to the money that came from subscribers to such sites as *Congressional Quarterly, Consumer Reports,* and *Cook's Illustrated* as evidence that Isaacson, who had made his case first at a speech this winter at the Aspen Institute and then on the cover of *Time,* had been right. Readers not only would pay, but were already paying. They paid for information and for access to newspaper websites, too—in places like Little Rock, Albuquerque, and Lewiston, Idaho. They paid by the year, the month, the week. Perhaps they might even pay by the story—a micropayment, like for a song on iTunes.

But then, as often happens when euphoria is built on hope born of despair, the good feelings began to recede. The readers-will-pay chorus was ever more drowned out by the voices of the doomsayers, the apostles of information-wants-to-be-free.

Paid content, they insisted, was an illusion. Take a closer look at the sites that charge, they argued, and you will see flaws in your logic: for one, many of them cater to audiences of narrow interest—lobbyists compelled to follow legislation through every subcommittee; business people whose firms cover the costs, so that they might make a buck at the expense of their competitors; lovers of the best, kitchen-tested recipe for Yankee pot roast. And as for those few newspapers that had gotten away with charging for Web access, note that almost all were small, or the sole purveyors of news for hundreds of miles around. These voices were joined by those who saw in the vanishing of the American newspaper a necessary death—much like the Israelites wandering the desert for forty years, waiting for those wed to the old ways to die out.

And so it went, variations on familiar themes that tended to leave little room for the clutter of a middle ground. The back and forth produced a stalemate on the difficult question of whether it was possible, or reasonable, to expect people to pay for news that they had come to believe should be free.

But it obscured the big questions that, logic suggested, would have to come next: If you were going to charge, what, precisely, were you going to sell? And if you sold something new, would that alter, or even revolutionize, the nature of the news?

One

In the beginning, there was the 900 number.

The service had been around for decades when, in 1987, AT&T allowed businesses leasing 900 numbers to charge for calls. People started to pay—for sports scores, news, weather, and stock quotes. Men also paid, sometimes quite a lot, to listen to women talk dirty. The change in dialing habits revolutionized the *idea* of the phone call. The telephone was no longer merely a device that allowed for remote conversation at minimal cost. It became a vehicle for running a business—you could make money with a phone, so long as you sold what people wanted to buy.

That lesson was not lost with the coming of the Internet. Even as people fretted about whether anyone would figure out a way to make a buck online, the pornographers, ever on the vanguard, shifted technologies and began charging not merely for a voice, but for a peek. Others took notice, with higher aspirations. Even as the early apostles of Web culture extolled the virtues of every-man-a-publisher, content did, in fact, go on sale.

Some of it sold. Much didn't—or at least not enough, in the news business, to make up for all the potential lost advertising revenue that has always been the financial backbone of the industry. Slate charged for access for about a year, only to reverse itself in 1999. The *Los Angeles Times* charged for CalenderLive, only to drop the fee in 2005, after twenty-one months of declining page views and modest revenue. *Variety* and Salon took down their paywalls, as did many of the handful of small newspapers that had charged—among them the *Creston* (Iowa) *News Advertiser,* the *Newton* (Iowa) *Daily News,* and the *Aiken* (South Carolina) *Standard,* whose page views tripled after its wall came down in 2007. The *New York Times* ended Times-Select in 2007, having calculated—at that time—that it could more than make up for the $10 million in lost revenue with the advertising generated by all the many new visitors to its site.

Still, there were holdouts, and the titan among the paid-content stalwarts was and remains *The Wall Street Journal,* which continues to charge subscribers $100 annually. While the number of subscribers has grown steadily to its present one million, they pale in comparison to the 20 million monthly unique visitors to The *New York Times,* which, for the moment, remains entirely free—but may not be for much longer.

The sense among the free-content advocates, though, is that the *Journal,* great as it is, is an outlier, a publication not written for a general audience but for the world of commerce. The same was being said of other specialized online publications that cater to people with a financial stake in the news they provided. The growing online presence of the trade press, in the view of the believers in free content, meant only that people already conditioned to spending hundreds or thousands of dollars a year for the brand of news that served their particular needs were now logging on, and not waiting for the newsletter to arrive.

Besides, walled-off content meant content that was not searchable, which meant that it did not draw the great flows of online traffic in a world where the hyperlink had become the coin of commerce and notice.

Sites like CQ.com—which boasted a multitude of databases, brought in about 43 percent of *CQ*'s annual revenue (somewhere between $50 million and $100 million; the company is privately held and will be no more precise about earnings), and had a large editorial staff (CQ Inc. employs more than 165 people)—while admired for the work they produced, were nonetheless relegated to the fringe because they were not part of the greater, link-driven conversation. And hadn't *CQ* subsequently started a free site, CQ Politics, which, while it generated less than 2 percent of the company's revenue, did attract an average of 450,000 uniques a month, ensuring that *CQ* was not left out of Washington's overheated political conversation?

The criticism was much the same for those sites that sold news whose value was not necessarily fungible—politically or financially, either in money earned (the business-to-business press) or in money well spent (*Consumer Reports*). These sites sold news that mattered only because everyone in particular slivers of the online world was talking about it. These were the sites that had occupied small pockets of Chris Anderson's Long Tail, his theory about the rise of niche businesses online. Places like Orangebloods.com.

Orangebloods is a site that, depending on the time of year, has between eight thousand and ten thousand subscribers paying $9.99 a month, or $100 annually, for steady updates about all known thought regarding the University of Texas football team. The site covers practices and assesses the team's strengths and potential worries, but the least important thing it does is cover games. Everyone covers games, the reasoning went, and everyone *watches* games. So instead, Orangebloods found a niche within a niche: it reports and sells what no one else can provide, which is year-round coverage of Longhorns recruiting. Its reporters fan out across the state, and sometimes across the nation, meeting, observing, and collecting footage of leading high-school football players. They then pour all this into the Orangebloods site along with information about those potential Longhorns' size, speed, bench-pressing capacity, and GPAs, all the while offering interviews, commentary, starred rankings, and candid assessments of the Longhorns' chances of securing a commitment: *Solid verbal!*

Orangebloods is one of the 130 paid college-football sites that are part of Rivals.com, which Yahoo bought in 2007 for $100 million. Rivals is run by Bobby Burton, who in the early 1990s, as an undergraduate at Texas, worked in the football team's film library, converting film to video and then editing the footage so that coaches could study, say, tendencies on third and long. Burton took that passion—he uses the word often—to the *National Recruiting Advisor,* a newsletter that reported on recruiting and augmented its service with updates on, yes, a 900 number.

The business went through several iterations—free, then paid, then failing—before re-emerging in 2001. By then Burton had abandoned the idea of using citizen journalists to do his reporting for him, having determined that he needed professionals. In time, the combined editorial staff at Rivals grew to over three hundred and, as the site's reputation grew among the college-football cognoscenti, its subscriptions rose to its present 200,000; Orangebloods is among the most popular.

And that popularity, that desire to subscribe, says its editor, Geoff Ketchum, is as much about the news it reports as it is about the talking and ruminating with an audience that cares beyond all apparent reason about Longhorn football. They make full use of the site's message board, offering lengthy and deeply-felt opinions, and talk with one another with such familiarity that when one subscriber's child was diagnosed with cancer, his online friends raised money for treatment.

> ## "We're like heroin for UT football fans. We've got all the nuts that exist. We cover what the people want to pay for."
>
> —Geoff Ketchum

"We're like heroin for UT football fans," Ketchum says. "We've got all the nuts that exist." He says this with the affection of someone who recognizes his own. "We don't cover all the sports," he adds. "We cover what the people want to pay for."

Two

But would the people pay for news aimed not at the few but at the many? As zealots on either side of the pay divide duked it out, Nancy Wang ran the numbers. The news was not good. For either side.

Wang, who with her husband, Jeff Mignon, runs a Manhattan media consulting firm, crunched nine different scenarios for newspapers of two different approximate sizes—100,000 paid circulation and 50,000. (Here her base scenario was for a most typical American paper, which has 50,000 circulation, publishes seven days a week, charges $17 a month for print subscribers, has a website with 250,000 unique visitors, and online revenues of $700,000.) The analysis, Wang says, were based on real numbers, but were intended as projections of potential, not actual, revenue.

Her conclusions, which were reported in March 2009 by the Newspaper Association of America, essentially boiled down to this: once a newspaper put all its content behind a paywall, online subscriptions dropped dramatically and those subscriptions did not come close to making up lost advertising revenue. The advertising projections, she explains, were based on "very conservative," pre-recession numbers. "It's hard to say that putting in a paid model for content would pay on its own," she says.

But her results were not all that encouraging for the free-content crowd, either—those who advocate an advertising-only model despite the fact that revenue for online ads, though rising, is a fraction of what it is for print.

The online scenario that worked best, she concluded, was a compromise—combining free and paid content, at a percentage of 80 to 20, free to paid. But, she cautions, "there has to be something that people are willing to pay for."

Could that "something" be local news? Wang built her analysis on numbers from the NAA, the media buyers AdPerfect and Centro, as well as from Borrell Associates, a Virginia consulting firm whose president, Gordon Borrell, had for years preached that publishers were wrong if they continued to believe that local news as currently constituted would sell.

Borrell had begun his career as a reporter for *The Virginian-Pilot,* and so came to his conclusion with an understanding and empathy for the work reporters do. The problem, as he saw it, was that newspapers assumed they could continue to sell what he regarded as a tired and tedious product in a new medium simply because they had done so well selling it in an old one.

Borrell had issued his first comprehensive study on paid content shortly after the 9/11 attacks, a time when the public was devouring news, and so a moment when the prospect of online revenue would be running high. He surveyed nearly 1,900 online-newspaper readers and discovered that while people were willing to register for sites—a necessity in attracting advertisers—and might be willing to pay for some news, they were not about to start paying for general online news they had become accustomed to getting for free. He had thought at the time that they might, one day.

But now, eight years later, he saw no evidence of that happening. Readers simply did not value local news enough to pay for it. Borrell found only about 12 percent of most markets went to the Web for local news.

They still bought newspapers, though in diminishing numbers, and quite often not with the same imperative that drove Borrell's one-time newsroom colleagues. While journalists envision people tossing out the coupons to get to the news, many readers perform the ritual in reverse—tossing the news to get to the coupons, a practice confirmed by an NAA study that found that fully half of all readers bought local papers for the ads. Such, Borrell concluded, was the fate of a product that, in the eyes of its intended audience, was "not that compelling."

But wait. Hadn't the industry been pinning its hopes for well over a generation on local news, on bringing to suburban readers targeted versions of the traditional mix of local politics, cops, fires, courts, and the occasional strange doings that used to fill the big-city papers that everyone in town read? And hadn't the mix grown to include dispatches on schools and zoning and features of local interest? And hadn't some of that work been of consequence, hadn't it won awards and allowed publishers to speak of their "watchdog" role and to suggest, channeling Jefferson, that their work kept the citizenry informed and enlightened? *Not that compelling?*

Or did Borrell have a point? Was it possible that the self-satisfaction with which news organizations regarded themselves and their role had been undermined and diluted? The news purists had been warning for years of the danger of a culture in which publishers cheapened the value of their content with cutbacks intended to satisfy investors and media analysts. But no one had paid them much mind, because even in a diminished state the product still sold. If you could do it on the cheap, why not?

Lack of competition was good for profits but turned many dailies into vanilla approximations of themselves.

But it was not just the shareholders' fault. Competition, the catalyst that drove journalists, that fueled their anxiety, fear, ruthless streaks—qualities of personality that propelled them to succeed—had been vanishing for decades. Fewer newspapers in fewer towns found themselves in direct competition for stories, and while this helped make a good many papers very profitable (Exhibit A: Gannett), it also had the effect of rendering many newspapers into vanilla approximations of themselves. The papers weren't necessarily bad; they looked good and read well enough. But it was hard to imagine anyone standing on a street corner shouting, "Extra! Extra! Read all about it!" when the headline screamed ZONING DISPUTE.

The problem with the content, however, did not stop there. Stories were ever more routine, in the subject and in the way they were told—so much so that news, as defined and presented, had for years been an ongoing object of parody in, most famously, *The Onion.*

The pity of it was that in the decades that preceded the recent downsizing of content, newspapers had been stretching the definition of news in ways that made papers of the more distant past seem hopelessly narrow. *Front Page* romanticism aside, readers of, say, the *St. Louis Star* in 1942 would have had no sense of the dark and frightened mood in town in the first winter of World War II, because the paper did not consider such matters news. A generation later, everyone, it seemed, had an investigative team, as well as education, immigration, and health-care reporters, and a local columnist or two. The best writing was no longer necessarily on the sports pages and there was no shortage of FOIA requests. The definition of news expanded, as did the way news was told.

But then, over a stretch of years long enough that it was hard to notice, the reports that came back from once-proud-and-lively newsrooms were that it was getting very hard to, say, sniff out local corruption or capture the zeitgeist of a community when your beat had expanded from three towns to ten, and when the unspoken but well-understood directive from above was to feed the beast, in print and, in time, online. Newspapers still produced admirable work, but the appearance of another plaque on the newsroom wall tended to obscure the fact that while great work was still being accomplished, a good deal of what was otherwise being done was of diminishing value and allure.

So for Borrell, editors and publishers and owners who rallied to the cry of paid content were working under the misapprehension that what they had given away or sold very cheaply would suddenly be regarded as having value by readers whose needs had been sadly undervalued for a long time.

But Borrell still believed that there was money to be made in the news business—online and in print. Print was the place for display advertising, and for all those coupons and end-of-summer ads. Free online access brought the readers—the eyeballs—advertisers wanted. As for paid content, Nancy Wang and Jeff Mignon had for some time been preaching the virtues of a hybrid approach of mixing paid and free online content to the fifty or so news organizations of various sizes they consulted for, and the result, she says, was almost always the same: the young, Web-savvy people would get excited by the possibilities, and their older, more tradition-bound editors, she says, would scream, "NO!"

The resistance, she explains, was not a function of blind stubbornness, but rather a fear that that which they hold sacred was about to be diluted in the name of making a buck. And they were not altogether wrong.

It was at this moment in the conversation that publishers and editors were forced to confront a difficult choice: if a newsroom had a finite number of reporters, and if that newsroom needed a new revenue stream to make up for declining circulation and lower ad rates, it needed to report something that people wanted enough to pay for. Not all people. Just some, with the money and the willingness to pay.

That, in turn, meant *not* devoting the time, the staff, and the money to report on what was presumably of interest to everyone. It meant making the choice to provide content that was exclusive to paying customers. It meant satisfying the core readership at the expense of those unwilling, or perhaps unable, to prove their loyalty with a check or money order.

Something had to go, if you were going to stay in business. But if you were going to start selling news, you had decide what you could offer that people might buy.

And so once the conversation moved past the arguments about the *idea* of paying, and it became ever more apparent that news organizations would do well to charge for *something,* the word heard most often was "value."

Three

Peter Fader was such a fan of TimesSelect—the opinion-oriented section that *The New York Times* briefly put behind a paywall—that had the price doubled he would gladly have paid it. Times-Select represented value for Fader, a quality, he says, that always eclipses price when a purchase is being considered. Fader is a professor of marketing at the Wharton School at the University of Pennsylvania. He explains that pricing "is a trade-off attitude." Economists, Fader says, often make the mistake of building projections upon the supposition that people are rational beings. But people, he says, will perform the irrational act of paying for all kinds of things that they can otherwise get for nothing.

They will, for instance, pay 99 cents for songs on iTunes that can be downloaded for free because Apple makes the transactional experience not only legal, but easy, attractive, and accessible. People will also pay for subscriptions. They will, for example, willingly allow their bank accounts to be dunned $17 a month for Netflix even though weeks may pass without a rental or download. No matter, Fader says; those subscribers have fallen into an "electronic trance" in which they refuse to cancel because they anticipate renting one day, real soon.

Perhaps the best and most alluring analogy for selling news online is cable television. TV used to be free and in some places still is. But cable transformed the idea that the medium came without cost by making it into a medium that provided a wide choice of occasionally terrific content that was exclusive to those who paid for it.

The transformation did not come instantly, and despite all the new channels, the experience of watching cable TV is often as it was in the old five channels-plus-UHF days: *Nothing's on.* But cable offers lots of choices, on a sliding scale, and Fader says people will continue to pay for the promise of value because whatever disappointments they might have experienced—for instance, a weeper on Lifetime—have been outweighed by, say, *The Sopranos.*

New technologies arrive with lamentations for the institutions and traditions and old technologies sure to die out. It was that way with television—*the death of movie theaters!* And with FM radio—*the end of live concerts!* But new technologies do not replace the old, they merely take a place at their side. Grand and aging movie palaces became multiplexes, and owners did such a brisk business that people decided it was worth spending an extra $1.50 to pre-order tickets on Fandango. So it is that Fandango sells what once came without cost, but which now represents admission denied to someone else.

That, in a sense, is also the calculus for success at *Congressional Quarterly,* which sells information that is available elsewhere at no cost but at considerable hassle. If you are, for instance, a lobbyist who needs to know the status of a particularly worrisome piece of legislation, *CQ* can sell you, through its BillTrack database, the full text and an analysis of the bill, its status in committee, a profile of that committee, a district-by-district breakdown of the members of the committee, a dollar-by-dollar breakdown of those members' campaign contributors—in short, everything a clever lobbyist needs to know *before* that information comes to another clever lobbyist for the opposition. This is what Robert Merry, *CQ*'s president and editor-in-chief, calls "information paranoia," a particularly virulent affliction in Washington.

CQ sells access to thirty-five different databases. It has four niche verticals—homeland security, health, a budget tracker, and its political money line. It does give some information away for free. So do *The Wall Street Journal*—a story at a time—and the *Financial Times*—a limited number of stories each month, before the paywall goes up. But these are, from a marketing standpoint, the journalistic equivalent of movie trailers on Fandango: *If you loved our report on this stimulus package, you'll want to see . . .*

Merry thinks of *CQ* as a pyramid. At its base are the many visitors to CQPolitics who pay nothing but who do deliver eyeballs. At the top are those so ravenous for particular slices of news they can use that they will pay $10,000 or more a year for access. In other words, *CQ* sells various products for various media to audiences who differ not by geography or income but by need. It was doing so well before analysts like Wang and Mignon began preaching the virtues of the "hybrid" model to their sometimes-reluctant clients.

The Wall Street Journal will soon expand its existing free-for-a-single-story "hybrid" model into one that includes micropayments. The *New York Times* is considering such revenue streams as metered payments (like those at the *FT*) and premium content memberships that presumably would cater to the paper's most loyal readers. It is one thing for the *Times*, the *Journal*, and the *FT* to impose fees on some of their content because their content is so highly regarded by so many. But what of those general news publications that have done away with so much of their original coverage of anything that is not local, and have diminished even that? Are they doomed? Or can they save themselves by redefining their content, and by extension, news?

General news has long been predicated on the idea that people's primary interest in news was defined by where they lived. But that was never completely so. The ethnic press, for instance, is as much about where you are from as about where you landed. Similarly, magazines are now almost exclusively defined by the particular interests of their readers. (The demise of the general-interest magazine offers a powerful and emotional parallel to the fate of the general-interest newspaper: a generation ago it seemed impossible to envision an America without *The Saturday Evening Post, Life,* and *Look.*)

Yet most newspapers still represent a model defined by borders. This makes for a relatively easy business to run when most readers lived in one place—a small town or a city. With the post-World War II exodus to the suburbs, however, the urban newspaper model built on cops, courts, fires, and politics was essentially picked up and transplanted not to one locality but to many disparate places where, it was assumed, readers had little interest in the goings-on across the town line, and the ever more remote downtown. Gone was the big-city paper; in its place came the regional daily.

But now, *The Washington Post,* for one, has begun to embrace the idea of defining itself not as the newspaper of Washington, the physical entity, but as Washington, the idea—just as *The Wall Street Journal,* which the *Post*'s new editor, Marcus Brauchli, used to run, is not about Wall Street, a district in lower Manhattan. In a memo to her staff last December, the *Post*'s publisher, Katharine Weymouth, wrote of the paper as "being about Washington, for Washingtonians and those affected by it." The latter phrase is key. It suggests that the paper is both acknowledging the physical boundaries of a portion of its coverage—"the indispensable guide to Washington"—while expanding beyond them. It means that Washington is, in a sense, everywhere—in every tax dollar, FAA hearing, wherever Washington's institutions and influence reach. A new and different hyper-local.

If this succeeds, what's to stop, say, the *Detroit Free Press* from augmenting its definition of Detroit as a municipality with Detroit as an idea—say, all things automotive? There is news in cars, lots of it. And there are people who need to know it, not all of them residents of greater Detroit. One wonders what the denuded *San Jose Mercury News,* a paper that had been a model of the regional news organization, might have become had it positioned itself as the definitive source of tech news for a readership well beyond Silicon Valley.

Once a news organization sees itself as something more than in service of a place, it puts itself in a position to tap into one of the emotional imperatives that sustain the niche sites. Geoff Ketchum's Orangebloods, for instance, is not limited to resident Texans. Regardless of where they live, his core readers have proven themselves willing to pay for the knowledge his site offers so that they can remain a part of a conversation. "Newspapers can't entice us into small payment systems," argues the media thinker Clay Shirky, "because we care too much about our conversation with one another. . . ." Newspapers, as presently defined, cannot. But if Orangebloods can, why can't a vertical on what is otherwise a general news site?

Those conversations can be inclusive (pay $9.95 a month and become an Orangeblood) or exclusive (CQ BillTrack), but what they have in common is that each, in a sense, represents what might best be called a Community of Need. The need is for the news that fuels a particular conversation. So long as there is something new to report.

Niche sites succeed, in large measure, by staking out a line of coverage that represents precisely the kinds of stories that newspapers decided to abandon years ago because so many readers found them so tedious: process stories. The relentless journey of a bill through a legislative body—*cloture vote!* Tracking a running back as he decides between Baylor and Texas. But process stories are stories that, by their nature, offer an endless source of developments; there is always something new happening, even if to those on the outside of the conversation, it is news of little value. Robert Merry wonders, for instance, why so many newspapers abandoned their statehouse bureaus when those capital cities were awash in money, lobbyists, legislators, and eager-beaver aides who'd be willing to pay quite a lot for information that might give them an edge. They did so because most readers said the stories were boring—and that was true for most readers, but not all.

But there is an important caveat: such projects do not succeed if they're done on the cheap. They require reporters whose primary responsibility is to supply the endless news that feeds those relatively few readers' needs. The need is for news. Not opinion. (Bobby Burton is not alone in believing the *Times* erred in what it chose to place behind its TimesSelect paywall, which was not news but the opinions of its famous columnists.) The problem with opinion is that the Web has made everyone a columnist precisely because it costs nothing to offer a point of view. Nor does it cost very much, or sometimes nothing at all, to fill a site with well-intentioned work, and opinion, provided by citizen journalists. But as Burton discovered in the early days of Rivals, those amateur journalists may have wise and clever things to say, but when he wanted to regularly break news he went out and hired people who knew how to do it—and he pays them between $30,000 and more than $150,000 a year.

Orangebloods is only as good as its next scoop; because if its stories begin appearing with any frequency someplace else—and perhaps, for free—the compact that Ketchum has with his readers is in jeopardy. Which is why there is nothing passive or reactive about the site's approach to its work. That, however, has not always been the case for general news that has traditionally defined itself by default: it's news because it's always been news. This, in turn, has created a culture of news in which the operative verb, far too often, is *said,* a culture in which all a reporter needs to do is listen and record.

As a result, too much of what fills the news pages is, as is often said, stenography. And because it can be done quickly, and at great volume, and with relatively little effort, it endures. The timing could not be more dispiriting, given that the generation in power in journalism now came to the field with a sense of journalism's possibilities, and broadened the idea of what news could be. But this generation also came of age at a time of growing newsroom prosperity.

This expanded sense of what the content could be made newspapers fatter; new sections appeared; nothing had to go, save for those process stories that no one wanted to read. Not a tough choice. Not like now, when the redefinition of news may mean deciding what you can sell to those willing to pay, and, by extension, what you will give up in the rest of the day's report so that you can redeploy your shrinking staff.

Inevitably, this raises an existential issue: What are newspapers for? Do they exist to serve narrow bands of interest? Or are there issues that transcend the paying niches, journalistic responsibilities that we should worry might well be overlooked and ignored in the interests of satisfying those who foot the bill?

It is not enough to simply hope that editors and publishers will retain their nobler instincts, not when times are tough. But, at the risk of sounding cynical, there is every reason to believe that they might continue offering stories of consequence for a larger, and perhaps unpaying audience for another reason—because it

might be good for business. There are stories that transcend demographic borders. They are stories that are universal in their appeal, and infectious in their presentation. Not all novels, after all, are written for niche audiences; some speak to people who, on the surface, have nothing in common with one another. And as it is with novels, and movies, and television shows that attract wide followings, there are stories that capture the eye and the imagination, and which lure readers who might stick around, or even come back, and bring advertisers with them. The burden rests on the news organization to do what news people have always done: find those stories.

Transform the everyday work of journalism from a reactive, money-losing proposition into a more selective enterprise.

So it is that journalism's crisis offers an opportunity to transform the everyday work of journalism from a reactive and money-losing proposition into a more selective enterprise of reporting things that no one else knows. And choosing, quite deliberately, to ignore much of what can be found elsewhere.

People will pay for news they deem essential, and depending on the depth and urgency of their need, they will pay a lot. Their subscriptions, in turn, might well help to underwrite the cost of producing original work that might remain free and be of interest to more than a select few.

Those subscriptions will not save newspapers. They alone will not pay for the cost of reporting. No one revenue stream will—not online or print advertising, or alerts on handheld devices, or new electronic readers that display stories handsomely. The hope is that they *all* will.

The means of distributing the news will change, but what is clear and unchanging is people's desire to know things, to be told a story, and to be able talk about it all with other people—for such things matter.

Extra! Extra! Read all about it!

Critical Thinking

1. Which do you predict is more likely: (a) Niche media will replace true mass-mass media; or (b) The most popular niche media formats will become the new mass-mass media (survival of the biggest sellers)? Why?

2. Construct your own survey to investigate what kinds of online content people you know would be willing to pay for, and how much they would be willing to pay for each hypothetical site. Summarize and analyze your results.

MICHAEL SHAPIRO, a contributing editor to *CJR*, teaches at Columbia's Graduate School of Journalism. His most recent book is *Bottom of the Ninth: Branch Rickey, Casey Stengel, and the Daring Scheme to Save Baseball From Itself.*

Nonprofit News

As news organizations continue to cut back, investigative and enterprise journalism funded by foundations and the like is coming to the fore.

CAROL GUENSBURG

Since 1993, the Henry J. Kaiser Family Foundation has funded journalism training on health issues, including funneling up to $50,000 to a handful of fellows each year to support reporting projects. But, dismayed by cuts in newsroom staffing, newsholes and airtime—and the sketchy reporting that can result—foundation officials began kicking around other ways to ensure solid coverage of topics they consider crucial.

One possibility: a nonprofit health news service of their own. Matt James, senior vice president for the California-based foundation, remembers running the idea past longtime editor Bill Kovach, founding director of the Committee of Concerned Journalists and an adviser to Kaiser's media fellows program. James chuckles, a little uncomfortably, recalling the start of Kovach's generally encouraging response during a meeting last May. "He basically said, 'Five years ago . . . I would have told you to go to hell and shown you the door.' "

These days, foundations and philanthropists are finding a warmer reception.

Beleaguered journalists who once clung solely to the business model of paid advertising and circulation now recognize the urgency of developing new revenue sources for labor-intensive newsgathering. For some, foundations hold increasing promise as allies in meeting the public's information needs—beyond superficial headlines and celebrity sexploits—so long as there are safeguards for editorial independence.

"The fact of the matter is philanthropic institutions have provided millions of dollars over the years to help journalists do their work. Journalists have an unfortunate habit of not acknowledging that," says Charles Lewis, head of the nonprofit Fund for Independence in Journalism. From 1989 through 2004, he served as founding executive director of the Center for Public Integrity, which "raised and spent $30 million [on journalism projects] in the years I was there."

New forms of nonprofit, grant-funded news operations are proliferating. The lineup includes the Pulitzer Center on Crisis Reporting (see "Funding for Foreign Forays," page 173), Brandeis University's Schuster Institute for Investigative Journalism, MinnPost.com (see Drop Cap) and at least two state-level health news sites (see "Healthy Initiatives," page 172). The Washington Independent, freshly minted in January, joined the Center for Independent Media's network of four related sites in Colorado, Iowa, Michigan and Minnesota. And there are many more in the mix.

The highest-profile newcomer is ProPublica (propublica.org), an investigative news operation that opened shop in Manhattan in January (see "Big Bucks for Investigative Reporting"). California philanthropists Herbert M. and Marion O. Sandler dreamed up the project—which they're bankrolling at $10 million annually for at least three years—and hired former Wall Street Journal Managing Editor Paul E. Steiger as editor in chief. He and Managing Editor Stephen Engelberg, a former investigative editor at the New York Times, eventually will oversee a staff of about 25 reporters, editors and researchers charged with producing public interest stories of "moral force," as the website proclaims. These will be offered free to select news outlets, whose own staffs may join in the newsgathering, as well as being showcased on ProPublica's site.

The Sandlers, who made $2.4 billion when they sold the Golden West Financial Corp. savings and loan in 2006, have given millions to Democratic Party causes over the years, according to news accounts. That—and donors' often heightened emotional investment in money they've earned—prompted Slate media critic Jack Shafer to question Herbert Sandler's role as Propublica chairman (slate.com/id/2175942/). Even though the couple pledged not to interfere with editorial content, Shafer recommended that Sandler guarantee at least 10 years' funding and then resign his position, "so he'll never be tempted to bollix up what might turn out to be a good thing."

Some prominent media leaders and innovators have called for even more philanthropic support to ensure journalism's vital watchdog role.

Geneva Overholser, writing in "On Behalf of Journalism: A Manifesto for Change" (annenbergpublicpolicycenter.org/Overholser/20061011_JournStudy.pdf), urged a greater role for nonprofits in assisting news media. Her 2006 treatise advanced journalist Lewis' suggestion that foundations and philanthropists create a "Marshall Plan" to create more public-minded forms of news coverage. Grantmakers could "increase support for nonprofit media organizations" and "foster new nonprofit media models," wrote Overholser, a Missouri School of Journalism professor. She also recommended steps for corporations, journalists, government and the public.

Jan Schaffer, executive director of the interactive journalism incubator J-Lab, introduced a "Citizen Media" report (kcnn .org/research/citmedia_introduction/) last February by writing that community foundations should "be alert to real possibilities for building community capacity" by supporting citizen media. "Journalism alone will not suffice," she elaborated in a phone interview. "I think foundations and philanthropies will play a role in supplementing that information landscape."

Dan Gillmor, in a September 17 op-ed published in the San Francisco Chronicle (sfgate.com/cgi-bin/article.cgi?file=/ c/a/2007/09/17/ED1OS4OIU.DTL) and timed for a Council on Foundations' conference there, urged community foundations to "put the survival of quality local journalism squarely on their own agendas." Gillmor—who in January launched the Knight Center for Digital Media Entrepreneurship at Arizona State University's Walter Cronkite School of Journalism—suggested measures such as paying the salary of a local investigative journalist or providing seed funding for a network of local blogs and media sites, adding journalism training for participants.

And Alberto Ibargüen, president and CEO of the John S. and James L. Knight Foundation, publicly addressed those San Francisco conferees with a like-minded appeal, warning: "If the citizens are unaware, then the democracy is in peril." Knight and the council will cohost a seminar February 20 and 21 on communities' information needs in a democracy. Up to 200 community-foundation representatives will meet in Coral Gables, Florida, to consider media trends, the digital revolution, gaps in coverage and how these might be filled.

Foundations see their growing involvement as compensating for newsrooms' diminished coverage of civic issues. They're stepping in because "the traditional news business is not investing as much as it needs to . . . in getting reporters out to cover stories," Kaiser's James pointedly notes. "We as nonprofits have a duty to figure out: Is there a role for us, in increased training, in direct partnerships with news organizations or even [in] creating a new news service to fill that void?

"What we're talking about is supporting real journalism, not advocacy," adds James, whose foundation already partners with National Public Radio, USA Today, the Washington Post and other news media on public opinion research projects. "We're big believers in the role of journalism in democracy. We believe it's important for nonprofits to find ways to support it."

With newspaper revenue tanking as classified and retail advertisers migrate to the Web and Wall Street tightens its grip, journalists are casting about for financial lifelines. Foundations have the wherewithal to throw some: By law, they must spend a minimum 5 percent of their net assets each year on charitable causes. In 2005, U.S. foundations granted $158 million for media and communications, the Foundation Center reports, though it doesn't break down whether the payouts went for journalism per se or marketing or research dissemination. Nor does that figure necessarily reflect spending on journalism-related education.

Journalism's funders include those affiliated with legacy news media—such as Annenberg, Scripps, Tribune, Reynolds, Gannett—plus longtime supporters like Carnegie, Ford and the Pew Charitable Trusts. (AJR has received support from the Freedom Forum, Ford, Knight, Pew and Carnegie.)

Knight, the leading journalism funder overall, announced more than $21 million in journalism grants in 2006 and more than $50 million in 2007, though some of these are multiyear grants and won't be paid out all at once. "There are years when we are not the largest [journalism] grantmaker," Eric Newton, its vice president for journalism initiatives, said in an e-mail interview. Since the foundation's start in 1950, it has invested nearly $300 million in U.S. and global journalism—emphasizing midcareer training in the 1980s, journalism education in the 1990s and digital media innovation in the current decade.

Knight has contributed to journalism philanthropy in another fundamental way. Shortly after joining the foundation in 2001, Newton—former managing editor of the Newseum and, before that, the Oakland Tribune—helped pull together an informal group of program officers from legacy media foundations and others interested in journalism. Participants included the Bill & Melinda Gates Foundation, which in November announced a three-year, $1.7 million grant to the International Center for Journalists to support Knight health fellowships in sub-Saharan Africa.

"We think all foundations should care about the information needs of communities in a democracy," Newton says.

Done right, the journalism-funder relationship benefits both parties as well as the public they aim to serve. It supplies important news resources, and it satisfies a grantmaker's mission—maybe even bringing a touch of prestige. Done wrong, the association raises concerns about editorial objectivity and whether it has been compromised by a funder's agenda.

It's instructive to look at, or listen to, NPR, perhaps the most successful model of nonprofit journalism. The privately supported membership organization derived a third of its revenue from grants, contributions and sponsorships in 2005. Its biggest revenue share (39 percent) came from programming fees paid by member stations, which conduct their own fundraising.

"We're always engaged in very constructive discussions with the world of philanthropy," says NPR President Kevin Klose, who describes himself as an active participant. The conversations emphasize editorial control, "the starting point for us. . . . One of the reasons why we are attractive to foundations and to corporate sponsorship is because of the integrity and independence of what we do. They wish to align themselves with that set of values."

They probably don't mind that their names, and information they care about, reach 26 million pairs of ears.

Klose says he engages with the foundation world not just to gain financial support. "It's also important to us," he explains,

Big Bucks for Investigative Reporting

When its imminent launch was announced last fall, Pro-Publica brought a double-barreled blast of attention to nonprofit news media. It wasn't just the premise of an independent newsroom devoted to investigative reporting, an endangered species in an era of down-sizing; it was the promise of $10 million-a-year backing to ensure hard-hitting stories that would be given away to other news outlets.

Founders Herbert M. and Marion O. Sandler committed that chunk of their personal fortune—burnished by the 2006 sale of their Golden West Financial Corp. savings and loan to the Wachovia Corp.—to support the stated mission of "producing journalism that shines a light on exploitation of the weak by the strong and on the failures of those with power to vindicate the trust placed in them."

Additional one-time grants are coming from the John D. and Catherine T. MacArthur Foundation ($250,000) and the Atlantic Philanthropies and JEHT Foundation ($25,000 each).

ProPublica's editor in chief is Paul E. Steiger, who led the Wall Street Journal to 16 Pulitzer Prizes while serving as managing editor from 1991 until last May. As his managing editor, Steiger tapped Stephen Engelberg, a managing editor at Portland's Oregonian who'd earlier been an investigative editor for the New York Times. They'll direct a staff of about 25 reporters, editors and researchers based in a Manhattan newsroom and doing stories of national import.

By mid-November, ProPublica had received roughly 400 résumés "from essentially every major news organization in the country," says General Manager Richard Tofel, who worked with Steiger at the Wall Street Journal and most recently was a vice president of the Rockefeller Foundation.

The organization, which launched in January, will gear up during early 2008, regularly spotlighting others' investigative reports on its website (propublica.org) while developing its own projects.

Steiger says he has spoken with representatives of leading newspapers, magazines and television news outlets about carrying ProPublica projects. With those that are "90 percent done, we'll be looking for a collaborator who can give the most impact and visibility," Steiger says. "For collaborations that we might start at an early stage, we'll be looking at where there would be mutual advantage" for another news outlet to join in the reporting and editing. ProPublica will publish the work on its own site, in some cases simultaneously with the news organization.

As Michael Miner observed in the Chicago Reader, this approach probably cuts out news organizations—especially those far from population centers—with the fewest resources to keep the powerful in check.

Editorial independence will be crucial not just to Pro-Publica but to the news organizations disseminating or partnering on its stories. And it may be a challenge to overcome newsrooms' preference for stories they've produced internally.

For example, Philadelphia Inquirer Editor William K. Marimow says he's "agonized a lot about ProPublica." Though he's confident that, "with Paul at the helm, they'll do great work," Marimow expressed concern about a news organization ceding any editorial control. "When it comes to investigative reporting, it's my belief that top editors need to take responsibility from the get-go," he says. "A hybrid project creates diffuse responsibility."

—C.G.

---

to learn "what people are thinking about. These are often very socially aware organizations that track issues naturally of interest to news organizations."

A sturdy firewall separates NPR's news and business operations. Barbara Hall spent more than 14 years on its fundraising side, serving as vice president of development through late August 2006. (Near the end of her run her group generated more than $50 million a year, excluding a $230 million bequest from Joan B. Kroc in 2004.)

Over that time, Hall saw a shift in funders' strategies. "The best gift any nonprofit can get is unrestricted support. But the trend we've seen with foundations, and increasingly with individuals, is wanting to designate their support for specific issues and topics," says Hall, who left to head development for the Phillips Collection, an art museum in Washington, D.C. While "most foundations understand that news organizations are not advocacy groups," she adds, "now they're being very focused on what they're supporting and its impact."

"Funders may have their own interests—they often do," Klose says, but they can't dictate story focus. "We're very interested in philanthropic support of a whole range of activities: coverage of foreign news, coverage of children, family and education. We have a foreign desk, a national desk, a political desk. That's what people fund."

By designating funding, a grantmaker aims to raise the visibility of an issue or area and expand public knowledge.

The Carnegie Corp. of New York, for instance, gave NPR $200,000 last year to support education coverage. It began subsidizing that around the 2000 election, says Susan Robinson King, vice president of external affairs and director of the journalism initiative at Carnegie. Back then, NPR "had one reporter who sometimes covered education. . . . They were able with our money to hire a producer and really increase the level of reporting."

Dynamic social forces affect nonprofit journalism as readily as commercial news operations. Shifts in the economy boost or deflate endowments. Developments in research, demographics or regional politics, changes in leadership or board structure—all can affect attitudes and funding priorities. No wonder only a quarter of all grants get renewed.

I absorbed these lessons as founding director of Journalism Fellowships in Child and Family Policy from early 2000

Healthy Initiatives

Carol Gentry doesn't think "it's any mystery why health care is bubbling up so early" as the focus of at least two non-profit, state-level news services. "People don't understand how it works," says Gentry, founding editor of the year-old FloridaHealthNews.org. "It's hard to get good coverage, particularly at the local and state level."

There's another basic reason. "It's where the money is," explains Carol DeVita, a researcher at the Urban Institute's Center on Nonprofits and Philanthropy. The news services largely are supported by so-called "conversion" foundations, created when nonprofit hospitals were sold to for-profit providers. Dozens of states have required that proceeds from charitable assets be redirected to support community health—through efforts such as clinics, immunization programs and research.

The Kansas Health Institute, an independent, nonprofit policy and research organization in Topeka, in January 2007 introduced the online KHI News Service to cover state health policy. It has four staff journalists with newspaper backgrounds. It features daily spot news stories and a weekly centerpiece. A recent one examined whether a proposed tobacco tax increase could provide reliable funding for health reform.

Vice President for Public Affairs Jim McLean says the free service primarily reaches legislators, government staffers and lobbyists, though it's also intended for consumers. KHI stories have been picked up by the Topeka Capital-Journal (where McLean was a managing editor) and assorted small papers. McLean hopes to increase distribution this year by introducing story budgets to help editors plan.

The institute gets its funding mostly from philanthropy, with some project-based funding from state and federal agencies. The editorial staff works independently, McLean emphasizes, and "there's no advocacy mission at all."

Florida's independent online news service covers a wide range of state and local health issues. Launched in March 2007 primarily as a news aggregator, the St. Petersburg-based FloridaHealthNews.org tracked health care bills when the Legislature was in session and posted original stories. Until mid-December, it had one paid staffer, part-time Managing Editor Pat Curtis, as well as a paid intern. Gentry has signed up a Tallahassee correspondent and is recruiting stringers around the state. She herself didn't start drawing a paycheck until mid-December, instead logging volunteer hours while reporting on health full time for the Tampa Tribune. She resigned from the paper in late November, after the Florida Health Policy Center—a partnership of eight foundations—approved $183,000 in new grants. The center had provided seed money of $59,200 for the news service's first year.

Gentry says she'll "outsource the fundraising, the marketing, the advertising. We want, as much as we can, to have a firewall between the newsroom and the business side. . . . That's the most important thing, that people can trust us as journalists."

A decade ago, the Oakland-based nonprofit California HealthCare Foundation introduced a health news aggregation site, California Healthline. Now, it may add experienced journalists to produce "in-depth health care reporting in partnership with media organizations," says David Olmos, a former Los Angeles Times reporter and editor who in the fall stepped down as the foundation's communications director. He's researching the project, which might entail partnering with newspapers, public radio and television stations or other news organizations. Like ProPublica, the new nonprofit news outlet for investigative reporting, its services "almost certainly would be free," Olmos says.

Its mission would be "tackling some larger issues that are not sufficiently covered in California," which Olmos describes as "a proving ground or laboratory for some of the health efforts" relevant nationwide.

Both he and Gentry say these niche news services may serve as templates for other areas of coverage, such as education or the environment. Says Olmos: "It's going to be really important that these start-up ventures are thoughtful."

—C.G.

through mid-2005. The professional development program, based at the Philip Merrill College of Journalism at the University of Maryland, awarded competitive fellowships for all-expense-paid conferences featuring expert briefings and skills training. Select fellows also received project support of up to $25,000 for six months. They contributed to scores of outlets, including NPR, the Chicago Tribune, the Austin American-Statesman, Reuters, Salon, Mother Jones, Reader's Digest, Portland's Oregonian, the Milwaukee Journal Sentinel, the Village Voice, WBUR-FM in Boston and Pacific News Service.

Ruby Takanishi, president of the Foundation for Child Development, a private philanthropy in New York, helped conceive the program and make sure it was funded generously. Her goal was to invest in journalists, particularly young ones who might have a more lasting impact in shaping the news, and "really improve the depth of reporting" on child and family policy, she says. Initially there was no limit to what fellows might explore in conference briefings or their own research: the impact of welfare reform on families, harsh "zero-tolerance" policies that criminalized youth, brain research on toddlers, the growing reliance on grandparents for foster care.

The expansive approach began to narrow after four years. The foundation had been concentrating its other funding on three subjects—children of immigrants, education from pre-kindergarten through third grade and an index of child well-being—and "some very strong voices on our board" wondered why these weren't getting more coverage from the news media, Takanishi recalls. The board decided the fellowship program's training and projects should be more clearly aligned with those issues for any future grants. At the time, we had a multiyear grant good through mid-2005.

I'd come out of newspapers, editing and reporting mostly on the features side. I tried to equate the tightening scope as something akin to the challenge of producing stories for the ad-driven annual dining guide or cruise travel section or the fall prep sports guide. With some effort, you could come up

Funding for Foreign Forays

With backing from one of journalism's pedigreed families, the Pulitzer Center on Crisis Reporting opened in early 2006 to promote foreign affairs coverage in U.S. media.

The center provides travel grants to journalists—mostly freelancers but also news organization staffers—to do in-depth stories about war-torn, exploited or overlooked lands and people. For instance, it helped send a reporter and photographer from North Carolina's Fayetteville Observer to Afghanistan to chronicle U.S. soldiers' rebuilding efforts there at "Fort Bragg East." It has subsidized stories exploring government corruption in Colombia, Maoist activity in India and an American-led effort to save a Mozambique national park devastated by civil war. It has awarded at least 40 grants to date, with most ranging from $3,000 to $10,000.

"I knew from my own experience that if you got a small grant that got you somewhere, you could turn it into something important," says Jon Sawyer, the center's director. He'd reported from five dozen countries while working in the St. Louis Post-Dispatch's Washington bureau from 1980 through 2005. In that last year, as his paper and other Pulitzer holdings were being sold to Lee Enterprises (see "Lee *Who?*" June/July 2005), Sawyer proposed the center.

He found a backer in Emily Rauh Pulitzer, once his former chain's principal shareholder. "There's [been] a terrible diminution of quality and a strong cutting back of information about what's going on in the rest of the world," says Pulitzer, a center trustee. "That's incomprehensible, because as the world gets smaller, we need to understand more about it."

She put up $250,000 annually for four years to launch the center and another $250,000 to support educational outreach. Other initial donors include David Moore—a grandson of the first Joseph Pulitzer and a longtime Pulitzer Inc. director—and his wife, Katherine.

The initiative started out as "a modest idea," Sawyer says, but it has quickly grown in scope and reach. The Pulitzer Center is an independent division of the World Security Institute—itself a sponsor of journalism and scholarship—which provides office space in Washington, D.C., staff resources and plenty of synergy. The institute produces "Foreign Exchange," a weekly global affairs program for public television. Pulitzer is the primary supplier of its "In Focus" slice-of-life video segment. Pulitzercenter.org features grantees' blogs from the field. The center also set up a channel on YouTube, whose editors in December featured Pulitzercenter.org at the top of their "News and Politics" page and praised its videos as "some of the most moving journalism you'll find on this site."

Sawyer speaks enviously of the financing of ProPublica, a lavishly funded new investigative reporting enterprise (see "Big Bucks for Investigative Reporting," page 171), even though it's clear he's mastering the art of the deal. He assembled multiple supporters for a Palm Beach Post series last November on "Heroes of HIV" in the Caribbean. First, Pulitzer sponsored reporter Antigone Barton's fellowship with the International Center for Journalists to spend three weeks reporting in Haiti and the Dominican Republic. Then Sawyer arranged for Barton to get a National Press Foundation fellowship to the International AIDS Society conference in Sydney, Australia, which included a week's training on HIV. With part of a $102,000 grant from New York's MAC AIDS Fund, the center hired a videographer and Web producer to accompany Barton to the Caribbean. Three of their videos appeared on "Foreign Exchange"; all are on the Pulitzer website, along with interviews and other materials. "He is extremely resourceful," Barton says of Sawyer. "He had a vision of what this could be."

Pulitzer grantees' work has been carried by the Post-Dispatch, Smithsonian magazine, NPR, the New York Times, the Washington Times, the Christian Science Monitor and other outlets. But if Sawyer and Associate Director Nathalie Applewhite believe in an idea, they'll approve funding even without a news organization's prior commitment.

They invested $13,000 to help Utah-based freelance reporter Loretta Tofani travel several times to China for a project on how the lack of safety precautions led to sometimes fatal injuries and illnesses in almost every Chinese industry that exports to the United States. Tofani—who won a Pulitzer Prize reporting for the Washington Post before joining the Philadelphia Inquirer and spending years as its China correspondent—had lined up a news outlet, but that fell through with a change in management. She offered the nearly complete project to the Salt Lake Tribune, which accepted it overnight with the proviso that Tofani localize the story. Tofani says she gladly spent the next month "running all over the state and talking with people about work conditions in the factories they were using."

In October, the Tribune published a four-part series, "American Imports, Chinese Deaths." Editor Nancy Conway says she's "glad that we had the opportunity to work with Loretta and to publish the stories," for which she paid $5,000. The only drawback, says Conway: "It would have been better if we had been in on the story from the beginning."

Sawyer agrees. He wants newsrooms "to be as closely involved as they can be. We're not competing with anybody. We're trying to partner with everybody."

—Carol Guensburg

with fresh, worthwhile stories for the dedicated space. But there was a crucial difference: While it was relatively easy to develop briefings and story ideas for covering immigrants and early education, there was no guarantee of real estate or airtime in others' newsrooms.

Our program's compressed focus, combined with industry-wide newsroom cuts in staffing and newsholes, made the fellowships a tougher sell. In the end, my advisory board, my boss at the college of journalism and I decided to seek a final, year-long grant—which we got—and then put the program to rest.

Most of the former fellows who'd gotten project support said their work wouldn't have proceeded as quickly—or at all—without financial assistance and guidance. Their comments dovetail with those of other journalists who've received fellowships elsewhere—from the Alicia Patterson Foundation, Kaiser and the New America Foundation, to name a few.

Funding enabled them to report on issues they cared about passionately. And it's important work, judging from some stories' impact and honors.

Out of my program alone, for instance, reporting by Barbara White Stack of the Pittsburgh Post-Gazette ultimately led the Pennsylvania Superior Court to rule that child-welfare dependency courts should be open to the public. Eric Eyre of the Charleston Gazette, reporting with then-colleague Scott Finn, exposed the high social costs of school consolidation in rural West Virginia. That project, which documented schoolchildren's hours-long bus rides, slowed the consolidation movement and won the Education Writers Association's grand prize in 2003.

Over the years, newsroom leaders and staff repeatedly told me that outside funding from various nonprofit programs validated their journalistic ambitions for projects while delivering vital budget relief.

"It's made a huge difference here. The majority of the long-term investigative projects that we do here would not have been possible" otherwise, says Eyre, a nine-year veteran of the Gazette. The privately owned paper circulates 48,000 copies daily and 74,000 on Sunday. Eyre also won a 2006 Kaiser Media Fellowship in health, which equipped him to do a project on poor oral health in his state.

Colleague Ken Ward received an Alicia Patterson fellowship to examine the coal industry—in December 2005, a month before the deadly Sago mine collapse. He delayed starting the fellowship while contributing breaking stories, then used it to produce a Gazette series on U.S. mine safety and a Washington Monthly article on the Bush administration's mine safety policies. Investigative Reporters and Editors honored Ward's series with a medal—its highest award—and the PBS documentary series "Exposé" focused on Ward's work in a program originally broadcast in November. "We were pretty happy for them to do this," Ward says. "It certainly made us look good."

Editors in some other places endorse training but decline grant support for newsroom projects. If a story is important enough, they say, they'll find money for it in the budget. They don't want the merest hint of outside influence. Nor do they want to be constrained by a donor's funding scope.

In 2006, as editor of the Lexington Herald-Leader in Kentucky, Marilyn W. Thompson wanted her paper to undertake a major project examining Republican Sen. Mitch McConnell's political fundraising practices and suggestions of influence peddling. When she realized her lean newsroom budget alone wouldn't cover it, Thompson got her Knight Ridder bosses' enthusiastic approval to seek a grant from the nonprofit Center for Investigative Reporting. The California-based center provided $37,500 to underwrite the salary of reporter John Cheves, who took an unpaid six-month leave of absence to do the project, as well as to cover expenses.

Just before the October publication of Cheves' four-part series, "Price Tag Politics," McConnell staff members complained of liberal bias—at the center. They cited center board and staff members' donations to Democratic candidates or causes. They called it "a known liberal entity, but what they seized on was the underlying funding," Thompson remembers. In particular, the McConnell

camp objected to involvement by the Deer Creek Foundation of St. Louis, which had funded groups seeking campaign finance reform. McConnell had led the fight against the bipartisan measure in Congress and in court. He was the lead plaintiff in McConnell v. Federal Election Commission, an unsuccessful U.S. Supreme Court challenge to the 2002 law.

By the time the McConnell complaints surfaced, both the newsroom's ownership and leadership had changed. In June, the paper had been acquired by McClatchy; in July, Thompson had gone to the Los Angeles Times as national investigations editor. McClatchy officials "brought me in on several conference calls" before deciding to reimburse the funder, Thompson says. Now an investigative reporter for the New York Times, Thompson says she was disappointed by the decision. Cheves' work—published that October—was excellent and error-free, she says, and "no one likes the suggestion that their reporting was in any way biased."

That was precisely why McClatchy's vice president for news, Howard Weaver, returned the center's grant. "I'm not uncomfortable with the journalism, and I'm certainly not uncomfortable with the journalist," the Herald-Leader quoted Weaver as saying at the time. "I just think that the relationship [with the outside groups] was sufficiently unorthodox that we don't need to do it."

The incident made a lasting impression at the center. While there always has been "a complete firewall" between editorial and fundraising, since then "we have made the case more strenuously to funders that we would prefer general operating support as opposed to project-specific support," says Christa Scharfenberg, the center's associate director. (Funding for the McConnell project had come from money Deer Creek had designated for campaign finance coverage.)

And in mid-December, the center's board voted to offer the executive director job to Robert J. Rosenthal, former managing editor of the San Francisco Chronicle. He accepted. "We decided the organization was ready to grow and evolve," Scharfenberg says. "We wanted an experienced, highly regarded journalist at the helm, which we think also will deflect concerns about the journalistic integrity of the organization."

Takanishi of the Foundation for Child Development believes foundations and journalists have "a shared future" because of the public's right to know. She also encourages "more critical coverage of philanthropy. . . . It exists in the public trust, so it should be open for examination." But "how do foundations, by making grants, [best] support journalism?" she muses. "How does journalism cover philanthropy? It's sort of biting the hand that feeds you."

Edward Wasserman, the Knight Professor of Journalism Ethics at Washington and Lee University in Lexington, Virginia, agrees that foundation handouts can put recipients at a disadvantage. "Who's going to do the story on the Knight Foundation?" he asks rhetorically, noting his own endowed teaching position. The funder does "a good but not infallible job. The news organizations that should be reporting on them can't," at least not impartially. "Most of the people in media have one eye out for where the money might be coming from."

The plight is a familiar one in many newsrooms, though with different players. Is there "any real difference between advertiser influence and donor influence on editorial sanctity? There shouldn't be," says Lewis, of the Fund for Independence in Journalism. A journalist in residence at American University, he maintains that nonprofit journalism ventures can "basically ensure transparency and credibility, sometimes more so than a commercial outlet does."

To preserve newsgathering integrity, nonprofits "must disclose their donors," Lewis says. "I happen to think it's important to have some discretion about whose money you accept. There are some other schools of thought about that," he acknowledges. "Make sure, to the extent possible, that the journalist inside the nonprofit newsroom doesn't have substantial interaction with the donors"—a condition he couldn't follow as both editor and publisher at the Center for Public Integrity, he admits.

Wasserman says he's especially uneasy with "an almost direct line between funder and news organization," a structure emerging in health news services. "I could very readily see that this opens the door for various trade coalitions to bankroll reporting that could in itself be perfectly OK, but, in terms of subject matter, would have a tilt toward topics of greatest interest to the funders: biofuels coverage funded by Archer Daniels Midland. You get into a murky area pretty quickly."

But Missouri's Overholser is less wary of foundations developing their own news media outlets. "There are a lot of ways to do journalism in the public interest," says Overholser, who also chairs the Center for Public Integrity's board and serves on a handful of other nonprofit journalism boards. "The only key here is transparency. . . . An educated consumer should be able to see who put [a report] together, who funded it, what are the underlying goals. . . . I welcome partisan information, as long as it's labeled. What worries me is deceit, when we get people playing on the public stage who don't acknowledge their money is coming from the left wing or the right wing. . . . We need to have some reliable sources whose goal is to be nonpartisan, to report whatever they find—no matter how unsettling to their funders."

Overholser, like others interviewed for this story, expresses confidence that nonprofit news operations will flourish. She believes these may even bolster their for-profit counterparts.

"I never for a moment think nonprofits are going to supplant commercial media," she says. "The existence of nonprofits can strengthen the journalism done by commercial media. Nonprofits can be more fearless, in some ways, because they don't have to worry" about offending the powerful or risking popularity.

CAROL GUENSBURG (carol.guensburg@verizon.net) is senior editor for the *Journalism Center on Children & Families,* a University of Maryland professional program—and a nonprofit. It receives primary support from the Annie E. Casey Foundation. Guensburg spent 14 years as an editor and reporter for the *Milwaukee Journal Sentinel* after working for three other papers.

Arianna's Answer

The Huffington Post may have figured out the future of journalism. But it's going to be a very difficult future.

DANIEL LYONS

If you had to declare a winner among Internet media companies today, the victor easily would be Arianna Huffington. Her site, The Huffington Post, attracted 24.3 million unique visitors last month, five times as much traffic as many new-media rivals, more than *The Washington Post* and *USA Today*, and nearly as many as *The New York Times*. HuffPo's revenue this year will be about $30 -million—peanuts compared with the old-media dinosaurs, but way better than most digital competitors. And HuffPo has finally started to eke out a profit.

Those numbers, however, don't fully convey the site's place in this new-media world. What began five years ago as a spot for Huffington and her lefty celebrity friends to vent about the Bush administration has become one of the most important news sites on the Web, covering politics, sports, entertainment, business—along with plenty of tabloidy stuff to drive clicks, like photos of "Jennifer Aniston's topless perfume ad." HuffPo's mission, Huffington says, is "to provide a platform for a really important national conversation."

It's a humid July afternoon in New York—Huffington's 60th birthday—and she's sipping San Pellegrino water and nibbling on apple slices in her tiny office on the third floor of a building in New York's SoHo. Minions rush in and out, bringing chocolates, messages, and a BlackBerry, with her ex-husband, former Republican congressman Michael Huffington, on the line. Arianna has just come from speaking at an advertising conference—she gives more than 100 speeches a year, addressing techies and publishing types, who view her as the patron saint of new media, the queen of bloggers, the one person who's figured out the future of journalism.

But a closer look at HuffPo's financials shows just how tough that future is turning out to be. HuffPo has a big audience, but like most websites, it can't monetize it very well. Right now, HuffPo generates just over $1 per reader per year. That's nothing compared with the mainstream-media outlets that HuffPo hopes to displace. Cable-TV networks and print newspapers collect hundreds of dollars per year from each subscriber, and then generate hundreds of millions in ad revenue on top of that. The comparison isn't perfect—TV and newspapers have higher fixed costs than websites—but it gives you a sense of how radically things are changing.

Yes, money is gushing out of old media—nobody knows this better than NEWSWEEK, which is struggling financially and has been put up for sale by its parent, The Washington Post Company—and some of that money is flowing onto the Internet. But something strange happens to those ad dollars as they make the journey from old media to the Web—somehow, by some weird, bad voodoo, those dollars turn into dimes. Or nickels. Or even pennies. A recent report by eMarketer, a leading researcher of Internet media, says online ad spending will grow more than 10 percent per year over the next few years, approaching $100 billion by 2014. That will still represent only 17 percent of all advertising spending.

Ce-web-rities

The hard truth is that advertisers want to put messages on websites, but they just don't want to pay very much for that privilege. And perhaps for good reason. When was the last time you clicked on an Internet ad? Or even noticed one? "Maybe it's time that someone says the unsayable—that online advertising just doesn't work. A website turns out to be a not very good advertising vehicle," says Michael Wolff, the *Vanity Fair* columnist who also runs Newser, an ad-supported news-aggregation website that attracts 2 million unique visitors a month and will generate a few million in revenue this year. Online advertising rates have been dropping for a decade. Wolff says his average CPM (what he can charge for delivering 1,000 impressions of an ad) fell 20 percent in the past two years, from $10 to $8. The average for the Internet is only $2.43, according to comScore, a market-research firm that tracks Internet traffic and ad spending. And nobody expects ad rates to bounce back up—ever.

HuffPo CEO Eric Hippeau says the site charges well above the average for its advertising space by creating a better-than-average experience for its audience. Even so, HuffPo and other online publications must find ways to acquire content at low cost. These sites run lean; HuffPo has 88 editorial employees, while big newspapers might have several times that many. Online jobs used to pay far less than print jobs, but now salaries for entry-level staffers are comparable: $35,000 to $40,000. To hold down the costs, sites get a lot of content free, aggregating articles from other sites and getting readers to create the content themselves, as HuffPo does via its 6,000 unpaid bloggers. Cheap content, however, begets cheaper ad rates. Social networks like Facebook, the ultimate creator of user-generated content, get only 56 cents per thousand ad impressions, according to comScore.

In this low-margin world, companies that operate on a massive scale have a big advantage. Google reaps billions of dollars by showing zillions of cheapo ads. That's why Internet giants AOL and Yahoo now are pushing into the online content business, hiring journalists. But both are also pursuing a low-cost, low-value strategy, as evidenced by Yahoo's recent acquisition of Associated Content, whose business involves paying freelancers $100 or less to churn out stories based on whatever keywords are most popular on search engines. The growing presence of big players will likely put even more pressure on ad rates, further squeezing the little guys.

This is what The Huffington Post—and every other online news site—is up against. She has lots of company: one block over from HuffPo's SoHo headquarters are the offices of Mediaite, run by TV journalist Dan Abrams. A few blocks away is Gawker Media, led by Internet guru Nick Denton. Also in the neighborhood: Wolff's Newser. Over on Fifth Avenue is Business Insider, started by ex–Wall Street analyst Henry Blodget. Not far away, in Chelsea, Tina Brown runs her news site, The Daily Beast. There's also Politico, in Washington, D.C., and a slew of tech blogs out in Silicon Valley, including TechCrunch, GigaOm, AllThingsD—and on and on.

Of all these, HuffPo is the biggest and best-known, and if Huffington is worried about the future, it doesn't show. That's partly just her personality—she's a force of nature. She seems to be everywhere at once. She posts items on HuffPo. She has a book coming out called *Third World America*—it's her 13th. She does two weekly shows, including *Left, Right & Center* on public radio. She's on TV all the time, often arguing politics with some conservative. She even lends her voice to a character on *The Cleveland Show*, an animated comedy series on Fox.

In person, she's charming and a bit overwhelming. She offers snacks or drinks to everyone who comes near her. "I'm so Greek," she says. "I can't help it." Arianna made her name as a conservative commentator, but switched sides in 1996 and became a liberal. Huffington and a partner, media executive Kenneth Lerer, raised $4 million to start the site. Since then, HuffPo has raised $33 million more from venture-capital firms. The company now has 178 employees.

How has HuffPo managed to leap so far ahead of almost everyone else in its space? The deep pockets help. But another key is how quickly The Huffington Post embraces new technologies. The lifeblood of a big website is what's called a "content-management system," meaning a bunch of software programs that handle how stories get published. HuffPo has one of the best and most advanced systems on the Internet, and it's constantly evolving. The site has 30 techies strung around the globe, in the United States, Ukraine, India, Chile, the Philippines, and Vietnam—"so we have developers working 24/7," says Hippeau. That publishing system enables HuffPo's editors to create new ways to tell stories, mixing links and videos and slide shows and comments, grabbing bits and pieces from other sources and sprinkling on some topspin from HuffPo's writers, all while measuring traffic to see what's working and what's not.

While some HuffPo reporters do the old-fashioned work of going out and interviewing people, the job for a lot of HuffPo editorial staffers involves sitting at long tables in a big room in New York grabbing sexy stuff from other websites—photos of Leonardo DiCaprio shirtless, a video of a baseball player getting hit in the groin. Editors watch Google to see which search terms are hot at any moment, then craft stories that will show up in response to those searches. The stories might be written by a HuffPo staffer, or might be grabbed from some other site, or might be a mix of both. (About 40 percent of what HuffPo runs is stuff that originated somewhere else.) The trick is to design stories in such a way that they will get pushed toward the top of search rankings—a black art known as "search-engine optimization," and an area in which HuffPo excels.

Huffington acknowledges the importance of technology, but insists "there's no way you can supersede human editing." She's proud of HuffPo's original journalism, and her explanation for the site's success is that from the start it went after news with a passion and a point of view—there was no pretending to be neutral or unbiased. "We have a clear attitude. On the Afghan war, for example, we've been clear that we believe it's an unnecessary war," Huffington says. "The whole thing is about editors following their passions."

Probably the most stunning thing about The Huffington Post is the number of comments its readers post. It's not unusual to see more than 5,000 comments posted on a story; one recent piece about Jeb Bush possibly running for president in 2012 has generated more than 8,000. In June the site received 3.1 million comments. Huffington credits her decision early on to moderate comments and keep things civil rather than allowing the typical Internet free-for-all. It's a lot of work—HuffPo has 20 people who do nothing but weed out the nasties. "Self-expression is the new entertainment," Huffington says. "People don't want to just consume information, they want to participate. Recognizing that impulse is the future of journalism." HuffPo now bills itself as being similar to a social-networking site. Instead of just cruising into HuffPo to read a story, people stick around to talk about it. In the business that's known as "engagement," and when you are trying to attract advertisers, engagement is a priceless commodity. "We're doing social news," Huffington says.

Sure, some of this is just spin. It's also a sign that HuffPo is still evolving, and nobody, not even Arianna, knows where it will all end up. One outcome would involve being acquired by a big media company. There have been rumors of offers from MSNBC and Yahoo, as well as rumors that HuffPo may try to sell shares to the public. Hippeau won't comment on any of this, and just says that he and Huffington are trying to build a "strong and independent" business. Hippeau says these are still early days on the Web, and that HuffPo has big potential. There are some encouraging signs. Last quarter *The New York Times* generated $50 million in Internet advertising from an audience that's not much bigger than HuffPo's. That puts it on track to generate $200 million a year, versus $30 million for HuffPo. An optimist would say it shows HuffPo has a lot of room to grow. "What if I can get to $100 million in revenues with 30 percent EBITDA margins?" Hippeau says, meaning earnings before interest, taxes, depreciation, and amortization. "I have the inventory. I have a very attractive audience. This can be a very profitable organization."

It's easy to say that, but not so easy to see how HuffPo gets there. Huffington, for her part, seems totally unconcerned. She's becoming a new-media baron, a modern-day Citizen Kane. And she's loving every minute of it. Who can blame her?

Critical Thinking

1. Do you believe HuffPo will be around 5, 10, 15 years from now? If so, describe how you see the make-up of media in the future. If not, what do you think will replace it (and other such sites)?

2. Describe the differences between journalists operating under the old media system versus journalists who are hired by sites such as Huffpo. Do you see the quality of content suffering or improving under the new type of journalism displayed on the internet?

Test-Your-Knowledge Form

We encourage you to photocopy and use this page as a tool to assess how the articles in *Annual Editions* expand on the information in your textbook. By reflecting on the articles you will gain enhanced text information. You can also access this useful form on a product's book support website at www.mhhe.com/cls.

NAME:

DATE:

TITLE AND NUMBER OF ARTICLE:

BRIEFLY STATE THE MAIN IDEA OF THIS ARTICLE:

LIST THREE IMPORTANT FACTS THAT THE AUTHOR USES TO SUPPORT THE MAIN IDEA:

WHAT INFORMATION OR IDEAS DISCUSSED IN THIS ARTICLE ARE ALSO DISCUSSED IN YOUR TEXTBOOK OR OTHER READINGS THAT YOU HAVE DONE? LIST THE TEXTBOOK CHAPTERS AND PAGE NUMBERS:

LIST ANY EXAMPLES OF BIAS OR FAULTY REASONING THAT YOU FOUND IN THE ARTICLE:

LIST ANY NEW TERMS/CONCEPTS THAT WERE DISCUSSED IN THE ARTICLE, AND WRITE A SHORT DEFINITION:

We Want Your Advice

ANNUAL EDITIONS revisions depend on two major opinion sources: one is our Advisory Board, listed in the front of this volume, which works with us in scanning the thousands of articles published in the public press each year; the other is you—the person actually using the book. Please help us and the users of the next edition by completing the prepaid article rating form on this page and returning it to us. Thank you for your help!

ANNUAL EDITIONS: Mass Media 11/12

ARTICLE RATING FORM

Here is an opportunity for you to have direct input into the next revision of this volume.
We would like you to rate each of the articles listed below, using the following scale:

1. **Excellent: should definitely be retained**
2. **Above average: should probably be retained**
3. **Below average: should probably be deleted**
4. **Poor: should definitely be deleted**

Your ratings will play a vital part in the next revision.
Please mail this prepaid form to us as soon as possible.
Thanks for your help!

RATING	ARTICLE	RATING	ARTICLE
	1. In the Beginning Was the Word		16. Economic and Business Dimensions: Is the Internet a Maturing Market?
	2. Revolution in a Box		17. Ideastream: *The New* "Public Media
	3. Tele[re]vision		18. Too Graphic?
	4. Research on the Effects of Media Violence		19. Carnage.com
	5. Wikipedia in the Newsroom		20. Distorted Picture
	6. Journalist Bites Reality!		21. The Quality-Control Quandary
	7. Girls Gone Anti-Feminist		22. What Would You Do?: The Journalism That Tweaks Reality, Then Reports What Happens
	8. The Reconstruction of American Journalism		23. The Lives of Others: What Does It Mean to 'Tell Someone's Story'?
	9. Peytonplace.com		24. A Porous Wall
	10. Capital Flight		25. How Can YouTube Survive?
	11. Overload!: Journalism's Battle for Relevance in an Age of Too Much Information		26. But Who's Counting?
	12. Don't Blame the Journalism: The Economic and Technological Forces behind the Collapse of Newspapers		27. Brain Candy
			28. Multitasking Youth
	13. What the Mainstream Media Can Learn from Jon Stewart		29. Tossed by a Gale
	14. Whatever Happened to Iraq?: How the Media Lost Interest in a Long-Running War with No End in Sight		30. Open for Business
			31. Nonprofit News
	15. What's a Fair Share in the Age of Google?: How to Think about News in the Link Economy		32. Arianna's Answer

173

BUSINESS REPLY MAIL
FIRST CLASS MAIL PERMIT NO. 551 DUBUQUE IA

POSTAGE WILL BE PAID BY ADDRESSEE

McGraw-Hill Contemporary Learning Series
501 BELL STREET
DUBUQUE, IA 52001

ABOUT YOU

Name   Date

Are you a teacher? ❏ A student? ❏
Your school's name

Department

Address   City   State   Zip

School telephone #

YOUR COMMENTS ARE IMPORTANT TO US!

Please fill in the following information:
For which course did you use this book?

Did you use a text with this ANNUAL EDITION? ❏ yes ❏ no
What was the title of the text?

What are your general reactions to the Annual Editions concept?

Have you read any pertinent articles recently that you think should be included in the next edition? Explain.

Are there any articles that you feel should be replaced in the next edition? Why?

Are there any World Wide Websites that you feel should be included in the next edition? Please annotate.

May we contact you for editorial input? ❏ yes ❏ no
May we quote your comments? ❏ yes ❏ no

NOTES

NOTES